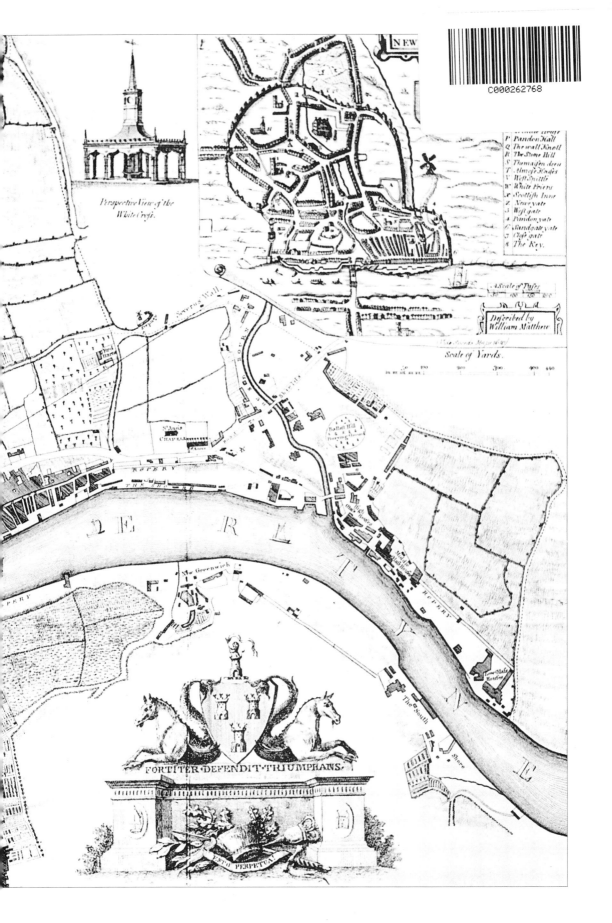

Perspective View of the
White Crofs.

P Pandon Hall
Q The wall Knoll
R The Stone Hill
S Thornaton dene
T Almefe Houfes
V Weft Spittle
W White Friers
x Scottifh Inne
y Neur yate
3 Weft gate
4 Pandon yate
6 Sandgate yate
7 Clofe gate
8 The Key.

A Scale of Pafes

Defcribed by
William Matthew

Scale of Yards.

FORTITER·DEFENDIT·TRIUMPHANS.

ESTO·PERPETUA.

C000262768

# NEWCASTLE
## UPON TYNE

### A Modern History

# NEWCASTLE
## UPON TYNE
## A Modern History

*edited by*

*Robert Colls & Bill Lancaster*

Phillimore

2001

Published by
PHILLIMORE & CO. LTD.
Shopwyke Manor Barn, Chichester, West Sussex

ISBN   1 86077 167 X

Previous page: *Newcastle upon Tyne, from Gateshead*, 1896, by Niels Lund (1863-1916)

Printed and bound in Great Britain by
BUTLER & TANNER LTD.
London and Frome

# Contents

Preface and Acknowledgements   vii
Notes on Contributors   viii

1   The 'Black Indies': Economic Development of Newcastle, *c.*1700-1840
    JOYCE ELLIS   1

2   An Integrated Elite: Newcastle's Economic Development 1840-1914
    OLIVER LENDRUM   27

3   The Emergence of the Post-Industrial Economy in Newcastle 1914-2000
    NATASHA VALL   47

4   The Governance of the Victorian City
    MAUREEN CALLCOTT   71

5   The Making of a Diocese 1851-1882
    JEFF SMITH   93

6   Print and Preach: The Entrepreneurial Spirit of Nineteenth-Century Newcastle
    JOAN HUGMAN   113

7   The People of Newcastle: A Demographic History
    MIKE BARKE   133

8   Drink in Newcastle
    BRIAN BENNISON   167

9   Sport on Tyneside
    RICHARD HOLT & RAY PHYSICK   193

10  Architecture in Newcastle
    THOMAS FAULKNER   213

11   Art on the Margins: from Bewick to Baltic
     PAUL USHERWOOD   245

12   Remembering George Stephenson: Genius and Modern Memory
     ROBERT COLLS   267

13   Winged Words: Literature of Newcastle
     ALAN MYERS   293

14   Sociability and the City
     BILL LANCASTER   319

15   The Reconstruction of Newcastle: Planning since 1945
     DAVID BYRNE   341

16   Last Word: Dialect
     BILL GRIFFITHS   361

Index   367

## Illustration Acknowledgements

Newcastle City Library Local Studies Collection, Tyne and Wear Museum Service and the University of Northumbria Library supplied the majority of illustrations. Jimmy Forsyth and West Newcastle Local Studies kindly supplied illustrations 8.8, 8.9 and 11.7. The following courteously provided illustrations for chapter 13: The Royal College of Physicians 13.1, The Directors and University Librarian of the John Rylands University Library Of Manchester 13.2, The National Portrait Gallery 13.3, Mrs. Rene Chaplin 13.5, Michael Standen 13.6 and the Basil Bunting Poetry Centre, University of Durham 13.7. Two contributors provided illustrations from their personal collections: Natasha Vall provided 3.4 and Joan Hugman 8.8 and 8.9. Every effort has been made to obtain permission from copyright owners. The editors apologise for any inadvertent breach of copyright convention.

# Preface and Acknowledgements

This has been an easy and enjoyable book to make because all those involved in its making have been such good colleagues. We thank the contributors who clearly believed in this book as much as we did, and stuck with us through thick and thin. Their enthusiasm was infectious. They put up with us. We thank also the librarians and archivists who were unstinting in their help – in particular, the staffs of the Local Studies Unit of Newcastle Central Library, the Tyne and Wear Archive and Museum Service, and the libraries of the universities of Northumbria and Newcastle. We extend our special thanks and gratitude to Dilys Harding and Patricia Sheldon of the Central Library, who went way beyond the call (not for the first time or, we hope, the last), and to John Millard of Tyne & Wear Museum Service, who got us some perfect pictures. Finally we would like to thank Noel Osborne and his team at Phillimore, especially Simon Thraves and Nicola Willmot. We remember the relief we felt on our first meeting with Noel in the British Library in November 1999: at last, a proper publisher who actually wanted to publish books (rather than tell editors how to edit them).

It is over fifty years since Middlebrook's last major history, *Newcastle upon Tyne. Its Growth and Achievement*, published in 1950. It is surprising that so little scholarly work on the city has been carried out between then and now. There can be no doubt that a new history is long overdue. City and region currently find themselves at a historic crossroads. The old has gone and the new has yet to take shape. In 1992, our book *Geordies. Roots of Regionalism* addressed these concerns for the region. We now turn our attention to the city, and we offer this book in the certain knowledge that a city in the throes of redefining itself needs its history most.

Since 1950, Newcastle upon Tyne and the way history is written have both changed immensely. Yet we hope for the same old things: that we have got it 'right', and that it is a pleasure to read.

ROBERT COLLS AND BILL LANCASTER
Centre for Northern Studies

June 2001

# Notes on Contributors

**Mike Barke**, a geography graduate from Liverpool University, went on to complete his doctorate at Glasgow University in historical geography. He teaches at the University of Northumbria where his special interests include social geography, housing studies and the historical geography of North East England.

**Brian Bennison**, a native of Stockton-on-Tees, teaches at the University of Northumbria. He has published widely on the brewing and drink trades, including a three-volume history of Newcastle's public houses and articles in *Northern History*, *North East History*, *Tyne & Tweed*, *The Local Historian*, *The Journal of Regional & Local Studies* and *Archaeologia Aeliana*.

**David Byrne** is Reader in Sociology and Social Policy at the University of Durham. He is the author of *Beyond the Inner City* (Open University Press, 1989), *Complexity Theory and the Social Sciences* (Routledge, 1998), and *Social Exclusion* (Open University Press 1999). He is a native of Tyneside who has been involved in community action and politics since the middle 1960s.

**Maureen Callcott** lectured in History at Kenton Lodge College of Education and Newcastle upon Tyne Polytechnic, now the University of Northumbria, and The Open University. She has research degrees from the University of Newcastle and has researched, written and broadcast on various aspects of local political and social history, women's history and oral history. Her last book was *A Pilgrimage of Grace: The Diaries of Ruth Dodds 1905-1974* (1995).

**Robert Colls** teaches in the Department of Economic and Social History at the University of Leicester. He is an Honorary Fellow of the Centre for Northern Studies.

**Joyce Ellis** is Senior Lecturer in History at the University of Nottingham. She studied at the University of Oxford and in 1975-77 held the Sir James Knott Fellowship at the University of Newcastle. She subsequently taught at Leicester and Loughborough universities, and at Trinity College, Oxford, before moving to Nottingham in 1988. She has published widely on the economic and social development of Newcastle and the coalfield 1660-1840, and is currently working on the urban history of Britain in the long 18th century.

**Thomas Faulkner** is Senior Lecturer in the History of Architecture and Design at the University of Northumbria and has written and lectured on many aspects of the architecture of Newcastle and the North East. A Fellow of the Society of Antiquaries of London, he is also a member of the Society of Architectural Historians of Great Britain, the Georgian Group and the Victorian Society and is Chairman of the Northern Architectural History Society. His publications include *John Dobson: Newcastle Architect, 1787-1865* (1987), *Northumbrian Panorama: Studies in the History and Culture of North East England* (edited, 1996), and *Lost Houses of Newcastle and Northumberland* (1996).

**Bill Griffiths** lives in Seaham on the Durham coast, and has published several dialect items with the Centre for Northern Studies and on the web at www.indigogroup.co.uk's site. His affinity to North East dialect was prompted by study of Old English.

**Richard Holt** was born in Monkseaton in 1948 and still returns regularly to Tyneside. He read history at St John's College, Oxford and was Lecturer in History at Stirling University from 1974-1990. Amongst other works, he is author of *Sport and the British* (Oxford University Press, 1989) and jointly with Tony Mason of *Sport in Britain, 1945-2000* (Blackwell, 2000). He is currently Research Professor at the International Centre for Sports History and Culture at De Montfort University, Leicester.

**Joan Hugman** studied for her Ph.D on 19th-Century North East Radical Politics at the University of Northumbria. She has published several articles on 19th-Century politics and now teaches at Newcastle University.

**Bill Lancaster** is Director of the Centre for Northern Studies, University of Northumbria.

**Oliver Lendrum** studied history at the University of Durham where he completed an MA focusing upon the industrial development of North East England in the period 1840-1914, with special reference to entrepreneurship. He is currently working at the Home Office in London.

**Alan Myers** was born in South Shields in 1933. After attending London and Moscow Universities, he taught in Hertfordshire for many years before becoming a professional translator. His work includes Dostoevsky's *The Idiot* and Pushkin's *Queen of Spades*, as well as poetry and prose by Joseph Brodsky, Nobel laureate. *Myers Literary Guide: The North East* was published by MidNAG/Carcanet in 1995.

**Ray Physick** is studying for a Ph.D at De Montfort University on the 'Development of Professional Golf circa 1875-1975'. He has published work on sports history with Dick Holt and he is presently employed at John Moores University, Liverpool preparing an on-line history of Liverpool from 1207 to the present day.

**Jeff Smith** was born in Chopwell, near Newcastle, in 1926. He gave up law for 18th-century English history, particularly the North East. He is currently working on a study of the cultural history of Georgian Newcastle.

**Paul Usherwood** is an art critic and historian teaching at the University of Northumbria. His recent publications include *Public Sculpture of North-East England* (Liverpool University Press, 2000).

**Natasha Vall** is an AHRB research fellow in the Centre for Northern Studies at the University of Northumbria. She recently completed a doctoral thesis comparing Malmö and Newcastle in the 20th century and is currently researching 20th-century regional culture.

THIS BOOK IS DEDICATED TO
**Keith Wrightson**,
doyen of northern historians
and an inspiration to so many contributors to this volume.

I

# The 'Black Indies'
## The Economic Development of Newcastle, c.1700-1840

## JOYCE ELLIS

The roads of 18th-century Britain seem to have been crowded with tourists intent on exploring their native land and on committing their impressions to paper. Some of these intrepid travellers ventured as far north as the Tyne valley and, guided by the strong smell of sulphur and by the sight of coal waggons rolling down to the river, came at last to a vantage point overlooking the 'glory of the North', the town of Newcastle. Most of them found the view disappointing, having expected something more obviously impressive than the huddle of buildings that clung to the riverbanks beneath them. The river and its teeming traffic certainly excited admiration but, as Defoe pointed out with commendable restraint,

> The situation of the town to the landward is exceedingly unpleasant, and the buildings very close and old, standing on the declivity of two exceeding high hills, which, together with the smoke of the coals, makes it not the pleasantest place in the world to live in.[1]

However, none of these earlier visitors went as far as a tourist of the 1790s who made no secret of his relief at escaping from 'this nasty, sooty, smoky chaos of a town' to the rural haven of Morpeth. Most travellers in the early 18th century were not particularly interested in rural havens. They measured interest in terms of economic and especially commercial success and to that extent they found in Newcastle exactly what they had expected, a town which 'next to *Bristol*, may be called the greatest trading Town in *England*' and which was consequently 'large, populous and rich'.[2]

---

[1] Morris, C. (ed.), *The Journeys of Celia Fiennes* (1947), p.209; Hodgson Hinde, J. (ed.), *Inedited Contributions to the History of Northumberland* (Newcastle, 1869), p.42; Defoe, D., *A Tour Thro' the Whole Island of Great Britain* (1727), vol.iii, p.158.

[2] MacRitchie, W., *Diary of a Tour Through Great Britain in 1795* (1897), p.137; Macky, J., *A Journey Through England in Familiar Letters* (1722), vol.ii, pp.216-7; Brome, J., *Travels over England, Scotland and Wales* (1700), p.171. This change in attitude over the century is discussed in Sweet, R., *The Writing of Urban Histories in Eighteenth-century England* (Oxford, 1997), especially pp.131-41.

## Trade and Industry

Newcastle's status as a port and commercial centre ranking fourth in the urban hierarchy after London, Norwich and Bristol is apparent in all contemporary accounts from the early years of the century. It was in fact an ideal example of Defoe's sea-port towns 'where Trade flourishes, as well foreign Trade and home Trade, and where Navigation, Manufacturing, and Merchandize seem to assist one another'.[3] In terms of the volume of shipping trading at the port it was already one of the busiest in the country and its inhabitants were clearly proud of its facilities, above all the famous broad, stone-faced quay, 'soe full of merchants walking to-an-againe', the busy customs house on the Sandhill, the wharfs, cellars and warehouses lining the town's densely-packed foreshore, and the taverns, alehouses and coffee houses crowded into the narrow streets behind.[4] Visitors were dazzled by the sheer number of vessels entering and leaving the Tyne at the height of the summer shipping season, giving observers the impression that 'the River seemed every where to be in motion': between 10 and 19 September 1734, for instance, around 579 ships entered the river while 500 sailed out.[5] Many of these vessels would have been locally owned: in 1709 Newcastle investors owned 11,500 tons of shipping, a figure exceeded only by London, Scarborough and Bristol and representing just under 4 per cent of national shipping capacity. By 1751 this had risen to 21,600 tons, just over 5 per cent of the total. 'A spirit of adventure' was invoked by one contemporary commentator to explain the willingness of a surprisingly wide spectrum of the local population – from widowed gentlewomen to linen-drapers and biscuit-makers – to sink their capital (sometimes literally) in such a speculative investment. The risks involved were instrumental in the dramatic downturn in cargoes moving through the port in the winter months [see Figure 1.1], a pattern that persisted well into the century, most owners preferring to lay their ships up in safe havens rather than run the gauntlet of the open sea and harbours inadequately protected from rough weather. Many investors also cautiously hedged their bets by buying small shares in a large number of vessels, an arrangement that benefited merchants and traders in Newcastle's highly integrated economy by extending their business patronage and market influence for a relatively modest outlay.[6]

[3] Defoe, D., *A Plan of the English Commerce* (1728), p.85; Ellis, J., 'Regional and county centres c1700-1840', in Clark, P. (ed.), *The Cambridge Urban History of Britain, vol.ii. c1540-c1840* (Cambridge, 2000), pp.674-6.

[4] Morris (ed.), *Journeys*, p.210; Bourne, H., *The History of Newcastle on Tyne: or, the Ancient and Present State of that Town* (Newcastle, 1736), pp.123,133.

[5] Birley, E., 'Sir John Clerk's Visit to the North of England in 1724', *Transactions of the Architectural and Archaeological Society of Durham and Northumberland*, vol.11 (1958-65), p.228; *Newcastle Courant*, 21 Sept.1734.

[6] Corfield, P.J., *The Impact of English Towns 1700-1800* (1982), pp.36-7; Ville, S.P.,'Patterns of shipping investment in the port of Newcastle upon Tyne 1750-1850', *Northern History*, vol.25 (1989), pp.210-13 [quotation p.210]; Defoe, *Tour*, vol.iii, p.159; Ellis, J.M., *The Business Fortunes of William Cotesworth c.1668-1726* (New York, 1981), pp.43-5.

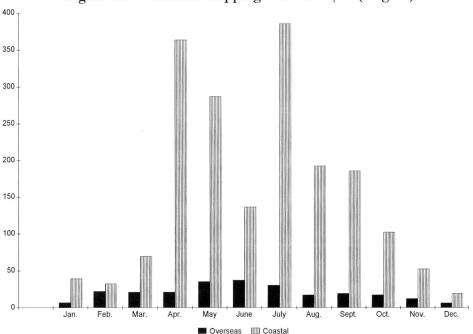

Figure 1.1    Seasonal Shipping Patterns 1706 (cargoes)

By far the greatest number of the vessels entering and leaving the port in the early years of the century were engaged in the domestic trade, which was itself dominated by the London market: two-thirds of the 1,862 coastal shipments from Newcastle in 1706, for instance, were bound for London, while a quarter of the 221 inbound cargoes originated in the capital. Newcastle's foreign trade in the early decades of the century was comparatively limited in quantity and equally narrow in its concentration on the ports of Holland and the western Baltic.[7] Given that it was foreign trade, particularly with Britain's trans-Atlantic colonies, which was the principal engine of wealth and expansion in 18th-century ports, this could be interpreted as a flaw in Newcastle's otherwise impressive record; in London and Bristol, for instance, a much higher proportion of trading activity was engaged in servicing colonial demand and in redistributing colonial imports. It is also undeniable that the high volumes of goods shipped out of the Tyne [see Figure 1.2] can give a misleading impression of Newcastle's relative standing when compared with the trade of ports handling smaller, more compact cargoes of higher valued goods. The

[7]    Public Record Office (hereafter P.R.O.), Newcastle Port Books, E190/212/10, 211/3. Until 1848 the 'port' of Newcastle included not only the whole of the Tyne down to the river mouth but also small harbours such as Blyth and Seaton.

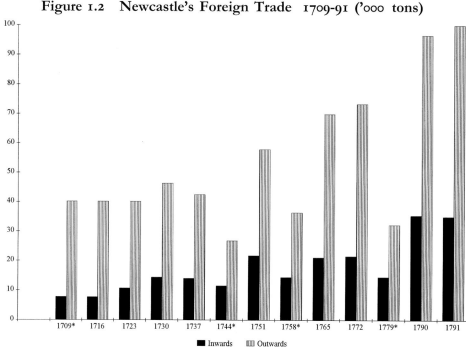

Figure 1.2 Newcastle's Foreign Trade 1709-91 ('000 tons)

■ Inwards ▥ Outwards

'one-way' nature of so much of Newcastle's trade, evident from the disparity between the number of vessels entering and leaving the port, as well as from the quantities of ballast deposited along the banks of the Tyne downstream from the town, was also a handicap to merchants. Return cargoes not only reduced freight charges on the outward voyage but also minimised the difficulties of securing payment at a time when there was no regular rate of exchange quoted between Newcastle and the major Dutch ports, let alone further afield. However, contemporaries who commented dismissively that 'the Inhabitants maintain little or no foreign trade' and that most of Newcastle's merchants 'drive small Pedling Retaile trades' were clearly underestimating both the volume and the value of the trade concerned.[8] Even in the early years of the century several Newcastle merchants were operating extensive and varied commercial networks through a complex chain of contacts and commission agents stretching from Bordeaux to Narva on the Gulf of Finland, while by the 1730s significant trading links had been established with markets in the Mediterranean and north America. There was 'no place in England', Ralph Carr

---

[8]   Ellis, *Business Fortunes*, pp.52,175; Jackson, G., 'Ports 1700-1840', in Clark (ed.), *Cambridge Urban History, vol.ii*, pp.707-10; Cox, T., *Magna Britania et Hibernia, Antiqua et Nova, or, a New Survey of Great Britain* (Durham, 1720), vol.i, p.624; Gateshead Public Library (hereafter G.P.L.), Cotesworth MSS. CG/5/84: The case of the freemen of Newcastle, 1722.

**Figure 1.3   Coal exports from the Tyne 1699-1799 ('000 tons)**

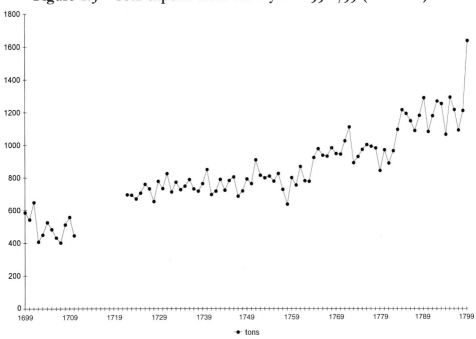

informed his correspondents in New York in 1750, where a cargo to the colonies could be provided more cheaply, with the result that 'I ship great quantities yearly for all parts of America, as crown glass, bottles, sheet lead shot all sorts of woolens … nails, edge tools and every kind of iron ware, coarse felt hats and coarse earthenware'.[9]

As Carr's correspondence indicates, the basis of Newcastle's continuing success as a port rested on its complementary role as the centre of a thriving industrial region. In the middle ages its unspectacular prosperity had been founded on the export of agricultural produce and grindstones, but the rapid expansion of the coal industry in the 16th century had resulted in the development of an industrial hinterland which supplied and fostered a trade that was virtually unique in being characterised by the exchange of industrial for agricultural goods. The basis of this exchange was and remained the coal trade. The annual average export of coal from the Tyne rose from about 413,000 tons in the 1660s to 777,000 tons in the 1750s, with the steepest rise occurring in the first three decades of the 18th century [see Figure 1.3]: less than 4 per cent of vessels clearing customs from the Tyne in the

9   Ellis, *Business Fortunes*, pp.33-5; Roberts, W.I., 'Ralph Carr: a Newcastle merchant and the American colonial trade', *Business History Review*, vol.42 (1968), pp.73-4.

1730s did *not* carry any coal, which was even included in cargoes bound for Lisbon, Marseilles and south Carolina.[10] Although the mines themselves were located in the countryside, rather than in the town, Newcastle was renowned as the place where 'the perfection of coalery' was to be found in terms of financial, legal and commercial, as well as mining, expertise. Keelmen employed in transporting coal from staiths upriver to ships anchored downstream appear to have been the largest male occupational group in the town in the early decades of the century, closely followed by pitmen and coal-workers employed in nearby collieries. The keelmen and their families dominated the eastern parish of All Saints, congregating in crowded riverside districts such as Sandgate. Even the aristocratic 'Lords of Coal' found it necessary to keep a presence in the town to protect their interests; within its walls they found themselves 'under the domination of the god of mines … The conversation always turns upon money; the moment you name a man, you are told what he is worth; the losses he has had, or the profit he has made by coal-mines'.[11] However, Newcastle's popular reputation as the 'Black Indies' reflected not simply the profits to be made by individual coal-owners but the extent to which the prosperity of the town as a whole depended on the growing turnover of the Tyneside coal industry. It was estimated in the 1720s that the coal trade earned £250,000 a year for Newcastle and thus financed not only a vast return trade in foodstuffs and commercial goods but also the circulation of capital and credit. Contemporaries were well aware that 'when the Coal Trade is brisk, that all other Business is so too; and when it is otherwise … there is a certain Deadness in all Trafick': a long-term decline in exports would have such a disastrous effect on employment, land values, shipping and local industries dependent on the coal trade it was all too clear that 'there is not a Cobler that will not suffer greatly'.[12]

One of the most important of these local industries was salt making, for the conjunction of salt water and cheap pancoal had produced a flourishing industry downstream from Newcastle at the mouth of the Tyne. The close connection between coal and salt was illustrated by the growing level of multiple ownership in the two industries, as coal-owners sought a profitable outlet for the 'crusty, drossy,

[10] Willan, T.S., *The English Coasting Trade 1600-1750* (Manchester, 1938), pp.114-5; P.R.O., E190/235/5, 241/7, 242/3.

[11] Birley, 'Sir John Clerk's visit', p.228; Ellis, J., 'A dynamic society: social relations in Newcastle upon Tyne', in Clark, P. (ed.), *The Transformation of English Provincial Towns* (1984), pp.217-20; Bourne, *History*, pp.154-5; Climenson, E.J. (ed.), *Elizabeth Montagu. Her Correspondence 1720-61* (1906), vol.i, p.149.

[12] Houghton, J., *A Collection for the Improvement of Husbandry and Trade* (1727), vol.ii, p.155; Historical Manuscripts Commission (hereafter H.M.C.), *Portland MSS*, vol.vi (1901), p.106; Bourne, *History*, p.158; Northumberland Record Office (hereafter N.R.O.), Carr-Ellison (Hedgeley) MSS. ZCE 10/6: Cotesworth to Sanderson, 15 Apr. 1722. Key works on the Tyneside coal industry include: David Levine and Keith Wrightson, *The Making of an Industrial Society. Whickham 1560-1765* (Oxford,1991); M.W. Flinn and David Stoker, *History of the British Coal Industry 1700-1830* (Oxford, 1983); Robert Colls, *The Pitmen of the Northern Coalfield 1790-1850* (Manchester, 1987).

mouldering coal' which was the inescapable by-product of mining operations geared to the production of high-quality shipcoal for sale in the coastal and export markets. In 1716 there were over 170 salt-pans in operation at North and South Shields, forming the largest concentration of salt-works in Britain and producing, according to one estimate, around 15 per cent of the total national salt output. The salt trade served a wide market, both domestic and foreign, although not as wide as that of the coal trade: in 1706, for instance, 10,392 tons of salt were shipped to 15 ports in the Baltic and northern Europe and 27 English ports, while 431,950 tons of coal went to 38 foreign and 40 English ports.[13]

Multiple ownership was also a feature of the expanding glass-making industry, emphasising once again both the close connections between the coal trade and Newcastle's wider industrial profile and the ingenuity with which local entrepreneurs contrived to turn 'waste' products into profitable manufactures. As an admiring visitor remarked, Newcastle was a town where 'industry seems to vie with conveniency for the better carrying on of trade'. Since salt and coal were two of the bulkiest of all commodities in proportion to their value, immense quantities of sand were brought into the port every year by ships returning without a full cargo and were deposited on ballast heaps outside the walls where they were utilised by a growing number of glassworks, many of them founded by refugee families in the later 17th and early 18th centuries. By 1696 there were six window glass, four bottle glass and one flint glass-works on the Tyne, numbers which grew steadily throughout the century despite occasional complaints from the genteel residents of Westgate about smoke drifting over from those in the Closegate district on the western outskirts of the town.[14] Like coal and salt, glass was shipped in large quantities to a wide variety of foreign and domestic markets. The coarse brown earthenware produced using local supplies of clay in potteries established at the Skinnerburn, on the South Shore and upstream at Newburn had a much more restricted appeal, although cheap imports of special clays as ballast in returning colliers allowed a few firms to start producing finer wares from the 1730s: in 1735, for example, Stourbridge clay was arriving in ships that had unloaded in Bristol. Pipeclay to supply the 40 or so tobacco pipe-makers who were operating in Newcastle and Gateshead around 1700 was also imported.[15]

[13] Ellis, J., 'The decline and fall of the Tyneside salt industry 1660-1790: a re-examination', *Economic History Review*, vol.33 (1980), pp.45-8, 58 [quotation p.47]; P.R.O., E190/211.3, 212.10.

[14] Birley, 'Clerk's visit', p.228; Bourne, *History*, pp.154-5; Loveday, J., *Diary of a Tour in 1732* (Edinburgh, 1890), p.171; Buckley, F., 'Glasshouses on the Tyne in the 18th century', *Journal of the Society of Glass Technology*, vol.10 (1926), pp.26-52.

[15] Buckley, F., 'Potteries on the Tyne and other northern potteries during the 18th century', *Archaeologia Aeliana*, vol. 4 (1927), pp.68-82; Edwards, L., 'Seventeenth and 18th-century Tyneside tobacco pipemakers and tobacconists', *The Archaeology of the Clay Tobacco Pipe* (BAR British series, 192, 1988), pp.3-5. Note that specialist clays were also used in the glass-making industries.

The intimate connection between coal, cheap transport for bulky goods and industrial progress in other sectors of the local economy can also be seen in connection with growth of the metallurgical industries on Tyneside. Lead-mining in south Tynedale, Derwentdale, Allendale and Alston Moor flourished as firms such as the London Lead Company and landowners such as the Blacketts expanded their operations, bringing a significant proportion of their output down to smelt mills and refineries upstream from Newcastle and exporting both lead and silver through established agents and merchants in the port. Lead was one of Newcastle's major foreign exports in terms of value, with annual shipments of around 1,500 tons in the 1730s worth between £15,000 and £20,000.[16] By 1700 Newcastle's hinterland was also one of the country's leading centres in the production of iron and steel. In the late 17th century Ambrose Crowley, the well-known iron master, had moved his works to Winlaton and Swalwell in the Derwent valley, prompted by the availability of locally mined supplies of iron, and water power from the Derwent river, as well as by the accessibility of imported Swedish wrought iron. The Crowley works not only catered for local demands for nails, files, spades, picks, steel-edged tools, chains and anchors but also supplied the Royal Navy and the East India Company as well as feeding into both the coastal and export trades. It rapidly became one of the essential tourist sights of the area, recognised as 'the source of great riches to this town' and astonishing visitors with the scale and mechanical ingenuity of its operations. The Crowleys' advanced techniques in steel-making were eagerly copied by other centres such as Sheffield, while their success inspired other local firms, albeit on a much more modest scale, such as the Team works established in Gateshead in 1747 by the Hawks family to process old iron brought into the port as ballast into heavy chains and anchors.[17]

The rapid expansion of these advanced industrial sectors had stimulated rather than supplanted the trade in Newcastle's traditional merchandise, such as grindstones and agricultural produce. Grindstones were still mined in the coal measures above the High Main seam in valuable beds of fine grained sandstone which outcropped on both sides of the river. A contemporary writer believed that few ships left the Tyne without one or two stones on board, and they were certainly shipped to a wide variety of markets: the 1731 Port Book shows that just under 6,000 tons were exported to at least 30 foreign and 17 English ports.[18] The wool trade had declined

[16] Hughes, M., 'Lead, land and coal as sources of landlord income in Northumberland 1700-1850' (PhD thesis, University of Newcastle, 1963), pp.69-115; Ellis, *Business Fortunes*, p.13; P.R.O., E190/235/5, 242/3, 242/15.

[17] Flinn, M.W., 'Industry and technology in the Derwent valley in the 18th century', *Transactions of the Newcomen Society*, vol.19 (1953-5), pp.255-62; Spencer, N., *The Complete English Traveller; or a New Survey and Description of England and Wales* (1771), p.571; G.P.L. CA/2/65: lease to I.Cookson & J.Bulton, 25 Mar.1722.

[18] Cox, *Magna Britania*, vol.iii, p.608; P.R.O., E190/235/5, 236/7.

in importance after centuries as Newcastle's major exporter but the export market still absorbed moderate quantities of dozens, kersies, stuffs, bays and cottons. There was a flourishing local textile industry, represented in both Gateshead and Newcastle by companies of dyers, fullers and weavers: fulling mills were in operation at Urpeth in 1712 and the local craftsmen must have had a certain reputation since in 1715 serge was being sent up from London for fulling there.[19] Animal products like leather, butter and tallow also continued to play an important part in Newcastle's trade. The town became a heavy shipper of butter later in the century but it had a wide export market even as early as 1706. The pastoral economy of the areas around the port provided a reservoir of hides, tallow and glue which was drawn on by merchants: it was reported in 1723 that over 3,000 sheep were killed weekly in Newcastle in the four months before Christmas, with other animals in proportion, figures which had risen by the 1780s to annual totals of 143,000 sheep and lambs, 10,000 calves and 5,000 beef cattle. Judith Milbanke bemoaned the 'Fragrance' of the three tanyards that surrounded her rented house in the city and ridiculed the women who carried freshly butchered carcasses through the streets on market days, 'dangling over their Brawny Arms', but the town as a whole profited considerably from these noisome activities. Tallow chandlers in Newcastle and Gateshead drew additional supplies of raw animal fat from as far afield as Carlisle, refined it in their own workshops and then exported casks of tallow to London and other southern ports: contemporary estimates suggest that 2,000 tons a year were exported in the early 1770s. Such journeys across country cannot have been unusual, since one important aspect of Newcastle's foreign trade was the export of tobacco brought into the country through Whitehaven, although direct imports from Virginia and New York were not unknown.[20]

Finally, the increased volume and variety of Newcastle's trade during the 17th and early 18th centuries had encouraged the growth not only of ship-ownership, as discussed above, but also of a Tyneside shipbuilding and repairing industry. According to Defoe, 'they build Ships here to Perfection as to Strength and Firmness, and to bear the Sea, the Coal trade demanding such', although the frequent repairs or even wholesale reconstruction occasioned by the rough handling of bulky goods in transit probably accounted for a considerable proportion of the shipwrights' business. Above the Ouseburn, shipyards and rope-yards spread along the ballast shores lining the north bank of the Tyne as far as Sandgate, while others sprang up

[19]  P.R.O., E190/211.3, 235/5; Brand, *History*, p.33; Ellis, *Business Fortunes*, pp.13-14.
[20]  Willan, *English Coasting Trade*, p.116; P.R.O., E190/211/3, 212/10; H.M.C. *Portland MSS*, vol.vi, p.106; Brand, J., *The History and Antiquities of the Town and County of Newcastle upon Tyne* (1789), vol.i, pp.19, 36n; Elwin, M., *The Noels and the Milbankes: Their Letters for Twenty-five Years 1767-92* (1967), pp.107,145; Edwards, *Archaeology*, p.110; Ellis, *Business Fortunes*, p.15.

on the south bank of the river downstream from Gateshead. Many of the vessels turned out by these yards were of medium size, sturdy two-masted brigantines of between 100 and 300 tons which were economical to operate and adaptable to a number of uses.[21] The growth of shipbuilding, together with the wider concentration of industrial activity on Tyneside, in turn contributed to a growing demand for raw materials which locally available resources could not meet. Shipbuilding and coal mining were both voracious consumers of timber and the demand for oak-timber, staithings, masts and spars on the one hand, and cheap pine and fir as pit-props, shaft linings and barrel staves on the other, was not easily satisfied. Over half of the ships entering Newcastle in 1706 from foreign ports carried timber, mainly in whole cargoes from Scandinavia, while the coastal trade also brought beech rails from Chichester, deals from Berwick and oak timber, rails and sleepers from Hull. Imports of tar, tow and hemp were also closely associated with the needs of the coal and shipping industries.[22]

The result of this concentration of industrial activity in and around the valleys of the Tyne and its tributaries was a significant concentration of population. Studies of agriculture in the area have suggested that the population of Northumberland and Durham increased by about 50 per cent between 1660s and 1730s and that this growth was accompanied by a marked redistribution of population away from the uplands and towards the industrial area, a development which enhanced Newcastle's well-established role as 'the great *Emporium* of all the Northern Parts'. In fact the Tyne valley experienced a 'thickening of the countryside' as riverside settlements expanded and villages grew up along a waggonway network carrying coal down to the waiting keels.[23] This expansion of the local industrial and commercial workforce, nearly all of them consumers rather than producers of food, required the services of an efficient and sophisticated market which could obtain supplies from a wide area and channel them into the shops, public houses and specialised street markets which so impressed contemporary visitors. The Saturday Flesh market, 'which is like a faire for all sorts of provision and goods and very cheape', attracted particular attention, 'not only as it supplies the Town in a very great Measure, but … also furnishes the country for several Miles round', as well as provisioning the coal fleets that gathered in Tynemouth haven. Moreover, the growing demand from Newcastle's customers for the basic necessities of life provided a market for the products of the town's manufacturing sector, in which clothing, shoemaking and construction were

[21]  Defoe, *Tour*, vol.iii, p.159; G.P.L. CG/5/1: minutes of evidence, 1722, f.8; Davis, R., *Rise of the English Shipping Industry in the Seventeenth and Eighteenth Centuries* (1962), pp.61-66.

[22]  P.R.O., E190/211.3, 212/10; Tyne and Wear Archives, Chamberlain's Accounts, 543/98, 99.

[23]  Brassley, P.W.,'The agricultural economy of Northumberland and Durham in the period 1640-1750' (BLitt thesis, University of Oxford, 1974) pp.21,33-4; Cox, *Magna Britania*, vol.iii, p.608.

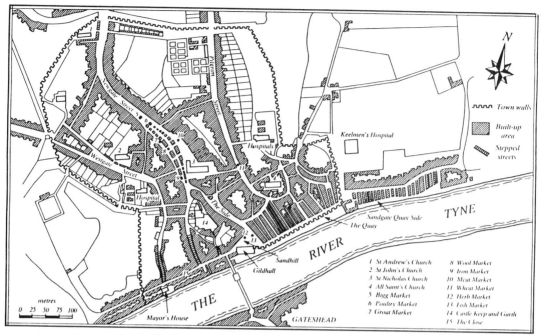

Town walls
Built-up area
Stepped streets

Keelmen's Hospital

Hospitals

TYNE

Sandgate Quay Side
The Quay

1  St Andrew's Church      8  Wool Market
2  St John's Church        9  Iron Market
3  St Nicholas Church     10  Meat Market
4  All Saint's Church     11  Wheat Market
5  Bigg Market            12  Herb Market
6  Poultry Market         13  Fish Market
7  Groat Market           14  Castle Keep and Garth
                          15  The Close

Sandhill
Gildhall

RIVER

THE

metres
0  25  50  75  100

Mayor's House                    GATESHEAD

**1.1**  Newcastle upon Tyne in the 1730s.

prominent. In fact Defoe's analysis of the strength of popular purchasing power in the national economy seems particularly appropriate to Newcastle: 'These are the People that carry off the Gross of your Consumption; 'tis for these your markets are kept open on Saturday nights; ... in a Word, these are the Life of our whole Commerce, and all by their Multitude.'[24]

At a more sophisticated level, the town was the main distributor of the wines, groceries and consumer goods that were imported from London or abroad. Its wholesale merchants supplied customers over a wide area in Cumberland, Westmorland and north Yorkshire in addition to Northumberland and Durham, while retailers operated from shops which Celia Fiennes was already praising in the 1690s as being 'of distinct trades, not selling many things in one shop as is the custom in most country towns and cittys'. The complex occupational structure which had evolved to match the growth of demand meant that goods and services appropriate to every level of society were available: surgeons and bonesetters, cobblers and mantua-makers, butchers and confectioners, pot-founders and makers of musical instruments. Despite its overwhelming commercial character, the presence in the town of an impressive range of luxury trades and services clearly indicates

[24]  Morris (ed.), *Journeys*, p.211; Bourne, *History*, p.54; Defoe, *Plan*, p.217.

[11]

that Newcastle was large and wealthy enough in its own right to generate a market for leisure and luxury among the middling ranks of urban merchants, tradesmen and professionals as well as to exert some social 'pull' over the gentry and nobility within its extensive hinterland.[25] John Macky remarked in the 1720s, there was 'as much good Company, as can well be expected in a place of so much Business', a phenomenon that was encouraged by the evolution of a summer season marked by race and Assize weeks, assemblies, theatre performances, and subscription concerts. By the 1760s such activities had expanded, augmented in the following decades by the construction of elegant new assembly rooms in Westgate Street and the Theatre Royal in Mosley Street. In spite of its smoky, 'industrious' character, Newcastle was not even a particularly unpleasant place in which to live permanently as long as you avoided the jostling lower town behind the waterfront and chose instead the pleasantly 'retir'd' areas amid meadows and gardens which survived into the 19th century in the northern parishes of St Andrew's and St John's.[26] As in Britain's other great regional centres, the purchasing power of this urban elite made a major contribution to the vitality and diversity of Newcastle's economy.

## The 'river dragon'

The underlying dynamism of Newcastle in the early 18th century was reflected in the diversity and accessibility of its society. Its social pluralism was undoubtedly influenced by the shared interest of its inhabitants in the fortunes of the port: despite the well-documented social and political divisions between the 'double gilted gentry' on the one hand and the 'leather aprons' and 'raggamuffins' who made up the lower ranks of Newcastle's freemen on the other, they were united in their dependence on the tidal and seasonal rhythms of trade flowing up and down the Tyne. It was noted that 'Every gentleman in the county, from the least to the greatest, is as solicitous in the pursuit of gain as a tradesman', while humbler citizens backed their rulers to the hilt in defending the town's commercial interests from outside attack.[27] Many of these humbler citizens undoubtedly derived a comfortable livelihood from these interests, benefiting from the relatively high money wages and low prices for both food and fuel that prevailed in the local economy. Both pitmen and keelmen 'got Money fast … when Trade was good' and were renowned

[25] Ellis, *Business Fortunes*, pp 28-32; Willan, T.S., *An Eighteenth-century Shopkeeper. Abraham Dent of Kirkby Stephen* (Manchester, 1970), pp.38-40; Morris (ed.), *Journeys*, pp.210-11. Information on trades and occupations pre-1778 is taken from parish register samples, poll books and local newspapers.

[26] Macky, *Journey*, vol.ii, p.217; Montagu, *Correspondence*, vol.ii, pp.205-7; Brand, *History*, vol.i, pp.121-2; Loveday, *Diary*, pp.168-9; Bourne, *History*, p.22.

[27] Knox, T.R., 'Wilkesism and the Newcastle election of 1774', *Durham University Journal*, vol. 72 (1979), pp.23-38 [quotations p.28]; Montagu, *Correspondence*, vol.ii, p.149. For an analysis of the political struggle and its context see: Wilson, K., *The Sense of the People. Politics, Culture and Imperialism in England 1715-85* (Cambridge, 1995), pp.315-75.

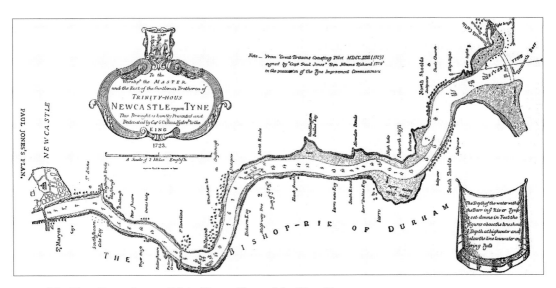

**1.2** 'The River Dragon': 1723 Trinity House Chart of the River Tyne.

for spending it equally rapidly: probate records, however, demonstrate that individuals could accumulate a modest amount of property over their lifetimes, owning their own keels as well as shares in a number of ships, and disposing in their wills of considerable stocks of household goods and plate. A handbill issued by striking seamen in 1793 tells much the same story, claiming that in peacetime 'We can then live comfortably, support our Families decently, give our Children an honest and useful Education'. This relative prosperity combined with the contemporary ethos of improvement and 'clubability' among both artisans and skilled labourers to support a wide range of associational activities within the town, including around fifty formal clubs and societies as well as 'combinations' to defend wage levels and working conditions.[28]

However, the prominence of these defensive associations and the frequency with which sections of Newcastle's workers were forced into militant action is a clear indication that comfortable livelihoods were neither typical nor reliable over the longer term. The town had in fact an unenviable reputation for the 'prodigious number' of its poor. The nature of the local economy had created an unusually uneven distribution of wealth and status in the town, leaving the quasi-proletarian multitude of the poor acutely vulnerable to the fluctuating nature of the trade on which so much of their employment was based. Downturns in the London market

---

[28] Young, A., *A Six Month's Tour Through the North of England* (1770), vol.iii, pp.9,12; iv.321-2; Chicken, E., *The Collier's Wedding. A Poem* (Newcastle, 1764), pp.3-5; McCord, N. & Brewster, D.E., 'Some labour troubles of the 1790s in north-east England', *International Review of Social History*, vol.13 (1968), p.379: Brewer, J., *The Pleasures of the Imagination. English Culture in the Eighteenth Century* (1997), pp.507-11.

for coal, outbreaks of warfare or the onset of hard weather which disrupted shipping in the port and interrupted the flow of funds necessary to maintain payments to the industrial workforce, all had the potential to throw 'promiscuous numbers' out of work. These occasional crises should not, however, obscure the less dramatic but more insidious effects of seasonal unemployment, which made it difficult for keelmen and casual labourers alike to maintain their precarious hold on solvency.[29] Over-manning and under-employment were endemic in Newcastle, as in all busy ports, breeding chronic insecurity and exacerbating the grinding poverty that was all too evident in the narrow alleys leading back from the waterfront below the bridge, 'the poorest and most contemptible part of the town'. In such circumstances, the 8.6 inhabitants per house recorded for Newcastle as a whole in 1801, the highest in the country, clearly indicates that the lodging houses and tenements of Sandgate were appallingly overcrowded; perhaps even 'the most crowded with buildings of any part of his majesty's dominions'.[30]

It was an environment that encouraged a proliferation of 'lewd and disorderly houses' as desperate women struggled to make a living alongside people often represented by outsiders as 'dirty Savages' or 'Brutes', prone to drunken and irrational violence. Certainly many of Newcastle's inhabitants worked in conditions that could legitimately be described as brutalising. The 'nervous and muscular strength' of the keelmen was tested to the full as they transferred their bulky, backbreaking cargoes up and downstream in all weathers and states of the tide; while visitors were horrified by the 'soar labour' of the men, women and children who worked in the salt and glass-making industries. The film of coal-dust and smoke which obscured the features of so many inhabitants of 'the Black Indies' seemed to horrify and alarm southern visitors, evoking colonial imagery and attitudes that encouraged them to exaggerate the depravity and understate the humanity of the poor. While no-one could doubt that Newcastle society as a whole, from the great families who controlled the Corporation down to the poorest labourer on the waterfront, was noticeably competitive and aggressive, and prone to drunkenness, cursing, swearing and internal recriminations, John Wesley was one of the few contemporary observers to acknowledge that 'the very mob of Newcastle, in the height of their rudeness, have commonly some humanity left'.[31]

---

[29] Defoe, *Tour*, vol.iii, p.159; Ellis, 'Social relations', pp.197-8,207,212; G.P.L. Ellison MSS.A32/21: Liddell to Ellison, 14 Jan.1729. The seasonal pattern of trade is discussed above, p.2.

[30] Curnock, N. (ed.), *The Journal of the Rev.John Wesley* (1938), vol.iii, p.14; Warner, R., *A Tour Through the Northern Counties of England and the Borders of Scotland* (1802), pp.313-14; Mackenzie, E., *A Descriptive and Historical Account of the Town and County of Newcastle upon Tyne, including Gateshead* (Newcastle, 1827), p.163. Comparative figures are available in Corfield, *Impact of English Towns*, p.183.

[31] Elwin (ed.), *Noels*, p.107; Baillie, J., *An Impartial History of the Town and County of Newcastle upon Tyne and its Vicinity* (Newcastle, 1801), p.142; Birley, 'Clerk's visit', p.228; Wesley, *Journal*, vol.iii, p.81.

1.3 Late 18th-century engraving of Newcastle keelmen.

In any case, neither aggression nor insecurity was unique to the poorer sections of society in any trading city. Newcastle indeed owed its reputation as the 'river dragon' to the fierce determination with which the Corporation defended its trading privileges over local rivals who appeared to pose an ever-increasing threat. Although the town's economy continued to attract admiring comments in the second half of the century, these conventional panegyrics were becoming increasingly divorced from reality, mere 'pages of inanity' copied uncritically from one publication to another, as Arthur Young complained, and merely repeating 'in the common hackneyed style, *That Newcastle is a place of very considerable trade, her merchants possessing a very extensive commerce, exporting this, that and the other, and importing such and such commodities*, etc. etc.'. As Young himself recognised, contemporaries had great difficulty in getting beyond these generalities given that few statistics were available locally except those generated by trade passing through the port and by the Corporation's own revenues; since both these series seemed to be rising steadily, observers could perhaps be forgiven for their optimistic assumption that the town 'has not only maintained its rank, but even risen in the scale of national importance'. As a result, the census enumeration of 1801 was greeted in Newcastle with 'universal surprise' and its outraged citizens virtually demanded a recount. They were used to thinking

**1.4**  Hedley's locomotive transporting keels: strike breaking, 1822.

of themselves as operating in the premier urban league: the official figure of 33,048, which appeared to indicate that the town had slipped well down the urban hierarchy, coming to rest just below Portsmouth and Bath, was simply unacceptable.[32] It was little comfort, presumably, that the same figures revealed a high level of positive urban growth in the town's immediate vicinity, creating what has been termed an 'urban doughnut' coupling together the economies of the Tyne and Wear. Indeed, the rapid advance of Sunderland and the startling gains made by Gateshead, Tynemouth and North and South Shields only added insult to injury.

There are several possible explanations of Newcastle's temporary eclipse within its flourishing and populous region but one of the most cogent highlights, somewhat paradoxically, the inherent disadvantages of its location at the lowest crossing point of the Tyne. A great port which lay ten or twelve miles upstream could not be described as ideally placed, especially when the long, winding passage upriver was often made impossible by high winds and stormy weather. Moreover, the problems of masters trying to reach the town from the sea were increased by the condition of the channel, which was perilously shallow in places, making navigation above the

---

[32] Surtees, R., *The History and Antiquities of the County Palatine of Durham* (1820), vol.ii, p.94; Young, *Six Months Tour*, vol.iii, pp.2-8; Langton, J., 'Urban growth and economic change: from the late 17th century to 1841', in Clark (ed), *Cambridge Urban History of Britain, vol.ii*, p.473.

'Natural Dock' at Tynemouth difficult, dangerous, and time-consuming. The river's natural tendency to silt up was aggravated by the vast quantities of sand and gravel ballast which had built up over the years and which the Newcastle authorities insisted should be deposited at official ballast shores; a sliding scale of charges encouraged masters to use quays as close to the town as possible and, moreover, penalised them if they used agents rather than coming up to town in person to pay their fees and clear their cargoes. In 1765 it was calculated that 100,000 tons of ballast was carried upstream in this way every year, a high proportion of which was either dumped illicitly overboard to avoid paying the allegedly exorbitant fees, or simply swept back into the river by floods and high winds from inadequate, badly-sited riverside dumps. In December 1764, for instance, 1,000 tons of ballast was washed off St Anthony's Quay in a single night. Although the Corporation claimed to spend large sums in maintaining the channel, there were constant allegations that they neglected their obligations even in the immediate vicinity of Newcastle's famous quay. In 1722 an aggrieved merchant complained that a vessel carrying his goods had actually overturned at the quay because of the 'ill-groundage': only ships under 200 tons could actually get alongside and their masters had to take careful soundings to ensure that loading did not leave them hopelessly aground.[33]

The shallowness of the river and the difficulties of loading caused particular problems in the coal trade: colliers grew steadily larger over time to reduce the costs of transporting so bulky a cargo and were therefore less able to penetrate very far upstream. The coal fleet therefore anchored in the famous deep water haven at the mouth of the river and were loaded from keels that plied between Tynemouth and staiths located further upriver, sometimes several miles beyond the Tyne bridge. The fact that so many of Newcastle's principal exports were both produced and trans-shipped outside its boundaries made the Corporation particularly sensitive to the danger that the port's effective centre of gravity would move downstream and that an alternative commercial centre would develop at Tynemouth and the Shields. In their eyes, all that was keeping Newcastle from sharing the fate of other inland ports were its traditional 'rights and privileges' – which sharpened the teeth of the old river dragon, deployed in the 18th century as they had been for generations to suppress dangerous competition from the lower reaches of the Tyne.[34] Unsurprisingly, perhaps, this policy was overwhelmingly popular with the Newcastle electorate but equally unpopular with the majority of those using the river. The Crowleys, for

[33] Guthrie, J., *The River Tyne: its History and Resources* (Newcastle, 1880), p.62; *Newcastle Journal*, 16 Dec.1764; G.P.L. CG/5/52: A remonstance of grievances suffered by Edward Fairless of South Shields in importing corn, 1722; Ellis, *Business Fortunes*, pp.18-21.

[34] Hausman, W.J., 'The size and profitability of English colliers in the 18th century', *Business History Review*, vol.11 (1977), pp.460-73; North, R., *The Lives of the Norths* (1826), vol i, p.249; Brome, *Travels*, p.172.

instance, kept up a running battle over several decades with the Corporation, persistently evading port regulations and tolls on goods passing between Swalwell and Tynemouth, while those aristocratic coal-owners who dominated the coalfield south of the Tyne were prepared to offer the government a collective bribe of £8,000 a year in return for their support against the tyranny of 'a few ill-bred, ill-natured and insolent inferiors'; what they envisaged was nothing less than amending or even rescinding Newcastle's charter. On this occasion the Corporation successfully defended its position as it was to do until nationwide municipal reform in the 1830s. In 1725 the town's income from rents, dues and tolls was some £12,500 a year, rising by the 1780s to almost £20,000.[35]

However, despite the magistrates' vigilance they were unable to prevent industrial and residential development spreading downstream and consolidating at the river-mouth. Despite the fact that key trades such as carpenters, anchorsmiths, blacksmiths, bakers and brewers were officially prohibited from servicing vessels anchored in the haven, visitors in the early years of the century were already describing Shields as 'the harbour of Newcastle ... large, well built and populous' and noting that it was 'well inhabited by ... such tradesmen and artificers as are necessary and depend upon the sea service'. As the century wore on shipbuilding in particular tended to be located nearer to the sea. Between 1786 and 1800, only 30 per cent of the vessels built on the Tyne and registered in the port were actually constructed upstream near Newcastle. Moreover, Newcastle shipyards tended to turn out vessels that were significantly smaller than those built at North and South Shields or at Howdon-pans. In many respects this was a simple matter of common sense, given the pressure on suitable waterfront sites near Newcastle's historic centre. However, the contrast between the modest yard operated from 1756 by William Rowe at St Peter's, which consisted of little more than an open slipway on the riverbank, and the ambitious scale of Hurry's shipyard at Howdon, constructed in 1758-9 complete with a substantial dry dock, and an 800-foot quay and ancillary industries operating on site, may indicate a significant reduction in the confidence and ambition of Newcastle's business community.[36]

This is certainly an argument that would have appealed to the growing number of contemporary writers who claimed that the very rights and privileges on which Newcastle relied had in reality fatally weakened the town's ability to respond to economic opportunity. As the century wore on, it became widely accepted that

[35] Flinn, M.W., *Men of Iron. The Crowleys in the Early Iron Industry* (Edinburgh, 1962), pp.120-3; G.P.L. CK/1/47: Ellison to Cotesworth, 17 Aug.1722; N.R.O. ZCE 10/4: Cotesworth to Banks, 30 Oct.1719; Wilson, *Sense of the People*, pp.293, 323.

[36] Cox, *Magna Britania*, vol.iii, p.606; *The Universal Magazine* (1748), p.354; MacRitchie, *Diary of a Tour*, p.137; Ville, S.P., 'Shipping in the port of Newcastle 1780-1800', *Journal of Transport History*, vols 9-10 (1988-9), pp.66-7; Richardson, W., *History of the Parish of Wallsend* (1923), pp.199-204.

'Charters and Corporations are of eminent Prejudice to a Town, as they exclude Strangers, Stop the Growth of Trade, and ... prevent Ingenuity and Improvements', creating an apparently inevitable connection between 'Corporation-Tyranny' and stagnation. Newcastle's entrenched oligarchy, it could be argued, had become so preoccupied with defending the *status quo* and collecting its substantial revenues that it had neglected the long-term interests of its citizens: the Corporation's inertia thus encouraged complacency and business conservatism in a period which demanded enterprise and action.[37] This discourse was readily adopted by their political opponents, who consistently accused the magistrates of neglecting the commercial infrastructure of the port while spending the town's revenues lavishly on feasts, ceremonies and amenities that benefited Newcastle's social and political elite more than the majority of the population. In the 1774 parliamentary election campaign, for instance, the opposition candidates pointedly inspected the quays down to Shields and anti-Corporation campaigners contrasted the elite's readiness to subscribe large sums of money to the new assembly rooms with the slow progress made in rebuilding the vital Tyne Bridge, destroyed in a disastrous flood in November 1771. This latter charge was blatantly unfair: restoring the road link over the Tyne was a major public engineering project involving difficult negotiations with the bishop of Durham and expenditure of well over £30,000, while the assembly room subscription of around £6,000 was only little more than the £4,000 raised for the relief of the flood victims three years earlier. It is also worth noting that George Grieve, chairman of the radical Constitutional Club, had himself subscribed £25 to the rooms, as had several other prominent opposition figures including Richard Lacy and Thomas Maude. Moreover the Corporation resisted the temptation to recoup its outlay on the bridge by charging tolls, a strategy which in Bristol provoked serious civil unrest.[38]

On the other hand, the disputes of the 1770s reveal a level of disenchantment with the Corporation which severely undermined its credibility, especially as little was done to satisfy the opposition's basic grievances. A report on the state of the river submitted in 1816 by John Rennie, the greatest dock engineer of his day, outlined conditions virtually identical to those described in affidavits collected from ship-masters and keelmen in 1722. A further enquiry in 1848 by the Harbour Department of the Admiralty detected very little improvement, even after the establishment of a River Improvement Commission in 1836. Throughout the period, therefore, vessels using the river ran the risk of fouling their anchors on abandoned

[37] Short, T., *New Observations on City, Town and County Bills of Mortality* (1750), p.79; Hinde (ed.), *Inedited Contributions*, p.6; Mackenzie, *Historical Account*, p.197; Ellis, 'Regional and county centres', pp.678-80.

[38] *Newcastle Chronicle*, 13 Aug.1774; Knox, T.R., 'Popular politics and provincial radicalism: Newcastle upon Tyne 1769-85', *Albion*, vol.11 (1979), pp.223-41; Brand, *History*, vol.i, p.121-2; G.P.L. CJ/6/12: list of subscribers, 10 Feb.1774; Newcastle City Library, L942.82/N5370: subscription ledger, 1776; Harrison, M., '"To raise and dare resentment": the Bristol bridge riot of 1793 re-examined', *Historical Journal*, vol. 26 (1983), pp.557-85.

wrecks and of running aground on the massive shoals which obstructed the navigable channel all the way down to Tynemouth. Even the entrance to the harbour was unsafe, especially in a north-east wind. It was reported that you could walk from North to South Shields at low water springs: certainly ships often stuck fast on the bar, as did HMS *Greyhound* in 1711 and HMS *Martin* in 1792. In the latter case it was particularly embarrassing for the Corporation as Conservators of the Tyne that the warship had to be pulled off the shoal on which it had grounded by the very seamen whose 'mutiny' it was meant to suppress. Conditions may even have become worse as property prices along the river rose and existing ballast shores reached their capacity, with the result that masters had to bear the additional cost of moving large quantities of sand and gravel back from the waterfront to cheaper sites inland. Yet the response of the Corporation was wholly inadequate. Rather than putting back the immense revenues they had derived from the river into a coherent effort to maintain the channel, which would have had the added benefit of providing work for keelmen and casual labourers when trade was slack, the town council seems to have given priority to the interests of urban ratepayers, spending heavily on public services such as lighting, paving and scavenging: in the 40 years 1809-49, for instance, only 41 per cent of the £957,973 collected in river dues was actually spent on the river itself.[39]

Moreover the unreformed Corporation seems to have had a very narrow interpretation of its duties as 'conservator', rejecting and indeed often actively opposing any proposals that would actually *improve* conditions on the Tyne. A scheme which was first proposed in 1755 to load incoming ballast straight into specially-built hoppers so that it could be safely dumped at sea was said to have 'much allarm'd' the magistrates, who were said to have been more concerned to protect the Corporation's income than to promote the long-term prosperity of the port. In a similar vein they consistently opposed schemes to extend the navigable waterway upstream through a river navigation or a canal. Preoccupied as they were with maintaining Newcastle's unique hold on the trade of the river, they appeared oblivious to the fact that successful urban centres depended on developing good communications with their hinterlands. While Liverpool and Hull, for example, were investing heavily in canal and dock developments, in 1797 only 258 Newcastle residents could summon up the enthusiasm to petition Parliament in support of a canal projected to link the northern outskirts of the town with Carlisle. Admittedly the goods likely to benefit in the immediate future from better access to the Newcastle market – limestone from Corbridge, coarse felt hats from Hexham, slate from Shap

---

[39]  G.P.L. CG/5/1: minutes of evidence, 1722; Burn, W.L., 'Newcastle upon Tyne in the early 19th century', *Archaeologia Aeliana*, vol.34 (1956), pp.1-13; *Newcastle Courant*, 25-27 Aug.1711; *Newcastle Chronicle*, 1 Dec.1792.

– were likely to be much less profitable than the 50,000 quarters of corn that were estimated in 1793 to be flowing annually into Hull down the Derwent navigation from Malton.[40] On the other hand the long-term benefits of investment in improved transport links, as well as in the basic infrastructure of the port, could have given Newcastle a much-needed boost at a time when its previously dynamic expansion seems to have faltered.

## Newcastle's Economic Performance

However, it has to be accepted that many of the problems faced by long-established urban centres in the later years of the 18th century were not susceptible to easy solutions and that even the most astute, energetic civic leadership could struggle in vain to adapt to changing circumstances. There was no guarantee, for instance, that a canal network centred on Newcastle would have the same impact as those centring on Liverpool or Hull, while many ports found that the steamship and railway revolution of the early 19th century rendered much of their expensive capital investment obsolete.[41] In some ways, indeed, Newcastle's civic leaders revealed a far-sighted perception of the town's long-term interests precisely in the amount of money invested by the Corporation in public amenities and urban improvement schemes from the 1770s onwards: almost £100,000 was spent on town improvement. Far from being a selfish luxury of benefit only to a narrow social elite, the facilities which towns could offer wealthy residents and visitors were crucial to their continued success as centres of both wholesale and retail trade. Faster transport systems were rapidly concentrating trade in the best-positioned and best-provisioned centres, while towns which failed to develop the smart, sophisticated residential and commercial areas, which well-travelled visitors now expected to find, risked becoming locked into a spiral of decline. It may be an early sign of this anxiety that Sir Charles Brandling, an unsuccessful candidate in the 1784 parliamentary election, was criticised in the local press for 'sending to London or York for what Newcastle could supply as well'.[42]

On the other hand, Newcastle was not as badly placed in this competitive market as its 'forbidding appearance' and congested, polluted environment might suggest.[43] Although complaints about the ugliness, noise and squalor generated by

---

[40] North of England Institute of Mining and Mechanical Engineers, Brown Letter Book 16/2, 7 Feb.1765; Guthrie, *River Tyne*, pp.39-40; *Journal of the House of Commons*, lii (1796-7), pp.345, 446; Jackson, G., *Hull in the Eighteenth Century: a Study in Economic and Social History* (Oxford, 1972), pp.21-2.

[41] Jackson, G., *The History and Archaeology of Ports* (Tadworth, 1983), pp.73-6.

[42] Ellis, 'Regional and county centres', pp.681-2; *Newcastle Chronicle*, 3 Apr.1784.

[43] Spencer, *Complete English Traveller*, p.571. Spencer seems to have been particularly sensitive to environmental problems; see Sweet, *Urban Histories*, pp.132-3.

industrial and commercial processes grew more and more insistent over the century, it is clear that these perceptions did not prevent 'industrious' towns which were also major regional centres from developing impressive leisure and retail infrastructures to service their increasingly wealthy hinterlands. Size mattered: there were thus more luxury trades and traders in Bristol in the 1790s than there were in Bath. It also seems likely that most people who were exposed to the latest fashions in consumer goods in the 'showcase' settings of London, Brighton or Bath went on to purchase them much nearer home. The woman who visited Joseph Harris's china shop in old Pullen market in 1780 looking for a Wedgwood dinner service of 'Arabesque Border' before Mr. Harris had even heard of the pattern falls into this category; she rejected his current stock, insisting that she wanted it because it was 'much used in London at present'. A comparative analysis of the trade directories of the period indicates that Newcastle in fact rose remarkably well to the challenge. By the 1790s Newcastle consumers had a choice of four china-dealers, a number which fell well below the eight recorded in Liverpool but put Newcastle roughly on a par with Manchester and Bristol, a comparison borne out across the whole 'luxury sector' of trades and services.[44] These positive developments were reinforced after the end of the long and costly wars with France by an ambitious scheme of town improvement, inspired by Nash's work in London, which for a few brief years made Newcastle 'Britain's most handsome industrial city'. In the years between 1825 and 1840 Grainger in effect created a new city centre, one which included a network of high-status shopping streets, including a Royal Arcade, as an essential adjunct to the impressive public buildings and smart housing. The Royal Arcade in particular indicated that Newcastle's fashionable retail facilities were keeping pace with those of London and Britain's other great regional centres.[45]

This evidence of Newcastle's ability to respond to economic change in the early 19th century is somewhat at variance with perceptions of its relative failure before that. And indeed arguments which equate Newcastle's apparently sluggish population growth in the 18th century with economic 'failure' may be badly mistaken. Local perceptions of Newcastle's size and status, which were so confounded by the results of the 1801 census, would undoubtedly have included the 'suburb' of Gateshead rather than regarding it as a separate town, and would have been based on the actual built-up area rather than on the formal boundaries of the town's official jurisdiction: the *de facto* population of this aggregate settlement in 1801 can be calculated as

[44] Stobart, J., 'In search of a leisure hierarchy: English spa towns and their place in the urban system', in Borsay, P., Hirschfelder, G., and Mohrmann, R. (eds), *New Directions in Urban History* (Munster/New York, 2000), pp.19-40; McKendrick, N., *The Birth of a Consumer Society. The Commercialization of Eighteenth-century England* (1982), p.120; *Whitehead's Newcastle Directory for 1778*, p.15; Whitehead, J., *Newcastle and Gateshead Directory for 1790* (Newcastle, 1790), p.65.

[45] Best, G., 'The Scottish Victorian city', *Victorian Studies*, vol.11 (1968), p.336; see below, chapter 10.

41,645, which goes some way to substantiate the estimates of 30-40,000 made by 'sensible inhabitants' in the 1770s.[46] Yet there is sufficient evidence of significant weaknesses in several key sectors of Newcastle's industrial base to indicate that the second half of the 18th century in particular *was* a time of lost opportunity. Its lead in steel-making technology, for instance, was not maintained and the initiative passed to Sheffield. Even the wonders of the massive Crowley ironworks became somewhat outdated with the passage of time; Arthur Young, for instance, questioned the amount of routine work that was still carried out there by manual labour and was puzzled by their apparent inability to obtain adequate supplies of American bar iron. Meanwhile the once-flourishing salt industry faltered in the 1730s and went downhill rapidly after 1760 as the impact of falling transport costs in the Cheshire salt-field undermined its economic base. Even the coal trade, the mainstay of the town's prosperity, gave cause for concern as demand failed to keep pace with rapidly rising production costs, creating a relative oversupply of coal on Tyneside just as competition from alternative sources of supply, notably from the rapidly developing port of Sunderland, began to cut into Newcastle's markets. Given that coal imports into London stagnated between 1725 and the 1760s, Newcastle's growing dependence on demand from the metropolis in this period was doubly unfortunate.[47]

The impact of cut-throat competition on coal-owners' profits, and thus on the entire Tyneside economy, could well have contributed to a local business culture that arguably discouraged enterprise. In relative terms, the high entry thresholds of capital-intensive industries such as coal, salt and glass-making, and the high recurrent costs of sustaining the necessary flow of investment, undoubtedly deterred many potentially able businessmen while encouraging in those who did succeed a potentially inefficient mix of excessive caution on the one hand and equally excessive, ill-judged speculation on the other. Newcastle merchants found it difficult to break into the buoyant colonial market for manufactured goods, for instance, partly because they refused to follow the example of their Dutch and English rivals by extending credit and selling on consignment. It was also unhelpful that Newcastle manufacturers tended to concentrate on lower-quality goods aimed at mass markets rather than to refine their production techniques and widen their appeal: the only earthenware which interested Ralph Carr's New York correspondents in the 1750s was the fine tea, sugar and milk pots typical of Staffordshire wares, goods which local potteries did not attempt to produce in any quantity until the late 1760s.[48]

---

[46] Langton, 'Urban growth', pp.457-60; Young, *Six Months' Tour*, pp.5-8; Brand, *History*, vol.i, p.19.

[47] McCord, N., *North East England* (1979), p.15; Young, *Six Month's Tour*, vol.iii, pp.9-11; Ellis, 'Decline and fall', pp.53-7; Ellis, J.M., 'Cartels in the coal industry on Tyneside 1699-1750', *Northern History*, vol.24 (1998), pp.137-9.

[48] Ellis, J.M., 'Risk, capital and credit on Tyneside c1690-1780', in Bruland, K. and O'Brien, P. (eds.), *From Family Firms to Corporate Capitalism. Essays in Business and Industrial History in Honour of Peter Mathias* (Oxford, 1998), pp.84-111; Roberts, 'Ralph Carr', pp.275-6; Buckley, 'Potteries', pp.77-8.

Subsequent recovery can be attributed to the renewed surge of coal exports through the port that followed the end of the Seven Years War in 1775. Stimulated by the combined effects of population growth and industrial expansion, the London market in particular embarked on a 12-year period of steadily increasing demand and stable prices which coincided with a huge injection of new capital into the Newcastle coalfield and a significant expansion of mining to the north and east of the town. Equally significant was the fact that the bulk of this investment came not from the aristocratic landowners who had dominated the coal industry for so long, but from local entrepreneurs such as Matthew Bell, John Cookson and William Brown, using funds channelled through Newcastle's growing number of local banks. These were people with a vested interest in ploughing their profits back into the local economy, unlike many of the wealthy land-owning families who had tended to spend their profits in fashionable London or on their southern estates. Elizabeth Montagu, for example, had consoled herself during her exile among the 'bleak' prospects of Northumberland with the thought that 'I shall see its produce at Sir James Colebrook's in Threadneedle Street'.[49] Coal exports moved sharply upwards from the 1790s, reaching two million tons a year by 1830, an expansion that carried with it an equivalent rise in both the total tonnage being handled by the port and in local investment in shipping. By 1801, 632 vessels were registered at Newcastle representing a tonnage of 140,055, narrowly beating Liverpool for second place behind London. The aggregate value of Newcastle-registered ships at the end of the 18th century was estimated at £950,000. There were other clear signs that Newcastle was keeping pace with national trends in the industry, with much greater concentration of ownership in the hands of professional shipowners and the growth of marine insurance. The port was renowned as a centre of mutual insurance clubs operating alongside a growing number of specialist brokers. In 1790 there were already six firms of ship and insurance brokers listed in the Newcastle directory and, although there was as yet no separate entry for 'shipowners', by 1827 this had emerged as a substantial occupational category.[50]

Other sectors of Newcastle's industrial economy also benefited from the area's hard-won expertise in handling coal-based sources of energy. Although salt manufacture had dwindled to a shadow of its former glory, powerful synergies still bound many of the town's other industries together in a close-knit association that once again established Tyneside in the vanguard of technical progress. The glass-

[49] Flinn, M.W., *The History of the British Coal Industry, vol.ii, 1700-1830* (Oxford, 1984), pp.40-1,208; Cromar, P., 'Economic power and organization: the development of the coal industry on Tyneside 1700-1828' (PhD thesis, Cambridge University, 1976), pp.107-12, 119-22; Montagu, *Correspondence*, vol.ii, p.202.

[50] Flinn, *Coal Industry*, pp.218, 226; Ville, 'Patterns of shipping', pp.209-19; Dunn, M., *An Historical, Geological and Descriptive View of the Coal Trade of the North of England* (Newcastle, 1844), p.64.

making industry, for instance, was well placed to take advantage of the rise in popularity of high-quality crown glass for domestic glazing, leading to significant expansion in the Skinnerburn glassworks to the west of the town and those at Ouseburn to the east, as well as to the construction in 1787 of one of the largest glass cones in the country at Lemington by the newly formed Northumberland Glass Company. In 1772 there had been 16 relatively modest glassworks on Tyneside as a whole; by 1812 this number had risen to 30 and within 15 years the region was responsible for around forty per cent of the national glass output. The continuing utility of securing a profitable outlet for 'waste' coal from the collieries encouraged the Ridley family to acquire a large interest in the window and bottle glass trade; conversely, it was probably John Cookson's experience as a glassmaker that had led him into investment in mining. It is also worth noting that Cookson and John Airey, partners in the Close glassworks, were also partners in Newcastle's original bank, founded in 1755. The coal-owner Matthew Bell was another founding partner, while Matthew White Ridley joined the firm in 1787.[51] The close-knit integrated nature of this local business world was also pivotal in stimulating the growth of the chemical industry, another staple of the town's 19th-century prosperity. Soda or alkali was crucial to the glass-making process, among others, while on the other hand the production of soda depended on abundant supplies of cheap fuel and brine-salt. William Losh, a trained chemist who had inherited a considerable interest in Walker colliery, was ideally placed to build at Walker the first British alkali works using the Leblanc process and so spark off a period of massive growth of the industry on Tyneside.[52]

The final link in this chain of integrated business enterprise was represented by the iron-working and engineering industries. Losh himself diversified his activities through his involvement in the firm of Losh, Wilson and Bell at Walker ironworks, while Cookson & Co. had been running an iron and brass foundry near Closegate as early as 1778. The expanding coal industry was a voracious consumer of metal goods, from basic tools such as picks and shovels through the increasing quantity of iron wheels and rails used in the waggonway network that led coals down to the riverside staiths, culminating in the sophisticated engineering required by the coal-fired colliery drainage machinery that had proliferated during the 18th century. George Stephenson, for instance, began his career as a colliery engineman and his development work on steam locomotives was prompted purely by the demands of

[51] Buckley, 'Glasshouses', pp.27-32; Mackenzie, *History*, vol.ii, p.383; Parson and White, *Directory of Northumberland and Durham* (1828), vol.ii, pp.374-5; *The Penny Magazine*, vol.13 (1844), pp.249-52; Phillips, M., 'The "Old Bank" (Bell, Cookson, Carr and Airey), Newcastle-upon-Tyne', *Archaeologia Aeliana*, vol.16 (1894), pp.452-70.

[52] Warner, *Tour*, p.315; Baillie, *Impartial History*, pp.441-533; Richardson, M.A., *Descriptive Companion through Newcastle* (Newcastle, 1838), pp.165-7.

the coal industry, while Robert and William Hawthorn who established an engineering workshop at Forth Banks in 1817, were themselves sons of a colliery engineer. In 1820 the Hawthorn Company built a steam-driven crane for lifting ballast out of vessels using St Anthony's Quay and in 1824 they built an engine for Cookson and Cuthbert's plate glassworks. The links which bound together so much of Newcastle's industrial base meant that technical and managerial innovation in one industry was rapidly and widely disseminated in another, a feature which continued throughout the 19th century.[53]

The launch of the first steam-powered boat on the Tyne on Ascension day in 1814, an event which combined a traditional ceremony in which 'Cheerful libations are offered … to the genius of our wealthy flood' with a technological breakthrough that was to revolutionise the local economy, in many ways symbolised Newcastle's successful transition from Georgian to Victorian Britain. Newcastle remained very proud of its heritage: there were few other towns that could boast a similar continuity of historical importance and its inhabitants were conscious of living surrounded by what Defoe had termed 'abundant business for an antiquary'. The corporation indeed demonstrated its concern to preserve this antiquarian heritage by purchasing the derelict castle in 1809, adding a roof and a set of crenellations to the 12th-century Norman keep. Yet even in the 17th century Newcastle's inhabitants had been equally aware of the town's changing role and of the part played by the coal industry as a force in this process. In 1721 one local coal-owner compared his waggonways, modestly, with the Via Appia, and Bourne's history (1736) had continued the allusion, claiming that 'these Waggon-ways, a small part of the whole Coal Works, may Vie with some of the great Works of the Roman Empire'.[54] It was with an equal confidence that the ancient walls, gates and street plan were gradually sacrificed to the demands of 'improvement', a process that culminated in the ruthless determination shown in driving the railways through the heart of the historic city centre. 'This mart of trade' entered the Victorian age with its eyes set firmly on the future.[55]

[53] Ellis, *Business Fortunes*, pp.61-2; *1778 Directory*, p.24; Flinn, *Coal Industry*, p.454.

[54] Brand, J., *Observations on Popular Antiquities* (1777), pp.269-70; Sweet, *Urban Histories*, pp.83-4; Defoe, *Tour*, vol.iii, pp.159-60; British Library, Additional MSS 40747, fols.184-5; Bourne, *History*, p.159.

[55] Richardson, *Descriptive Companion*, p.58; Baillie, *Impartial History*, p.142; *Newcastle Journal*, 25 Aug.1838.

# An Integrated Elite

## Newcastle's Economic Development 1840-1914

### OLIVER LENDRUM

It is easy to assume that Newcastle's economic development followed the same path as that of Tyneside generally during the years 1840-1914. However, while on Tyneside the economy became overwhelmingly dominated by heavy industry this was not so much the case in Newcastle itself. Though it always possessed industries common to the rest of Tyneside, and especially so after its boundaries were expanded in the early 20th century to include areas such as Walker and Benwell, Newcastle in fact developed more as a service and commercial centre for the surrounding industrial region. A substantial minority of male workers (16,000 or 29 per cent) were employed in traditional heavy industries, such as metal manufacture, shipbuilding and engineering, but these groups never came to dominate as they did elsewhere. The employment structure of Newcastle was instead dominated by service and commercial interests such as transport and retailing of various types. Large numbers of people were also employed in the manufacture of products needed for these service and commercial interests. From this it also becomes clear that, although different, the economies of Newcastle and Tyneside were heavily interdependent. For that reason, in order to understand the economic development of Tyneside in the later 19th and early 20th centuries it is vitally important to understand the development of Newcastle's own rather different economy in its own right. Similarly, in order to understand Newcastle's economy it is necessary to view its development within the wider context of the regional economy.

## An Integrated Elite

One of the driving forces behind Newcastle's economic development was the existence of a highly successful local entrepreneurial elite. The entrepreneurs who made up this elite came from a wide variety of backgrounds, some being local and some coming from abroad, some having the most humble of births while others were born into the aristocracy. However, once in business on Tyneside they gelled to form an elite, united not only through common business interests, but also often through marriage. Although external factors of supply and demand were crucial in determining the region's progress, so were the actions of this group. As they were personally responsible for what types of technology and business practices were adopted, and also in which areas they invested their money, they were responsible to a considerable extent for which industries and services prospered and which declined or failed. Many of the figures who were primarily associated with industrial development were also involved in services and commerce and vice versa. This interaction is a further indication of the interdependent relationship that existed between the different sectors of the economy. Indeed, it was also common to find a combination of entrepreneurs with expertise in manufacturing and finance among the directors of a single company, in order that their different skills could be combined to aid a firm's success. Historians have often attempted to explain Britain's relative economic decline in the late 19th and early 20th centuries in terms of a decline in entrepreneurial ability through this period within British manufacturing industry. While other historians have challenged this view, there is still a great deal of work to be done on the subject before this long running debate can be settled.[1] Such was the importance of Tyneside as a manufacturing centre, and such was the level of integration between all sectors of Newcastle's economy, that the history of the town's entrepreneurial elite provides important insights into this debate regarding British entrepreneurial quality in the latter 19th and early 20th centuries.

## Transport

Efficient transport links, not only with the rest of Britain but also with the world, were naturally crucial to the success of the region's industries. Transport became of considerable importance to Newcastle's economy not only in terms of the support it gave to other activities, but also as an industry in its own right, employing a significant proportion of the local population. Shipping, both coastal and overseas, expanded greatly in terms of imports and exports from the 1830s onwards.[2] An annual average of 209,000 tons was exported over the ten years to 1834, but over the next ten years the figure was 477,815 tons. In 1854 about 3,000,000 tons were

---

[1] A good introduction to this debate can be found in Payne, P.L., *British Entrepreneurship in the Nineteenth Century* (London, 1988). Key works promoting the hypothesis of entrepreneurial decline include Landes, D.S., 'Technological Change and Development in Western Europe, 1750-1914', in Habakkuk, H.J. and Postan, M. (eds.), *The Cambridge Economic History of Europe*, VI. *The Industrial Revolutions and After, Part 1* (Cambridge, 1965), and Burnham, T.H. and Hoskins, G.O., *Iron and Steel in Britain 1870-1930* (London, 1943). Works challenging this view include McCloskey, D.N. and Sandberg, L.G., 'From Damnation to Redemption: Judgements on the Late Victorian entrepreneur', *Explorations in Economic History*, IX (1971).

[2] Official records attributed to Newcastle included Blyth (until 1897), Amble, North and South Shields until the Shields towns acquired their own custom houses. Therefore for a number of years returns are for the Tyne ports.

exported and this figure had risen to almost 10,000,000 by 1912. By 1883 Newcastle had become the second most important port in the country in terms of export tonnage, although the low value of the export commodities ensured that it occupied a significantly lower position in terms of the value of those exports, coming in sixth. The commodities exported broadly reflected the industrial development of the surrounding region. Coal was unsurprisingly the dominant export throughout the period. Until the industry declined in the 1880s, substantial quantities of alkali were also exported. In 1874, 120,000 tons of alkali were exported overseas from Newcastle, the principal destination being Germany, while 54,000 tons were exported down the coast.

Unlike other major British ports, the quantity of goods imported was significantly lower than those exported. The smaller imports sector was in many respects a natural consequence of there being significant deposits in the local area of many of the raw materials required by industry, although some did have to be brought from elsewhere, including for example, brimstone and sulphur for the chemical industry and numerous materials for the leather industry including seal skins and bark. However, the fact that many of the imports into Newcastle were consumer goods provides an important indication of the commercial nature of the town's economy as a supply centre for the surrounding region.

As a result of the undoubted importance of shipping to all aspects of the local economy, it is hardly surprising that the local entrepreneurial elite took a considerable interest in the shipping industry. The professional shipowner had come to dominate investment in Newcastle shipping by 1850, partly as a result of the growth of marine insurance, but supporting investment still came from a very wide range of sources, particularly from those occupations most closely associated with shipping, and therefore with most to gain, such as shipbuilders and merchants.[3] Indeed, the professional shipowner did not come to dominate Newcastle shipping to quite the same extent as was the case in London. Many local coal magnates found it more economic to move coal in their own vessels rather than use the shipping companies. This is understandable when one considers the cost of shipowning compared with the very high capital expenditure involved in mining itself.[4] Similarly, the whole entrepreneurial elite took an active interest in the condition of the river. Prior to 1850, the condition of the Tyne was the responsibility of the Town Corporation which had utilised its large annual revenues for town purposes, when some of this money would have been better spent on improvements to the river. Consequently, in 1840 the Tyne was in a very poor condition and was facing increased local

---

[3] Ville, S.P., 'Patterns of shipping investment in the port of Newcastle-upon-Tyne', *Northern History*, Vol. XXV (1989), p.218.
[4] *Ibid.*, p.220.

**2.1** King's Meadows: final dredging, 1885.

competition as a result of improved facilities at Sunderland and the new harbour at Seaham. The granting of MPs and borough councils to towns such as Gateshead, Tynemouth and South Shields provided them with sufficient political power to overcome the control that the Town Corporation exercised.[5] After protracted parliamentary debates, The Tyne Improvement Commission was established in 1850 to enable necessary improvements to be made to the river, and represented a great victory for those whose livelihoods depended on the river as an efficient transport link. Although the Commission was plagued with difficulties throughout the 1850s, substantial progress was made in terms of dredging and pier construction. The interest and influence that the entrepreneurial elite had in this process is shown by the stance taken by the Newcastle Chamber of Commerce towards it, and also by their involvement in the election of Commissioners. The Chamber of Commerce, which had been formed in 1815 and possessed about 150 member firms by the mid-1860s, was strongly in favour of deepening the channel, believing that this would benefit all those engaged in commerce. After 1875 the composition of the Commission was revised, with two commissioners each being elected by the shipowners, coal-owners and trades. Several key figures within the entrepreneurial elite, including W.G. Armstrong, were also themselves elected to the Commission

[5] McCord, N., *The Banks of Tyne: A Historical Survey* (Newcastle-upon-Tyne, n.d.), p.6.

which was chaired by Joseph Cowen from 1853 to 1873, who was knighted for his efforts in 1872.

Railways also played a vital part in the economy of Newcastle throughout the period. The railways first reached Newcastle in 1838 with the opening of the Newcastle and Carlisle Railway and the network quickly expanded to provide a complicated system of local lines linking Newcastle to the coast and coal fields, as well as invaluable links with Scotland and the rest of England. The development of this new locomotive-powered network was an immeasurable improvement on the local network of waggonways that had been transporting coal from collieries to port facilities since the 17th century. Although passenger receipts grew from £1,400,000 to £3,134,736 from 1873 to 1913, this only formed about a quarter of gross income in the Newcastle area, freight being much more important. General goods accounted for around a third of total income over the same period, and minerals 35 per cent. As in the case of shipping, coal and coke dominated, the quantity carried rising from around 16 million tons per annum in the early 1870s to an average of 41 million tons during the period 1907-1911. As well as coal and coke, mineral traffic also included an average of 5 million tons of ironstone per annum over the years 1873-1912 and increasing amounts of limestone. Aside from providing an efficient means of transport which benefited other industrial activities, and providing another source of employment, the railways, like shipping, provided new markets for locally produced goods. In addition to their demand for coal, the advent of the railways was a catalyst for the expansion of mechanical engineering. Ten of the Newcastle and Carlisle Railway's first 14 locomotives were built in Newcastle and a further three in Gateshead. Robert Stephenson designed the new rail bridge across the Tyne, opened in 1849.

There was involvement from both the commercial and industrial sides of the economy in the railway industry. For example William Losh, the Walker iron and alkali manufacturer, and the Newcastle banker, William Woods, were among the directors of the Newcastle and Carlisle Railway at its opening, the latter later becoming company chairman.[6] The Newcastle Chamber of Commerce also took an interest in railway promotion, as they had done with the Tyne Improvement Commission, supporting various projects to link Newcastle to the rest of Britain and contributing large sums of money to cover the surveying costs involved in railway construction. The development of railways also provides an example of one of the features of the British economy in this period: the decreasingly regional and increasingly national nature of the economy. Amalgamations aimed at creating larger, more competitive and cost effective organisations, but also led to a dilution of local control. In 1854

[6]   McClean, J.S., *The Newcastle & Carlisle Railway 1825-62* (Newcastle-upon-Tyne, 1948), pp.111-12.

**2.2**   Metro ahead of the 'Metro'. Tyneside electrified suburban line, 1904.

several companies serving Newcastle merged to form the North Eastern Railway which dominated north-eastern England until 1923. However, the railways remained vitally important to the Newcastle economy and there was still considerable involvement from the local elite in this company. William Woods also became a director of the North Eastern Railway in 1862, as did other local entrepreneurs including Lowthian Bell in 1865 and W.G. Armstrong in 1901.[7]

The activities of Newcastle's entrepreneurial elite in transport can also be seen towards the end of the period in the development of an electrified suburban passenger transport system. Although horse-drawn trams had been working in Newcastle since the end of the 1870s, the introduction of the electric tram in 1902 was such a successful breakthrough that 42,800,000 tickets were issued in 1905 alone. This severely affected numbers travelling on the North Eastern Railway's suburban lines, as passenger receipts fell by £30,000 in the following six months, a third of which 'was certainly due to tramway competition'.[8] To meet this threat the suburban lines to the coast were electrified in 1904 at a cost of more than £250,000, five years

[7]   Tomlinson, W.W., *The North Eastern Railway: Its Rise and Development* (London, 1914), p.768.
[8]   *Ibid.*, p.97.

before similar developments were made in London. It was, as it were, a Metro ahead of the Metro, and even covered sections of line incorporated in the more recent scheme. This truly revolutionary development was the result of the work of Charles Merz, a Newcastle electrical engineering consultant who had established the firm of Merz & McLellan around the turn of the century. In 1904 the chairman of the North Eastern Railway asked him to complete a report on the electrification of these suburban lines and as a result of the success of the Newcastle scheme he was later involved in similar electrification schemes abroad, most notably in Chicago and Melbourne. He was also involved in an early scheme to electrify the east coast main line between Newcastle and York, although this was abandoned amid the chaos created by the formation of the LNER in 1923.

## Energy

In the same way as transport methods were important facilitators of industrial growth while at the same time becoming important parts of the local economy in their own right, so were the public utilities companies. Towards the end of the period Merz was also heavily involved in the electricity supply industry in Newcastle. It was largely as a result of his innovations in terms of power station design and the creation of a regional grid that the Newcastle-upon-Tyne Electric Supply Company (NESCo) became a model for others to follow. Despite competition from the Newcastle & District Electrical Lighting Co., NESCo came to dominate electricity supply in the area. From an area of 16 square miles in 1900, its supply area expanded to 1,400 square miles by 1914, making it Europe's largest integrated power system. The involvement of Charles Merz provides an excellent example of business and family interaction within the entrepreneurial elite, and it was undoubtedly partly as a result of this that the firm's success was achieved. His father, Theodore, had been one of the founders of NESCo in 1889 and after returning to Newcastle to become involved in electricity supply at the request of his father, Charles' revolutionary innovations in this field not only contributed to NESCo's success, but also to the creation and subsequent success of Merz & McLellan. Both also benefited from the family link with marine engineering and shipbuilding: John Wigham Richardson was Charles Merz's uncle and was instrumental in persuading shipbuilders and engineers to use electricity at the same time that his nephew was promoting his ideas in electricity generation.[9] That they were successful in this is reflected in the fact that by 1913 almost 90 per cent of NESCo's sales were made to industry. Before

---

[9] Hennessey, R.A.S., 'Early Electrical Engineering and Supply in North East England', in Institution of Electrical Engineers, *The History of Electrical Engineering: Papers presented at the 4th I.E.E. Weekend Meeting* (Durham, 1976), p.4.

founding NESCo, John Merz was a leading figure in the Tyneside chemical industry, working at Tennants' Hebburn works, while one of NESCo's earliest directors, Sir Lindsay Wood, was also a director of John Bowes and Partners and the Harton Coal Co.[10] The development of the electrical supply industry led to the development of a successful heavy electrical engineering industry on Tyneside, in the van of which was the Heaton works of Charles Parsons.

For much the same reasons the entrepreneurial elite invested heavily in the other major public utilities, namely water and gas. Gas was mainly supplied by the Newcastle and Gateshead Union Gas Co. which was formed in 1830. Its list of original subscribers included two future partners at Armstrong's, A.L. Potter and Armorer Donkin, as well as the mechanical engineer Robert Hawthorn, Aubone Surtees of Benwell Colliery and John Clayton. An important landowner and solicitor with Clayton & Gibson, John Clayton was a very significant figure in Victorian Newcastle. He took over from his father, Nathaniel, as Town Clerk in 1822 and held the post until 1867, and was also a legal advisor and financial backer to the city centre developer, Richard Grainger.[11] Water was supplied by the Whittle Dean Water Co., which changed its name in 1863 to become the Newcastle and Gateshead Water Co. Potter, Hawthorn and Donkin were on the provisional committee of this company along with several other leading figures including two other partners in Armstrong's, George Cruddas and R. Lambert.

## Finance

During the 19th century Newcastle developed an important financial services industry vital to the success of the local industrial economy. Despite the uncertain nature of the local banking industry, there was considerable involvement by the local business elite in this sector in the first half of the 19th century. However the collapse of the Northumberland and Durham District Bank in 1857 marked something of a watershed in the history of Newcastle banking. As a result of its leading position in the banking industry of northern England, its failure was especially damaging. Not only did it adversely affect several leading entrepreneurial families, including the Richardsons, but it also led to a 'fracturing of business confidence in banking generally'.[12] In the immediate aftermath of this failure two important new banks were set up: Woods and Co., and Hodgkin, Barnett, Pease and Spence. Following the loss of business confidence in banking caused by the 1857 crisis, there was at

---

[10] Benwell Community Project Final Report Series No. 6, *The Making of a Ruling Class* (Newcastle-upon-Tyne, 1976), p.33.
[11] *Ibid.*, p.97.
[12] *Ibid.*, p.32.

first perhaps more limited involvement than previously from Newcastle's leading entrepreneurial families. The founders of these new banks either had backgrounds specifically in the local banking industry or came from outside the local area altogether. William Woods had previously been involved in the management of the Newcastle Shields and Union Bank which had folded in the commercial slump of 1846-7. Spence had previously been a manager of the Union Bank while Pease's family was already heavily involved in banking in the Teesside area. Of their partners, Hodgkin and Barnett both came up from London to join them and were the sons of a solicitor and a stockbroker.[13]

Increasingly effective legislative controls and the lessons learnt from past failures resulted in the banking facilities of the second half of the century being more responsible and better managed.[14] As a result of this greater stability the city's leading families again became more heavily involved in banking. Richard Clayton became a partner in Woods & Co. in 1868, and was followed ten years later by John Coppin Straker. Despite this greater stability, bank failures did not entirely become a thing of the past. Just ten years after its opening in 1871, the Northern Counties Bank folded while the Industrial Bank Ltd. lasted for an even shorter period, closing in 1876. The North Eastern Banking Co. was founded in 1872 and epitomised the increased stability of the banking industry, going on to considerable success before eventually merging with the Bank of Liverpool in 1914. The involvement of the Noble family in the senior management of this bank towards the end of the period is another example of the interaction that existed between different parts of the economy. The same family held simultaneously the chairmanship of Armstrong's, Newcastle's most important engineering firm. The merger of the North Eastern with the Bank of Liverpool is an indication of the increasingly national nature of Britain's financial services industry at this time. Hodgkin, Barnett, Pease and Spence were taken over by Lloyds in 1903 following the takeover of Woods and Co. by Barclays in 1897. Although it was one bank among many regional ones, the Bank of England had possessed a regional branch in Newcastle since 1828, and there was nearly £500,000 of its notes in circulation in Newcastle in 1842, so a national banking system was nothing new.[15]

The growth of marine insurance was important in the rise of the professional shipowner in Newcastle in the mid-19th century. The 'port was renowned, in particular, as a centre of mutual insurance clubs'.[16] Consequently, insurance became

[13]  *Ibid.*

[14]  McCord, N., *North East England: An Economic and Social History 1760-1960* (Newcastle-upon-Tyne, 1979), pp.64-5.

[15]  Remarkably little has been published on the history of Newcastle banking. In addition to useful sections in McCord, *North East England* and Benwell, *Ruling Class*, further information can be found in Phillips, M., *A History of Banks, Bankers and Banking in Northumberland, Durham and North Yorkshire* (1894).

[16]  Ville, 'Shipping Investment', p.219.

**2.3** Bank of England, Grey Street, 1860.

an important commercial activity in its own right while at the same time influencing the development of the very risky shipping industry. Consisting of cohesive groups of shipowners, these associations charged premiums 'far cheaper'[17] than those charged by Lloyds and several survived into the 20th century. One such association was the Newcastle Protection & Indemnity Association, formed in 1886, which grew to cover 672,341 tons of steamers before the end of 1909. Reflecting the same trend as banking, it included vessels registered at ports beyond Tyneside and merged with the North of England Iron Steam Ship Association in 1911.

So called railway mania led to share booms in 1836 and 1844-5 and therefore also to the growth of share dealing and regional stock exchanges across northern England. In Newcastle a Stock and Shareholders Association was formed in 1840 and in the following year there were nine brokers in the city. Such was the growth in this sector that by 1845 there were 20 brokers and a stock exchange was formed in April of that year. Originally it met daily, but like many other provincial exchanges it suffered badly as a result of the collapse in share prices in the autumn of 1845

[17]  Ville, 'Shipping Investment', p.219.

and thereafter resorted to the regular sale of shares by auction. Although the rules of the Newcastle exchange forbade members from being engaged in any other business, its stockbrokers were well integrated with the local business community, many of them having been engaged in other commercial activities before entering the exchange. For example, two of the earliest Newcastle brokers, John Drewry and J.J. Kimpster, who entered the profession in 1836, had previously been involved in the grocery trade.[18] Finance also encouraged the professions, especially accountants and solicitors, who were also heavily integrated into the local entrepreneurial elite.

## Retail

The near fourfold increase in population that Newcastle experienced between 1841 and 1911 (71,000 to 267,000), and its development as the service centre for the surrounding region, inevitably resulted in the development of a very considerable retail sector which was of great importance to the local economy. The importance of this sector is reflected in the aforementioned large quantities of consumer goods that were shipped into Tyneside. The growth of retailing is also reflected in the city's census returns: in 1851 about 3,500 people were engaged in selling activities, excluding shoemakers, milliners and tailors. This figure had risen to 5,000 or more by 1881 and had doubled again by 1911. Although debates surrounding entrepreneurship normally focus on manufacturing industry, the development of Newcastle's retail sector saw revolutionary entrepreneurial developments that easily matched its groundbreaking industrial sector. In 1838, following two years at the Regent Street store of Lewis & Albany, Emerson Bainbridge opened a drapery store in Newcastle which rapidly expanded its product lines to become arguably the first department store in England. Such was the success of the store that trade doubled between 1857 and 1888, and by 1897, when the firm became a private limited company, it possessed a capital of £471,000 with sales exceeding £500,000 per annum.

The key to Bainbridge's success was the way he recognised and capitalised on the changing social structure of the city. Aside from the fact that working-class wages were often high on Tyneside by national standards, the city's development as the centre of the world's coal trade resulted in the creation of a large lower-middle class. Many people in Newcastle enjoyed increasing levels of disposable income, and one way in which this new found respectability could be expressed was in the purchase of drapery. However these people were not attracted to traditional drapery stores which were very much the preserve of the wealthy with their reliance

[18] Killick, J.R. and Thomas, W.A., 'The Stock Exchanges of the North of England 1836-1850', *Northern History*, Vol. V (1970), pp.114-30.

**2.4**   Grainger Market, *c.*1900.

on high mark-ups and credit transactions. Bainbridge successfully provided for lower-middle-class and upper-working-class needs by offering, in addition to an insistence on cash payment, 'clearly marked prices, good quality products considerably cheaper than his rivals':[19] in other words, a highly desirable risk-free shopping experience. The inspiration for this came from another revolutionary retail development that had occurred some years earlier: the Grainger Market, which also utilised marked prices, a surveyor and corporation weigh house. Built in 1835 to house those displaced by Grainger's redevelopment of the city centre, it came to house 143 butchers, 60 greengrocers and numerous other traders.[20]

Bainbridge's was followed in 1882 by a second major department store, opened by J.J. Fenwick, a young man who had been employed by the Newcastle silk mercers Charles Bragg after his arrival from Stockton in 1868. Although intended to be rather more exclusive than Bainbridge's, this store was also very successful, employing around 200 staff in 1900 and double that by 1914. Fenwick displayed considerable marketing tact through the effective use of window displays and press advertising, including the front page of the first issue of the *Daily Mail* in 1896. Like Bainbridge, he also recognised the needs of the expanding middle classes, opening a separate

[19]   Lancaster, B., *The Department Store: A Social History* (London, 1992), p.9.
[20]   *Ibid.*

**2.5** Fenwick's Sale, late 1890s.

store to meet demand for ready made wear. The increasingly national nature of the economy towards the end of the period is also reflected in the development of Fenwick's and Bainbridge's. Fenwick's opened a London store on Oxford Street in 1891 and Bainbridge's had transferred boot and shoe manufacturing to Leeds by 1890, having already started making men's and boys' clothing there a few years earlier. The entrepreneurs responsible for these developments were also fully integrated into the local business elite, possessing extensive business interests. For example, aside from being chairman of Bainbridge's, T.H. Bainbridge had extensive industrial interests, sitting on the boards of the Wallsend Slipway Co., Consett Iron Co., Swan Hunter, Wigham Richardson, and Cairn Shipping Line.[21]

## Engineering

Although Newcastle was primarily a commercial and service centre, its economy always had a strong industrial element that became more important in the early years of the 20th century with the extension of the city boundaries. By 1840 a considerable mechanical engineering industry had evolved in Newcastle through the creation of firms such as Robert Stephenson & Co. (1823) and R. & W. Hawthorn (1817), both

[21] Airey, A. and J., *Bainbridges of Newcastle* (Newcastle-upon-Tyne, 1976), pp.105-8.

on the Forth Banks and both originally set up to build railway locomotives. Other early Newcastle engineering firms included Losh, Wilson & Bell at Walker. The industry continued to grow throughout the 19th century with the continuing expansion of these older firms and the creation of new firms, such as J. & G. Joicey at Forth Banks in 1849 and, most famously of all, W.G. Armstrong & Co. at Elswick in 1847. By 1862-3 Armstrong's had become the largest engineering employer in Newcastle when one also takes into account their successful armaments business providing work for 3,800 from a total of 8,534 men employed in engineering.[22] The case of mechanical engineering gives yet another clear example of the close relationships that linked different forms of industry and business activity. In their managers, the vast majority of Newcastle engineering firms had very considerable links with the coal industry, a fact that is hardly surprising given the natural overlap between the two in terms of products and markets. Indeed it is significant that most of these firms were located in west Newcastle, precisely the same area as the city's coal mines. Of Armstrong's original partners, A.L. Potter was the senior partner in the Walbottle Colliery while George Cruddas had interests in the Oxclose Colliery.[23] Similarly the Joicey family were themselves heavily involved in coal prior to the opening of their Forth Banks works, and it is therefore little surprise that they originally produced winding engines in addition to railway locomotives. After Benjamin Browne's takeover of Hawthorn's in 1870, the Strakers, a wealthy Durham coal-owning family, acquired substantial interests in the firm which lasted until the Second World War.[24] There were two Newcastle solicitors among Armstrong's original partners, perhaps not so surprising when one considers that Armstrong himself had trained as a solicitor.

Amalgamation and the creation of larger more competitive firms occurred in manufacturing industry as well as the service sector. Mergers were aimed at creating cross-sector local firms, a further reflection of the considerable business acumen of the region's entrepreneurs. This led to further integration within the local entrepreneurial elite although at the same time it also led to some dilution in the control that that elite held over the region. Armstrong's merged with Charles Mitchell's shipyard at Low Walker in 1882, and then with the Manchester armaments works of Whitworth in 1897. Similarly, in 1886 R. & W. Hawthorn merged with the Hebburn shipbuilding firm of Andrew Leslie. That local entrepreneurs had the commercial acumen to seize opportunities presented by new areas of demand is reflected in the increasingly diverse range of products that they produced. Armstrong's was initially created for crane manufacture but it soon moved into

[22] A comprehensive history of Armstrong's can be found in Warren, K., *Armstrong's of Elswick: Growth in Engineering and Armaments to the Merger with Vickers* (London, 1989).
[23] Benwell, *Ruling Class*, p.24.
[24] *Ibid.*, pp.26-7.

bridge manufacture, while the opportunity presented by the Crimean War prompted it to start armaments production and create the highly successful subsidiary, Elswick Ordnance Co. It was this involvement in armaments that led not only to the merger with Whitworth but also that with Mitchell, as the two firms had in fact worked in close cooperation since the 1860s with Mitchell building warships that Armstrong then armed.

The development of iron shipbuilding in the mid-19th century resulted in the Tyne recapturing its position from the Wear as the main shipbuilding river. Many Newcastle mechanical engineering firms expanded their activities into marine engineering. Prior to their merger with Andrew Leslie, Hawthorn's had themselves moved into marine engineering. Although they continued to produce railway locomotives at Forth Banks after Browne's 1870 takeover, they also established the St Peter's Marine Engine Works where they became a major supplier of warship engines both to Armstrong's and to the Admiralty. In the 1850s Robert Morrison set up his engineering works at Ouseburn and produced marine engines in addition to a wide range of other goods including steam hammers and cranes, as did Thomas Clark at Elswick. Newcastle entrepreneurs involved in mechanical engineering had sufficient vision to transform their industry in the face of changing circumstances in terms of both products and commercial structure.

As ships became larger most yards were located further downstream towards the coast. In addition to Charles Mitchell & Co., there was also the Neptune yard of John Wigham Richardson at Walker which opened in 1860. He took over the yard previously used by Charles Coutts whose firm had led a troubled existence from its founding in 1840 until its final demise in 1856. The failure of Coutts' yard is a clear reminder that, even in the case of Newcastle's most successful industries, not all entrepreneurs shared that success. Despite being an excellent innovator, the first Tyne shipbuilder to use iron, and his progress being hindered by the shipbuilding depression of the 1840s, Coutts was to a certain extent responsible for his own downfall. Unlike most successful entrepreneurs he did not form partnerships with others who would compensate for his lack of knowledge in some areas. He seemed 'to have been a man who wanted to be his own master, whereas Charles Mitchell went from strength to strength ... using the talents and abilities of the many able men around him'.[25]

Coutts and Mitchell had very similar backgrounds, both having been born and brought up in Aberdeen, and apprenticed to the same firm there before spending time at the London marine engineering company of Maudslay Son & Field and finally settling on Tyneside. However, Mitchell was the one who very rapidly integrated himself into the local entrepreneurial elite and was able to benefit from

---

[25] McGuire, D.F., *Charles Mitchell 1820-1895: Victorian Shipbuilder* (Newcastle-upon-Tyne, 1988), p.54.

all the advantages which that brought. Mitchell married Anne Swan which brought him valuable local business and social contacts, and perhaps as a result he was introduced to Matthew Biggs, a wealthy local banker and coal owner, who provided him with ready cash, something that Coutts among others struggled to raise. Coutts' lack of involvement in the local elite seems to have contributed to his downfall. Coutts' successor at Walker, John Wigham Richardson, was much more successful and his firm, like Mitchell's, eventually merged to create a larger, more competitive unit, this time with Swan & Hunter of Wallsend in 1903. Significantly John was also deeply integrated into the local business elite, being the son of Edward Richardson, a leading local coal-owner, banker and leather manufacturer.

## One Failure

While industries such as shipbuilding and mechanical engineering grew in importance in Newcastle, and on Tyneside as a whole throughout the period, other important industries declined to the point of extinction. The most notable example of this was the alkali industry which declined from a peak in the early 1880s to almost total oblivion by 1900. In the 1860s Tyneside was producing more than half the national output of alkali and the local industry included '… some of the most prominent men in the regional economy'.[26] By 1895, the number of Alkali works on Tyneside had fallen from a peak of 25 in the early 1870s to just 10, of which only four were actually still in production and 'their days were numbered'.[27] This decline reflects the wider decline that took place in the British alkali industry at this time. In the 1880s Britain was by far the largest producer of chemicals in the world but by 1913 was a very poor third behind Germany and the USA.[28] Although many of the more important firms were located elsewhere on Tyneside, several were located in the Walker area, and all had disappeared by the time the city boundaries were expanded to include that area. The most important was the Walker Alkali Co., originally formed by William Losh in 1796. These works provide another clear example of the local entrepreneurial elite's involvement across the sectors. Losh became a partner in the Walker Iron Foundry along with Thomas Wilson and Thomas Bell and in 1841 these partners then took over Losh's alkali works. This firm in fact folded before the decline on Tyneside really got started, closing in the early 1870s, never having recovered from William Losh's death in 1861.[29] This was not the end of

---

[26] McCord, *North East England*, pp.42-3.

[27] *Ibid.*, p.140.

[28] Richardson, H.W., 'Chemicals' in Aldcroft, D.H. (ed.), *The Development of British Industry and Foreign Competition 1875-1914* (London, 1968), p.227.

[29] Campbell, W.A., *The Old Tyneside Chemical Trade* (Newcastle-upon-Tyne, 1964), p.14.

Walker alkali production, however, as these works were subsequently used for a time by John Lomas, while John Cook's works survived until the rationalisation of the industry brought about by the creation of the national United Alkali Co. (UAC) in 1890.

The creation of the UAC is a further example of control of the local economy being removed from the hands of local entrepreneurs towards the end of the period. Nevertheless, the death of the local alkali industry should not be seen as a consequence of this loss of control, as the industry was in terminal decline well before the trend to national merger. Despite the fact that Losh's works seem to have failed partly as a result of there being no suitable replacement after his death, the fact that Losh had no worthy successor is more a reflection of the good business sense of local entrepreneurs: they were increasingly unwilling to invest capital in an industry that was increasingly seen as flawed, especially when the region presented so many better investment opportunities. As a result of insufficient local demand, the Tyneside alkali industry was largely dependent on exports to northern Europe and consequently was hit hard by the development of the European chemical industry in the later years of the century. This problem was further compounded by the increasingly protectionist trade policies of many European countries, most especially Germany in the 1870s, which resulted in, for example, exports of soda crystals from Tyneside to Germany falling from 281,000 cwt to 39,000 cwt over the years 1883-7.[30] As a result of this loss of its overseas markets, and the decline of local consuming industries such as glass manufacture, the alkali industry therefore presented a steadily decreasing investment opportunity for the local entrepreneurial elite.

## Modern Products

Towards the end of the period there were attempts to establish several new industries in Newcastle including the production of consumer electrical goods and motor cars, but they did not meet with the same levels of success as their more illustrious and longer established counterparts. However, as in the case of alkali production, there is little indication that this failure occurred as a result of entrepreneurial weakness. The contribution of men such as Charles Merz to the development of a successful heavy electrical engineering industry has already been mentioned, and there was also an attempt at producing small consumer electrical goods, in the form of light bulbs, at Benwell by Sir Joseph Swan. He established his factory there in 1881 but production ceased in 1886. Far from being a failure, however, Swan was apparently not only a great innovator, but also a businessman of considerable ability.

[30]   Warren, K., *Chemical Foundations: The Alkali Industry in Britain to 1926* (Oxford, 1980), p.125.

He and his partners were also very well integrated into the local business elite, as they included leading industrialists from the chemical trade including James Cochran Stevenson and Theodore Merz, colliery owner Hilton Philipson, and Tynemouth merchant James Craig. The firm was therefore in an excellent position to gain advantages that firms such as Coutts' could not. The firm's disappearance was therefore not a result of entrepreneurial failure or a lack of integration with the business elite, but was the result of the increasingly national economy that developed towards the end of the period, which saw control of this firm removed from the locality. The works had prospered until 1886, but after the firm's merger with Edison to form the Edison & Swan United Electric Light Company in 1883 the practicalities of continuing to produce bulbs in the North East became increasingly questionable. The decision to transfer production to Ponders End in Middlesex was taken because the company was now based in London and there appears to have been more demand for its services in the south of England.[31]

Newcastle's involvement in motor car production was brought about by Armstrong's takeover of the London car manufacturer Wilson, Pilcher & Co. early in 1904 and ended shortly after the outbreak of the First World War, when the Scotswood works were once again devoted to the production of munitions. Despite the fact that disagreements at board level had delayed the original takeover of the London firm and had hampered early development, after the creation of a Motor Committee in 1908 production increased steadily. In 1912, 344 chassis were produced, placing Armstrong-Whitworth on a par with Morris and Vauxhall. While it is possible to argue that the disagreements at board level and the apparently autocratic management style of the ageing Andrew Noble held back Armstrong's production initially, the eventual termination of car production cannot be attributed to entrepreneurial failure. The demands of wartime armaments production were the true cause of this. It must be remembered that motor manufacture was only a very small part of Armstrong's activities, activities which were directed mainly at highly profitable military work. It is hardly surprising that investment in motor manufacture was only modest compared with that in armaments. Indeed, in 1910 and 1911, when motor car production was more profitable than commercial shipbuilding, it attracted more of the firm's investment capital, demonstrating that the directors were in no way unresponsive to the rates of return on its different production lines.[32]

[31] Lendrum, O.D.R., 'Enterprise in Industry: Manufacturing in North East England 1850-1914' (unpublished MA dissertation, University of Durham, 1999), pp.54-60.
[32] Irving, R.J., 'New Industries for old? Some Investment Decisions of Sir W.G. Armstrong, Whitworth & Co Ltd 1900-14', *Business History*, 17 (1975), p.166.

**2.6** Quayside Extension Works, 1908.

## *Other Industries*

Other Tyneside industries represented in the Newcastle economy throughout the period included construction, brickworks, coal mining, pottery, glass, lead, and other sectors of the chemical industry that did not experience the same dramatic collapse as alkali, such as fertiliser and paints. Space does not permit detailed discussion of these other activities but in the majority of cases their managers were also heavily integrated into the area's entrepreneurial elite. The leather industry is especially interesting as, unlike those above, it was originally based in unexpanded central Newcastle – although Richardson later opened a factory in Elswick. By the 1860s Newcastle had lost to Leeds its position as the leading leather producing centre in Britain, but the industry was still of considerable importance. The Richardsons had family involvement in numerous other industries, most notably in shipbuilding through John Wigham Richardson, but also in fertilisers, through their ownership of the Blaydon Manure and Alkali Co. The success of local entrepreneurs in the leather industry and the increasingly national nature of the economy are also reflected in the expansion of George Angus' firm. Following the addition of India rubber to its product range in the 1840s, it became a limited liability company in 1888 and had a national network of warehouses and a branch in Johannesburg.

## *Entrepreneurial Success?*

In conclusion it can be seen that, throughout the period 1840-1914, Newcastle possessed a highly dynamic economy. Although there was a very considerable amount of industrial activity following a broadly similar pattern to that of Tyneside as a whole, Newcastle was more important as a commercial and service centre for the surrounding region. The ways in which members of a local entrepreneurial elite interacted with each other in business and personal terms was central to their success and the development of the regional economy. Indeed there is even the suggestion that failure to integrate fully with this elite could place an entrepreneur at a serious disadvantage. Although there was a loss of some control in all sectors of the local economy towards the end of the period, the activities of these entrepreneurs raise some important points with regard to wider debates concerning entrepreneurship in the later 19th century. Throughout the entire period the entrepreneurial elite responded positively to the challenges presented to them in areas such as transport, utilities, the retail sector, financial services and general business organisation. It is also the case that in areas where they were more cautious in their involvement, such as banking or alkali manufacture, they were in fact displaying considerable business acumen, recognising the relatively greater risks involved in such areas. In the case of industries that declined or failed to become established it appears that entrepreneurial failure was not primarily responsible, although it may have been a factor in the case of certain individual firms as it was in all industries throughout the whole period. There is therefore little indication of a decline in entrepreneurial spirit from the 1880s onwards that could have contributed to Britain's overall economic decline, as some historians would have us believe. Indeed, the activities of the entrepreneurial elite in all areas of the Newcastle economy contributed to the town's high levels of prosperity and innovation. Despite these high levels, it should be remembered that Newcastle's economic development through this period was not without setbacks. Indeed, due to the city's close links with capital goods industries, cyclical fluctuations in its economy were of greater severity than those of the nation in general.

# 3

# The Emergence of the Post-Industrial Economy in Newcastle 1914-2000

## NATASHA VALL

> Industrially it is a port, it has three collieries, and a large mining population, it has shipyards and a number of heavy engineering works, including the famous Armstrong Whitworth works. Commercially, it is the capital of a large exporting area.[1]

Newcastle's historic role as England's 'Black Indies' and its domination of the regional economy still resonates in this description of the city by Henry Mess in 1928. But even then its position was being severely undermined by competition in the coal trade, as this uneasy lament published by *Newcastle Chamber of Commerce Journal* in 1932 makes clear:

### Coffee and Cigarettes: a Quayside Rejoinder

If you want to know the reason why the
Quayside's up the pole,
Why so many pits are idle and we cannot sell our coal
Just read the 'Monthly Journal' which is
published from the Quay …
While tons and tons of Polish coal are expected from Gdynia
They actually sit and talk and
Smoke the products of Virginia![2]

During the 1930s, the flow of cheap Polish and German coal caused irrevocable damage to exports from Tyneside. For instance, by the late 1920s, British imports of coal into Scandinavia had dropped from 92 per cent of the trade to 54 per cent. Annual shipments of coal from the Tyne declined from 21 million to 13 million between 1925 and 1935, incurring a £200,000 deficit for the Tyne Improvement

---

[1] Mess, H., *Industrial Tyneside, A Social Survey* (1928), p.19.
[2] *Newcastle and Gateshead Chamber of Commerce Journal*, Volume XII, March 1932, No. 137, p.89.

Commission.³ This was also causing problems for Tyneside shipowners given that the Baltic trade had been based on round trips – outward with coal and back with timber. Nevertheless, it needs to be emphasised that, since the creation of the Tyne Improvement Commission in the middle of the 19th century, shipments of coal did not generate revenue exclusively for the Corporation of Newcastle itself; moreover, during the early 20th century, Tyne figures increasingly reflected coal mined and shipped outside the city from locations such as Jarrow Staithes. Although collieries like the Montagu at Scotswood remained working in Newcastle until after the Second World War, there can be little doubt that coal played a less decisive part in shaping Newcastle's 20th-century economy than it did during the 18th and 19th centuries.

The *Rejoinder*'s tone also captures the Quayside's long reputation as a sociable place, but the observer of the 1930s cannot have been aware of how more true this would become as the century progressed. Without wishing to diminish the overall importance of 20th-century industrial decline, comparisons with the 19th century often treat the experience of the 20th century – particularly the growth of the service sector – as a diversion from the industrial norm. But it is clear that the changes over the last 100 years need to be viewed against the reality of a *longstanding* service sector development. Whilst Newcastle's commercial and retail economy was well advanced by the end of the 19th century, the development of the city's service sector occurred in conjunction with its dislocation from the regional industrial base in the 20th century. Therefore, an assessment of Newcastle's economy since 1914 needs to contend with the complexities of this transition by acknowledging the elements of continuity with the previous century, whilst at the same time recognising that 20th-century developments had a dynamic of their own.

Newcastle manufacturing in the early 1900s can be related to some of the most prominent arguments surrounding the causes of relative economic decline in Britain. Picking up where the last chapter on economy left off, it is clear that the explanation of relative economic decline in terms of entrepreneurial failure also has relevance to 20th-century Newcastle. The close of the 19th century saw high levels of entrepreneurial innovation in Newcastle's principal manufacturing companies, albeit in firms heavily dependent upon the fortunes of the region's capital goods industries.⁴ This longstanding tendency towards the concentration of capital in narrowly integrated growth sectors increased during the First World War. The rapid advances made in marine engineering, particularly the production of steam engines for naval vessels, often depended upon continued use of existing plants rather than

³ *Proceedings of the Tyne Improvement Commission*, 19 November, 1935, p.3 .
⁴ See Oliver Lendrum's chapter in this volume, above.

new investment into plants capable of diversifying manufacturing potential.[5] Moreover, there can be little doubt that the severe labour shortages which ensued after the outbreak of war in August 1914 also caused a degree of dislocation in industrial production. By September 1914 nearly two thousand men from Armstrong's company alone had enlisted, whilst Hawthorn & Leslie had lost nearly one thousand.[6]

Whether innovation within manufacturing was effectively halted by the war nevertheless remains a complex issue. The First World War produced unprecedented demand for armaments, which the country's existing Royal Ordnance factories were unable to meet. Subsequently, Lloyd George chose a small group of trustworthy armament firms to provide assistance. Armstrong Whitworth Ltd. was part of this select group, alongside Coventry Ordnance Works, Vickers and William Beardmore & Co. Ltd.[7] In 1915, the Munitions of War Act stipulated that munitions workers could not enlist without employer consent, ensuring that any interruption of production was kept to a minimum. Armstrong's, alongside Vickers, was largely responsible for the production of the gun that was 'the backbone of the British artillery effort', the 18-pounder, while a new shop at Elswick and an extension at Openshaw were built for the production of the 60-pounder, for which Armstrong's were solely responsible.[8] On the other hand it has also been suggested that the company lost much of its earlier entrepreneurial zeal during the war. Compared with the innovative steps taken to attract foreign clientele during the late 19th century, the success during the war was guaranteed by a profitable and seemingly secure government market.[9] The company's 'golden years' as a chief government contractor, during which record profits were made, nevertheless contributed to difficulties in adjusting to peacetime circumstances because the vastly expanded plants were suited primarily to the production of war materials.

The accelerated levels of production for the war effort also had a profound impact upon the labour market in Newcastle. In November 1913 Armstrong Whitworth Ltd. employed 20,669 on the Tyne, and by November 1918 the numbers employed had reached just under 60,000.[10] In Newcastle, one firm overwhelmingly dominated the historic concentration of manufacturing labour in heavy engineering. But the war also broke some traditions. Women were allowed to work in the shipyards for the first time in 1916, albeit with the proviso that 'as soon as women become

[5] N. McCord, *North East England, The Region's Development 1760-1960* (1979), p.153.

[6] J. Clarke, *Building Ships on the North East Coast, a Labour of Love, Risk and Pain (Part 2: c.1914-1980)* (1998), p.192.

[7] J. D. Scott, *Vickers. A History* (1962), p.97.

[8] *Ibid.*, p.104.

[9] See Kaldor, M., *The Baroque Arsenal* (1989) for extensive coverage of this theme.

[10] Warren, K., *Armstrong's of Elswick, Growth in Engineering and Armaments to the Merger with Vickers* (1989), pp.192-8.

[11] Clarke, *Building Ships*, p.207.

unremunerative they should be dispensed with'. By 1918, St Peter's Engine Works on the Forth banks (Hawthorn & Leslie) employed 150 women, or 7 per cent of the workforce. Such figures nevertheless compared poorly with the national average of 31 per cent for engineering.[11]

Several commentators on regional industry during the early years of the 20th century have noted that wartime levels of industrial militancy in Newcastle remained low compared with other British cities. Despite a Tyneside engineering strike in 1917, the conurbation was relatively free from industrial unrest. More importantly, workers in Newcastle appeared to be less opposed to the dilution of skill imposed during the war years than were their industrial counterparts in Glasgow. When the Minister for Munitions met trade unionists and Arthur Henderson in Newcastle in 1915, Lloyd George reputedly received 'a most enthusiastic reception'.[12] The overwhelming dominance of one firm in the munitions sector has been offered as partial explanation for the absence of a workers' committee in the city. Attempts to create a workers' committee in Newcastle, as in Glasgow, had in fact been so strongly opposed that James Hinton concluded that 'Tyneside was the most important gap in the development of the shop stewards' movement'.[13] Nevertheless, this cannot be attributed to one-firm paternalism alone, and it seems the explanation should also be sought in the exceptionally good dilution settlement achieved by male workers on the Tyne. As a precondition of this settlement, the number of women allowed into munitions was kept to a minimum, which in turn probably explains the low rate of female employment in engineering, relative to national levels before 1921.[14] This favourable (male worker) outcome has been attributed to the ineptness of the Chairman of the Tyneside Dilution Commission, Sir Croydon Marks MP, but Hinton also suggests that a pre-existing and independently organised local labour force helped to negotiate the agreement, thereby circumventing the fledgling wartime shop stewards' movement. The question of labour relations certainly needs closer attention than can be afforded here; nevertheless, it appears that worker truculence is not easily used to explain the problems that the Tyneside manufacturing sector experienced later in the century.

Whilst many Tyneside shipyards did well out of the demand for naval vessels during the war, the resulting backlog of mercantile orders also produced a building boom after 1918 which lasted well into the summer of 1920. Initially, new firms such as the Newcastle Shipbuilding Company established under the chairmanship of John Crass in 1919 were able to capitalise on this backlog. But the downturn of

[12] Clarke, *Building Ships*, p.207.
[13] Hinton, J., *The First Shop Stewards' Movement* (1973), p.189.
[14] The dilution agreement for Armstrong's workers also ensured that they would be paid full skilled rates without deductions for toolsettings or supervisions, Hinton, J., *op.cit.*, p.70.

1919-20 saw a sharp fall in foreign orders by the autumn of 1920. Merchant work in hand at Newcastle yards fell drastically. Not that this problem was exclusive to the Tyne. In March 1922 the Shipbuilding Employers' Federation reported that 56 per cent of all Britain's shipbuilding births were idle.[15] Nevertheless, European yards, particularly in Holland and Italy, continued to remain competitive. One explanation for this has been sought in the decisions taken at Versailles which not only offloaded German coal onto the world export market and severely damaged Britain's own export market, but also required Germany to cede its fleets. After 1921, former Tyneside clients such as the New Zealand Shipping and Federal Line, which had previously bought ships from the Tyne and turbines from Parson's, obtained vessels from Germany.[16] It is therefore important to note that the repercussions of the decisions taken as part of the Treaty of Versailles were not exclusive to the regional coal trade, but *also* restricted newer growth areas such as marine and electrical engineering. Newly established yards such as John Crass's perished in this harsh climate and, despite a reprieve in the late 1920s, the rates of unemployment in shipbuilding in the North East consistently exceeded 40 per cent, the highest recorded occupational rates in the country. In Newcastle the proposal to build a new road bridge over the Tyne in 1924 was supported by the local labour exchange as a means to provide work for the 50,000 unemployed skilled engineers and shipbuilders.[17] Standards of living in Newcastle nevertheless varied immensely from ward to ward, with the highest levels of deprivation in the city's riverside areas. Yet, official sources suggest that the experience of poverty was typical of many other British cities during this period. In 1918, for instance, Newcastle had 1,954 indoor paupers and 3,126 outdoor paupers, or 102 per 10,000 population. This figure was lower than Bristol, and lower also than both Manchester and Liverpool, but considerably higher than other northern industrial cities such as Bradford and Leeds.[18]

Although high wages and pronounced skill classifications may have exacerbated the problems of British industrial competitiveness, on the whole the crisis of the 1920s was largely caused by factors outside the control of individual firms. Technical innovation continued to flourish. For instance, Charles Parsons completed his third great invention in 1926 with the first high-pressure turbine driven steamship.[19] And prior to its enforced merger with Vickers, there were also clear efforts at Armstrong's to diversify into commercial areas that were more profitable than

[15] Dougan, D., *The History of North East Shipbuilding* (1968), pp.139-42.
[16] Clarke, *Building Ships*, p.217.
[17] Newcastle City Council Minutes, Meeting of the Council and Members of the Newcastle and Gateshead Chamber of Commerce, 9 January 1924.
[18] *The Labour Gazette*, February 1918, p.78.
[19] Dougan, *North East Shipbuilding*, pp.151-2.

shipbuilding.[20] At the same time, the 1920s also highlighted the failure of leading local companies to move beyond their trade links with Commonwealth countries, or to penetrate European markets. Given the increasingly narrow client base for heavy goods, the failure of Newcastle's largest employer to secure long-term gains in the 'new' inter-war industries undeniably weakened the manufacturing potential of Newcastle for the rest of the 20th century.

'Built like a battle ship' was the rather inevitable comparison used to advertise Armstrong's first car, a sturdy promise confirmed by the many reliability awards which it won in its first few years of production. In May 1904, Armstrong Whitworth Ltd. had agreed to pay the London-based Wilson, Pilcher & Co. £500 a year to produce their car at Elswick. But early losses resulted in the cancellation of the Wilson Pilcher deal in 1907. Although patents for the car, later marketed as the 'Armstrong Whitworth', were bought for £8,500, this made poor comparison with the £200,000 spent on shares in the Whitehead Torpedo Company for extensions to the Ordnance department in the same year. More significant than the actual amount, the company's strategy for investment in cars was increasingly incompatible with the demands of the modern motor industry.[21] Armstrong's may well have produced 344 chassis of five different types over the course of 1912, but in that same year Henry Ford established a plant in Detroit with the capacity to produce 1,000 Model Ts *per day*.[22]

Despite the interruptions of the war and the 'psychological blockages' of the company's 'old guard', Armstrong Whitworth continued to expand their interest in the motor industry after 1918. In 1919, it emerged that they had a controlling interest in the Siddeley Deasey Motor Company. Crucially, however, this very important appreciation of the potential long-term gains available in motor vehicle production saw this development removed from Tyneside. By the early 1920s a decision to move the production of the Armstrong car to 'the extensive and modern works of the company at Coventry' had been taken, probably in recognition of the advanced components and supply industry that flourished in the Midlands but was underdeveloped on Tyneside.[23] In 1923, Armstrong Whitworth entered a further agreement to undertake all their aeronautical work in Coventry, another move that did nothing to further Newcastle but helped secure Coventry's position of strength in the new industry.[24]

[20]  Irving, R.J., 'New Industries for Old? Some Investment Decisions at W.G. Armstrong Whitworth & Co. Ltd., 1900-14', *Business History*, 1975, p.166.
[21]  Warren, *Armstrong's of Elswick*, pp.149-52.
[22]  *Ibid.*
[23]  Warren, *Armstrong's of Elswick*, pp.155-8.
[24]  Thomas, D.W. and Donelly, T., 'Coventry's Industrial Economy, 1880-1980' in Lancaster, B. and Mason, T. (eds.), *Life and Labour in a Twentieth Century City, The Experience of Coventry* (1986) pp.11-57.

**3.1**   Armstrong car
and aircraft, *c*.1914.

Similarly, despite early innovation, the most impressive gains made by Newcastle's electrical engineering and supply industry were destined to evade the city and region. During the First World War, Mr. McLellan of Merz & McLellan became director of electric supply at the Ministry of Munitions. He brought his wartime expertise in electrical research for the Admiralty back to Tyneside after 1918, when he came to work as a consultant engineer in the city's new centre for electricity supply on Pilgrim Street. Apart from representing some of the finest Newcastle architecture of the inter-war years, Carliol House was designed specifically to display new electrical goods such as heated boilers and high-speed electric lifts. This building symbolised the triumph of Newcastle's electrical engineering and electricity supply industry. Carliol House was also the headquarters for NESCo, the Newcastle Electric Supply Company.[25]

Founded by Theodore Merz and Robert Spence Watson in 1889, NESCo expanded to take over the entire regional suppliers and finally merged in 1932 under the name North East Electrical Supply Company. This company supplied an area of over 4,000 square miles, the largest transmission network of any European power supply company at that time.[26] The creation of such an advanced electricity network was, in a way, the pinnacle of the previous century's progress, but, at the same time, this source of energy underpinned the 'new industrial' revolution, which took the motor industry from Tyneside to a new centre of industrial gravity in the

[25] Linsley, S.M, 'Industrial Archaeology of Electricity Around the Tyne and Wear' in 'The History of Electrical Engineering', Papers Presented at the 4th Institute of Electrical Engineers weekend meeting, Durham, July 1976, p.12.
[26] Waghorn, H., *North East Coast Countryside Electrical Development* (1931), p.14.

**3.2** Carliol House lit up for an exhibition in 1934.

Midlands and the South East. Charles Merz had certainly recognised early that large-scale returns for his company lay outside the region. He had already established an office in London by 1901 and he was employed by Samuel Consul to oversee the electrification of Chicago in 1911.[27] During the 1920s, Merz spent much of his time working on electrical supply projects in the Commonwealth, particularly South Africa, and, whilst there is little doubt that his company continued to innovate, by the Second World War the firm had lost its regional focus.

Conclusions about the city's diminishing manufacturing base, derived from assessment of the *large and familiar* companies, nevertheless tend to buttress a regional policy tradition, in which work opportunities for women after 1945 only get recognised as part of structural investment in 'development areas'.[28] Many of Newcastle's *less familiar* manufacturing companies, however, in what could loosely be defined as the 'lighter manufacturing' sector, flourished during the 1930s to provide new employment opportunities for women. The significance of brewing to the local economy is dealt with elsewhere in this volume, but expansion in Newcastle's consumer goods sector was not confined to beer.[29] Firms such as Hedley & Sons, the soap manufacturers, expanded rapidly during the 1920s and by the 1930s they were associated with Procter and Gamble, employing numerous local women to produce their famous 'Olive Suds' and 'Fairy Soap'.[30] During the 1930s, Newcastle Corporation was forthcoming with financial support for industrial diversification on the Tyne; for instance, Spiller's Mill received £130,000 as well as an extension of the Quayside in the area adjacent to it in 1934. The early 20th century also saw the confectionery industry established as a notable female employer. College Sweets, formerly of College Street in Newcastle, prospered before the expansion of branded confectionery after the Second World War. In their new properties overlooking the river, many 'nimble fingered girls' could be found, wrapping toffees, caramels and soft centres, '… labelled and dispatched to various buyers at home and abroad with "Messages of Goodness from Tyneside".'[31]

The official low rates of economic activity for women, upheld by female experience of the city's heavy engineering and shipbuilding firms, obscure this early 20th-century experience of employment in less notable companies. In 1921, 825 women were employed in the manufacture of food, drink and tobacco products, but only 43 of them were sugar and sweet boilers. Local employers' objection to the

[27] Burns, J.M., 'Charles H. Merz 1874-1940' in *The History of Electrical Engineering, op.cit.,* pp.26-7.

[28] Knox, E., 'Keep Your Feet Still Geordie Hinnie' in Colls, R. and Lancaster, B. (eds.), *Geordies. Roots of Regionalism* (1992), p.98.

[29] See Brian Bennison's chapter in this volume, below.

[30] *Newcastle and Gateshead Chamber of Commerce Journal,* Vol. XVIII, January 1938, No. 27, p.61.

[31] *Newcastle and Gateshead Chamber of Commerce Journal,* Vol. III, November 1927, No. 85, p.3.

**3.3** Female toothpaste packers at the Winthrop Laboratories at Fawdon.

1924 Factory Act requirement, that women workers be provided with chairs on the grounds that 'the average female worker would be much better off at work than at home', provides churlish testimony of the increasing presence of women in factories.[32] Ten years later there were over 2,000 women employed in food, drink and tobacco manufacture, with 700 women sugar confectioners.[33] The neglect of women's work early in the century has meant that expansion after 1945 is apt to be seen as a cause of the decline of the male manufacturing job. On closer inspection, however, this causal relationship is not easy to sustain. The Imperial Group opened their Wills cigarette factory in Newcastle in 1950, and the Rowntree Mackintosh factory was established in 1956. Similarly, at Fawdon the Winthrop Laboratories were established during the late 1950s, and many women were employed there in the manufacture of toothpaste and liver salts. All three companies benefited from the grants available for investing in Newcastle as a Development Area.

The clothing industry also made notable advances in providing work opportunities for women during the post-war period. During the Second World War many light clothing manufacturers based in London and the South East relocated to the North East to avail themselves of female labour, and by 1946 there were 10,500 employed in the clothing industry. This expansion meant that, starting in 1946, Newcastle was able to mount an important national fashion show each year. At the first show, the acclaimed designer Hyndman Gillespie created a futuristic catwalk especially for the occasion, decorated with 12 ft. high plaster hands reputedly inspired by the fast-moving hands of the girl machinists he saw in Newcastle factories.

[32] *Newcastle and Gateshead Chamber of Commerce Journal*, Vol. V, November 1924, No. 49, p.17.
[33] Census of England and Wales, 1921, Co. Northumberland, & Census of England and Wales, 1931, Co. Northumberland, London (1923) and (1934).

Commentary was supplied by Lucy Clayton of Britain's most prestigious model agency and broadcast by the North of England Home Service.[34]

The rising prominence of factory work for women in the region reflected the spatial and gender division of labour underway nationally after 1945, but these 'branch plants' also built on a degree of tradition.[35] In the clothing sector the city built upon the legacy of Lionel Jacobson's company, Jackson the Tailor, who spearheaded mass-produced clothing during the 1950s with such success that the Leeds-based Burtons clothing company had negotiated a reverse takeover by 1953. By the early 1960s, Jacobson was Chairman of Burtons. Additionally, before the Second World War women makers of tobacco products in Newcastle far exceeded their male counterparts, and the majority of these women were classified as skilled.[36] In the light of these continuities it might be pertinent to address 'deskilling' as a process which women as well as men experienced in the post-war years.

The focus on heavy engineering can also obscure the fact that Newcastle did not always mirror regional economic development. The Special Areas recommendations of 1934 *excluded* Newcastle, Middlesbrough and Darlington, because none had sustained the required 40 per cent unemployment level. Newcastle was included in legislation for development areas after 1945, but primarily in recognition that planning measures could be more effective if the regional capital was incorporated. On the other hand, during the 1930s some of the worst examples of poverty and malnutrition in the United Kingdom were recorded in the city.[37] Notwithstanding the growth of city confectioners and their sugary 'Messages of Goodness', contemporary reports estimated that during the 1930s almost half the resident population had energy intakes as low as those in the 19th century.[38] The image of depression and unemployment is consistent with much of what was experienced in Newcastle, but there were also notable developments in industries characterised as 'new', such as electricity supply.

On the eve of the Second World War, a senior manager at Swan Hunter wrote to the Secretary of State for Air with a proposal to establish a modern factory for mass-produced aircraft on Tyneside. This project was to be carried out in collaboration with Anthony Fokker of Holland and D.W. Douglas of Santa Monica.

[34] *Newcastle Journal and North Mail*, Monday 4 November 1946, p.3; *Drapers Record*, 9 November 1946.

[35] *The North East Industrialist*, January 1951. For an example of the argument surrounding the peripheralisation of the northern economy following the growth of branch plant companies after 1945, see Massey D., *Spatial Divisions of Labour* (1984).

[36] Census of England and Wales, Co. Northumberland, 1921 & 1931. This conclusion is also relevant for Tyneside, as the work of Fred Robinson particularly makes clear. See Robinson, F. (ed.), *Post-Industrial Tyneside, An Economic and Social Survey of Tyneside in the 1980s* (1988), pp.66-74.

[37] Webster, C., 'Healthy or Hungry Thirties?', *History Workshop Journal*, issue 13, Spring 1982, p.120.

[38] Bennison, B., 'Feeding the People' in Flowers, A. and Histon, V. (eds.), *Water under the Bridges. Newcastle's Twentieth Century* (2000), p.45.

The intended British Fokker Douglas Aircraft Ltd. was to be located in the Newcastle area with a plant at Swan's shipyard on the Tyne and a new factory and assembly shed at the aerodrome in Woolsington. In addition to being compatible with production for the war effort (Swan Hunter was already on the Admiralty list), this proposal also recognised the high priority that would be given to the development of civil air communications after 1945. The minister's negative response was based on the vulnerability of the Tyne to future airborne enemy attacks.[39] After the outbreak of war, the impact of this perceived geographical disadvantage continued to trouble Newcastle's industrial elite. In 1942 a disconcerted Lord Ridley commented that, 'All the new factories and war work are in other parts of the country (ours being held to be a vulnerable area before the war) – the result shall be that we will be in a disadvantage when peace comes.'[40] After 1945, members of the Northern Industrial Group (NIG), established by Ridley in 1943 for collaboration between employers and unions, were amongst the first to confirm the fate of smaller companies. With their underdeveloped plants they could not return to their obsolete products, and they did not have the necessary capital with which to start new lines of production.[41]

As a result of this weakened manufacturing position in the new post-1945 markets, the tendency of surviving export-based manufacturing companies to rely upon Commonwealth markets became increasingly pronounced. Before the war Parson's had spent much time and money consolidating their Commonwealth trade links, particularly so following the development of turbo alternators at Heaton. Nevertheless, this innovation brought them no closer to the European markets which had been exploited by continental firms such as Siemens during the 1930s.[42] At this time, as well, the company suffered a personal setback following Charles Parson's death in 1931. Subsequently, the company merged with others involved in electrical engineering on Tyneside, such as Reyrolle and Clark Chapman, enabling it to exploit the growing home demand for heavy electrical generating equipment, led by the national grid.

At the same time changes in the nature of warfare provided a boost to the city's armaments producer as can be seen in the rates of naval output contained in Figure 3.1. Whilst the market for big guns had diminished significantly by 1939, the demand for new military equipment such as tanks and submarines meant that, in 1945, Vickers-Armstrongs' plants at Elswick and Scotswood together remained the

---

[39] Clarke, *Building Ships*, p.280.
[40] Ball, S. (ed.), *Parliament and Politics in the Age of Churchill and Attlee. The Headlam Diaries 1935-1951*, Camden series, 5, Vol. 14 (1999), p.338.
[41] NIG Memorandum to the Government, White Paper on Employment Policy, 1945, Cmnd 6527.
[42] Newcastle and Gateshead Incorporated Chamber of Commerce, *Electrical Engineering Supplement*, 1934, p.19.

## Figure 3.1
## Naval output 1939-45 on the north-east coast by firm (tons)

| Firm | Naval output 1939-45 |
|---|---|
| Armstrong | 147,481 |
| Swan Hunter | 131,702 |
| Hawthorn Leslie | 64,492 |
| Blyth | 24,405 |
| Redhead | 18,650 |
| Smiths Dock | 16,837 |
| Gray | 10,000 |
| Short | 10,000 |
| Bartram | 9,730 |
| Pickersgill | 8,996 |
| Crown | 6,220 |
| Others | 2,917 |

Source: J. Clarke, *Building Ships on the North East Coast*

city's largest employers. Ordering booms for the city's armament and shipbuilding companies were sustained until the early 1960s, with stimulus provided for the former by both the Korean War and the Suez crisis. In 1951, Vickers-Armstrongs Ltd. had orders worth £45 million, half of which were to be built on the Tyne.[43]

All the same, the 1950s were a portentous decade for Tyneside shipbuilders, particularly so once Japan overtook Britain in 1956 as the world leader in shipbuilding. Between 1960-5, British shipbuilding output fell 19 per cent, whereas Swedish output saw a 78 per cent increase, and Japan a staggering 210 per cent. Of the many explanations for the failure of British yards to keep pace with rival productivity, the increase in demand for bulk carriers and large oil tankers seems to have been particularly problematic for the British. Whereas competitor yards such as Kockums in Malmö had developed prefabricated welding techniques particularly suited for such vessels, the North East's traditional strength, particularly its ability to custom-build a diverse range of ships, had by the early 1960s become a deep-seated problem. Faced with the rise in international competition, Swan Hunter's earlier position of strength (most of Tyneside's tonnage was launched from the company's Neptune yard during the war) appeared to be on the wane. By the early 1960s, the Neptune yard was only able to offset foreign rivals for the order of a bulk cargo vessel for Ghana with the help of a substantial government loan.[44] Similarly, although Parson's,

[43]  Dougan, *North East Shipbuilding*, p.195.
[44]  Clarke, *Building Ships*, p.381.

as part of Northern Engineering plc, secured export orders for their turbine generators in India and China during the early 1980s, the company had proved far less successful in the era of nuclear power stations. Major redundancies were recorded by the late 1980s, and in 1997 their former European rivals, Siemens Power Generation Ltd., bought Parson's Heaton works.

Vickers-Armstrongs Ltd. retained its productive capacity late into the 20th century, but not as a local shipbuilding or engineering plant. The naval yard at Walker was sold in 1968 and, by the early 1970s, the site of the Scotswood engineering works had been sold to Vickers Property Ltd. to be sublet for warehousing and office space. During the 1970s property deals gave far greater profits for the company and its subsidiaries than did mechanical engineering.[45] This drew attention to the acute changes in the development of Western capitalism during the 1970s, and whilst by no means exclusive to Newcastle, the profound social and economic consequences for the city should not be underestimated. Indeed, the development of Vickers-Armstrongs Ltd. after 1945 captures the experience of Newcastle's manufacturing sector generally and is represented in the occupational structure of the city contained in Figure 3.2.

These figures also reflect the experience of the conurbation and therefore need to be considered in conjunction with those compiled by Fred Robinson for Tyneside.[46] Although Newcastle City Council had prided itself during the early 1960s that the city had suffered less than the region from the decline of the primary sector industries, by the 1970s, Newcastle's own manufacturing fragility was all too clear.[47] Between 1979-82, annual rates of unemployment in a city, which had been less hit by structural change earlier in the century, but more proportionally hit now, rose from eight to 18 per cent.[48] The unemployment statistics for the period after 1960 are contained in Figure 3.3.

In part, de-industrialisation after 1961 appeared to be so dramatic because, as was the case with manufacture, that statistical monolith, the 'service sector', actually represented diverse and fluctuating occupations. Indeed, in Newcastle City Council's *Development Plan Review* of 1963, the 'service sector' included *all* employment categories that fell outside manufacture and the primary sector. For representatives of the region's labour movement, the rise of the broadly defined 'service sector' was problematic because it rapidly became associated with the culture of the low-wage, part-time job, particularly so during the 1980s when the government utilised part-

---

[45] Chapman, P., 'A Comparative Perspective of Vickers on Tyneside and Kockums in Malmö 1945-1988', University of Northumbria, undergraduate special subject paper (1999), p.8.
[46] Robinson, *Post-Industrial Tyneside*, figure 2.1, pp.20-1.
[47] Newcastle upon Tyne City Council, *Newcastle upon Tyne Development Review 1963*, p.40.
[48] Newcastle City Council, Research Section, City Profiles 1991, pp.17-19.

**Figure 3.2**

**Economic structure of Newcastle 1961-91 by rates of occupation**

| | *percentages* | | | |
|---|---|---|---|---|
| | *1961* | *1971* | *1981* | *1991* |
| Manufacturing | 28.89 | 26.69 | 30.7 | 12.86 |
| Construction | 7 | 5.79 | 12.1 | 7.7 |
| Distribution and catering | 22.36 | 22.19 | 14.5 | 20.45 |
| Bank and finance | 2.94 | 4.39 | 9 | 8 |
| Communications | 8.97 | 7.35 | 7 | 6.32 |
| Services (including public sector) | 13.94 | 17.88 | 28.09 | 36.9 |
| Energy and water | 2.9 | 1.95 | 3.64 | 1.97 |

Source: Census of England and Wales, County Report Northumberland.

**Figure 3.3**

**Unemployment in Newcastle by gender 1971-91**

| | *percentages* | | |
|---|---|---|---|
| | *1971* | *1981* | *1991* |
| Men | 8.8 | 16.2 | 16 |
| Women | 3 | 5.6 | 6.6 |
| Total unemployed | 11.8 | 21.8 | 22.6 |

Source: Census of England and Wales, County Report Northumberland
and Department of Employment Gazette.

time employment increases to mask the loss of jobs in manufacture.[49] At the time quantitative increases in service sector occupations could not assuage the qualitative loss of work in heavy engineering and manufacture. But 15 years on, and with continued expansion in the service sector, particularly the 'retail-led' and 'leisure' services, it is clear that this has been no mere diversion from an industrial norm. Therefore, the present time is particularly appropriate to investigate claims that due to its earlier significance as regional provider of commercial and retailing services, Newcastle has been especially well placed to capitalise on their expansion.

---

[49] The New Earnings Survey published in 1985 confirmed that, at a time when unemployment was growing steadily in the city, wages in Tyne and Wear rose less than national levels, Tyne and Wear Research and Intelligence Unit, *Economic Progress* (1988).

It has now been widely acknowledged that the emphasis upon the decline of the British manufacturing economy has obscured the significance of the tertiary sector, particularly retailing, in the development of the economy over the last 200 years. Current scholarship recognises that through these sectors it is possible to understand better the growth and changing shape of consumption as well as production during that period. Modern retailing and commercial activity in Newcastle accounted for a significant proportion of economic development and, compared with the setbacks in manufacture during the early 20th century, the city's department stores progressed well.[50] In 1918 Fenwick's department store in Newcastle made flamboyant plans for the Christmas shopping season in their newly extended premises on Northumberland Street, which included inviting Armstrong Whitworth Ltd. to develop lines in mechanical toy production.[51] Moreover, Newcastle's retailing elites were well aware of their importance to the city economy and, more importantly, in consolidating Newcastle's position as the regional capital. In 1927 J. Robinson, Chairman of the Retail Section of the Chamber of Commerce, called for greater appreciation of the 'service' rendered to the city by its many shopkeepers, and particularly from the regional railway companies indebted to the retailers for encouraging 'people to travel in their 1,000's to Newcastle, where the life of the city is largely centred in its shops'.[52] The growth of shoppers travelling to Newcastle's city centre was clearly boosted by the arrival of the electric tram in 1901 and, by 1912, Bainbridge's department store could claim that 2,500 trams passed their door each day.[53] A brief glance at the census returns for the interwar years suggests that improvements in transport were also responding to city centre prosperity. Particularly noteworthy were the changes brought by retailing success to the occupational status of women in the city. Although domestic service remained the most significant form of female employment during the early 1900s, in 1921, 1,000 women were recorded as proprietors or managers of wholesale or retail businesses. Ten years later, 'commerce and finance' were closing the gap on domestic service with nearly 9,000 women occupied and within this sector the most common occupations were retail dealers of hosiery, drapery and millinery, or department store workers.[54]

The *Retail Supplement of the Newcastle and Gateshead Chamber of Commerce* journal, published during the 1930s, provides evidence of increasing female purchasing power as well as employment. In 1936 it introduced an anonymous female columnist

[50] See Lancaster, B., *The Department Store. A Social History* (1995), chapters five and six for a detailed account of retail developments in Newcastle and elsewhere during the inter-war years.

[51] Pound, R., *The Fenwick Story* (1972), p.71.

[52] J. Robinson, Chairman of the Retail Section of the Chamber of Commerce, *Retail Supplement of the Newcastle and Gateshead Chamber of Commerce*, November 1927.

[53] Lancaster, *Department Store*, p.13.

[54] Census of England and Wales, Co. Northumberland, 1921 & 1931.

known as 'The Lady Onlooker' to provide a commentary on the city's retailing trends. In particular, the shopkeepers' seasonal marketing techniques provided the material for several column inches:

> Each year these Christmas Bazaars are becoming earlier than preceding years and as I write, several of these have been formally opened, and others are on the point of revealing their many charms. Everything points to a very successful Christmas shopping season by reason of the increased employment in the district.[55]

This particular strategy may have been designed to bolster confidence following the worst years of the Depression; nevertheless, the most common complaint of the interwar period was reserved for Newcastle's exorbitant rates and, given that the level of local rates was set according to sales, this suggests that turnover was high. Newcastle's growing importance as a regional distributor of consumer durables was also verified by the contention of city traders that the Quayside was both an awkward and expensive location from which to unload foodstuffs. Moreover, whilst department stores dominated occupations for women in the 'commercial and financial' services, butchery remained the most common retail occupation for men. The growth in the distribution of foodstuffs can also be seen through the strength of Newcastle Co-operative Society, which was the city's largest retailer of food by 1914. In 1925, with 54,000 members, the Newcastle Co-operative Society sold 222 chests of tea during the Christmas period, by far the largest trade in the city.[56] Their impressive department store on Newgate Street was built in 1932, the same year that C & A Modes and Marks and Spencer purchased premises on Northumberland Street.

Overall, the steady growth of retailing in an otherwise fluctuating period underlines the significance of this sector to Newcastle's 20th-century economy. It also brings to light the extent to which the service sector was heavily biased towards the provision of retailing services, at the expense, it could even be argued, of other commercial services. For instance, although Newcastle's financial services had developed in conjunction with regional industry during the 19th century, in the 20th century the city did not continue to distinguish itself much as a financial centre. Many Victorian firms, such as the Newcastle upon Tyne Permanent Building Society, survived, but progress was not spectacular, total assets growing from £1m. in 1920 to £4m. in 1933.[57] The Northern Counties and Rock building societies had also made similar

---

[55] 'The Lady Onlooker', *Retail Supplement of the Newcastle and Gateshead Chamber of Commerce*, November 1936, p.1.
[56] *Co-operative News*, 3 January 1925, p.7.
[57] *Newcastle upon Tyne Official and Commercial Guide* (1961), p.277.

progress, increasing their assets from one and a half million pounds sterling in 1925 to £4m. in 1945. Nevertheless, in a region where expansion of owner occupancy was slow, the demand for savings was not matched by commensurate demand for mortgages. It was Lord Ridley who suggested that a move to London could overcome the limitations of the regional housing market.[58] The Rock subsequently opened premises in London in the early 1950s, a move which proved to be opportune after the Conservatives returned to power determined to increase the proportion of houses constructed for owner occupation. By 1977 the Northern Rock Building Society had assets of £435 million. Therefore, it could be argued that the boom in owner occupation in areas of suburban London such as Croydon during the early 1960s was financed in part by Tyneside savings.

Whilst the exigencies of war dealt a blow to both shoppers and shopkeepers, in Newcastle this was a temporary diversion from the most significant development in retailing prior to 1939: the centralisation of the city economy in Northumberland Street. The historic prosperity of the street clearly owed much to the location of Fenwick's department store, consolidated following the celebrated extension of the Fenwick building in 1913. But what also secured future prosperity and the concentration of Newcastle's service sector to the confines of this one street was the arrival of C&A Modes and Marks and Spencer in 1932.[59] Without this early retailing 'critical mass', it is unlikely that highly ambitious and contentious schemes such as the Eldon Square shopping centre would have proved so successful in the long run, or even got off the ground in the first place. In 1939 the economic spotlight shifted away from retailing and Northumberland Street, and back to armaments production on Scotswood Road. This temporarily obscured the growing reality of Newcastle's economy being based increasingly on the distribution of goods rather than their production. One of the most striking features of Newcastle's economy during the 20th century is that the old, highly successful integration of the commercial and industrial sectors was gradually undermined. Exceptions, such as the old Tyneside shipowning firm Hunting & Sons Ltd., who established a travel agency in Newcastle in 1956 and a connection between the 'old' capital goods sector and the 'new' consumer and leisure economy, were a rarity.

During the 1960s, Mr. T. Dan Smith attempted to reconcile Newcastle's retailing strength with regional economic developments. Keen to rid the North East of its heavy industrial mindset, Smith spoke fervently of 'the greater number of working people who … were beginning to shine in the fields of science and technology'. His

[58] Aris, S., *The Story of the Northern Rock* (2000), p.82. This theme has also been covered by the Benwell Community Development Project, *The Making of the Ruling Class* (1979).
[59] Pound, *Fenwick Story*, p.76.

**3.4**  Shopping on Northumberland Street, 2001.

views on regionalism similarly endeavoured to sweep fresh air into the city and 'reflect the consciousness of an age of increasing leisure'.[60] So while Smith wished to emphasise Newcastle's commercial rather than its industrial status as a regional capital, he also recognised the need for industrial modernisation and diversification. Nevertheless, before the arrival of the Siemens and Fujitsu plants during the early 1990s, the city and region were not distinguished by progress in the high technology industries. Rather than 'white hot technology', the 'T. Dan Smith era' of local government is associated with the redevelopment of the city centre, and in particular the development of the Eldon Square shopping centre.

In 1965 the City Council launched a strategic plan with proposals for the redevelopment of Eldon Square and the construction of a large indoor shopping complex, a highly ambitious and contentious programme of physical regeneration. (The architectural and planning issues associated with the redevelopment of central Newcastle during the 1960s and 1970s are dealt with elsewhere in this volume.)[61]

---

[60]  Smith, T.D., *An Autobiography* (1972), p.80.
[61]  See Byrne's and Faulkner's chapters in this volume, below.

On reflection, it is often overlooked that Northumberland Street was pedestrianised as a direct result of what has sometimes been called an 'ill-advised scheme of civic grandeur'. Moreover, the scheme sought to consolidate Newcastle's position as a regional shopping centre and in this it has met with considerable and sustained success. During the 1970s, the Eldon Square complex was the most advanced indoor shopping centre in the country. Whilst the impact of the redevelopment deserves much attention, the scheme was also responding to new demand for premises in the city, reflecting the rapid growth of retailing after 1945. Turnover for the shops in Newcastle's central area increased from £56m. in 1951 to £121m. in 1971, which confirms Newcastle's significance as a regional shopping centre, particularly in comparison with larger population centres such as Leeds, where increases in turnover were less dramatic.[62] Nevertheless, the most impressive gains have been made in recent years. In 1998 turnover for Fenwick's department store alone was £250m.[63]

But the redevelopment plans of the 1960s were not designed exclusively for shopping. They also included significant infrastructural expansion, particularly in higher education after the formation of Newcastle Polytechnic in 1968 adjacent to Newcastle University. This was a big step towards T. Dan Smith's vision of a city centre education precinct which would invigorate the cultural as well as the economic life of the city. Public sector expansion during this period reflected the growth of the welfare state more generally. Between 1961-71 there was a 70 per cent increase in public administration occupations in the city, followed by a further 25 per cent increase between 1971-8. In Newcastle the transfer of the headquarters of the Ministry of Social Security to the site at Longbenton also complemented this expansion during the late 1940s, where about 8,000 people, many of them women, were employed during the 1980s.[64] The better-paid public occupations are concentrated in such sectors as higher education, which generated 8 per cent of the city's total employment in 1995.[65] Compared with retailing and public sector employment, however, between 1960-90 the proportion employed in the financial services remained marginal. It is worth returning to the weakness of the financial sector again in order to understand the shape of the local economy during the late 20th century.

In 1965, the Newcastle Stock Exchange amalgamated with the other exchanges of northern England to form the Northern Stock Exchange. With almost 70 different firms and 350 members this formed the largest stock exchange outside London and meant that Newcastle stockbrokers gained access to a 'jobbing network' for the

[62] *Census of Distribution 1971*, table 5, p.4/20.
[63] *North East England plc. A Comprehensive Guide to the Business Region* (1998/9), p.85.
[64] Robinson, *Post-Industrial Tyneside*, p.41.
[65] Lincoln, I., Stone, I., Walker, A., 'The contribution of Newcastle's higher education to the local economy', *NERU Research Paper*, no.6 (1995), *passim*.

first time. This regional advantage was nonetheless short-lived, as in 1973 all British stock exchanges united to form The Stock Exchange.[66] Since then, the weakness of the financial sector in the city has been attributed to the international deregulation of financial services, which benefited large global centres such as London, Tokyo and New York more. As a result of the closure of the regional stock exchange, access to development or venture capital has been located far away from Newcastle, with few financial companies choosing the city for head office.[67] This relative weakness was recognised by QUANGO-driven regeneration initiatives of the late 1980s and early 1990s. The Armstrong Business Park, home to the AA Insurance processing centre and other business headquarters, reflects the ambitions of the various strategies for economic and urban regeneration which have proliferated since the late 1970s. Nevertheless, the high profile activities of the Tyne and Wear Development Corporation – who managed key industrial sites from the Quayside to the western districts – failed to produce wider growth in city finance and business-led sectors. This relative weakness, however, cannot be attributed to the process of internationalisation alone given that other regional centres outside London, notably Leeds and Edinburgh, have exhibited success in these areas. Historically the centre of gravity for the English building society movement was based in Yorkshire and, during the 20th century, Leeds was able to take a leading position in the building society sector, particularly in the development of a national branch structure. In the North East, by contrast, building societies such as the Northern Rock were not part of a similar financial critical mass and only developed a modest national branch structure during the second half of the 20th century. In addition, the peculiarities of the North East housing market exacerbated this position of comparative weakness. Just as relatively low rates of owner occupation helped explain the movement of finance capital out of the region earlier in the century, during the boom in house prices of the late 1980s Newcastle sustained lower than average rates of owner occupation and, compared with other British regions, house prices remained low.[68] Leeds, by contrast, by now the capital of the building society movement, was able to prosper from the national rise in house prices. Indeed, Leeds found itself in a virtuous cycle of growth as building societies attracted the movement of banking, insurance and other financial services.

[66] 'The Stock Exchange in Newcastle upon Tyne', Newcastle City Libraries Local Studies, typescript.

[67] Gentle, C., 'The Financial Services Industry in Northern England: A Branch Office Economy', *CURDS Discussion Paper 6A* (1993), *passim.*

[68] City Profiles, *op.cit.*, p.10; see also Lancaster, B. (ed.), *Working Class Housing on Tyneside 1850-1939* for details of the history of housing in the city. To follow the theme of late 20th-century regeneration in the north see particularly Byrne, D., 'What is the point of an Urban Development Corporation in the North East?' in *Northern Economic Review*, no. 15, 1986 and Shaw, K., 'The Development of a New Urban Corporation: the politics of Urban Regeneration in North East England' in *Regional Studies*, Vol. 27, no.3, 1993.

This is not to say that there has been no increase in consumer spending in Newcastle during the last 20 years. Indeed, according to research carried out recently by the University of Strathclyde, those in work in Newcastle have amongst the highest levels of disposable income in the country due in part to the combination of lower house expenditure (and greater council house occupation) and below average levels of car ownership. As has been shown, this has clearly benefited retailing, but the other area which is directly linked to consumer expenditure in Newcastle is the 'leisure industry'. In 1981, Newcastle Council inaugurated a rolling programme of regeneration for the Quayside, an area whose former prosperity diminished after the completion of the Tyne Bridge in 1928. The Quayside programme set out specifically to stimulate economic, recreational and social life in that 'historic' part of the city, for which the Tyne and Wear Urban Development Corporation assumed responsibility in 1987. Since then the director Alistair Ball's pledge to 'replace old industries and bring new life' to the Quayside has been fulfilled, but the bias towards 'coffee and cigarettes' has produced hostilities from other quarters, particularly from the Quayside's Residents' Association who spent most of the early 1990s disputing the steady stream of applications for new bars and clubs. Others have celebrated the rebirth of the Quayside as much more than somewhere to drink. It is becoming a site where pride of place is reaffirmed, or, in the scholarly perspective, the Quayside bears witness to the growing influence of the new 'place entrepreneur', skilled in the business of packaging and selling 'place' as human sociability. Either way, it is perhaps the Quayside which best captures the nature of Newcastle's 20th-century economic development. The historic dependence upon the 'seasonal rhythms of trade flowing up and down the Tyne' can still be seen clearly in Newcastle's Quayside at the start of the 20th century.[69] By the 1990s, the economy of urban sociability dominated the Quayside area and little remained of the river's earlier commercial functions. This urban sociability represents a central part of the economic development which has sustained the city since the 1950s and, far more than just a story of manufacturing decline, it demonstrates that the 20th century was complex and not best analysed sector by sector.

Perhaps more than any previous era, the 20th century represented the closing of an epoch for Newcastle's economy. On Nationalisation vesting day in 1947 the Montagu was the only operative pit in Newcastle. When it closed in 1956, 209 years of mining came to an end. This striking discontinuity has come at a price. Given that Newcastle's earlier trading privileges depended upon a thriving industrial region, the decline of a North East industrial base during the 20th century severely undermined Newcastle's status as an industrial port and as capital and proprietor

---

[69] See Joyce Ellis' chapter in this volume, above.

**3.5** 'Party City', 1996.

of a large exporting area. The 18th- and 19th-century legacy depended upon close links between regional industrial and city commercial concerns but it failed to secure Newcastle's position of strength in the industrial developments of the 20th century. The alacrity with which the region's economic elite were willing to transfer resources from the local industrial sector to the metropolitan and global financial markets helped in the rapid erosion of the city's great industrial economy. At the same time, there were many profound discontinuities which were *not* related to the provenance of the North East coal trade or its business leaders. The most significant of these was the experience of two world wars. Whilst W.G. Armstrong & Co. had been Newcastle's largest engineering employer during the 19th century, it needs to be emphasised that the sustained dominance by Armstrong Whitworth Ltd. and subsequently Vickers-Armstrongs Ltd. was driven more by a series of international wars and crises than by anything to do with local industrial or entrepreneurial skill or innovation. Military expansion began and ended (at least as far as mass employment is concerned) in the 20th century, leaving the city with some serious manufacturing problems of its own to contend with.

But Newcastle's contemporary economy also needs to be rescued from the stigma of industrial decline. In the long historical perspective, the 20th century also contained some striking continuities, particularly evident in the enduring resilience of popular purchasing power. In the Newcastle of the 18th century the city's 'traditional' strength was its function as a distributor of consumer goods suitable to a diverse and expanding population. This strength was in no way sidelined by the expansion of the heavy industrial sectors; indeed shipbuilding was positively stimulated by the expansion of trade in consumer goods throughout that period. Increasing levels of disposable income in the 19th century contributed in turn to ground-breaking developments in retailing following the opening of Bainbridge's, the world's first department store, in 1838. Retailing during the 20th century proved to be surprisingly independent of the economic turbulence that affected the region's traditional industries. During the late 20th century economists described the British economy as having undergone a paradigmatic shift from production to consumption. Newcastle has been in the forefront of this movement but it has been the city's old staples of commerce, leisure and retailing which have led the way.

4

# The Governance of the Victorian City

## MAUREEN CALLCOTT

### The Reformed Corporation from 1836: Electorate, Members and Politics

Before the Municipal Corporations Act of 1835, Newcastle had been governed by its Common Council, confirmed by grant of a Royal Charter in 1400 and the governing Charter of 1600. This body, elected by procedures of the utmost complexity,[1] had considerable privileges and enviable revenues from its monopoly of the River Tyne, and from rents, while its responsibilities were minimal. The Act was passed by a Whig Parliament in order to reform and bring some uniformity to the patchwork of English town government. Its immediate effect in Newcastle was to transform a closed, self-selecting, mainly Tory body in a condition of constitutional crisis, into an assembly elected according to a nationally regulated system. Its duties remained few at first and were reluctantly accepted, but in a century of huge industrial expansion and urban growth it had to be the responsible authority for an increasing range of regulations and administration. By 1900 the body created in 1835 could not have recognised itself for there had been a veritable municipal revolution.

The municipal electorate grew with the expansion of the boundaries of the town (granted city status in 1882) and with a more liberal franchise. In 1835 it numbered 2,485, 3.5 per cent of the population, an increase of only 703, and less than the parliamentary electorate. At first, every adult male occupier of property rated for relief of the poor within the borough for that year and the two preceding years and during that time an inhabitant householder within the borough or within seven miles of it would have the vote. By 1852 there were 4,363 borough voters and the Small Tenements Rating Act of 1850 raised the numbers to 7,983. In 1869 the period during which rates had to be paid to qualify for the vote was reduced to one year and women who met these qualifications were also enfranchised. This did not include married women who still had no property rights independent of their husbands. In 1880 there were 25,358 municipal voters in Newcastle, the number rising to 39,136 in 1900.

---

[1]  Cook, M., 'The Last Days of the Unreformed Corporation of Newcastle upon Tyne', in *Archaeologia Aeliana*, 4th series, vol.39, 1961, p.208.

Who were the members of Newcastle's ruling body during the Victorian period? Councillors themselves had to own real or personal estate valued at £100 or be rated for relief of the poor at not less than £30 per annum. Clergymen were excluded. Elections were held on 1 November and every year one third of councillors had to leave office. Initially there were eight wards with 14 aldermen, selected by the Council, who served for six years, and 42 councillors. Council membership remained confined to males. Even though women became eligible for municipal council election in 1907, Mary Laverick, Newcastle's first woman councillor, was not elected until 1919. Members had to be property holders, and as all Council meetings were held in the afternoons, the vast majority of people who worked were effectively excluded. The Council tended to be composed therefore of older men of established position and the gradual widening of the qualification for membership did not substantially affect this.

The eight Tories in the first reformed Council could all be described as businessmen, such as John Brandling, a coal-owner and younger brother of Charles John Brandling, former Tory MP for Newcastle. The professions were not strongly represented at this period, but three prominent lawyers were elected and another, James Losh, co-opted Alderman. Ralph Park Phillipson's influence became 'almost supreme'. He succeeded John Clayton as Town Clerk from 1857 to 1867. He was also a coal-owner and went on to be a River Tyne Improvement Commissioner. The other lawyers were Armorer Donkin and Abraham Dawson. The two medical doctors, John Fife and Thomas Headlam, had led the agitation for reform, but used their new-found powers to exclude opposition and turn on their former radical allies. Having been in the early '30s the 'idol of the mob', by 1839 Fife had cast them off 'like an old slipper'.[2] Afterwards, as Mayor, leading the forces which suppressed the Chartist riots in the town, he was knighted and it was observed that when he disembarked from the steamer which had brought him back from London his baggage was conspicuously labelled, 'Sir John Fife, Newcastle upon Tyne'.[3]

Decisions tended to be determined by the major committees, especially the Finance and Town Improvement committees. Both normally had powerful and long-serving chairmen. For example, James Hodgson, until 1850 proprietor and editor of the *Newcastle Chronicle*, was chairman of the Finance committee for 22 years from 1844. He was succeeded by Isaac Lowthian Bell, one of the region's most prominent industrialists, who was followed by Thomas Hedley, soap manufacturer and director and Chairman of the Newcastle and Gateshead Gas Company. Finally in our period, one of the most prominent of Tyneside's industrial

---

[2] *Newcastle Journal*, 3 November 1838. The Tory newspaper took every opportunity to ridicule the new Council, especially John Fife.
[3] *Ibid.*, 6 Nov. 1839.

elite with widespread financial interests, William Haswell Stephenson, was Finance committee chairman for 28 years from 1890 to 1918. He several times refused a safe Tory seat in Parliament, but clearly relished his civic role, accepting the Mayoral and Lord Mayoral role no fewer than seven times. These were outstanding civic leaders, but their backgrounds were not entirely untypical of a Council which in 1900, as in 1836, was still largely in the hands of men with a considerable stake in the trade and business of the town and region. These included the two Cowens, father and son, though both were also Members of Parliament and for neither was the Council their major arena. Joseph Cowen senior, a notable north-east radical and proprietor of the *Newcastle Daily Chronicle* from 1859, and Joseph Cowen junior, were both influential campaigners in causes which engaged them.[4]

Soon after the first couple of bitterly contested elections for the reformed Council, party politics virtually disappeared from Newcastle local government. The first Councils were clearly dominated by varieties of Liberals and they probably remained in the majority throughout the century, but political affiliation seems to have played little part in either deciding the election of a councillor or his progress thereafter. Until the 1890s contested elections were the exception. However, concern over rates was always a central issue and, after agitation over the 1853 and 1855 Improvement Acts, Newcastle's first Ratepayers' Association was formed in 1855.[5]

Another followed much later in 1881, but its promoter, an elected auditor and sharp critic of Council expenditure and administration, complained ten years later of the 'sleeping Fever' of Newcastle ratepayers.[6] Yet at the same time party politics outside the Council was fiercely combative, and Members of Parliament included men such as Alderman Charles Hamond (Conservative), Isaac Lowthian Bell (Liberal/Liberal Unionist), the two Cowens (Liberal/ Liberal Unionist) and Walter Richard Plummer (Conservative).

James Cuthbert Laird, sponsored by the predominantly Liberal Trades Council, was the first working man to stand for Council election and he won Elswick ward in a by-election in June 1883. As a tailor with flexible hours he was able to attend meetings in the afternoon, but he campaigned for meeting times which would accommodate the hours of other working men. This was not achieved, but he met more success in his advocacy of Sunday library opening, an extension of branch libraries, baths and washrooms, the wider use of parks, free concerts and more free places in local grammar schools. The only two other working men who stood for

---

[4] For example on 2 March 1899 the editorial of the *Newcastle Daily Chronicle*, under the headline 'Communism in the Council', attacked what were termed 'the schemes of reckless and ill-informed visionaries …', that is, those who favoured the municipalisation of the tramways.

[5] *Newcastle Chronicle*, 9 November 1855.

[6] C. Robinson, *A Chat With the Ratepayers of Newcastle upon Tyne*, 1891.

election in the 1880s were easily defeated, but in 1891 and 1892 J.J. Harris, secretary of the Trades Council, and Arthur Henderson (later Foreign Secretary in a Labour government) were elected. By the end of the 1890s the agenda was changing and in 1897 a Joint Municipal Reform committee was formed which included progressive Liberals, Independent Labour Party members, prominent Trades Councillors and municipalising radicals such as David Adams. Their main objective was the municipalisation of public services: gas, water, electricity and tramways.

Early in the 20th century Sidney and Beatrice Webb undertook a massive survey of English local government, most of which remains unpublished. In Newcastle, among those they interviewed was Tom Cairns, a Quayside shipowner, who described himself as a 'Progressive'. 'No one', he alleged, 'would take the slightest interest in what the Council did', and he thought it was 'made up of inferior people, dominated by a few strong men who were there to grind their own axes. It was virtually a closed body ... absolutely no party cleavage of any kind.'[7] Apathy towards elections, the undoubted control of a small number of businessmen together with the record, which we shall look at next, of reluctant activity in all major fields, makes this harsh judgement not entirely unfair.

By the 1890s, in terms of its size and responsibilities, the Council was a vastly different body from that elected in 1835. As the fine Guildhall buildings had long been inadequate, a new Town Hall was built between 1855 and 1858 in St Nicholas Square opposite the Cathedral, though this was a modest project compared with contemporary edifices in Leeds or Manchester. It was considered inadequate itself within 20 years but, despite several further proposals, the local administration was not adequately housed until the present Civic Centre was opened in 1968.

## The Accumulation of Powers

To begin with, the members of the newly elected Council in 1835 simply set about consolidating their own position while, with a fine show of indignation, they attacked Tory abuses and 'extravagances'. As Burn feelingly expressed it, 'The "brave new world" was inaugurated by an insensate and wasteful piece of vandalism, the sale of the Mansion House and its contents: there has probably never been a sale in Newcastle at which collector's items fetched as little as they did on that occasion.'[8]

Nonetheless the beginnings of modern town government came about through the duty, at once laid upon the Council, to establish a borough police. This was to

---

[7] Webb, Vol.217. Local Government Collections. British Library of Political and Economic Science, Accession No. 351. Newcastle volumes are 211-17.

[8] Burn, W.L., 'Newcastle upon Tyne in the early Nineteenth Century', *Archaeologia Aeliana*, 4th series, vol. 34, 1956, p.8.

be followed by the enforced reform of the management of the River Tyne, pressures of public health problems and issues of control over the development of gas and water supplies which impinged upon the streets. All of these matters involved the expenditure of ratepayers' money, the accumulation of greater powers and the employment of more and more Council staff.

## A Borough Police Force

**4.1**  Newcastle detectives, 1900.

The hand of central government was beginning to be felt in local affairs and the Municipal Corporations Act required the establishment of a local police force. Under the superintendence of John Stephen, formerly of the Metropolitan Police, Newcastle was to have for the first time a 'day' police of 20 men as well as two horses to be used in the 'country' townships of Jesmond and Byker. There was a good deal of opposition. The radical councillor Thomas Doubleday declared that 'this Frenchified thing called a police was decidedly unfit to parade before the free and well-behaved citizens of Newcastle …'.[9] Policing was but the first example of the Council's reluctance to accept a wider responsibility, but by 1871 the force numbered 160,

[9]  Newcastle Corporation Proceedings (NCP), 9 May 1836.

though the quality of policing was questionable at least until that date. After a dispute with the authority practically the whole force resigned and was replaced, largely by 'a good many Scotchmen'.[10] New scales of pay, ranging from 21s. per week for a third-class constable to 38s. 6d. rising to 50s. for a detective, were introduced and a more harmonious and efficient development began.

## The Council and the River Tyne

From time immemorial Newcastle had obtained enormous financial benefits from its 'conservatorship' of the River Tyne for the 17 miles of its tidal flow. Indeed the river provided up to half the town's income. During the ten years up to 1833, £137,319 had been raised from river dues while only £5,133 18s. was spent on improving the river. Quays were lacking and ships were sometimes beached and looted. The new forces of wealth and business from both banks of the Tyne clamoured for improvement. In 1839 a memorial from mercantile interests outside Newcastle pointed to the great increase in use of the river, over 300 vessels yearly, and argued that the Tyne would lose trade to ports such as Sunderland and Stockton where large sums were being spent on improvement.[11] Then, in 1840, Gateshead, South Shields and Tynemouth began an attempt to secure the conservancy of the river, and remove its control from Newcastle.

The resulting Admiralty inquiry, as well as criticising the navigable state of the river, emphasised the vast discrepancy between the wealth derived from it and the money expended upon it. The consequence was the River Tyne Improvement Act of 1850 by which a Conservancy Commission replaced Newcastle's traditional control. This consisted of six representatives from Newcastle, two from Gateshead and three each from Tynemouth (including North Shields) and South Shields, with two representatives from the Admiralty to be added later. Newcastle was to keep three-eighths of the coal dues (which were relinquished in 1872 in return for a lump sum of £130,000 paid in five yearly instalments). Enormous sums of money were needed for the construction of docks, piers, dredging and other necessary improvements, and disputes continued over Newcastle's encroachment on tidal waters by jetties, embankments and other works, which were said to hinder navigation. The great increase in the value of the foreshore lands owned by Newcastle was another issue, and it was late in the century before the work of the Commission was able to proceed without interruption and friction.

[10] NCP, 2 August 1871.
[11] The Sunderland River Commission formulated plans for new docks in the 1820s and 1830s and in the 1840s the South (or 'Hudson' after the 'Railway King') Dock made Sunderland the most successful port in the North East for a time.

## The Health of the Town

Although two of the most powerful councillors elected in 1836, John Fife and Thomas Headlam, were doctors involved in medical education, including the setting up of a Medical School, as was Thomas Gregson, elected to the Council in 1854 and a member for 30 years,[12] not one of them made the connection between political will and public health. However, the Council was compelled to respond to the Health of Towns Commission set up by Peel's Government in 1843. Newcastle Council (and others) was required to provide information under eight headings which produced the first statistical information which could be the basis of sanitary action in the town. Dr. D.R. Reid was the commissioner appointed to lead the inquiry at Newcastle and the ensuing report, published in 1845, was named after him.[13]

Press coverage meant that the findings became public knowledge. Reid emphasised the problems and suggested the remedies. There was no up-to-date plan of the town nor were there regulations relating to sewerage, drainage or paving. This caused difficulties for builders, engineers and sanitary reformers. Lack of building regulations meant, for example, that 'Pandon Dene, on the east side of the town, has now become little better than a public sewer'.[14] Water, provided by the Joint Stock Water Company, was in short supply. Its quality was also criticised: '... some water contaminated with the discharge of the excrementitious [sic] and other matters from the common sewers'.[15] There were very few building regulations, and such as there were remained unknown and unenforced. In the poorer parishes – All Saints, St John's and St Nicholas – the inhabitants lived in damp, over-crowded conditions, families often occupying one room, and, even where ash-pits were provided, 'filth and refuse accumulate in the lanes and vacant corners'.[16] Worst of all were the lodging-houses, presenting '... the most deplorable exhibitions of the want of sanatory [sic] regulations to be found in this country – crowded in the extreme, dirty, ill-managed, occupied promiscuously by both sexes ...'.[17] It was judged that '... tramps, foreign sailors, and Irishmen or Scotchmen seeking casual labour will reduce any accommodation ... by negligence and filth', and the need for public control was recognised in the interests of all classes.

The report anticipated that, as the Council was now informed of the evils, the benefits of 'a little timely assistance or interference' would be applied. But little was

[12] Bettenson, E.M., *The University of Newcastle upon Tyne, 1837-1971*.
[13] D.R. Reid, *Report on the State of Newcastle upon Tyne and other Large Towns*, 1845.
[14] *Ibid.*, p.73.
[15] *Ibid.*, p.80. Rennison, R.W., *Water to Tyneside* is a very good recent account of the history of the local water supply.
[16] *Ibid.*, p.85.
[17] *Ibid.*, p.93.

done. Pressure from the Poor Law Guardians and a new element, the first national Public Health Act in 1848, produced the first Sewers' Rate of 2d. in the pound. The Public Health Act could be imposed upon a town with an annual death rate over 23 per 1,000 or on the petition of ten per cent of the inhabitants. Newcastle's death rate had averaged 29.6 per 1,000 for the previous seven years and the Sanitary Association had petitioned the Board of Health, as established by the Act, to bring its provisions into operation in Newcastle.[18]

The history of the inquiry instituted by the Board of Health as a result of this memorial illustrates the limitations of the central authority in the face of local reluctance to act. This was recognised by Rawlinson, the Board of Health inspector, whose report remains in manuscript form.[19] He agreed with the petitioners but felt 'satisfied that any report I might write on Newcastle upon Tyne so far as the local authorities are concerned would be a dead letter'.[20] When the Council did agree to take any action (though it was not always implemented), it was often in the face of the threat to have the Public Health Act applied. This occurred when Dr. Henry Newton, a Poor Law medical officer, was elected to the Council and persuaded it to erect baths and a wash-house at the foot of Gallowgate and Bath Lane and to apply its bye-laws for the regulation of lodging-houses. As he warned, the alternative 'would make the Council the mere executive of a Board in London'.[21]

## The Cholera

The third and worst outbreak of cholera in Newcastle occurred in September 1853. It took the lives of 1,527 people, and apart from its devastating effect on the population it was also a significant test of the capacities and attitudes of the municipal authority. Three hundred and six people had died in the epidemic of 1831-2, but Newcastle had escaped fairly lightly in the 1849 outbreak. The immediate background to the 1853 outbreak was a long dry spell and the Water Company's decision to pump water from a tidal reach of the Tyne at Elswick, as from 2 July, to all its 18,000 customers. The combination of impure water and an unhealthy overcrowded environment was generally judged to have produced the epidemic. Within a week the daily death total rose at a terrifying rate, reaching 89 on 15 September and over 100 on each of the next five days. After about 9 October the disease appeared to be subsiding, though small numbers of deaths were reported daily until early November. Businesses were reported to be in a state of complete stagnation,

---

[18] Reid Report, 15 November 1848.
[19] Rawlinson, Report to the General Board of Health, 7 March 1853, PRO MH13/232.
[20] *Ibid.*
[21] NCP, 14 September 1851.

doctors worked to exhaustion and the cemeteries could not cope with the numbers of dead.

The Poor Law Guardians, the Poor Law Board and General Board of Health in London, and the Council, were all responsible and all were slow to respond. When the Central Board of Health in London sent its Superintendent Medical Inspector General, Dr. Grainger, he was very critical of the lack of enforcement of local sanitary legislation and urged the immediate enforcement of the Lodging Houses Act.

The Council did not even to meet to discuss the cholera until two weeks after the outbreak and some time after its epidemic proportions had been recognised. Grainger advised the implementation of the regulation of their two statutes regulating common lodging-houses, instancing the arrival of a steam-boat from Hull, with 100 to 150 Irish labourers on board who immediately descended on the overcrowded lodging-houses of Sandgate. He urged upon the Council the proper provision of privies, scavenging, the washing of the filthy courts, the removal of the sick to houses of refuge, the careful supervision of meats, fish and fruits, and the conveying to everyone of the need for the early treatment of bowel complaints which could arrest the onset of cholera.[22] The Council agreed to implement these measures and placed £500 at the disposal of the Guardians. Newcastle was fortunate not to be visited with another outbreak of cholera; for the warnings presented by both the epidemic itself and the concluding words of the inquiry commissioners went unheeded. Mortality rates remained very high and the local authorities in the 1850s and '60s ignored preventable causes of death just as they had in the 1840s.

During the 1860s, under the leadership in the council of such men as Isaac Lowthian Bell and encouraged by a growing campaign in the town itself, headed in this period by the medically qualified Congregationalist minister Rutherford, sanitary reform at last became a regular subject for Council debate, and the Improvement Committee pursued its role with slightly more vigour.

## The Medical Officer of Health

This did not augur well for the appointment of the town's first Medical Officer of Health (MOH). The 1872 Public Health Act made it compulsory for all local sanitary authorities in England and Wales to make such an appointment. Newcastle was not among the 50 authorities which had already done this and only carried out the ruling to do so after considerable opposition to the measure. When the town's first MOH, Dr. Henry Armstrong, was appointed in July 1873, Alderman Benjamin

---

[22] NCP, 14 September 1853.

Plummer opined that 'the appointment was no more use to the town than an umbrella to a duck'.[23]

Armstrong was then aged thirty. He remained in the post for 39 years and it is clear that he was a particularly able MOH. In his first year of office, 1873, the death rate in Newcastle was 30.1 per 1,000 in contrast to the average for 21 large towns in the United Kingdom of 24.3 persons. He emphasised that more than a quarter of these deaths were preventable, in particular those from scarlet fever and diarrhoea largely caused by 'the negligence of individuals and … sanitary imperfection',[24] describing the latter in great detail. Also the infant death rate was very high at 80 per 1,000. For what he termed 'the indefinite sub-class' of the population, it was an astronomical 284 per 1,000. He related most of this class to the large proportion of inhabitants born in Ireland.

Noticeably lacking was a vigorous leading personality committed to public health. In Newcastle there was no Joseph Chamberlain with a civic mission as there was in Birmingham, no John Simon as in London, and no Octavia Hill who rattled up the London landlords. But the work of Armstrong and his Health Department undoubtedly contributed to the reduction of the death rate by about 10 in every 1,000. In 1873 it had a staff of six. In 1889 there were 12 and by 1900 at least 24, an increase which exceeded the growth in population, dramatic though that was (from 128,443 to 266,671). Furthermore, the accumulation of information in annual reports and the diffusion of increased medical knowledge, together with the growing professionalism of local officers, provided a sound basis for remedial action.

## Water

There was a similar situation with the supply of water to the rapidly growing town. This became a concern for three main reasons. First, as has been described, in the 1840s central government had initiated a series of reports and inquiries into urban conditions. Water supply was central to all of these. Second, the supply of water, like the supply of gas, necessitated lifting roads and pavements, properties of the Council. Third, an ample supply of water was important to industrialists who were also concerned about increasing fire hazards. In 1854 an explosion and great fire at the Quayside killed 53 and damaged many businesses. The Reid Report of 1845 had recommended the provision of 'a constant supply by a disinterested body, if necessary by the local authority itself'.[25] Here, in other words, was a positive

[23] NCP, 2 July 1873.
[24] MOH Report, 1873.
[25] Reid Report, p.80.

encouragement to remove from the control of a private, profit-motivated concern a commodity vital to the health of all.

As with the gas supply, however, there was with water a close connection between leading aldermen and councillors and the commercial companies involved. In 1845 (coinciding with the Royal Commission on the Health of Towns report), reasons of public interest and private profit had encouraged the Council to co-operate with the promoters of a new water company being formed in that year. When Joseph Crawhall, chairman of the Improvement Committee, laid before the Council a list of the new company's provisional committee it 'contained names of the highest respectability' including the Mayor, T.G. Headlam (who in 1851 crushed the proposed municipalisation of the gas supply) and four previous holders of that office.[26] The future industrialist, W.G. Armstrong, one of the originators of the new company, initially acted as solicitor and then secretary to it and showed 'great astuteness in his choice of associates and his timing of events in that in 1845 his father, a successful merchant, was a member of the Newcastle Council, while his uncle, Addison Potter, was Mayor during the same critical period of Armstrong's venture'.[27]

Although the Corporation obtained powers to purchase the new company, the Whittle Dean Water Company, and became involved in some surveillance of its activities, it avoided takeover and the company continued to make a 'judicious' choice of directors from members of its own Council,[28] men such as Benjamin Plummer, Richard Burdon Sanderson and Addison Potter, son of the company's Chairman and later to be Chairman himself as well as proprietor of the Willington Gas Company. The question of ownership reappeared all through the 1860s, '70s and '80s. The Water Company was constantly criticised for its supply, but no action was taken. In this respect Newcastle was even more out of line with developments elsewhere. During the third quarter of the 19th century the trend was for local authorities to municipalise their water supply in order to make sufficient provision both for domestic, street-cleaning and industrial purposes, often regardless of profit. By 1897 there was a municipal supply in more than two-thirds of local authorities.[29]

## Libraries

Throughout Britain in the last quarter of the 19th century local authorities were becoming involved on such a broad front in the provision of public services that in 1890 Sidney Webb coined the term 'municipal socialism'. As we have seen though,

[26] NCP, 5 February 1845.
[27] Rennison, *Water to Tyneside*, p.39.
[28] *Ibid.*, p.94.
[29] Finer, H., *English Local Government*, 4th edition, 1950, p.28.

in Newcastle all such developments were reluctantly undertaken and the opportunity to municipalise the gas and water supplies had been rejected. Even so, by 1900 the Newcastle City Council was administering a range of services and considering others, all of which would have been inconceivable in 1836 and laughed out by members as recently as 1870. After 'sanitation', 'civilization', the provision of parks, libraries, public baths and museums followed, and by the 1890s the more complex and costly enterprises of transport and housing had become public considerations.

The establishment of the first free public library in Newcastle was the culmination of a 26-year struggle. Since the Public Libraries Act of 1850, libraries were seen as models of self-help and education. The campaign in Newcastle was led by Dr. Henry Newton and his son, also a doctor, councillor and sanitary reformer. It took off in the 1870s backed by the *Weekly Chronicle*, under the editorship of W.E. Adams, ex-Chartist and lifelong radical. It was supported by the Trades Act.[30] In the Council, Dr. Thomas Gregson, who continued to oppose the scheme, conceded 'that there was a majority for the Act but what was it composed of? A lot of hobbledehoys and people who would never be called upon to pay a 6d'.[31] The plans, finally approved in September 1878, utilised land belonging to the Corporation adjacent to the Mechanics' Institute and the Carliol or Weaver's Tower, part of the medieval town wall. There was to be a lending library costing a penny rate, two reading rooms, a reference library and the librarian's office, with provision for further enlargement. Alderman Joseph Cowen MP opened the library on 13 September. The new building on the site of the present Central Library was opened two years later.

The provision of the Central Library encouraged demand for branch libraries and in 1884 three branch newsrooms were opened at Byker, Elswick and Westgate using a large room in each of the chief Board Schools (established by the Education Act of 1870) in the evenings. The continued demand for branches was only met through the intervention of a private benefactor. Alderman William Haswell Stephenson offered to build a library in Elswick if the Council made land available in Elswick Park and this (the Stephenson Branch Library, now the Elswick branch) was opened on 2 December 1895. It was Stephenson's philanthropy which provided the east end with its first library too, the Victoria Jubilee Library (now the Heaton branch), situated in Armstrong Park, in February 1899.

There was a huge demand for books with almost one third of the readers aged between 14 and 20 in the early years. Hence by 1900, for those who would read, and at a relatively small cost to the ratepayers, there was a large and up-to-date stock of books and periodicals available at three libraries. They constituted a

[30] NCP, 1 April 1874.
[31] *Ibid.*, 2 February 1876.

considerable amenity in the town which had been only grudgingly provided after an arduous campaign, and which owed much to private philanthropy.[32]

## Places For Recreation

Reid's powerful recommendation for 'a place of recreation' near 'to the habitations of the poor'[33] was included in the report of the Health of Towns Commission visit to Newcastle in 1844. Yet, despite a rise in the population of 82 per cent over the following 30 years, no such provision was made prior to the 1870s. On the contrary, pleasant fields by the Forth (near the Central Station), for example, were lost and not replaced when the Council sold them to the railway companies and for Robert Stephenson's and Hawthorn's engineering works. Newcastle was exceptionally well endowed with open spaces, having in the Town Moor and the Leazes 1,227 acres, a total which exceeded all the parks in London.[34] But the Moor, at the extreme north edge of Newcastle, was not developed at all for recreation and in any case was not immediately accessible. Developing open spaces meant increasing the rates so Reid was ignored for 30 years, as was a petition in 1858 from almost 3,000 working men living in the west of the town, asking for open ground on Elswick Estate to be purchased and used as a park.[35] Newton, also leading the campaign for a public library, supported this petition with the help in Council of Hamond and Cowen, who was appointed Chairman of the new Parks Committee in 1870. The Improvement Act of that year included clauses enabling the Council to develop the Town Moor for public parks. The first was Leazes Park, opened in 1873, and between 1878 and 1880 further portions of the Town Moor were laid out as Bull Park and Brandling Park.

In the meantime demands continued for parks in the west and east ends of the town. Stephenson, as well as contributing to the expanding library system, supported this. He castigated the Council for being laggardly. 'In Newcastle we had the reputation of being about the last town in the kingdom to undertake any improvement and when we did undertake any improvements we did it in a half-hearted way.'[36] He was one of a group of six local businessmen, Council members, who purchased a portion of Elswick Park in the west end, including the hall, for the purpose of selling it to the town for a public park. Eight and three-quarter acres

[32] For a history of the libraries in Newcastle see Knott, J., 'A History of the Libraries of Newcastle upon Tyne to 1900', MLitt Thesis, Newcastle upon Tyne University, 1975, and *Newcastle upon Tyne City Libraries, The First Hundred Years*, 1980.

[33] Reid report, ch.2, pp.78 *et seq.*

[34] The four Royal Parks totalled 875 acres. Webb, *op.cit.*, vol.215.

[35] NCP, 23 September 1858.

[36] NCP, 29 January 1876.

4.2   City Library and Laing Art Gallery, 1920.

4.3   The New Bowling Green, Heaton Park.

were bought for £14,000.[37] At the same time 22 acres were bought from Addison Potter who then owned Heaton Hall. The decision to go ahead with Heaton Park produced the gift from William Armstrong of an additional 28 acres, which he purchased for the Council from Potter.[38] The park was named after Armstrong and three years later he added Jesmond Dene (including the banqueting hall with its furniture and pictures). The parks were all well maintained and developed. Encouraged by the philanthropy of leading citizens, therefore, the Council co-operated in the provision of five parks which gave the inhabitants of Newcastle better access than most to fresh air and open spaces with trees and flower-planted gardens and walkways, bandstands, lakes and games areas.

## Tramways in Newcastle

The exciting possibilities of a new local transport system were first considered in 1870 but it took 30 years before the Council operated its own system of some forty miles of tramways providing cheap and readily available public transport over large areas of the city. The tramways were the only major municipalised enterprise but in this case it was not possible to stand aside and allow commercial enterprise to advance unimpeded. Even more so than with gas and water supply, the introduction of a tramway system in a densely populated commercial area necessitated major street works for construction and repair and raised engineering problems as well as questions of ownership, management and control. Rapid technical developments which advanced the mode of traction from horses to cables to electricity produced further complications.

Newcastle was propelled into the tramway era late in 1870 when promoters asked permission to build a line from Blaydon to Barras Bridge. Did the town want tramways at all and, if so, should the Council or the promoters undertake their construction? Thomas Wilson, chairman of the Improvement Committee, was in favour of Council ownership but arguments raged for the next thirty years. Joseph Cowen MP, owner of the *Newcastle Chronicle*, led the opposition. His extraordinarily revealing indictment of the body of which he had been a member for 15 years included the observation that '... the Corporation have sufficient to do and what they did they did not do sufficiently well to warrant them in engaging in any speculation of that description ... [he was] much opposed to the Corporation engaging in any commercial undertaking or attempting to compete with private individuals'.[39] It was eventually agreed that the promoters' plans to build a line be

---

[37] NCP, 6 March 1878. The vendors retained 3½ acres for building ground.
[38] *Ibid.*, 2 October 1878.
[39] *Ibid.*, 13 March 1871.

accepted subject to certain conditions including a Council option to purchase, but negotiations were protracted and broke down in 1872. The matter then lapsed until 1875 when the merits of a system operative now in Middlesbrough, Stockton, Hull and Leeds were put forward. Stephenson described Sheffield where, 'It was delightful to see the ease with which 50 people could be whistled along the street.'[40] A year later a scheme drawn up by the Borough Surveyor was given near unanimous support and work was begun in 1878. The system was to be municipally owned and the operation leased for 21 years until 1899 to the Newcastle and Gateshead Tramways and Carriage Company Ltd. The first lines were partly double, partly single 'and ran from west to east, from Scotswood Road via Neville Street, Northumberland Street, Barras Bridge, Jesmond Road to Jesmond Church. In June 1879 a further section to Gosforth was opened.

The following two decades saw the rapid expansion of lines to a total of 17 miles with 44 horse trams using 272 horses and four steam tramway engines. The tramways became a welcome amenity and a main feature of city life. During the 1890s two major decisions had to be made and for several years tramways were the chief preoccupation of Council business. First it had to be decided whether or not to convert to the overhead cable system, but before this was resolved further technical improvements made it necessary to consider electrification and the merits of each were long debated. The other decision was about ownership. As the 21-year lease period of the operators drew to its close in 1899, the lobby for municipalisation gathered strength. The mobilisation of opinion and a town meeting secured the abandonment of the Parliamentary Bill for the adoption of a cable system in 1896 and the consequence was a delay of another three years before a further bill was presented.[41] Supporters of municipalisation, led this time by Cairns, were denounced in the new term of abuse as 'Communists' and their schemes those of 'reckless and ill-informed visionaries'.[42] In the end, statutory powers were obtained to construct an electric tramway system and some forty miles of tramways, including 21 miles of new tramways, were authorised, together with the purchase by compulsory powers of some tramways outside the city boundaries. The chaos produced by reconstruction resulted in a stopping of the tramways, and in April 1901 for the first time in 23 years Newcastle was tramless. People in and out of the Council competed with their stories of personal discomfiture.

[40]  NCP, 4 August 1875.
[41]  *The Tramways of North East England*, reprinted from Bett, W.H. and Gillham, J.C., *Great British Tramway Networks*, 1938, provides a brief account of Newcastle tramways. Most of the information here is gathered from the Town Improvement Committee Minute Books, the Proceedings of the Corporation and the local press which was much engaged by the issue.
[42]  *Newcastle Daily Chronicle*, 2 and 9 March 1899.

In a Council of free-enterprise businessmen, municipalisation was an emotive issue. Technical developments overtook decisions, and the influence of a generally hostile press, especially the unremitting hostility of Cowen, was difficult to counter in a Council lacking strong political leadership. Moreover, during the 1870s and 1880s a series of scandals in the key departments of Treasurer and Engineer had undermined what confidence there was in the Corporation's ability to administer anything. Nevertheless, when it was finally made, the decision to municipalise proved to be justified. By the early years of the 20th century, Newcastle, like most major cities, had an extensive electrified urban transport system which was to be steadily extended until the 1930s when trolley buses, and then motorbuses, began to replace tramways. From workmen in the early hours to large crowds at peak hours and at weekends, the benefits to all classes were soon apparent. Furthermore, profits were immediate.

## Housing

In the 20th century municipal responsibility for housing large numbers of the population came to be taken for granted but in the Victorian period it was an entirely novel phenomenon. As we have seen, in 1861 Newcastle headed the list for overcrowding in England and at the turn of the century this situation had scarcely improved. At times of crisis, at the insistence of the sanitary reformers, housing was discussed by the Council but it was never a major preoccupation. It was widely accepted that the provision of rented accommodation by private enterprise should be the norm, the Council using its powers only to intervene in cases of very serious negligence by builders and owners.

In 1861 Isaac Lowthian Bell took up the issue, basing his case on Newcastle's position as second in the death-rate league at 31-32 per 1,000, and much higher than that, at 46 and 54 per 1,000, in St Nicholas' and St Andrew's wards. In an impassioned speech he argued the need for the Council to provide lodging-houses through funds from the Loans Commissioners. He considered the investment would return 'a handsome surplus'.[43] The subsequent inquiry recommended the provision of what it called working-class dwellings. It was proposed to build the houses on land owned partly by the Corporation and partly available for purchase. The scheme was approved but came to nothing and the arguments on both sides are revealing. For example, the 'moral' arguments included both the view that the scheme would take away the self-respect of the working classes and also that the corridors would be 'nothing but scenes of clashing idleness and smoking and one would corrupt the

[43]  Report of the Public Health Sub-Committee presented to the Council, 6 March 1867.

other'.[44] Alderman Gregson also attacked the scale and supposed luxury of the enterprise: 'Four storeys. Why Charing Cross Hotel is something of that kind.' Perhaps the most potent argument against it, illustrating the self-doubt which was a persistent response when any new scheme was mounted, was that of the Councillor who 'did not see that they were to turn themselves into builders, especially considering how exceedingly badly they had managed almost every other affair where administration had to be considered'. Finally he warned how one thing would lead to another: 'What next? Slaughter-houses and sell cheap beef to the working class; erect bakeries and also have a fleet of tailors to make cheap clothes …' However, in 1900, a scheme proposed by the shipbuilder Councillor Cairns was successful and in 1906 the first Council scheme was opened at Walker, consisting of 112 two-roomed and 14 single-roomed dwellings. It was not until after the First World War that the Council seriously accepted responsibility for housing provision.

## Bureaucracy and Corruption

A comparison of the numbers and cost of Newcastle Council's employees in the 1830s and the late 1890s illustrates the scale of the development of local government. In 1833 the Common Council at a cost of about £2,835 employed 62 officials. In 1900 there were six major departments to which very shortly were added the extensive tramways enterprise and responsibility for education.[45] The heads of the six departments received salaries totalling £5,078: the Treasurer and Surveyor were each paid £1,000 per annum, the Town Clerk £1,500, the Medical Officer of Health £750, the Chief Constable £542, and the Chief Librarian £266. The overall bill for salaries and wages, not including those designated 'workmen', was some £40,000. Wages to workmen doubled that sum. There were now large new categories of Council employees: engineers, surveyors, accountants, analysts of food and drugs, gas and water workers, solicitors, baths and parks superintendents, gardeners, inspectors of weights and measures, estate managers, rate collectors, draughtsmen, a substantial police and fire service and health department. The statistics relating to refuse removal are just one example of explosive growth. In December 1833 scavenging was contracted out for five years at £250 per annum. This was performed by six men with three horses and carts, a further eight men sweeping, watering and depositing refuse in a public midden. In 1907 the work was done by the Engineering Department, with a cleansing superintendent in charge. Over five districts there was an inspector, two foremen and a staff of 530 men and boys, 10 women and 93

44 Alderman William Gregson, NCP, 4 December 1867.
45 By the Education Act of 1902.

**4.4** Town Hall, 1900.

horses. This cost the Council about £50,000 per annum. In Newcastle, there was an organisation for employees' social activities with its own monthly journal, *The Newcastle upon Tyne Municipal Officer.*

In a little-understood bureaucratic world of committees and departments there was room for corruption. It was not until the 1880s that the Report of an Inquiry into the Accounts and Business of the Corporation, set up because of a series of scandals in three major departments, informed Council and ratepayers of the scope, cost and structure of their affairs.[46] The first revelation came from the Treasurer's office in 1872, when Brummell, Borough Treasurer since 1859, resigned leaving a deficiency. At the same time irregularities were discovered in the Surveyor's department and this was followed by troubles in the Engineer's. Regular criticism by the official auditors had gone unheeded up to this time, but the press and ratepayers' meetings demanded information and action. In a new climate of mounting vigilance it is not surprising that, when a new Town Clerk was required at the end of 1879, a special committee was set up to inquire into the duties of town clerks in comparable boroughs. This would be only the third Town Clerk since 1835, John Clayton holding the office from 1822 to 1867 and Ralph Park Phillipson from 1867 to 1880 when he died, still in post, aged eighty. Both had enjoyed remarkable independence and combined highly lucrative private practice with their municipal duties. In 1880 the salary was raised from £1,200 to £1,500 per annum for Mr. Hill Motum, the new Town Clerk, but he was restricted to municipal work only.

The 1879 Inquiry took four years to complete. Even the Council lost interest in its findings and relevant committees were badly attended. But it provided a remarkable and detailed account of the work of a major municipal workforce in the late 19th century.

## Finance

In 1836 the reformed Corporation inherited a substantial private income. Several new councils began with a burden of debt as in the case of Leeds, where the old Corporation had alienated all funds to prevent them falling into the control of the new masters, but the corporate wealth of Newcastle was second only to that of Liverpool. In the five years preceding the Municipal Corporation Inquiry, the unreformed Newcastle borough enjoyed an average annual income of £43,000. The town's wealth, of great benefit to ratepayers throughout the 19th century, derived from the considerable properties owned by the Corporation, and from its highly privileged position as receiver of dues from the River Tyne. In 1836, £21,400 of the income of £36,942 was collected in port and harbour dues, while £7,700 came from rents from properties in the town itself and from the Walker estate, purchased in 1715, outside the town to the east and valued in total at £208,153 in 1836. A large proportion of Corporation property moreover consisted of property let on 21-year leases, and income from these enabled a relatively low rate to be charged for town improvements throughout the century. A further unusual source of revenue was the 'Thorough Toll', a charge of two pence on loaded vehicles entering and leaving

[46] Newcastle Corporation Inquiry into Accounts and Business, 1888.

the town. Such a toll existed only at Newcastle and Carlisle. In 1836 it produced £1,700, at the time not a negligible sum. The expenses of the watch, which was at night only, and lighting, were defrayed by powers received under a local act of 1812 which raised £1,201.

On the last audit day before the reform inquiry, the Corporation debt was £99,499. This was from sums borrowed for various purposes such as the purchase of the Walker estates, and for town improvements and repairs such as the cost of building a new bridge after the floods of 1771.

After 1836 the income and expenditure from all sources grew rapidly as a result of the growth of population and industry and the quantity of trade by river and by rail. Most dramatic of all was the rise in rateable values. As the Commissioners noted in 1833, 'the prosperity of the town is great and still progressing'. By 1895 the various landed estates together with the Thorough Toll possessed a value of some £1,370,000. The loss of a portion of the river dues, after the Tyne Improvement Act of 1850, made a rate rise necessary in 1855, though the coal dues brought in a total of about £200,000 from 1850 up to 1870, when they were ceded.

The townspeople remained relatively lightly burdened. This was recognised with admiration at the annual meeting of the Building Societies Association held at Newcastle in 1906. The speaker, Alderman Lowe of Bristol, observed that, 'Newcastle was not by any means a Sleepy hollow, and the surprise is that they are able to do so much at so little cost. Some of us who labour under the burden of very much heavier rates, look very enviously upon the moderate rates which the Mayor and Corporation of Newcastle are content to draw from their townspeople.'[47] In response, the Mayor, Alderman Baxter Ellis, conceded, 'It is almost impossible to realize that our rateable value has increased (since the 1860s) from £365,000 to more than one and a half million.'[48]

The rise in rateable value exceeded population growth by about four times in the Victorian period. The scale of this rise was spectacularly greater than the national average, which between 1842 and 1904 was 295.5 per cent against Newcastle's rise of 698 per cent.[49] Other sources of funding came from central government, the most important of these for policing.

The scale of the expansion of local government in Newcastle is perhaps nowhere better demonstrated than by a glance at the sums of money raised and spent at the end of the century in contrast with 1836. In 1836, £36,942 provided for the government of the town; in 1900 the sum handled was £3,330,269. The problems

[47] Building Societies Annual Meeting, Newcastle 1906 (London 1906), pp.63-4.
[48] *Ibid.*, p.68.
[49] Figure calculated from information in Finer, H., *English Local Government*, p.379.

and risks involved in the management of increasingly large accounts are illustrated by the difficulties which persisted in the Treasurer's and other departments discussed briefly above. It took almost thirty years before the advice of the auditors of the 1860s was implemented, but in the 1890s the introduction of a new double-entry system of book-keeping and other administrative improvements were established. Nonetheless, at the turn of the 20th century the bitter divisions over the control and ownership of the tramways reflected a lack of confidence in municipal government in the city. The limited and reluctantly agreed range of municipal activity in Newcastle as compared with some other Victorian cities has to be seen as resulting, in large part, from clear evidence of incompetence, mismanagement, nepotism, pilfering and absenteeism in major departments over a very long period. Active local government was normally costly, in the short term at least, and those who paid rates and taxes understandably lacked enthusiasm for higher taxation by a municipal authority whose reputation regularly came under fire.

The reforms of the 1890s brought the financial procedures of Newcastle into line with those of well managed businesses, and made the city capable of absorbing the still greater complexities of municipal government to come. No matter how its friends and critics judged it, the governance of Newcastle had been transformed during the Victorian period. As the town and its population and industry had grown, so too had the municipal authority and its resources and responsibilities. The limited objectives of 1835 had long been left behind as, however reluctantly and imperfectly, the Victorian Council responded to the requirements of a different age and established a framework of town government capable of accommodating even greater expansion in the 20th century.

5

# The Making of a Diocese 1851-1882

## JEFF SMITH

The modern religious life of Newcastle began in the 18th century when the main religious camps formed. In the 19th century, with the emergence of a confident middle class intent on reform, these camps became more aware of their civic duties and religious rivalries. The religious census of 1851 made them focus very sharply on their relative strengths and weaknesses. The formation of the diocese of Newcastle in 1882, with a bishop and Cathedral church, was intended to re-establish the power and glory of Anglicanism not only over its rivals, but also in the face of growing urban secularisation.

### Numbers in 1851

Relative to Anglicanism, Dissent was strong in the region, and most significantly the older forms of Dissent. In Newcastle, in terms of political influence, not numbers, it was the Quakers, Baptists and Independents who mattered. Taking the best attendance figures on census day in 1851, the Church of England drew more than half the total attenders in only two of the 14 Durham and Tyneside districts, and less than a third in five of them. In Newcastle, the attendance figures for morning worship (in a population of 87,874) are given in Figure 5.1. As a comparison of Anglican and non-Anglican strength on a basis of maximum numbers of all attendances throughout the day: in Newcastle, in 12 places of Anglican worship, 15,417 attended or 17 per cent of the population or 43 per cent of the total maximum of worshippers (total attendance); while in 42 places of non-Anglican worship, 20,590 attended or 23 per cent of the population or 57 per cent of total maximum of worshippers.[1]

For Northumberland, in a total of 154 Anglican places of worship, 47,395 attended at all services, or 16 per cent of the population, or 37 per cent of all attendances. In a total of 334 places of non-Anglican worship, 81,400 attended, or 27 per cent of the population, or 63 per cent of the total maximum of attenders.[2]

[1] Pickering, W.S.F., *A Social History of the Diocese of Newcastle* (Stocksfield, 1982), p.100.
[2] *Ibid.*, pp.84-5.

## Figure 5.1   Morning Worship Attendance, 1851

|  | No. attending | % of population |
|---|---|---|
| Church of England | 7,202 | 8.2 |
| Presbyterian | 2,499 | 2.8 |
| Roman Catholic | 3,389 | 3.9 |
| Baptist | 1,072 | 1.2 |
| Congregational | 826 | 0.9 |
| Quaker | 217 | 0.2 |
| Unitarian | 461 | 0.5 |
| Wesleyan Methodist | 1,270 | 1.4 |
| Primitive Methodist | 806 | 0.9 |
| United Meth.Free Ch.(2) | 630 | 0.7 |
| Meth.New Connexion | 210 | 0.2 |
| Jews | 50 | 0.05 |
| Undenominational | 8 | 0.01 |
| TOTALS[3] | 18,640 | 20.96 |

Of these, Methodists comprised 11 per cent, and Presbyterians 9 per cent. In Newcastle the maximum percentage of the population who did not attend a church or chapel was 78 per cent or, put another way, more than two-thirds of the population were non-attenders who may or may not have been non-believers but were nevertheless seen as a major urban problem of the age.[4]

In sheer numbers, Anglican strength was greatest in the two urban districts of the south-east corner of the county (Tynemouth and Newcastle) where over 47 per cent of all Anglican attendances were registered, worshipping (it may be noted) in 24 churches.[5] However, in proportion to the population as a whole and the kind of support the Church of England supposed it should have, these two districts were among its weakest areas. It appears that Church of England strength was proportionally weakest where the population growth had been most rapid. In 1851, in Northumberland, there was an average of one non-Anglican chapel for every 900 people compared with the Anglican ratio of one church to roughly 2,000 people.[6] Apart from Bellingham, where there were more Anglican churches than non-Anglican, the Church was outnumbered everywhere else and in Newcastle very much so. It was easier to build or inaugurate a non-Anglican place of worship, not needing a lengthy legal and ritualistic process.

[3] Pickering, *Diocese of Newcastle*, p.86.
[4] *Ibid.*, pp.92-3.
[5] *Ibid.*, p.88. These constituted only 16 per cent of the total number of places of worship belonging to the Church of England.
[6] *Ibid.*, p.80.

Religious provision overall in Northumberland fell far short of what was needed. Over the whole county there was room, according to the census, for 52,405 worshippers in all the Anglican places of worship. Thus the Church of England had seats for only just slightly more than 17 per cent of the county population. At 12 per cent, Newcastle had one of the lowest percentages of accommodation.[7] Those with the most chapels (198) were the Methodists, taking all kinds together; the Presbyterians (various) were next with 68; other Dissenters followed with a total of 38 chapels and the Roman Catholics with 20.[8] Of the total number of attendances at all churches and chapels, the non-Anglicans commanded 63 per cent, compared with 37 per cent for the Church of England. The weakness of the Anglicans compared with the other denominations in Newcastle and Northumberland is apparent from these figures.[9]

The numerical strength of the different nonconformist denominations varied from district to district though in Durham and Northumberland the Wesleyans were the most popular, followed in Durham by the Primitive Methodists and in Northumberland by the Presbyterians. Wesleyan Methodists tended to be respectable middle- or lower-middle-class tradespeople and merchants. In Sunderland and neighbouring ports, Wesleyan congregations constituted a broad cross-section of the working and middle class. In Newcastle they were sufficiently prosperous to form a majority of the Town Council in the 1850s.

Roman Catholics showed at about eight per cent of the English population in 1851, largely made up of ancient recusant gentry and immigrant Irish. The latter came in great numbers from the 1840s. This new migration to the North East was largely confined to Newcastle and Teesside, the emphasis switching from one to the other according to the demand for labour.

In Northumberland just over one third of all Anglican sittings in churches were free; the practice of pew renting was generally accepted as a regular means of income before weekly collections became customary. At the Evangelical Anglican church of St Thomas's, Newcastle, a good result is recorded:

> The weekly attendance was considerable, with an average of 1,000 adults in the morning and 500 adults in the evening. The Religious Census of 30 March 1851 recorded an adult attendance of 958 in the morning, 305 in the afternoon, and 441 in the evening, together with 314 Sunday School pupils on the morning and 318 in the afternoon.[10]

---

[7] *Ibid.*, p.83.
[8] *Ibid.*, p.92.
[9] *Ibid.*, pp.92-3.
[10] Munden, A.F., 'The Origin of Evangelical Anglicanism in Newcastle upon Tyne', *Archaeologia Aeliana*, 1983, vol.xi, p.302.

In spite of this mid-century near obsession with religion and religious attendance, it is clear as well that a majority of the population did not attend a place of worship at all. The total number of worshippers on census Sunday was in the region of 7.3 million, or just over 40 per cent of the population of England and Wales. In Newcastle the percentage of non-attendance was somewhere between 60 per cent minimum and, as we have seen, up to a 78 per cent maximum.[11] This evidence of widespread dissaffection was viewed with grave concern and was seen as a real challenge to all the churches. This and the greatly increasing population made the question of pastoral care an urgent matter.

Following the census, in June 1854, the Newcastle Town Council received a motion from a group of councillors on the subject of a diocese of Newcastle. Sir John Fife submitted that the subject was of equal importance to Churchmen and Dissenters alike, though the Dissenters on the Council could not see the advantage to them of having a bishop in their midst. They accepted that some means of acquiring money from the See of Durham to spend in Newcastle was desirable but that it was unlikely to be forthcoming without a bishop. It was said that 'Dissenters, especially political Dissenters, will oppose every attempt to extend the English episcopate, and thereby strengthen the national church'.[12]

## Influence

As early as 1739 George Whitefield and a growing number of young churchmen were expressing an organisational radicalism that was preparing the way for profound religious-cultural changes in the century ahead. Whitefield's irregular open-air preaching was a carefully considered response to an obvious failure of the Church of England to meet the religious needs of the whole of society.[13] The Church's failure to achieve the monopolistic ideal upon which it had been established was not recent. For some years before Whitefield and John Wesley's launching of what came to be the Methodist movement, in some areas of the country the services of the Church had broken down, encouraging the growth of alternative religious traditions. For the Church of England the period from 1740 to 1830 was unsuccessful, arriving at a point in the 1830s when it had slipped from its predominant denominational position.[14] By 1830, whilst there may have been more church-attending Anglicans than in 1740, there were vastly more non-Anglicans. As we shall see, the Established Church was to improve its performance later, but

---

[11]   Pickering, *Diocese of Newcastle*, pp.94-5.
[12]   *Ibid.*, pp.25-28.
[13]   Gilbert, A.D., *Religion and Society in Industrial England* (London,1976), p.3.
[14]   *Ibid.*, p.27.

it was never to regain the pre-eminence it had enjoyed before the Industrial Revolution.

In this period the North East was still seen as a world apart. Far away from the centres of power and governance, its main industry was coal mining and the coal trade, quite unlike most of the rest of England, and Newcastle had also begun to experience changes in urbanisation. Local landowners felt no stigma in trade, and the development of their mineral resources reinforced their influence and expanded their wealth. As gentry, they tended to be of the Established Church; nevertheless the Dissenting community in Newcastle was one of the largest in the north of England.[15] Though it lacked some of the rich Dissenting diversity of somewhere like Bristol, it made up for it in energy. Seven chapels belonged to the Scottish Presbyterians. The Scottish chapels were closely linked through the Newcastle presbytery which in 1783 included 13 ministers. There were two Unitarian chapels in the late 18th century, and also a group of Particular Baptists. The Quaker meeting house was situated in Pilgrim Street, and on 20 December 1742 the Methodists opened the Orphan House in Northumberland Street.[16]

The Reverend James Murray, mentor of Thomas Spence and minister of a large independent Presbyterian congregation, had a chapel in High Bridge until his death in 1782. Murray was a powerful, colourful preacher and educator with a fierce radical brand of politics who enlivened the religious life of the town. He was a champion of the underdog both in politics and religion and his influence was sufficiently strong that more than forty years after his death his tombstone was renewed in St Andrew's churchyard.[17] William Hone, the radical publisher, wrote of him in the Preface to the 1819 edition of Murray's *Sermons to Asses*:

> The author of the *Sermons to Asses* was not a little remarkable for possessing two opposite qualities, seldom found united in the same character. From a cheerful temperament of mind, he was on most topics facetious and playful; but in defending the rights of civil and religious liberty, either in private conversation, or from the pulpit, he was grave and stern as Diogenes himself. It was one of his maxims 'that no man could be a real Christian who was not a warm and zealous friend to civil and religious liberty' … He was indeed a man who would enter into no compromise with anyone on political truths …

[15] Nossiter, T.J., *Influence, Opinion and Political Idioms in Reformed England. Case Studies from the North East 1832-74* (Brighton,1975), p.2.

[16] Bradley, J., *Religion, Revolution and English Radicalism* (Cambridge,1970), p.255.

[17] Smith, Jeffrey, 'James Murray: His Ideas in Relation to His Circle and His Time' (unpublished M.Litt thesis, University of Newcastle, 1998).

Murray tried to be the voice of the labouring man, the artisan, and the small trader. He was also a thorn in the side of the Established Church and the ruling elite. Murray has been credited with inventing modern politics in the North East.[18]

John Seed describes the Newcastle Presbyterians thus:

> In the late 17th century Presbyterians had been immensely powerful in Newcastle and included an important section of the town's governing elite. In 1727 they were wealthy enough to finance the building of a new fashionable chapel, with seating for 600 people ... The site was called Hanover Square: 'in testimony of their attachment to the reigning family and the principles of revolution'. By the second half of the 18th centry Hanover Square had become a settled and respectable part of the town's life.[19]

That nonconformity in Newcastle was robust is demonstrated by Seed's extract from the study written by the Unitarian minister at Hanover Square:

> By 1782, an old Presbyterian congregation had a Unitarian minister William Turner, its members came from various religious backgrounds – many from traditional English liberal presbyterians, several from Anglican families, thus there was a wide diversity of belief within the congregation ... As William Turner explained in 1811, religious individualism was the cornerstone of the congregation: its members ... desire to be considered as a voluntary association, not Episcopalian, Presbyterian, or Independents ... of individual Christians; each one professing Christianity for himself according to his own views of it, formed upon a mature consideration of the Scriptures, and acknowledging the minister's right to do the same; and necessarily united in nothing but a desire to worship the Supreme Lord of all as disciples of one common Master.[20]

In analysing the congregation at Hanover Square chapel, Seed describes it as containing 13 professional people: one barrister, two solicitors, three physicians, two surgeons, four newspaper editors and publishers and a mining engineer, as well as 18 merchants and manufacturers, in which are included two shipbuilders and three shipowners. The rest of the congregation covered a variety of trades and minor professions. Medical practitioners were particularly prominent and included Dr. Thomas Greenhow, who built up a large practice and eventually became

[18] Ashraf, P.M., *The Life of Thomas Spence* (Newcastle, 1983), p.33.
[19] Seed, J., *The Role of Unitarianism in the Formation of Liberal Culture 1775-1851. A Social History* (PhD thesis, University of Hull, 1981), p.67.
[20] Turner, W.A., *A Short Sketch of the History of Protestant Nonconformity and the Society Assembling in Hanover Square Chapel, Newcastle upon Tyne* (Newcastle, 1811), pp.19-21.

professor of Medical Ethics at Durham University. John Buddle, the famous mining engineer and agent for Lord Londonderry, also had links with this congregation.[21] James Losh, the barrister and Recorder of Newcastle in 1833, was another prominent member of the chapel from 1800.

5.1   Rev. William Turner.

The Unitarians, in a period of Newcastle's history stretching from the mid-18th century until long after the retirement of William Turner in 1841, were a great influence on the religious, political and intellectual life of the city, an influence quite incommensurate with their numbers. Turner inspired the founding of the Literary and Philosophical Society in 1793, and his energy fuelled the influence it wielded, and the forum it provided for men of the stature of William George Armstrong and George Stephenson. Newcastle Unitarians led in the founding of the Jubilee School in 1811 for the children of the poor, that so influenced Robert Owen; the founding of the Society of Antiquaries in 1813; the founding of the Newcastle Mechanics Institute in 1824; and the founding of the Natural History Society and the Infants' School in 1825. In all these enterprises the Unitarians led the other churches, and in the 1820s and 1830s they spearheaded the Newcastle campaigns for reform of Parliament, the repeal of the Test and Corporation Act, Catholic emancipation, and the anti-slavery movement.[22]

The Anglican Evangelical movement raised its own distinctive voice early in the 19th century:

> On 28 May 1808 Robert Wasney was appointed chaplain of St Thomas' Chapel and was the first evangelical witness in the town, so that by 1879 J.C. Ryle noted that outside London, Newcastle was one of the twelve centres of Provincial Evangelicanism. Wasney's appointment at the beginning of the nineteenth century confirms G.R.Balleine's impression that there were no Evangelicans in Northumberland in the eighteenth century. By the end

[21]  Seed, *Role of Unitarianism*, pp.68-9.
[22]  Smith, Jeffrey, 'James Losh: His Ideas in Relation to His Circle and His Time' (unpublished PhD thesis, University of Northumbria, 1996).

of the eighteenth century there was an estimated three to five hundred Evangelican ministers in the Church of England ... But on his appointment, it being a novelty to have an Evangelican in Newcastle, Wasney attracted a large congregation.[23]

A consideration of the religious communities of Newcastle, Manchester, Leeds and Liverpool makes it clear that many provincial centres had similar characteristics: strong Dissenting communities that were each in their own way to transform their towns. It was also the case that these Dissenting communities were familiar with each other's political and religious activities, and in frequent contact. Dissenters were excluded from public office until the repeal of the Test and Corporation Acts in 1828, unless they sought an 'accommodation' by a form of annual pledge of conformity. Failure to do so, however, as we have seen, did not diminish their influence.

In 1801, the north Tyneside area (from Wylam to North Shields and extending north to include Throckley, Gosforth, Longbenton and Whitley Bay) had a population of 61,079, which meant that it was already the most significant centre of population in Northumberland, accounting for rather more than one third of the total. Over 34,000 lived in Newcastle alone. In the next fifty years this population would more than double.[24] But in an age of patronage and influence, mere superiority in numbers was not everything. Indeed it was often the educated and prosperous 'old' Dissenters who played leading political roles, most strikingly perhaps in Sunderland where the Quakers, who though never numerically strong contrived to elect a county member and run the town. On Teesside the Quaker Pease family, Edward, Henry, Joseph *et al.*, dictated economic development.[25]

> Judging from a note in the 1829 book of members there would have been some 200 members of the Society of Friends in Newcastle in 1829 ... Newcastle Friends were beginning to work more widely with other denominations rather than tending to restrict their support, however dedicated, to work on communities.[26]

It might be argued that the insignificance of the Church of England in Newcastle was a reflection of the enormous power south of the river in the Palatinate of Durham. Van Mildert was the last Prince Bishop and when he died in 1836 his staff of office was broken and laid to rest with him. By the early 1830s the feeling that the Church of England faced the alternatives of reform or destruction was sufficient

[23] Munden, *op.cit.*, pp.301-8.
[24] Pickering, *Diocese of Newcastle*, p.10.
[25] Nossiter, *Influence, Opinion and Political Idioms*, p.18.
[26] Sansbury, R., *Beyond the Blue Stone: 300 Years of Quakers in Newcastle* (Newcastle, 1998), pp.131-2.

**5.2** New Bridge Street Unitarian Church, 1850.

to break through the massive impediments to organisational innovation and pastoral renewal which had for so long retarded the Church's adjustment to the new society. The ranks of the reformers and the volume of their agitation had been swelling since the opening decade of the century, but in the 1820s the problems confronting the Church began to assume crisis proportions.

In 1828 the repeal of the Test and Corporation Acts and in 1829 the Roman Catholic Relief Act symbolised dramatically the failure of the old monopolistic conception of the Established Church. The passage of the legislation was evidence of the power of reform and the same forces which had won in these cases might sooner or later be expected to launch an offensive aimed at securing full religious parity. Because repeal had long been contested by the Church, its coming was a sign of the Church's vulnerability. The same was true of Catholic emancipation.[27] Two years later the Church was shocked by the opprobium it suffered for the part the bishops played in the House of Lords when it threw out the Reform Bill in October 1831.

Nevertheless the Catholic Relief Act had also met resistance from the Methodists, who by this time were a power to be reckoned with. Machin describes an incident in Manchester that had its parallel in Newcastle:

[27] Gilbert, *Religion and Society*, p.125.

Methodist ministers agreed to sign an anti-Catholic petition but the others refused ... Sometimes the Methodists appeared more anti-Catholic than the Anglicans.[28]

In Newcastle their opposition to the Act, as well as their growing numerical strength, can be seen in the diary entry of James Losh, a Unitarian who led the movement for reform in the town:

March 10, 1829
Public meeting for petitioning on the Catholic Question ... The clergy and the Methodists had formed a junction and bringing in a number of colliers etc., they outnumbered us ...[29]

In 1830 holy orders were still looked upon as an attractive proposition for the son of a gentleman, although it would become less so later when clergymen were no longer so readily found on the magistrates' bench; and, whilst a man might be 'half a doctor' or 'half a lawyer', he was no longer acceptable as 'half a minister'. It was becoming necessary for a minister to concentrate more on his secular responsibilities in order to complement his spiritual offices. In 1832, Thomas Arnold, in demanding Church reform, pointed particularly to the failure of the Church in its parochial duties. It needed to re-capture that sense of mission characteristic of early nonconformity. Additional curates and the involvement of lay workers would increase the scope and flexibility of the parochial ministry. But the time when the Church could have reformed itself was now past. Eventually it would be reformed by a Parliament dominated by laymen, not all of whom were Anglicans.

In Newcastle in 1832, Mackenzie could invoke some impressive authorities in his publication, *The Church, Its Evils and their Remedies*.[30] In a speech to the House of Lords on 29 March 1829, for example, Earl Grey said,

What think you of one of the greatest grievances under which the country labours? The *Church Establishment*, not as a religious sect, but as an institution of the state, instead of a blessing, has in reality become a curse ... Where is here Christian charity? ... She is always ready to assist authority and support oppression; she bands herself with corruption; uses her resources and means given for good, for evil purposes ... Her country is steeped to the lips in poverty ... 'there is an accumulation of church property, which did not operate for the useful purposes of religion ...'

[28]  Machin, G.I.T., *The Catholic Question in English Politics 1820-1830* (Oxford, 1964), p.55.
[29]  James Losh Diaries, Carlisle Public Library, vol.24.
[30]  Mackenzie, E., *The Church, Its Evils and their Remedies*, Newcastle Public Library (NPL), Local Tracts, ref.dy102, No.17.

In 1842, getting people to church on Sunday was seen as the central problem:

> This remembrance [of the anniversary of Waterloo] led him to observe that if they would preserve the high position of this country in the earth, they must preserve her religion and that day on which rested the whole foundation of her national faith and character.[31]

In 1846 a layman saw the problem facing the Church of England differently:

> ... I believe it is an acknowledged fact, that, for a series of years, the efforts made amongst us have been wholly inadequate ... that these efforts have been insufficient in *extent*, and that all the ministers labouring in this large town have felt themselves without doubt, *physically* unable to overtake the mass of ignorance around them ... Ignorance and spiritual destitution prevail to an alarming extent ... [in four years] 9,023 people have died ... Are they now ransomed spirits, rejoicing before the throne of God and the Lamb? Alas! No.[32]

## Urban Expansion: Churches and Chapels

In the decades following the census of 1851, all the denominations began building new churches, founding new parishes, organising all kinds of evangelical efforts and reorganising their adminstrative machinery. Outstanding in this respect was the episcopate of Bishop Charles Baring (1861-79) of Durham. By the mid-1850s a new energy and determination was reported. Bishop Selwyn, on his return from New Zealand, was to comment: 'It is now a rare thing to see a careless clergyman, a neglected parish or a descrated church.' And, of course, there was no longer the failure to see the need for reform.

Meanwhile, some nonconformists were being exhorted to provide new buildings; typically, in 1846 the members of the Groat Market Congregation were being reminded of their duty to do so:

> The progress of the scheme for a New Church [Presbyterian] ... has been hitherto most encouraging ... You have been without a settled minister since the 12 September 1843 ... you have been dependent upon temporary supplies, which have frequently failed ... in order to secure any minister of the 'standing' your circumstances require ... you must satisfy him that you

---

31 Larkin, *On the Sabbath Question* ... (1842), NPL, Local Tracts, ref.Cr5, No.6. The motion against the closing of the Central Exchange Newsroom on Sunday was defeated.
32 A Layman, *The Moral Condition of Newcastle upon Tyne. A Letter to the Vicar of Newcastle* (1846), NPL, Local Tracts, ref.dy75, No.7.

are prepared to do your part in securing him full scope for the exercising
of his efforts ... convince him that all that has been hitherto promised and
said has not been vainglorious boasting ... [33]

Between 1851 and 1882 Newcastle had a population growth of 61,000 (68 per cent)
which complicated the Church's effort to catch up. Though it had increased its
number of sittings by 4,500 (46 per cent), the nonconformists had increased theirs
by 14,500 (76 per cent). In 1866, Anglicanism had adopted the mantle of the early
Methodists. Its spontaneous evangelicanism and lay initiative was held up as an
example to the Wesleyans! The increased number of churches, general clerical
competence, and an orientation to a more dynamic, organised pastoral role carried
it forward. In 1856 the Evangelican Anglicans of St Thomas's Church, Newcastle,
were faced with a dilemma. In the light of the decision to appoint a non-Evangelical
minister they were determined to build their own church:

> Upon the death of minister Richard Clayton ... since there was no other
> Evangelical churches in the city, members of the congregation of St Thomas'
> decided to erect 'a proprietary or trustee church with or without a district
> assigned, in which Evangelical truth shall be declared'. The bishop of Durham
> recommended that it should be a district church and selected Jesmond,
> where the new church was consecrated on 20 October 1859.[34]

And the congregation at St John Baptist's were also looking for expansion:

> ... A large increase in accommodation will also be gained for whilst at
> present there are little more than 500 available seats on the ground floor,
> the new plan will provide nearly 900 ... the parish has a large population of
> 13,000 persons, chiefly of the poorer classes, and, consequently little help
> can be expected from them ...[35]

Meanwhile the Presbyterians were alerting the nonconformist community to Anglican
plans to found schools. The Reverend Thomas Duncan was fearful of a scheme put
forward by what he saw as a 'Romanized' Church of England:

> ... I hasten at the outset to present a statement of my reasons and motives
> for addressing you on your proposed scheme of scholastic education for
> this large and properous town. In establishing it, you professedly address
> yourself to the members of the Church of England, which may appear to
> deprive me, a minister of another ecclesiastical body, of any title to interfere

[33] Bell, T.G., *The Members of the Groat Market Congregation* (1846), NPL, Local Tracts, ref.Cr31, No.2.
[34] Munden, *op.cit.*, p.306.
[35] Houldey, W.E., *A Lecture* (1875), NPL, Local Tracts, ref.Cr5, No.23.

... I have revolved your recent plan about erecting public schools, which, it must be admitted, will be exclusive and irresponsible in their management, I cannot help coming to the conclusion, that every day's delay, in maturing and establishing a national scheme, is greatly to be deprecated by all men of liberal and tolerant opinions.[36]

In his *Culture and Anarchy* Matthew Arnold denigrated English nonconformity for its 'provincialism', for the 'narrow and partial view of humanity' which inspired it, for the endless round of disputes, tea-meetings, openings of chapels, sermons and the like which seemed to dominate it.[37] But the nonconformists were made of sterner stuff than this, and in places like Newcastle it is doubtful whether Arnold would have expected people to be Anglican anyway. Parliament became a battleground for a whole range of legislation that favoured the independence of the non-Anglican churches. It needed, however, to be won at an attendance and influence level and Churchmen and nonconformists, in Newcastle as elsewhere, showered the public with pamphlets, newspapers, petitions and meetings in a campaign for their support. Many of the issues of the day had a strong religious element, and all classes of society were pulled into the struggle. The main religious issue, however, emerged as the privilege of the Established Church now embodied in the singular matter of church rates and church schools. As one clergyman put it in 1880, 'If we in the Church of England do not deal with the masses, the masses will deal with us. We depend, as far as our organisation goes at present, on the popular vote of the country.'[38]

The *Newcastle Daily Chronicle* (whose proprietor Joseph Cowen had Unitarian sympathies) drew its own moral from the 1871 census findings: 'In spite of all her laudable activity for two decades the Protestant Episcopal Church is less truly the Church of the nation than it was in 1851.' Figures published by that newspaper in 1881 show how far the attendance at morning worship had declined (see Figure 5.2). The population between 1851 and 1881 had increased from 87,784 to 149,549.[39]

In 1881 organised religion was weaker than in 1851, with only 15 per cent of the population of Newcastle at morning worship compared with 21 per cent in the earlier census. The population had increased by 70 per cent, but the number of worshippers by only 20 per cent. The Wesleyan Methodists were the only denomination to show a significant improvement in strength relative to increase in the population. Even the Catholics and Presbyterians, with the migration of Scottish and Irish families, did not improve markedly. Though the Established Church

[36]  Duncan, Rev. Thomas, *A Letter to Rev. Clement Moody M.A. Vicar of Newcastle upon Tyne*, NPL, Local Tracts, ref.dy31, No.13.
[37]  Arnold, M., *Culture and Anarchy* (London, 1901), quoted in Gilbert, *Religion and Society*, p.158.
[38]  *Church Congress Report* (1880), quoted in Gilbert, *Religion and Society*, p.167.
[39]  Pickering, *Diocese of Newcastle*, p.100.

### Figure 5.2  Morning Worship Attendance, 1881

| | Population | percentage | increase | decrease |
|---|---|---|---|---|
| Church of England | 6,441 | 4.3 | | 761 |
| Presbyterian | 3,053 | 2.0 | 556 | |
| Roman Catholic | 3,845 | 2.6 | 456 | |
| Baptist | 805 | 0.5 | | 267 |
| Congregational | 1,290 | 0.9 | 464 | |
| Quaker | 124 | 0.08 | | 93 |
| Unitarian | 220 | 0.1 | | 241 |
| Wesleyan Meth. | 3,345 | 2.2 | 2,075 | |
| Primitive Meth. | 977 | 0.6 | 171 | |
| United Meth.Free Ch.(2) | 1,145 | 0.8 | 515 | |
| Meth.New Connexion | 369 | 0.2 | 159 | |
| Bible Christians | 200 | 0.1 | 200 | |
| Catholic Apostolic | 150 | 0.1 | 150 | |
| Danish Church | 70 | 0.04 | 70 | |
| Jews | 255 | 0.17 | 205 | |
| Undenominational | 245 | 0.17 | 237 | |
| TOTALS | 22,534 | 14.86 | 5,258 | 1,362 |

remained the largest single denomination, its support was only 29 per cent of all attendances on the Sunday morning in question. Yet with only four per cent of the Newcastle population attending Catholic churches on census day, it would appear that the Protestant churches were still unrealistically haunted by the historical threat of Roman Catholicism. The Established Church and the nonconformists had not only a hard struggle with each other, but were conscious throughout the Victorian period of the growing strength of the Roman Catholics. Between 1851 and 1901 there were never fewer than 425,000 Irish-born residents in England. Anti-Catholicism had deep roots in the consciousness of Protestant England, but its prominence during the Victorian era was a result of the sheer growth of the Catholic population and its exacerbation of the vexed and complex question of Anglo-Irish relations. On Tyneside, Catholics were a small but vocal part of the religious scene, and members of the Church of England were increasingly aware of their influence.[40]

When it came to its influence in schools (where tomorrow's congregations were being educated) the Established Church was also losing ground. In the first School Board elections in 1871 the nonconformists – with the single exception of Sunderland

---

[40]  Rev.H.Stowell, *On the Romish Priesthood* ... the lecture room in Nelson Street was very soon crowded ... the question which had brought them together ... was a great conflict between truth and error, light and darkness, freedom and slavery – and that being so, he considered it incumbent upon all Protestants ... to combine against the Romish Church to protect themselves ... *Newcastle upon Tyne and North of England Northern Alliance*, NCL, Local Tracts, ref.Cr31, No.15.

where they fell out among themselves – swept the board. In Darlington and Tynemouth the Anglicans managed only three out of nine places, in Newcastle five out of fifteen, and in South Shields four out of eleven.

As the congregation of All Saints knew, the answer to the problem lay in attracting the poor:

> How to bring the Church to the poor of this parish, and the poor to their Mother Church? … In the early part of 1881, the energetic Churchwardens pushed forward the scheme of the restoration … Last November the Bishop of Durham preached on the Opening Day … the real question arose 'How the poorest parishioners could be won to their Church, so that the Church, and not the gaol or the public house, might be felt to be their Father's house of prayer?[41]

## Diocese

There was a growing awareness that pastoral reforms were necessary if the Church was to minister effectively to a nation where spiritual destitution was reckoned to be widespread. In the third and final report of the Royal Commission of 1852 on the creation of additional bishoprics, Newcastle was not included in the list of places with special claims and facilities for the creation of an additional bishopric. But the debate had begun. Seventeen years later, a questionnaire from Lord Lyttelton to 740 rural deaneries in England and Wales enquired whether they supported the proposal to increase the episcopate. Ninety-eight per cent were in favour of the division of the larger sees into smaller ones.[42]

Whilst the Church was concerned with this large issue, at grass roots at least one Church of England minister was having his doubts about the efficacy of his church and its message. It is ironic that these doubts were occasioned by his speculations on the subject of Roman Catholicism:

> … I will only add that, during 20 years' ministrations in the Church of England, though having a general impression of 'Popish error and superstition', I never found or cared to find occasion for 'protesting' from the pulpit against doctrines or practices of the Roman Church … To myself there seemed a reasonable doubt whether a Church whose supreme governor was a lay person, whose chief spiritual pastors were selected by the Cabinet Minister … whether a Church thus permeated with secular influences

---

[41] Wardroper, A.S., *All Saints' Church … Twelve Months. Nov.1881 to Nov.1882*, NPL, Local Tracts, ref.Cr53, No.1.
[42] Gilbert, *Religion and Society*, pp.29-35.

sufficiently corresponded with that unworldly institution contemplated by our Lord and his Apostles.[43]

Whilst this soul searching was going on, the Anglican situation in Newcastle was not getting any better. In the 30 years from 1851 to 1882 the net increase in Northumberland's population was 43 per cent, and in Newcastle alone 68 per cent. The nonconformist increase was around 14,500 and that of Anglicans 4,500 in a period in which the net population of the town rose by almost 40,000. None of the denominations could afford to be smug. For Gilbert, the institutional decline in Anglicanism was due to 'a recovery that was too little and too late'.[44] One institution's progress suggests the ineffectual efforts of the Church to deal with a changing situation. The Newcastle upon Tyne Church of England Institute was founded in 1853 and incorporated in 1893. In its heyday in the mid-1890s its membership was 1,500 but this had slipped to 1,000 by the 1920s. That the Church of England was having some difficulty in influencing the non-attending public is suggested by the following, from 1882:

> Lords Day Observance Society. At the first meeting of your Committee, it was decided to issue an earnest appeal to the Christians of this Town, and 11,000 copies were distributed, inviting the receivers to enrol themselves as members of the Society ... the number of members is 587, small indeed compared with the numbers of those to whom the appeal was addressed ...[45]

Yet the Baptists appeared to be going from strength to strength:

> At length Mr. Riley was invited by the Baptist Home Mission to occupy the post of minister, and a Church was formed in April, 1877, thirty members being dismissed from Bewick Street for that purpose.
> The Lord made this effort very successful, and now we see a flourishing cause in Gateshead with a property worth over five thousand pounds and a membership of over two hundred and fifty persons.[46]

For all their self-berating on the need to keep pace with the Church's policy of expansion, the nonconformists were not dissatisfied with their institutional advancement over the past hundred years. They saw themselves as a modern force for progress.

---

[43]   He later added that he returned to Protestantism and the unity of the Church in January 1891. Bulmer, J., *Particulars of an Inquiry into the Catholic Controversy* (1896), NPL, Local Tracts, ref.dy103, No.9.
[44]   Gilbert, *Religion and Society*, p.29.
[45]   Harrison, A.P., *Lord's Day Observance Society* (1882), NPL, Local Tracts, ref.D53, No.6.
[46]   Bradburn, J., *History of the Berwick Street Baptist Church* (1883), NPL, Local Tracts, ref.dy75, No.15.

In the last decades of the 19th century, when the Church was struggling to deal with this changing situation, Newcastle was becoming more prosperous and more civic minded. Signs of increasing confidence can be seen in the public works instituted by the Council. The new public library of 1880 in New Bridge Street showed a willingness to spend money on large and expensive buildings; as had been spent on education with the Bath Lane Schools in 1871. In 1884 the Natural History Museum moved to the new Hancock Museum, and the Fleming Hospital was opened in 1887. In 1867 the Tyne Theatre in Westgate Road was opened and the Newcastle Chamber Music Society was established in 1880. At the same time, the Church believed it was becoming more and more alienated from those sections of the population who, it might be said, had the most to gain from civic-mindedness. In a pamphlet of 1888 the Reverend Marsden Gibson, Master of the Hospital of St Mary Magdalene, with St Thomas' Church attached, read a pamphlet at the Diocesan Conference which made this point:

> The conditions of life are so hard amongst those who live by daily wages that too many become indifferent to all but the supply of daily needs oppressed as they are by defective education and unceasing toil … What has the Church done for these men? … The question, how far the Church has won the better class of working men, is plainly an important one; but the answer is not encouraging, for it is feared that there is no class amongst whom she has been less successful, and no class for whom she has done so little.[47]

The rapid expansion in population, in industry, and in political and cultural activity, were all making it increasingly difficult for the old bishopric at Durham to maintain touch with the town. On 24 April 1876, Bishop Baring of Durham wrote, 'I have therefore no hesitation in expressing my conviction that it would be much benefit to the interests of the Church of England in these parts, if the county of Northumberland with a population of 386,959 and with 154 benefices were formed into a separate Diocese.' Even with the support of the bishop of Durham and the offer of £1,000 per annum from his own income, there was strong opposition. Among the many and various objections to the Bill, the most violent were expressed by the radical Liberal MP for Newcastle, Joseph Cowen:

> … Our philanthropy has become revolutionary. It wants not only fresh reforms but fresh principles. New circumstances require new men and a new creed. Modern society is made up of class layers, between whom there is little intercourse … Enlightened men do their best to bridge this gulf, but

---

[47] Gibson, Rev. Marsden, *Democracy and the Church* (1888), NPL, Local Tracts, ref.cr36, No.2.

**5.3**  St Nicholas Cathedral, Newcastle, 1888.

the system will not permit the restoration of that direct and friendly intercourse ... that used to exist.[48]

Cowen made no attempt to hide his antagonism towards the Church of England, or his rejection of her doctrines and ministry. 'If they took State pay,' he said, 'they must submit to State control.' He objected to a proposal for which there was no popular demand, ignoring the number of petitions that had been put forward in the previous three decades. The only people in favour of the Bill, he said, were women, clergymen, 'and that small but intelligent section of laymen who took an aesthetic and architectural interest in ecclesiastical matters'. The people of Newcastle needed a purer atmosphere and a higher culture for sure – but they did not want a bishopric.

For Bishop Baring, the Dissenters were involving themselves in a matter which did not concern them. They were trying to prevent an increase in the episcopate which would improve the efficiency of the Church of England. Despite the objections of people like Cowen, the Bill had its third reading on 14 August 1878 and received the Royal assent the following day. The Schedule to the Act stated that the Bishop was to be the Bishop of Newcastle; the diocese would consist of the county of Northumberland, and the counties of the towns of Newcastle upon Tyne and Berwick-upon-Tweed. St Nicholas Church, Newcastle upon Tyne, was to be the cathedral.

The new diocese did not happen quickly. Bishop Baring resigned on 3 December 1878 and his successor, the new Bishop Lightfoot, pressed for the creation of the new see at the Diocesan Conference of September 1880. Canon Ernest Roland Wilberforce was consecrated first Bishop of Newcastle at Durham Cathedral on Tuesday 25 July 1882. It had taken nearly four years since the passing of the Act, but once in place the diocese encouraged a note of optimism which was echoed in the Church Congresses which were held in Newcastle in 1881 and 1900. The leadership of Bishop Wilberforce generated a great amount of church building and the number of clergy considerably increased.

By 1901 the population of the diocese had increased from 438,000 in 1881 to 606,000. On Easter Day in 1885 there were 21,000 communicants which represented 7 per cent of the population 15 years of age and over. In the years that followed this was to be the highest percentage recorded. The percentage of marriages performed in Anglican churches also dropped, from 72.3 per cent in 1879 to 61.4 per cent in 1909. A number of Church leaders were worried about impending decline and secularisation. Notwithstanding the efforts made in church building and attempts at pastoral care, the Church was still failing to be the national church.

[48] Speech of Joseph Cowen MP in the Circus, Newcastle, 22 Dec., 1883, NPL, Local Tracts, ref.Cr5, No.26.

**5.4**  Westgate Hall Methodist Mission, 1932. Women's Choir play, *The Signpost*.

The failure was seen as related to the changed character of Sunday observance. A paper given by Commander F.R. Norman RN at the Diocesan Conference of 1901 made no apology for bringing up again the subject which had been discussed at the Diocesan Conference of 1892:

> ... there is no doubt that of late years our British Sunday has to a marked extent lost, and continues to lose, the character by which it was for so long distinguished, and has come to be regarded by a large and increasing number of our population more as a holiday than a holy day ... At the beginning of the 20th century, however, our effort is not to dissuade Christians from kneeling, but rather to persuade more of them to adopt that posture ... Nonconformist Communions are essentially at one with our own Church in this matter, and even more so![49]

The Anglican resurgence had been confined largely to a social constituency in which the working classes were grossly under-represented. The Church's failure, which would continue into the 20th century, rested on the fact that only a proportion of society owed any allegiance to it, while it claimed rights and privileges accorded to a national church. Its high points of influence and power were long gone by 1882 and attempts at restitution were too little and too late.

---

[49]  Norman, F.M., Commander RN, *Christian Common Sense on Sunday and its Observance.* Invited speaker to the Newcastle Diocesan Conference of 1901, NPL, Local Tracts, ref.Cr50, No.2.

# 6

# Print and Preach

## The Entrepreneurial Spirit of Nineteenth-Century Newcastle

### JOAN HUGMAN

### Charismatic Leader

A plain statue, inscribed simply with name and dates, stands at the foot of Westgate Road as solitary tribute from a grateful and admiring public to Joseph Cowen MP who, like his father before him, was the senior Liberal member for the city of Newcastle from 1874 to 1886.[1] John Tweed's sculpture captured Cowen in typical declamatory pose but, assuming recognition now long gone, there are no panegyrics to his political vision or his singular contribution to British Radicalism. McCalmont's authoritative *Parliamentary Poll Book*,[2] shows that Cowen's identity as a Radical was officially recognised and acknowledged in his own time. And yet, the parliamentary statistics upon which historians have tended to rely register only the consistency with which the Liberal members for Newcastle secured re-election, even at critical moments, such as 1874, when the party's national fortunes were under great strain. The dominance of local politics by the Cowen family, and a polarised political system, have served to invest Newcastle with sturdy Liberal credentials that are strangely at odds both with the city and with Cowen's Radicalism.

Cowen completely dominated city politics from the late 1850s until his death in 1900 and epitomised the entrepreneurial spirit of the age. The progressive political agenda he set for himself was ambitious and high risk, absorbing massive amounts of his time, money and energy. His vaulting self-belief was both a strength and weakness. Pursuing radical reform like a man possessed, Cowen brooked no opposition. He promulgated his egalitarian mission by all the means at his disposal, gaining many adherents along the way and some powerful enemies too. Although he undoubtedly plundered Tyneside's existing radical tradition in order to legitimise his own bid for power, Cowen's democratic manifesto went far beyond the ideas

[1] See Hugman, J., 'Joseph Cowen of Newcastle and Radical Liberalism', unpublished PhD thesis, Northumbria (1993); also Todd, N., *The Militant Democracy* (1990).
[2] Stanton, M. and Vincent, J. (eds.), *McCalmont's Parliamentary Poll Book* (reprint 1971, first published 1879).

and beliefs of his political forebears, and even many of his radical contemporaries. In his case, personal charisma was more than matched by intellectual agility and acclaimed rhetorical skills. Under his leadership, local politics diversified and became inextricably bound up in international causes such as the American Civil War, the struggle for Italian unification, and the Polish and Hungarian liberations – not just because he embraced republicanism but because of his close friendships with Garibaldi, Mazzini, Kossuth and other continental luminaries. Most of all, Cowen championed the fight for Irish Home Rule at a time when it was widely perceived to be 'disloyal, impractical, visionary and perilous'.[3] In defending the interests of his constituency's large Irish community he ensured that land reform remained at the heart of the city's political agenda. In so doing, he nurtured the tradition and protected the unity of the Tyneside radicals.

In recent years, as a genre political biography has fallen into disrepute. Political correctness apart, the 'great man' approach to the explanation of past events is widely held to be a crude way of explaining the complex interaction of events and their circumstances. But in Cowen's case, a strong case can be made for the great man approach. E.F. Biagini,[4] endorsing John Stuart Mill's belief in a community-centred liberalism, contends that 'community politics often generated charismatic leadership at the local level'.[5] After 1868, under the guidance of their own political 'preachers' or members of parliament, what he refers to as local 'Houses of Commons' are judged to have served as vital forums of debate in which a new style Athenian democracy could flourish.[6] Significantly, it is Cowen's influence upon Newcastle which Biagini cites as a telling example of the way that this operated.[7] An examination of Cowen's political career will throw considerable light both upon the local community-politics dimension of popular liberalism, as well as the workings of charismatic leadership. In doing so, it will be necessary to trace the developments in Cowen's political career from the late 1840s. The brief 12 years of his ministerial office completely belies the profound and lasting influence he wielded, not just on Newcastle but also in the arena of national and international politics.

Vision he had aplenty but, as everyone knows, politics is essentially a tactical game. Making sense of how and why Newcastle gained notoriety as one of the foremost radical cities in the 19th century requires close scrutiny of Cowen's game

[3] O'Connor, T.P., 'The Irish in Great Britain' in Lavery, F. (ed.), *Irish Heroes in the War* (1917), p.25.

[4] His revisionist work has been crucial in establishing the marked resilience of British radicalism, notably in Biagini, Eugenio F. and Reid, Alistair J. (eds.), *Currents of Radicalism. Popular radicalism, organised labour and party politics in Britain 1850-1914* (1991), but see also Lancaster, Bill, *Radicalism, Cooperation and Socialism. Leicester Working Class Politics 1860-1906* (1987).

[5] Biagini, E.F., 'Liberalism and direct democracy: John Stuart Mill and the model of ancient Athens' in Biagini, E.F. (ed.), *Citizenship and Community. Liberals, radicals and collective identities in the British Isles 1865-1931* (1996), p.40.

[6] *Ibid.*, p.41.

[7] *Ibid.*

plan. It is crucial to recognise that at the beginning Cowen was as much a preacher as a politician. He understood the power of propaganda and became adept at harnessing it to his radical causes. Some of that understanding rested on an enthusiasm for innovation and business enterprise garnered from working in his father's successful brick business.[8] In 1859, when he was eventually able to invest in his own newspaper, the *Newcastle Chronicle*, his management style accorded perfectly with what Aled Jones identifies as a modernisation process.[9] Living in a town like Newcastle at that time must have buttressed his confidence in the new technologies. The journalistic and techno-logical innovations which transformed the *Chronicle* from an ailing weekly into a great northern newspaper, with offices in Paris

**6.1**    Joseph Cowen.

and New York and a web of agents throughout the length and breadth of the British Isles,[10] were emphatic testimony to Cowen's belief in the 'paper pulpit'.[11] In due course, the pages of the *Chronicle* newspapers were pressed into service to promote the full range of what were seen as 'modern' or progressive movements. The Co-operative movement and the miners' associations as well as a gamut of related self-help organisations, and campaigns for electoral reform, trade union legislation and social welfare all received massive and sustained support.

The rise of Cowen's political career, and the radicalisation of his Newcastle electorate, was directly connected to the rise of the provincial press. Both reached their apogee in the early 1870s. However, in the end, mass democracy and the new sensationalist journalism fractured the old mutuality that had to exist and be seen to exist between preacher and pulpit. In a newly expanded press of cheap titles all competing for new readers, no single newspaper could afford to dedicate its resources to its own exclusive political message. To win a mass market it had to assume a

⁸   Joseph Cowen Obituary, *Sunderland Daily Echo*, 22 December 1873.
⁹   Jones, Aled, *Powers of the Press, Newspapers, Power and the Public in Nineteenth Century England* (1996), p.5.
¹⁰   Ashton, O.R., *W.E. Adams: Chartist, Radical and Journalist 1832-1906* (1991), pp.100-3. The *Chronicle* offices were the 'first English provincial establishment of its kind to possess a private telegraph system'.
¹¹   Jones, *Powers of the Press*, p.73.

*populist* stance. By the time this was obvious, in the 1890s, Cowen's health was broken and his political acumen had waned. What is more, his seemingly reactionary beliefs on the Empire isolated him from many of his older radical allies. As an archetypal radical, Joseph Cowen regarded political independence as sacrosanct. Unlike Joseph Chamberlain, he never mastered the art of compromise. His failure to make friends at court robbed him of ministerial office. Rigidly independent as a matter of principle and therefore incapable of modifying his views in line with the political exigencies of the day, including a party line, and unwilling to dissemble in public, Cowen found himself out of favour and out-manoeuvred. In 1886 he resigned his seat.

## Print Culture

Cowen's modernism was first and foremost a product of the age and the place. It is not necessary to dwell here on the region and Newcastle's economic development, for this is covered elsewhere in the volume. However, due account must be taken of the way in which such remarkable and rapid economic advances impacted upon the politics of the period. Urban historians have long acknowledged the precocity of Newcastle upon Tyne. In the mid-16th century the 'eye of the North' was the third largest town in England with a diverse economy that was, even then, indicative of the expansion that was to follow. As John Walton observes, 'Here was a face of the future.'[12] Over time, these dynamic forces gathered a certain inexorable power. By the 18th century, Newcastle exerted all the influence of a regional capital and more as the tentacles of its vast commercial and industrial empire greedily spanned the northern counties, reaching the Scottish border.[13]

Newcastle's 19th-century emergence as a progressive modern city with a pronounced willingness to embrace new ideas manifested itself most obviously in an 'impressive stream of invention and innovation'.[14] Men of invention and ideas such as Charles Mark Palmer, Joseph Swan, George and Robert Stephenson, Charles Parsons and William Armstrong, whose inventiveness gave us, respectively, the first commercially-viable iron cargo ship, the electric light bulb (same time as Edison), a vast railway network, turbines for marine propulsion and electricity generation, and a modern factory system that was the envy of national and international competitors, placed Newcastle at the cutting edge of industrial development. Cowen's father, through his work as Chairman of the River Tyne Commission, was closely

---

[12] Walton, John K., 'North' in Clark, P. (ed.), *The Cambridge Urban History of Britain, vol. ii: 1540-1840* (2000), p.122.

[13] Ellis, Joyce, 'Regional and County Centres 1700-1840' in Clark (ed.), *Cambridge Urban History of Britain, vol. ii*, p.675.

[14] Rowe, D.J., 'The North-East' in F.M.L. Thompson (ed.), *The Cambridge Social History of Britain 1750-1950*, vol. i (1990), p.464.

involved in all this modernising. The improvements put in place in the 1860s transformed the then heavily silted-up Tyne estuary into a major port capable of serving the region's vast commercial shipping activities, and earned him a knighthood. But this level of enterprise did not operate in an industrial vacuum. The same entrepreneurial spirit that imbued Newcastle's scientists and technologists with their enthusiasm for pushing forward the frontiers of human endeavour characterised Newcastle's cultural and political ethos as well. Both spheres shared the same optimistic view of progress. And while there is no doubt that their creativity had an impact far beyond the city and its region, Newcastle and its people were the most immediate beneficiaries. In due course, the abundant flow of wealth into the city coffers gave rise to the demand for a number of status-laden projects, all aimed at making the city not simply more stylish and grand but more distinctive. An imposing classical architecture created anew the city's heartland, giving it a metropolitan sense of self. Before the advent of the railways, the sheer time of travel between Newcastle and London effectively precluded any wholesale and indiscriminate subservience to London. The local population had their own view of the world.

Chris Hunt's exhaustive survey[15] and the supplementary work of Peter Wallis chart the dramatic expansion of print culture in Northumberland and Durham. Between 1626 and 1860 it has been estimated that more than 1,700 people in the two counties were employed in some aspect of the book trade.[16] Whether the appointments of Robert Barker and Stephen Bulkley as printers-in-residence when Charles I was based in Newcastle in 1639 and 1646[17] had any lasting impact would be difficult to prove, but certainly from then onwards the trade in books and printed material was an important factor in the city's commercial success. The distinctive engravings of Thomas Bewick and Ralph Beilby and the craftsmanship of London printers such as William Bulmer, who originally served their apprenticeships in Newcastle, all helped to establish the city's national reputation as a centre of printing.[18]

Thomas Spence[19] spent his formative years in Newcastle upon Tyne and made good use of the city's publishing facilities and the growing number of literary societies.

[15] Hunt, C.J., *The Book Trade in Northumberland and Durham to 1860* (1975); Wallis, P.J., *The Book Trade in Northumberland and Durham, A supplement to C.J. Hunt's Biographical Dictionary* (1981).
[16] Day, J.C. and Watson, W.M., 'History of the Book Trade in the North: The first twenty-five years' in Isaac, P. (ed.), *Six Centuries of the Provincial Book Trade in Britain* (1991), p.190.
[17] Allnutt, W.H., *English Provincial Presses* (n.d.). Barker remained in Newcastle for three months in 1639 and produced a series of news sheets and proclamations related to the war; Bulkley's connection lasted rather longer, from 1646 to 1661, pp.280-1, 290-2.
[18] Clair, C., *A History of Printing in Britain* (1965), p.197; Curwen, H., *A History of Booksellers, The Old and the New* (1873), p.448.
[19] Chase, M., *The People's Farm: English Agrarian Radicalism 1775-1840* (1988); see also Ashraf, P.M., *The Life and Times of Thomas Spence* (1983).

In his endeavour to publish an accessible English grammar book, assisted by Bewick and by the bookbinder Gilbert Gray, who also ran a lending library, Spence quite naturally emerged as an accomplished propagandist and publisher in his own right. The shaping of an ambitious land reform plan that Malcolm Chase[20] and others have judged to be more rigorous than that of Thomas Paine, was undoubtedly influenced by the Rev. James Murray, the Congregationalist minister and noted radical whose reforming tracts obtained a wide circulation, particularly so during the successful campaign to resist enclosure of the Town Moor in 1771 and 1774. It was Murray, in fact, who persuaded Spence to publish the controversial lecture he delivered to the Newcastle upon Tyne Literary and Philosophical Society, *The Rights of Man*, in 1775 as a cheap tract, thus incurring the wrath of the committee who promptly withdrew his membership.

Given the ready availability of printing skills and technology it is hardly surprising to find that, while most towns struggled to support a single newspaper, 18th-century Newcastle published three and was home to 10 periodicals. The atmosphere was strongly competitive, yet the *Newcastle Journal* bragged of selling 2,000 copies per week in its first year of operation.[21] Inevitably, some titles were short-lived but others, notably the *Newcastle Courant* (1711) and the *Newcastle Chronicle* (1764), weathered the shifting fashions and tastes of more than two centuries.[22] They did so by constantly upgrading their printing machines and techniques and by providing more political coverage. Jeremy Black is right to recommend caution when assessing the significance of the English press as a whole in the 18th century, concluding that it 'developed far less and was substantially less influential than is commonly believed',[23] but Newcastle can justifiably be regarded as an exceptional case. Newcastle newspapers, including the *Courant* and the *Journal*, served a vast region that stretched as far as Cumbria. This gave their proprietors access to an unusually large and stable pool of advertising revenue and, armed with a belief in their own superiority and regional importance,[24] their leader articles became ever more directorial.

By the 19th century, newspapers in Newcastle were undoubtedly performing a vital political function, not just as the 'campaigning and publicity arm for the middle classes'[25] but as well by profiling the voice of progressive reform. In the first half of the century, the *Newcastle Chronicle* is said to have been the 'leading political organ

[20] Chase, M., *The People's Farm*, pp.78f.

[21] *Newcastle Journal*, 8 September 1739.

[22] Founded in 1711, the *Courant* was incorporated into the *Newcastle Journal* in 1915; the *Newcastle Chronicle* first appeared in 1764 and continued until 1953. See Milne, M., *Newspapers of Northumberland and Durham* (1971).

[23] Black, Jeremy, *The English Press in the Eighteenth Century* (1987), p.306.

[24] *Ibid.*, p.55.

[25] Brett, Peter, 'Early Nineteenth-Century Reform Newspapers in the Provinces: The *Newcastle Chronicle* and *Bristol Mercury*' in *Studies in Newspaper and Periodical History 1995 Annual* (1997), p.53.

between York and Edinburgh',[26] playing a key role in all of the reform movements from 1810 onwards with its forceful, uncompromising editorial stance. Other local radicals sought and secured a newspaper platform: W.A. Mitchell, writing as Tim Tunbelly for the *Tyne Mercury*, waged his own war of attrition against the excesses of the unreformed Corporation, while Charles Larkin's short-lived paper, *The Newcastle Standard*, focused attention on corrupt electoral practices and church reform.[27] Emboldened by a tradition of agrarian radicalism, and nurtured by a print culture with a reforming mission, when Newcastle embraced that most radical of causes, Chartism, the first step for the newly reconstituted Northern Political Union was to establish its own newspaper.

Newspaper propaganda had proved a tactical success in the reform battles of 1832.[28] With Augustus Beaumont's robust political and journalistic experience at their disposal, Newcastle Chartists had every reason to feel confident. The *Northern Liberator* was launched in October 1837, just a few weeks earlier than O'Connor's Leeds-based *Northern Star*. Within three months it was outselling the five other local papers and proved to be such a strong competitor for readers and advertising revenue that the proprietors of the Whiggish *Gateshead Observer* took steps to sponsor a rival newspaper.[29] For three years the *Northern Liberator* acted as local Chartism's organising muscle, generating members and co-ordinating demonstrations and activities. Robert Blakey, who took over the paper after Beaumont's death in January 1838, and his fellow editor, Thomas Doubleday, flirted dangerously with the then-stringent laws of sedition. To escape prosecution, they dressed up their ultra-radical critique in a highly intellectualised form of satire. The *Liberator*'s editorials became the touchstone of policy and tactics. Short-lived or not, the 'physical force' character of Tyneside Chartism can be directly attributed to the paper's endorsement of violence as a 'last resort'. The appointment of 'one of the ablest London reporters'[30] was just one of many innovations: home deliveries, spin-off handbills and tracts, and the publication of several editions each week were as financially lucrative as they were politically adventurous. For instance, copies of a serialised satire, *The Political Pilgrim's Progress*, raised a handsome profit and were even reprinted in New York for sales across the United States.[31] By 1840, when Blakey finally fell foul of the law and was forced to sell off the paper to pay his fine, the *Northern Liberator*

[26]  *Ibid.*, p.54.
[27]  Hugman, Joan, '"A Small Drop of Ink": Tyneside Chartism and the *Northern Liberator*' in Ashton, O., Fyson R. and Roberts, S. (eds.), *The Chartist Legacy* (1999), pp.27-8.
[28]  Ridley, D., 'The Spital Fields Demonstration and the Parliamentary Reform Crisis in Newcastle Upon Tyne, May 1832' in *North East Labour History Society Bulletin*, No. 27, 1992.
[29]  Hugman, "A Small Drop of Ink", p.29.
[30]  *Northern Liberator*, 16 December 1837.
[31]  Hugman, "A Small Drop of Ink", p.36.

had a creditable national circulation, with agents in 112 towns and cities. In many respects, this newspaper anticipated many of the developments which were later to transform British journalism. Above all, the dynamic collaboration between Tyneside Chartists and the *Liberator*'s editorial team demonstrated that press coverage was the most essential ingredient of any political campaign.

Cowen was, of course, too young to be a participant in the local Chartist movement but growing up in notoriously radical Winlaton must have been a salutary experience.[32] His own parents had taken an active part in local reform campaigns and, given close contact with his father's influential circle of radical friends, he quickly acquired a sophisticated grasp of the arguments. An Edinburgh University education and the friendship of his tutor, Rev. John Ritchie, considerably widened these early political horizons by introducing him firsthand to the controversy over the Free Kirk movement, the abolition of slavery campaign and, most significantly of all, European republicanism.

## European Republicanism

It was while he was in Edinburgh that Cowen first made contact with Mazzini. A 'cordial and encouraging' response to his letter of support at the time of the Bandiera affair marked the beginning of a life-long friendship and commitment to the Italian cause.[33] By 1846, Cowen's views had become so revolutionary that even his liberal parents were alarmed. Mulishly obstinate, even then, the united opposition of family and friends simply made him more 'determined to stick fast to my present views'.[34] Whether it was intransigence or ill health which precipitated his premature return to Tyneside from Edinburgh is unclear. What is certain is that the attempt to channel his energies into the family business and away from potentially seditious activities failed completely. Although he did not stay long enough in Edinburgh to complete his studies – dividing his time instead between countless political activities and presiding over the Debating Society – he nevertheless 'graduated' as an experienced political organiser and an accomplished public speaker. Neither a deliberately punishing daily workload in the brick manufactory nor the additional responsibility of deputising for his father, dampened his enthusiasm. Somehow, he still managed to dedicate time to studying political tracts and to launching a number of reform projects. A subscription to George Julian Harney's *Democratic Review* and the *Red Republican* quite naturally drew him into membership of the newly formed People's

---

[32]   Flinn, M.W., *Men of Iron* (1962).

[33]   Jane Cowen Mss., Chapter 6, *The Cowen Papers*. The Papers also include Mazzini's vast correspondence with Cowen from 1860-72.

[34]   Joseph Cowen, 'Notes, Hints and Observations from Daily Life', July 1846, *Cowen Papers*, F12.

International League. Although he was still only 18 years old, his reputation as a young man of ultra-radical views who had the wherewithal to promote them was now beginning to take shape.

1848 was scarcely the most auspicious period in which to launch a political career as a British radical. Chartism lingered on in small cells of resistance in the North East but was no longer a force to be reckoned with. Equally, the virtual collapse of Chartism nationally had left an uneasy coalition of radical forces divided and in disarray, and the difficulties this created were made worse by the outbreak of violent revolutions across Europe that same year.[35] These revolutions thrived on the difference between the timid and partial democracy of the middle class and the proto social democracy advocated by the committed radicals and workers. A large Tyneside delegation, including Joseph Cowen Snr., attended the Paris Peace Conference in 1849 but the decision to implement a policy of non-intervention in the affairs of Hungary and Italy brought forth a torrent of criticism from radicals such as George Julian Harney (in 1839 one of three Newcastle delegates to the Chartist Convention) and his compatriot, the engraver W.J. Linton.[36] Harney mocked the 'solemn farce' of the Paris conference, claiming that the delegates were 'like the voluptuous aristocracy of Vienna [who] desire peace that they may enjoy themselves in safety'.[37] In the circumstances, it could not have made comfortable reading for the Cowens. Young Cowen appears to have had no hesitation in aligning himself with the Harney/Linton camp and, egged on by Mazzini, he began to engage more directly in the Italian cause. Even though the mid-century heralded a shift in England away from confrontational class politics,[38] the transition was slow and uneven. The radical rump, wholly resistant to the pressure to compromise, began to regroup themselves behind a new banner – 'the Charter and something more'.[39]

Slogans were all well and good but actually delivering revolutionary change was a major challenge, as Cowen was soon to discover. His ultra-radicalism, particularly his views on religion, was as yet a step too far for Newcastle. Even though disestablishment of the Church of England was an old idea and in recent times the Scottish secessionists had ensured that the debate was well aired,[40] the political climate in Britain as a whole was still far from conducive in spite of the power of nonconformity. Under the circumstances, Cowen's grand plan to set up a branch of the Anti-State Church Association in Blaydon and Winlaton was as ill-conceived

---

[35] See Finn, Margot, *After Chartism. Class and Nation in English Radical Politics, 1848-1874* (1993), chapter 2.

[36] Briggs, Asa, *Victorian People* (1954), p.223f; Smith, F.B., *Radical Artisan. W.J. Linton 1812-97* (1973), p.148.

[37] *Democratic Review*, October 1849.

[38] Belchem, John, *Popular Radicalism in Nineteenth Century Britain* (1996), p.99.

[39] *Democratic Review*, February 1850.

[40] Machin, Ian, 'Disestablishment and democracy, *c.*1840-1930' in Biagini, E.F. (ed.), *Citizenship and Community*, pp.121-2.

as it was badly organised. Discomfited by his failure, he was forced to abandon his plans and concede defeat.[41] While he maintained an active involvement in the national movement as a member of the Liberation Society, and counted noted secularists such as Bradlaugh and Holyoake among his closest friends, Cowen subsequently avoided being drawn into any public confession of his religious beliefs. In the aftermath Cowen began to take the view that substantive political progress would not be achieved unless educational opportunities for the working classes were dramatically improved.

His financial stake in the republican movement increased as he became ever more embroiled in the Italian cause. A lot of money was poured into promotional literature of one kind or another. A circular address aimed at raising money and support for the *Friends of European Freedom* was distributed to every Liberal newspaper in the United Kingdom.[42] Cowen continued to prop up Harney's ailing radical journals and sponsor Linton's zealous publication, *The English Republic*.[43] In November 1854, at the outbreak of war in the Crimea, Cowen persuaded a number of like-minded radicals to establish a Foreign Affairs Committee. Ostensibly, their aim was to monitor the progress of the war but a spin-off group, The Republican Brotherhood, had more ambitious aims. As the Brotherhood's newsletter proclaimed, they would be satisfied with nothing less than 'government of the people, by, and for, the people'.[44]

In keeping with Cowen's propagandist strategy he immediately set up a new journal, the *Northern Tribune*. Together with the *English Republic*, it was printed at Brantwood by Linton and W.E. Adams[45] (subsequently appointed editor of the *Newcastle Weekly Chronicle*) and constituted a finely balanced democratic manifesto for Britain and Europe. For Cowen, the war of words was not just a theoretical exercise, for he spent most of the 1850s secretly smuggling weapons and seditious literature on behalf of the Polish Democratic Society, raising money to supply arms for Garibaldi's Sicilian campaign and, it appears, even getting personally involved in a bomb plot to assassinate Napoleon III.[46]

Throughout this period, Cowen gave European republicanism a public platform, not least by offering hospitality to Garibaldi and Louis Kossuth and persuading the local people to provide shelter and jobs for a number of Hungarian refugees. He was, though, extremely careful to cover up his republican activities as he sought to

---

[41] Jane Cowen Mss., Chapter 3, *The Cowen Papers*.
[42] *Ibid.*, Chapter 9.
[43] Smith, *Radical Artisan*, p.60.
[44] *Republican Record*, January 1855.
[45] Ashton, *W.E. Adams*.
[46] *Cowen Papers*, various but see letter dated 4 January 1859. Also Holyoake, W.J., *Sixty Years of an Agitator's Life* (1906), vol.2.

establish himself as a respectable member of the Newcastle business community. Conspicuous philanthropy was the chief entry qualification and this was no problem, for Cowen was naturally altruistic and had the means to be. Cowen Senior was recruited as Chairman of the Winlaton Sanitary Association, which his son set up in 1847 along with the Literary and Scientific Institute, which he launched soon afterwards. Yet while he had no scruples about making use of his father's influential position on the City Council, he was not content simply to follow in his footsteps. He was active on his own account, sponsoring a number of self-improving and educational initiatives that directly benefited local people, as well as his own reputation.

**6.2** Giuseppe Garibaldi.

## *Institutes, Co-ops, Charisma*

He did not linger too long in his father's shadow. He had strong views on the failings of the Mechanics' Institute movement (his father was on the Newcastle Mechanics' Institute executive) and in planning to provide an institute for his home community he sought to eradicate what he regarded as its discriminatory practices. He was determined that his Blaydon Institute would be more egalitarian and enabling: 'open to all, irrespective of their mark or station, without regard to their religious or political sentiments … a campaign against ignorance, a battle against bigotry and prejudice'.[47] He encouraged working-class members to elect their own executive committee, cautioning against 'the machinations of unprincipled demagogues and aspirants to political power who might work to mislead them for … their own sinister and selfish purposes'.[48] This might seem somewhat disingenuous, given that Cowen was, to some extent, using the Institute to further his own political ambitions but, equally, his motives were not just self-serving. The open access policy, cheap subscription rates, children's educational facilities and a progressive lecture

[47] *Cowen Papers*, D5, 2 February 1847.
[48] Jane Cowen Mss., Chapter 3, *The Cowen Papers*.

programme were far removed from the more exclusive practices that prevailed elsewhere.[49] In complete contrast to the widespread embargo which forbade discussion of politics and religion in other institutes, the Blaydon Institute's lecture programme was dominated by politics and religion. Garibaldi and Kossuth, to name but two, were among the many guest speakers Cowen introduced. The new purpose-built Blaydon Institute was established in 1852 to become a model of good practice for others that were swiftly set up in the surrounding villages. When the Northern Union of Mechanics' Institutes was founded the subscribing institutes were readily persuaded to adopt Cowen's open admissions policy.

The network of Mechanics' Institutes aimed to inculcate the values of self-help and this was strengthened still further when in the autumn of 1858 Cowen introduced Holyoake's book on the Rochdale Co-operative Store, *Self Help By the People*. Urged on by Cowen's personal endorsement, the following December the Blaydon members set up the first co-operative store in the North East, initially hiring a few rooms to trade from, but within 12 months profits were sufficient to justify bigger premises. A proselytising mission to other mechanics' institutes was a resounding success and by 1862 Cowen judged that co-operation was sufficiently well established on Tyneside to merit the formation of a Central Co-operative Committee for the North of England. As usual, Cowen was so impatient to push ahead with his plans that he failed to anticipate the opposition such a scheme was bound to generate among co-operators, many of whom feared they might have to surrender control of their societies or, worse still, their hard-won profits to an anonymous regional committee. The Blaydon Society, needless to say, was one of the first to join the North of England Co-operative Wholesale Society when it was eventually set up in Manchester in 1864, but as late as 1870 some societies, such as Cramlington, were still unable to persuade their members that affiliation was in their best interests.

The phenomenal growth of the Co-operative movement in the North East which, when the first Co-operative Congress was held in Newcastle in 1873, comprised some 74 retail stores and several related enterprises (including an engine works, industrial bank, mining company, carpet manufactory, household furnishing company and a printing works) was central to Cowen's bid to 'make men citizens'. Radical reform lay at the heart of the 'new gospel he preached which would ultimately 'effect a better distribution of the wealth of the country'.[50] By 1873, after 15 years of intense political activity on not just one but on several fronts, Newcastle's citizens knew the radical creed by heart, and, more importantly, the working-class majority appear to have formed a deep attachment to their preacher-politician.

[49] Harrison, J.F.C., *Living and Learning 1790-1960* (1961), p.126.
[50] Joseph Cowen's speech to the Newcastle Co-operative Congress, *Cowen Papers*, B137, 13 April 1873.

**6.3** Newcastle upon Tyne Co-operative Society Limited.

When the Co-operative experiment was still in its infancy Cowen was just on the brink of launching a new suffrage campaign. The Northern Reform Union (NRU) was formed on 27 December 1857 and within three months had enlisted 481 members.[51] For Cowen, this was a personal campaign on every level and, although he could easily have delegated the responsibility of hosting meetings, he deliberately chose otherwise. This is not to suggest that he was consciously soliciting popular support. He had already a substantial power base at the municipal level, serving alongside Cowen Snr. for much of the period and, once his father was elected as Member of Parliament in 1865, Cowen's position on the Council became even stronger. A man of enormous self-confidence, he had an unshakeable faith in his own abilities. Quite simply, he believed that he alone was capable of tapping into the insecurities of the working classes and winning them over to his reforming agenda. In the long term, it was this personal appeal which underpinned his electoral success.

Setting himself a punishing schedule, he travelled throughout the North East mounting a major leafleting campaign and addressing gatherings almost every night. Mechanics' Institutes, especially in mining villages, were the obvious venues for his

[51] Northern Reform Union Minutes, *Cowen Papers*, C6, 5 April 1858.

reform meetings and, while the main purpose was to resurrect the suffrage campaign, he took advantage of the opportunity this presented to publicise other radical causes. The rapid expansion of co-operative societies can be directly attributed to Cowen's shrewd decision to promote the two campaigns in tandem. The middle classes, unfortunately, were not so easily cultivated. An intense lobbying campaign yielded little response, causing Cowen to denounce publicly their 'selfishness'. An open letter to the Radical Reformers of the United Kingdom called upon the working classes to be self-reliant, for 'Those who are not for you are against you'.[52] More and more he identified himself with the working classes, dressing in plain clothing and stoutly defending what he saw as their rights and interests. At the beginning of 1858, when Thomas Doubleday was recruited to help by assessing the potential levels of support elsewhere in the country, he advised Cowen that 'they are looking to the North for a movement and to Newcastle especially'.[53] Holyoake, called upon to undertake a similar task, corroborated Doubleday's assertion, exhorting Cowen to give a lead to cities such as Sheffield, Birmingham and Bradford. By the end of 1858, the NRU was being dubbed the 'Aurora Borealis of Reform' as the agitation began to have a regional then a national impact. Six hundred yards of petition, bearing 34,456 signatures from across the North East represented the culmination of feverish activity in the first six weeks of 1859. When the petition was presented to Parliament on 28 February it was estimated that more than half the adult male population of Northumberland and Durham officially backed the reform campaign.[54] An attempt was made to field an NRU candidate in the Newcastle elections that same year. P.A. Taylor, an ardent republican and radical activist, was put forward on Cowen's recommendation but his lack of local standing and religious prejudices operated against him.[55] Cowen himself was pressed to stand at Berwick to counter the corrupt practices that were held to be endemic in the borough, but he had other plans which would keep him in Newcastle.

While the NRU campaign conspicuously failed to achieve the aims of its sponsors, it nevertheless ensured that electoral reform was not lost sight of in the doldrum years between the end of Chartism and the Second Reform Act of 1867. Failure served another purpose too; it convinced Cowen of the need to acquire his own newspaper. In the latter stages of the campaign he had paid the owner of the *Newcastle Chronicle* handsomely to publish a number of supportive articles and to advertise the

[52] Northern Reform Union Minutes, *Cowen Papers*, C6, 11 October 1859.
[53] *Ibid.*, 4 October 1858.
[54] *Ibid.*, 28 February 1859.
[55] An attempt was made to split the radical vote by a group of 'moderate' reformers strongly influenced by Newcastle Nonconformism and opposed to the 'Blaydon atheists'. Taylor's secularist affiliations made him a particular target. See Todd, N., *The Militant Democracy: Joseph Cowen and Victorian Radicalism* (1991), pp.46-7.

NRU's activities. This 'political fund' was, to all intents and purposes, keeping the *Chronicle* afloat. Its circulation rates were by then pitifully small, and, armed with this knowledge, he was able to negotiate a keen price.

His acquisition of the *Chronicle* in 1859 and shortly afterwards its stablemate, the *Newcastle Weekly Chronicle*, enabled Cowen to achieve that which was physically impossible: to be a daily presence in the lives of the population, to drip-feed his ideas about society and democracy in countless ways and to win over the many sections of Newcastle society who, in the normal scheme of things, were unlikely to attend a political meeting or join a radical organisation. Cowen's charisma is not in doubt but the paper pulpit manifestly intensified its power. The power of newspapers had been the focus of considerable intellectual debate and not a little anxiety for much of the century.[56] Print still had a scarcity value then which invested it with an authority which is difficult to comprehend fully today. Cowen fully appreciated the extent to which the public still stood in awe of their newspapers, and willingly invested more than £40,000 in the first four years as part of his drive to make the *Chronicle* the '*Times* of the North'.[57] By 1873, daily sales figures for the second quarter were estimated to be 35,534 and the *Weekly*'s were just slightly less.[58] Few papers outside London could match that and, increasingly, the views expressed in Cowen's newspapers attracted national attention.

On a practical day-to-day basis the *Newcastle Chronicle* offered the usual mixture of news and views associated with other provincial newspapers. Important weapons in Cowen's political armoury, sports reports, serialised literature, domestic anecdotes and local gossip were all offered as sweeteners to advance the paper's more serious intent: that of giving the people a radical education. Special features ranged from a lengthy promotional series on local co-operative societies to the co-ordination of an aggressive campaign by the Reform League. The *Chronicle* championed the miners' claim for an amendment to the 1867 Act and, perhaps most controversially of all, took a leading role in the 1871 engineers' strike on Tyneside. George Julian Harney, who had by then left England and settled in Boston, Massachusetts, was recruited to promote American democracy through a series of leading articles in the *Weekly*.[59] His 'Letters From America' was part travelogue, part political instruction. Opening up debates about abolition, republicanism, democracy and civil rights, he even used his column to shame members of Newcastle Council into approving the increased rates necessary for a Free Public Library.

---

[56] Jones, *Powers of the Press*, chapter 4.
[57] Ashton, *W.E. Adams*, p.102.
[58] Brown, Lucy, *Victorian News and Newspapers* (1985), p.53.
[59] Ashton, Owen R. and Hugman, Joan, 'Letters From America: George Julian Harney, Boston, USA, and Newcastle upon Tyne, England, 1863-1888' in *Proceedings*, Massachusetts Historical Society, vol. cvii, 1995.

Thomas Burt's[60] election to Parliament in 1873 as one of the first working-class members owed much to the *Chronicle*'s support. When the death of Cowen Senior in 1873 forced his hand and Cowen finally decided to secure the Liberal representation the respect and support of local mining communities was crucial. The Gateshead Representation League, originally intent upon fielding a 'bona fide representative of Labour', accepted Cowen's candidacy as a perfectly acceptable compromise. There had not been a single reform or campaign during those 15 years with which Cowen had not been associated; there had not been a single issue of public interest in which he had not voiced an opinion. His newspapers carried verbatim copies of his speeches, the editorials acted as his mouthpiece, the 'voice of the North' trained Newcastle in the art of popular politics. Arguably, the style of Gladstone's Midlothian campaign in 1879-80 and the adulation it aroused was not an innovatory 'solution to the problem of marrying a representative system to a large style franchise'.[61] It had already been tried and tested, and perfected, by Cowen, years earlier, with considerable success.

## *Ireland*

Thus far, this analysis has tried to demonstrate the centrality of Cowen's propagandist tactics to his ability to claim and hold the electorate's loyalties. It would be misleading, however, to suggest that this was his only strategy. A shrewd politician, he knew better than to cultivate a faction or an interest group; he had to be seen to meet all of his constituents' needs. In the 19th century Newcastle had the 'fourth largest ratio of Irish to English in England and Wales'.[62] On the basis of numerical strength alone, the Irish were bound to have an impact upon local politics. While sectarian attitudes undermined the assimilation of the Irish in most, if not all, of the major centres in which they settled, on Tyneside they not only benefited from the relative absence of sectarianism but their political influence far outweighed their minority status. On the political front, the alliance that was brokered between the Irish nationalists and the indigenous population rested mainly on the way that Tyneside radicalism was able to serve the interests of both groups. The ideological roots of English agrarianism and international republicanism acted as common currency, fostering the identification of shared objectives. In a powerful sense, the Irish represented a highly visible test case for both – a graphic example of the corruption of the British political system. Like his father before him, Cowen applied his

[60]   Satre, Lowell, J., *Thomas Burt, Miners' M.P., 1837-1921* (1999).
[61]   Matthew, H.C.G., as cited in Biagini, E.F., *Citizenship and Community*, p.42.
[62]   Nicholson, R.J., 'Irish Priests in the North East in the 19th Century' in *Northern Catholic History*, Spring 1985, vol. xxi.

considerable influence to the forging of good Anglo-Irish relations, opposing a succession of coercive statutes intended for Ireland, championing Home Rule and providing favourable and sympathetic coverage of Irish affairs in his newspapers.

Links between Irish and Tyneside radicals were detectable at the time of the Spital Fields demonstration in 1819 when reformers showed their solidarity by carrying a distinctive banner emblazoned with entwined roses, thistles and shamrock. The Spencean connection with such symbolism is significant. Moreover, as the Brassfounders and Brassfinishers Union resurrected the self-same banner at the time of the Tyneside Reform League demonstration in 1867, it is reasonable to assume that such solidarities were long-standing.[63] The Chartists, too, took a similar stance, with poetry, songs and banners all proclaiming that theirs was a united British front which included Ireland. Even so, there were times when that close relationship was vulnerable and liable to fracture. The rise of Fenianism in the 1860s fuelled popular prejudices, especially in places such as Manchester, Liverpool and Glasgow where the Irish presence put pressure on local jobs and resources.

The North East was reputed to have been 'honeycombed with Fenians'[64] and, despite a successful recruitment drive by the 'Constitutionalists', in 1884 regional membership of the Irish Republican Brotherhood was judged to be over 6,000.[65] The Cowen press was notably pro-Irish, reporting outbreaks of violence and swift enough to condemn them, but, at the same time, constantly reminding readers that local Irish people were not to be held responsible for outrages carried out elsewhere. Following the Clerkenwell explosion (1867), when Newcastle became a particular target for government surveillance and several hundred special constables were sworn in at North Shields, the *Chronicle* mounted a campaign to establish the unquestionable loyalty of the Tyneside Irish. A forthright editorial even went so far as to insist that 'The people at all times have the right to revolt against their rulers' and called upon English and Irish radicals to work together to instigate constitutional change.[66] As if this level of support was not enough, Cowen's *Chronicle* operated as a *bona fide* Irish newspaper: Irish elections, Irish political meetings, Irish eviction statistics and parliamentary divisions of Irish members were given such extensive coverage as to obviate the necessity for a separate Irish journal to be published in Newcastle until after 1884. Sharing the same radical newspaper was bound to have a positive outcome and, ultimately, this stress on collective rather than ethnic goals became a rallying point for all sections of the community.

---

[63] *Newcastle Daily Chronicle*, 29 January 1867.
[64] O'Connor, T.P., 'The Irish in Great Britain', p.47.
[65] Quoted by Fitzpatrick, D., 'A Curious Middle Place' in Swift, R. and Gilley, S. (eds.), *The Irish in Britain, 1815-1939* (1989), p.33; see also *Newcastle Weekly Chronicle*, 2 February 1864.
[66] *Newcastle Daily Chronicle*, 25 November 1867.

Of course, Cowen's role was not confined to ensuring that Irish affairs were sympathetically reported. Through his close friendships with activists such as John Barry, Timothy Healy, Joseph Biggar and Alex Sullivan, editor of *The Nation*, Isaac Butt was persuaded to host the first Home Rule Conference in Newcastle in August 1873 with Parnell. Cowen was directly involved in Irish politics at the highest level. As John Martin MP told those who had gathered in Gateshead Town Hall to celebrate St Patrick's Day in 1875: 'Cowen was the most valuable friend that Ireland had among Englishmen'.[67] As one of the most implacable opponents of Gladstone's 'Ministry of Coercion', his position among the Liberal faithful was decidedly weak and becoming weaker. Unseating him was out of the question, as was the possibility of countering the *Chronicle*'s attacks on Gladstonian Liberalism. In 1881 the government judged the *Chronicle* to be just as seditious as the Irish nationalist press and prohibited its circulation in Kilmainham jail. For their part, the Newcastle Liberal Association tried to silence the Cowenite opposition by offering to endow his press. When that failed, they were forced to finance their own newspaper.[68] If, by 1881, Cowen was unloved and unwanted by the Liberals, the Irish Nationalists were not slow to express their desire to claim him as one of their own. They invited him to become an executive member of the National Land League of Great Britain – a singular honour for an English politician – and they even offered him an Irish seat. He might, they said, 'have his pick of twenty'.[69]

## The Last Radical

It has been suggested that electoral reform in 1867 recast the nature of the relationship between politicians and the voting public. Politics became more personal and success at the polls rested more with those key individuals whose rhetorical and leadership skills were such that they were able to tap into the prejudices and passions of the masses.[70] This view can certainly be upheld in Newcastle. Armed with all the necessary personal and intellectual skills, endowed with a popular radical political inheritance and enabled by wealth, Cowen made Newcastle politics in his own image: heretical, independent-minded, community-centred, *progressive*. He seized the opportunities presented by the new print technology and this too became an essential part of his armoury. In claiming to represent *the city* – not party or faction – he outgunned the Conservative official opposition and marginalised the Liberal unofficial opposition at one and the same time. He never canvassed support, claiming that his views were

---

[67] *Newcastle Weekly Chronicle*, 20 March 1883.
[68] *Minutes*, Newcastle Liberal Association, 31 December 1881.
[69] *Newcastle Weekly Chronicle*, 17 March 1881.
[70] Beetham, D., *Max Weber and the Theory of Modern Politics* (1985), p.227.

so well known as to render such 'humiliating' supplication unnecessary. Once elected, he believed he had a mandate to exercise his own judgement. Unfortunately, in 1874 the imposition of party discipline had already begun to erode parliamentary independence. Out in the constituencies, members were increasingly expected to uphold party policy on a national stage.

In the end, Cowen's hold on the Newcastle electorate weakened. The painstaking community building undertaken in the early years had endowed him with an apparently unbreakable power base. But the strength of that leadership depended entirely on Cowen's ability to maintain a close relationship with his people. Between 1874 and 1877 serious illness and the demands of Westminster created a level of disengagement that he never quite fully resisted. By the early 1880s, the introduction of more sophisticated party machinery imposed new constraints on members of both parties. Cowen's maverick approach to his parliamentary responsibilities and his frosty relationship with Gladstone made it difficult for the Newcastle Liberal Association to promote party policy. Robert Spence Watson, a prominent Quaker businessman and the prime mover of constituency politics, had been the architect of Cowen's election victories in 1873 and 1874. Notwithstanding his long friendship with Cowen, however, Watson's first loyalty was to Gladstone and the party. In 1880 Spence Watson deliberately brought in Ashton Dilke to fight for the second Liberal seat and to lend more credibility to Newcastle Liberalism in general. Cowen made his feelings plain, refusing to share a platform with Dilke. With the *Chronicle* to co-ordinate and promote his campaign, Cowen stood as an Independent, topping the poll by 11,766 to 10,404 votes. Yet, although his independent candidacy finally relieved him of what had become by then an irksome obligation to the Liberals, it also left him politically isolated and ever more vulnerable.

On a personal level, he had become increasingly disenchanted with political life. To put it bluntly, by the mid-1880s Cowen was frustrated by the slow pace of reform. As radicalism declined into the kind of single issue, sectional activity that had made the Tichborne Claimant a 'vulgar hero', Cowen no longer had any faith in its ability to deliver general reforms such as universal suffrage or an increase in working-class representation. In June 1881, he was clearly looking for a way forward. He flirted briefly with Hyndman's Democratic Federation – lured on by his avowed commitment to fight for Irish reforms if he became a founder member. But as the Federation assumed a more overtly socialist profile, he withdrew. Socialism, he said, 'would reduce man to a cypher or to a machine ... his free will would disappear. It would be the serfdom of the Middle Ages without the hope of Manumission.'[71] In 1883 and again in 1885 he 'interfered' in local by-elections and promoted the

---

[71] *Cowen Papers*, B349, 1885.

Labour Representation Committee's candidate. He had long been frustrated that, despite all his efforts, so little progress had been made towards increasing the numbers of working-class MPs. What Cowen failed to appreciate, however, was the extent to which this was a minority view. In the past, he had been able to impose his opinions fairly easily because of the respect in which he was held and the inherent deference of local working-class constituents. The Durham Miners' Association had already passed a resolution affirming their decision to field a candidate 'in connection with the Liberals'.[72] Cowen's futile attempt to railroad the Durham Miners' Association into accepting his own candidate caused a serious rift with the miners who had long been the backbone of his support.[73] Equally, in 1883 when Ashton Dilke became ill and a replacement candidate had to be found, Gladstone's staunch ally John Morley was selected to contest the seat. Cowen was, as ever, confident of success and seemed scarcely aware of the favourable impression which John Morley made on the Newcastle electorate. With the backing of Spence Watson and the Newcastle Liberal Association, Morley won the seat comfortably. For his part, Cowen was, by his own admission, completely astonished that 'a stranger to Newcastle would ever be elected that way'.[74]

Electoral triumph in the 1885 election was little comfort to Cowen who was forced to confront the unpalatable reality that Tory votes had secured his victory. Fatally out of step with his constituents, and dogged by ill health, he resigned his seat. His departure was a source of regret to the Newcastle electorate who tried to persuade him to change his mind. The general consensus was that if he had 'flattered Ministers, had he generally voted with his party, had he exercised less independence and shown less acrimony, he might have been Chief Secretary for Ireland with a seat in the Cabinet'.[75]

After Cowen's resignation, Newcastle politics settled into less oppositional mode and became, at last, a proper Liberal constituency. It was not destined to last. The radicalism that had been a defining characteristic of city politics and culture for over two centuries lingered on and became a source of inspiration for the nascent Independent Labour Party. When the ILP launched the *Northern Democrat* in August 1906 it was, they said, inspired by Cowen's *Northern Tribune*.[76]

[72]  Wilson, J., *A History of the Durham Miners' Association 1870-1904* (1907), p.194.
[73]  Biagini, E.F., *Liberty, Retrenchment and Reform* (1992), p.367.
[74]  Hirst, F.W. (ed.), *The Life and Letters of John Morley M.P. vol.ii 1875-1885* (1927), p.122.
[75]  *Cowen Papers*, unidentified newspaper cutting, 12 February 1886.
[76]  Todd, N., *The Militant Democracy*, p.162.

# 7

# The People of Newcastle
## A Demographic History

MIKE BARKE

## The World of Albert Moore

Early in 1890, Elizabeth Moore of 3 Pitt Lane in the Westgate district of Newcastle gave birth to Albert. Albert, her ninth child, was one of 6,936 children born in the Newcastle upon Tyne Registration District that year, over a thousand of whom were to die before reaching their first birthday. Having survived that first year of life, however, Albert's chances of a reasonable natural life span were actually quite good, at least, up until war in 1914-18.

The 11 members of the Moore family lived in two rooms, sharing 3 Pitt Lane with three other households – a further 16 people.[1] Each of these households lived in just one room. Elizabeth, now aged 38, was born in Walker and had married William, a 41-year-old chainsmith from Gateshead, 20 years earlier. All their children were born in Newcastle and the eldest, 19-year-old John, was a coal miner, along with the 15-year-old William, whilst the eldest daughter, 17-year-old Dinah, was in domestic service. The younger children had been born at regular intervals: Elizabeth (13), George (10), Joseph (9), Ann (7), Robert (3), and now Albert (1). In many ways the Moore family appear to fit the stereotype of a late Victorian working-class household: large, overcrowded, the parents marrying relatively early and, from the gap in the sequence of children, possibly having suffered the loss of at least one child, either in pregnancy or early in life.

This simple description of one late 19th-century Newcastle family raises a number of questions. To what extent was early marriage (probably at age 18) responsible for high fertility? How common was the experience of infant death? The Moores were clearly a nuclear family but what other family and household structures characterised 19th-century Newcastle? How much did household and family structures vary? How typical was local migration and how did this vary by social group? Finally,

---

[1] Census Enumeration Books, Newcastle upon Tyne Registration District (1891).

despite four incomes coming into the household, the Moores were extremely overcrowded. To what extent was this a 'normal' situation in Newcastle?

Early 19th-century Newcastle experienced substantial industrial growth but at mid-century the occupational pattern indicated an emergent, rather than a mature, industrial structure (Table 1).

### Table 1    Occupations in Newcastle, 1851 and 1891[2]

| | 1851 | | 1891 | | % change, |
|---|---|---|---|---|---|
| | No. | % | No. | % | 1851-1891 |
| Food and drink | 3,381 | 8.7 | 5,891 | 7.5 | + 74.2 |
| Services(*) | 694 | 1.8 | 1,821 | 2.3 | + 162.4 |
| Shipbuilding | 608 | 1.6 | 2,124 | 2.7 | + 249.3 |
| Building | 2908 | 7.5 | 5,429 | 6.9 | + 86.7 |
| Clothes and shoes | 4,927 | 12.7 | 7,217 | 9.2 | + 46.5 |
| Blacksmiths & metal workers | 2,619 | 6.7 | 4,534 | 5.8 | + 73.1 |
| Engineers | 1,034 | 2.7 | 7,130 | 9.1 | + 589.5 |
| Horse & horse transport | 960 | 2.5 | 2,761 | 3.5 | + 187.6 |
| Coal | 511 | 1.3 | 1,059 | 1.3 | +107.2 |
| Glass, pottery, chemicals | 1,398 | 3.6 | 893 | 1.1 | - 36.1 |
| Sea and boatmen | 2,078 | 5.3 | 1,555 | 2.0 | - 25.2 |
| Agriculture | 633 | 1.6 | 500 | 0.6 | - 21.0 |
| Government service | 141 | 0.4 | 469 | 0.6 | + 232.6 |
| Labourers | 2,540 | 6.5 | 4,911 | 6.2 | + 93.3 |
| Teachers | 372 | 1.0 | 1,123 | 1.4 | + 201.9 |
| Domestic service | 5,356 | 13.8 | 9,917 | 12.6 | + 85.2 |
| Railway service | 427 | 1.1 | 1,678 | 2.1 | + 293.0 |
| Commercial/business clerks | 253 | 0.7 | 2,674 | 3.4 | + 956.9 |
| Total | 38,784 | 100.0 | 78,708 | 100.0 | + 102.9 |

(*) includes legal, medical and commercial (accountants, brokers, insurance and banking) employees and self-employed

The largest single category of employment was domestic service, followed by the manufacture and sale of clothes and shoes. Third came the manufacture of food and drink. More people living in the city were employed in agriculture than were employed in shipbuilding. Despite the broader regional significance of the coal industry, only 500 people living in the city were employed in it. The employment structure at mid-century does not fit the 19th-century industrial stereotype. The next 40 years saw substantial change with a massive 103 per cent growth in employment, or the equivalent of 1,000 new jobs each year. A more important

[2]  Rowe, D.J., 'Occupations in Northumberland and Durham, 1851-1911', *Northern History*, vol. VIII (1973).

change, however, was the rise to dominance of much larger units of production, a factor of significance for the nature of the workforce and their relationships to employers.[3] Metal industries provided the most spectacular examples of the growth of the large firm in Newcastle.[4] Newcastle was a very different place at the end of the 19th century from what it was at the beginning or, indeed, in the middle. However, a large proportion of the jobs created in the course of the century were problematic in that they were either seasonal (for example, building, dock labour, external painting and decorating),[5] casualised (for example, street hawking, some domestic service, carting and general labouring in many industries),[6] or subject to the trade cycle (shipbuilding and related heavy engineering).[7] Whilst economic and social conditions overall gradually improved for the majority of its population, late 19th-century Newcastle continued to demonstrate widespread poverty.

## Population Growth

Table II shows the estimated growth and the rate of growth of Newcastle's population from the mid-18th century up to 1911. Where available, data are shown for *both* the 'town' of Newcastle upon Tyne and the Newcastle upon Tyne Registration District. Although the registration district only came into existence in 1837, it forms the most useful geographical basis for demographic analysis because it comprises the basic unit for which continuous population registration is available for most of the 19th century. It changed its boundaries only once in the study period (1905) and for most of the century it approximates closely to the functional reality of Newcastle. The second half of the 18th century and the first decade of the 19th was a period of sluggish growth mixed with periods of absolute decline. The next 50 years showed growth rates generally well in excess of two per cent per annum. In the 1860s and '70s, however, a considerable slackening of the rate of growth took place, followed by very rapid increase in the 1880s but then a further slackening of the rate approaching the First World War.

Table III shows the components of change of the population of Newcastle upon Tyne. Only after 1841 with the availability of both census data and continuous

[3] Benwell Community Project, 'The making of a Ruling Class', Final Report Series, No. 6 (1978) .

[4] McCord, N. and Rowe, D.J., 'Industrialisation and urban growth in north-east England', *International Review of Social History*, vol. 22 (1977).

[5] Stedman Jones, G., *Outcast London* (1971).

[6] Treble, J.H., *Urban Poverty in Britain, 1830-1914* (1979).

[7] *Royal Commission on the Depression of Trade and Industry*, cmnd. 4621 (1886).

[8] Chalklin, C.W., *The Provincial Towns of Georgian England: A Study of the Building Process, 1740-1820* (1974).

[9] Middlebrook, S., *Newcastle upon Tyne: Its Growth and Achievement* (1950).

[10] Law, C.M., 'Some notes on the urban population of England and Wales in the 18th century', *The Local Historian*, vol. 10 (1972).

## Table II    Population of Newcastle and growth rates, 1700-1911 (*)

| Year | 'Town' of Newcastle | Change | % change per annum | Newcastle reg. dist. (*) | Change | % change per annum |
|---|---|---|---|---|---|---|
| 1700 | 14,000 (Chalkin,1974)[8] | | | | | |
| 1740 | 21,000 (Middlebrook, 1950)[9] | +7,000 | + 1.25% | | | |
| 1750 | 29,000 (Law, 1972)[10] | | | | | |
| 1770 | 24,000 (Middlebrook, 1950) | +3,000 | + 0.48% | 27,600 | | |
| 1775 | 33,000 (Law, 1972) | | | | | |
| 1801 | 28,366 | +4,366 | + 0.59% | 34,092 | +6,492 | +0.76 |
| 1811 | 27,587 | -779 | - 0.27% | 33,723 | -369 | -0.11 |
| 1821 | 35,181 | +7,594 | + 2.75 | 43,177 | +9,454 | +2.80 |
| 1831 | 42,760 | +7,579 | + 2.15 | 54,991 | +11,814 | +2.74 |
| 1841 | | | | 71,844 | +16,853 | +3.06 |
| 1851 | | | | 89,156 | +17,312 | +2.41 |
| 1861 | | | | 110,968 | +21,812 | +2.45 |
| 1871 | | | | 131,198 | +20,230 | +1.82 |
| 1881 | | | | 150,252 | +19,054 | +1.45 |
| 1891 | | | | 196,817 | +46,565 | +3.10 |
| 1901 | | | | 233,644 | +36,827 | +1.87 |
| 1911 | | | | 250,825 | +17,181 | +0.73 |

(*) Only estimates of population are available prior to 1801. Most of these are inadequate or unreliable. The Registration District did not exist until the 1830s. Population totals for 1801-31 include Westgate, Elswick, Jesmond, Heaton and Byker (incorporated into the 'Town' in 1835), that is, the area that ultimately became the Newcastle upon Tyne Registration District. Law's figures probably include Gateshead. References 8-10 on p.135.

## Table III
### Components of Population Change, Newcastle upon Tyne, 1770-1911

| Period | No. births | No. deaths | Births - deaths | Population change | Assumed migration |
|---|---|---|---|---|---|
| 1770-1800 (*) | 25,848 | 27,411 | -1,563 | +6,492 | +8,055 |
| 1801-1810 (*) | 12,147 | 9,160 | +2,899 | -369 | -3,268 |
| 1811-1820 (*) | 15,261 | 9,537 | +5,724 | +9,454 | +3,730 |
| 1821-1830 (*) | 20,737 | 12,909 | +7,828 | +11,814 | +3,986 |
| 1831-1840 (*) | 24,521 | 19,921 | +4,600 | +16,853 | +12,253 |
| 1841-1850 | 26,150 | 21,598 | +4,552 | +17,312 | +12,760 |
| 1851-1860 | 35,691 | 27,379 | +8,312 | +21,812 | +13,500 |
| 1861-1870 | 48,097 | 34,128 | +13,969 | +20,230 | +6,261 |
| 1871-1880 | 56,239 | 36,484 | +19,755 | +19,054 | -701 |
| 1881-1890 | 62,375 | 38,424 | +23,951 | +46,565 | +22,614 |
| 1891-1900 | 72,301 | 43,982 | +28,319 | +36,827 | +8,508 |
| 1901-1910 | 76,478 | 44,353 | +32,125 | +17,181 | -14,944 |

(*) Calculations are for the area that subsequently became the Newcastle Registration District

registration of population, can confident estimates be made.[11] The figures prior to 1841 should therefore be treated with extreme caution.

At the end of the 18th century it appears that the city was growing solely through migration gain. This was not enormous, averaging only 269 per year, but sufficient to counter what seems to have been an excess of deaths over births in several years. But by the first decade of the 19th century this situation was reversed and there was migration loss which, despite the surplus of births over deaths, still resulted in an absolute population decline for the town in total. Contemporary accounts[12] and local histories have described the first decade of the century as one of near 'famine conditions' in several years,[13] so outward migration should not be too surprising. The 1810s and 1820s experienced both natural gain and migration gain with the former being more significant. The period from the 1830s to the 1850s was different and was characterised by large influxes of migrants who accounted for more of the increase than the continued surplus of births over deaths. Subsequently, the relative significance of migration's contribution to growth declined and, although the largest number of migrants arrived in the decade of the 1880s (22,614), that number was exceeded by natural increase. Apart from this decade, Newcastle, at the turn of the 19th and 20th centuries, experienced fairly weak migration growth with a period of net loss in the 1870s and a very substantial one in the 1900s.

For each decade from the 1860s, natural gain was substantial. The reasons for these variations are partly because of the fluctuating economic fortunes of the city and partly because, in the longer term, Newcastle reflected national changes in the basic demographic variables. Despite these oscillations, the structure of the population in terms of age and sex remained remarkably constant. In 1851, when census data on ages became available for the first time, 33.9 per cent of the population were aged under 14 years and only 8.3 per cent over 64. The city's population grew marginally 'older' by 1911 but only 9.6 per cent were aged over 64 at that date and 32.2 per cent were under 14. Yet, despite a relatively unchanging age structure, the main demographic variables of marriage, fertility, mortality and migration changed considerably over the same period and earlier.

---

[11] Methods and problems in estimating vital events at the national scale for the pre-civil registration period are discussed in Wrigley, E.A. and Schofield, R.S., *The Population History of England, 1541-1871* (1981). However, it is clear that factors such as non-registration of births and the significance of nonconformity were likely to have been higher in Newcastle than is allowed for in Wrigley and Schofield's *nationally* based formula. See Barke, M., 'The pre-civil registration population of Newcastle', *Division of Geography and Environmental Management, Occasional Paper, no.* 37 (2000) for a discussion of the method of calculation of Newcastle's pre-civil registration births and deaths.

[12] Parson and White, *Directory*, vol.i (1827).

[13] Middlebrook, *Newcastle upon Tyne*, p.164.

## Marriage

In past societies, fluctuations in marriage often represented an important means of controlling fertility, with those oscillations themselves likely to be responses to economic fluctuations.[14] In Newcastle, two possible scales of change in marriage rates may be recognised: one that is short term and a response to economic fluctuations of, say, a few years or even one year; and another which may be regarded as more fundamental, producing a wholly different set of norms.[15]

From Figure 7.1 four broad phases in the period 1754 to 1830 may be identified, one from 1754 to 1762 with, apparently, a relatively low and marginally declining number of marriages. From 1763 to 1795 a moderate and slightly fluctuating number of marriages took place, but fluctuating on an annual basis rather than showing a trend over several years. From 1796 to 1819, *on average* the number of marriages increased but there was a significant negative tendency in the years 1800 and 1801. Finally, from 1820 through to 1830 a further general increase took place, albeit with significant reductions in 1822, 1823 and 1829. There was a remarkably close statistical relationship between the annual number of marriages and coal shipments from Newcastle ( $r = +0.866$ )[16] which indicates that, at this period, local economic fluctuations explain fluctuations in marriage rates. However, an important question is how this relationship changed in the course of the 19th century as the urban economy diversified.

Availability of civil registration data from the 1830s allows a more detailed analysis. There was an upward trend from the 1830s to the mid-1870s (Figure 7.2), albeit with some minor 'dips', most notably in the mid-1840s and later 1860s. The 1870s show considerably more volatility with a tendency to a lower number of marriages, and this subsequently continues. The trends in marriage demonstrate a generally upward trajectory, but it is clear that the overall increase does not parallel the increase in population (in the area covered by the registration district population increased by a factor of 4.5–4.6 between 1831 and 1911 but only by 2.3 in the case of marriages). This implies *either* some fundamental changes in population structure (e.g. age structures or sex ratios), or in Newcastle marriage behaviour itself. The propensity for marriage (i.e. the marriage *rate*) was above the national average although there is a convergence towards the national norms by the later 19th century. The high marriage rate, noted from early in the century, carries on right through to 1871.

[14] Kabir, M., 'Regional variations in nuptiality in England and Wales during the demographic transition', *Genus*, vol. 36 (1980).

[15] Compulsory registration of marriages dated from 1837 with the establishment of the Newcastle Registration District. Prior to this, data are available from the Parish Register Abstracts, published with the decennial censuses from 1801 to 1841.

[16] Coal shipment data are given in Mitchell, B.R. and Deane, P., *Abstract of British Historical Statistics* (1971).

**Figure 7.1    Trend of marriages, pre-civil registration, 1754-1830**

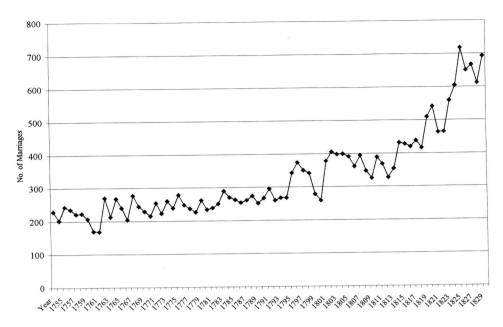

**Figure 7.2    Trend of marriages, 1831-1911**

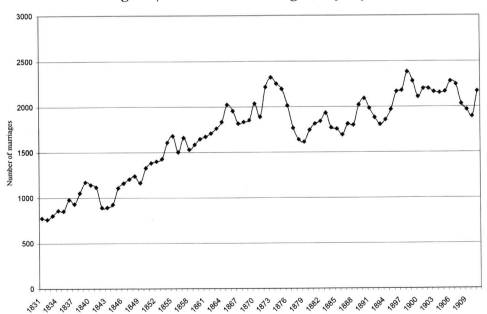

Comparisons with other urban industrial areas[17] confirm this higher propensity for marriage in Newcastle. Only Sheffield approaches the Newcastle marriage rate. As far as marriage is concerned, mid-19th-century Newcastle appears to have entered a completely different demographic regime compared with the 18th and early 19th centuries. However, this greater propensity for marriage could be nothing more than a product of population structure in terms of age and sex.

At all periods from 1861 to 1891 a slightly higher proportion of the total population in Newcastle were either married or widowed, suggesting a greater propensity towards marriage than the national average. The most marked differences occurred in the 20-24 age group. A considerably higher proportion of Newcastle's population in this age group were married than was the case in England and Wales, an excess of 7.1, 9.5, 6.1 and 8.7 percentage points for 1861, 1871, 1881 and 1891 respectively. Similar differences are apparent for the 25-34 age group, also for all four periods. There is very little difference between the figures for Newcastle and those for England and Wales in the middle age groups but for older age groups, especially those over 65, there appears to be a tendency for a greater proportion to be never married in Newcastle than in England and Wales. In other words a reversal of the situation for the younger age groups. This again suggests some important secular changes in marriage patterns in the course of the 19th century. This excess of spinsters and bachelors at the older age groups could, in part, be due to age cohorts passing through the life cycle. That is, they reflect the relatively low marriage rates of the early decades of the century although this, of course, assumes relatively limited geographical mobility. However, the main conclusion to be drawn is that, up until 1891, there was an overall greater propensity for marriage in Newcastle and a tendency to marriage at younger ages. Thereafter, a convergence towards national trends took place.[18]

Neither Newcastle's sex ratio nor its age structure provides particularly significant explanations for this pattern. Detailed investigations of marriage rates at the national scale by Anderson[19] and Woods and Hinde[20] and more localised studies (for example, Haines[21]) have noted the significance of fluctuations in occupational structures and their implications for changes in propensity to marry and marital fertility. In particular, 'the role of female employment outside the home, especially in domestic service

[17] Brown, G., 'Marriage data as indicators of urban prosperity', *Urban History Yearbook* (1978).
[18] The crude marriage rate (marriages per 1,000 people) declined from a mean of 15.7 in 1869-73 to 11.9 in 1879-83, 9.9 in 1889-93, 9.4 in 1899-1903 and 7.8 in 1908-10.
[19] Anderson. M., 'Marriage patterns in Victorian Britain: an analysis based on registration district data for England and Wales, 1861', *Journal of Family History* (1976).
[20] Woods, R.I. and Hinde, P.R.A., 'Nuptiality and age at marriage in 19th-century England', *Journal of Family History* (1985).
[21] Haines, M., *Fertility and Occupation* (1979).

was … important in delaying marriage and reducing the proportion married'.[22] Limited female employment in Newcastle for most of the century could explain the generally high marriage rate. However, from 1891 this declines. Between 1841 and 1911 the proportion of women working at all ages increased from 16.6 per cent to 21.1 per cent and, for those aged over 20, from 20.7 per cent to 25.7 per cent.[23] This represents an increase in the propensity of women to work but such a small increment would, in itself, be unlikely to explain the reduction in marriage rate. More significant was the increase in females employed in domestic service between 1841 and 1891, from 2,785 to 11,038, an increase of 296 per cent. However, the actual proportion of total female employment taken by domestic service actually declined between those two dates, from 65.2 per cent to 38.6 per cent. Potentially more significant than general domestic service, however, is the proportion of *resident* domestic servants, that is, living in the same households in which they were in service. The working environment and conditions of the latter were much more likely to reduce the opportunities for meeting potential partners. Published census data does not make this distinction until 1911 but the unpublished census enumeration books allow such a difference to be calculated. Sample data for 1851 and 1891 show an increase of 6.2 per cent in resident female domestic servants. A slight increase in female activity rates and, especially, an increase in the employment of resident domestic servants in late 19th-century Newcastle served to reduce the overall propensity to marry and encourage a convergence towards national norms.

## Fertility and Mortality

Figure 7.3 shows the total annual births in Newcastle Registration District from 1831 to 1911 and Figure 7.4 the crude birth rate (births per 1,000 total population). The crude birth rate fluctuates quite considerably with a significant fall in the 1840s and a long-term decline beginning in the mid-1870s. The latter is of course, consistent with national trends;[24] the former, however, is somewhat unexpected. Although it could be partially explained by deficiencies in recording in the early years of civil registration,[25] it would be strange if the quality of the data seriously declined. Even if the precise figures may be open to question, evidence suggests a broad trend of birth-rate decline in Newcastle in the 1840s. First, as we have already seen, the

[22] Woods and Hinde, 'Nuptiality and age at marriage', p.120.
[23] Before 1891 employment data is divided into two broad age groups only, those over and those under 20 years. Due to legislation with regard to education, from 1891 employment data is given for those aged over 10 years only. For comparability, therefore, activity rates are calculated for total female population for 1841 and 1911.
[24] Woods, R.I., *The Population of Britain in the Nineteenth Century* (1992).
[25] Glass, D.V., 'Population and population movements in England and Wales, 1700 to 1850', in Glass, D.V. and Eversley, D.E.C. (eds.), *Population in History* (1965).

## Figure 7.3　Total births, 1831-1911

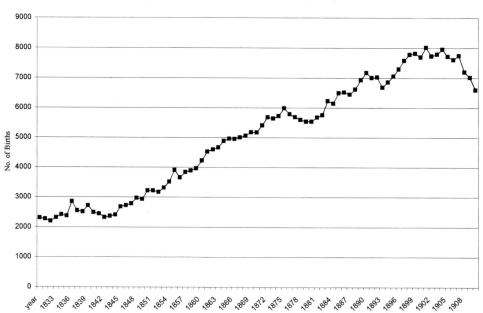

## Figure 7.4　Crude birth rate, 1831-1911

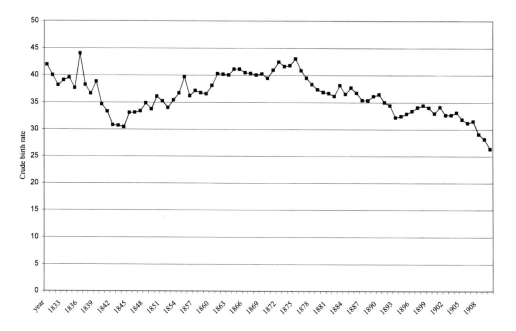

number of marriages 'dipped' in the 1840s (Figure 7.2) as did the marriage rate. It is widely accepted that at this time fertility was largely conditioned by marriage or the expectation of marriage.[26] Conceptions would predominantly take place within marriage or be soon followed by marriage. It follows, therefore, that a decline in the number and rate of marriages would lead to a decline in the number of births and (unless there were significant changes in the behaviour of those already married) declines in the birth rate.

Socially and economically, the 1840s were a very difficult period and the problems of most of that decade were thrown into sharper relief by the fact that the 1830s had been relatively prosperous on Tyneside.[27] During the 1840s, Chartist agitation and the campaign for the repeal of the Corn Laws were fuelled by economic depression and genuine distress.[28] In 1842 it was noted that 'three fourths of the mechanics are out of employment and the demand for labour is less than at any preceding period since the [Poor Law] Union's formation in 1836'.[29] The 1840s decline in the birth rate appears 'real' and the reduction in marriage rate, consequent upon economic hardship, appears to be the main explanation for it.[30]

The other main feature of Figure 7.4 is the decline in the birth rate in the late Victorian period. This, of course, has excited the interest of scholars for many years.[31] However, we can ask, was this also due to reductions in the marriage rate (as in the 1840s) or due to changes in marital fertility? The marriage rate decreased, especially from 1881, and this could be a major contributory factor. However, the increased practice of various forms of birth control within marriage could be equally or more significant.[32]

In the Newcastle case it seems highly likely that the causes were several. The gradually increasing tendency for women to be employed in waged work and, especially, an increase in resident domestic service, combined with the reduced earning power of children stemming from the imposition of state schooling and

[26] Woods, *The Population of Britain*.
[27] McCord, N., 'The implementation of the Poor Law Amendment Act on Tyneside', *International Review of Social History*, vol. xiv (1969).
[28] Middlebrook, *Newcastle upon Tyne*, p.180.
[29] Quoted in Dunkley, P., 'The "Hungry Forties" and the New Poor Law: a case study', *The Historical Journal*, vol. xviii (1974), p.332.
[30] Despite the problems of the 1840s it appears that Newcastle experienced substantial in-migration. This apparent contradiction is explained by two processes. Newcastle was the natural centre of the region and, in times of distress was the one place where relatively 'local' people would be likely to converge in search of the possibility of employment. Secondly, longer distance Irish migration resulted from the famine in the 1840s. For the latter, see MacDermott, T.P., 'Irish workers on Tyneside in the 19th Century' in McCord, N. (ed.), *Essays in Tyneside Labour History* (1977).
[31] Woods, R.I. and Smith, C.W., 'The decline of marital fertility in the late 19th century: the case of England and Wales', *Population Studies*, vol. xxxvii (1983).
[32] For a summary of the debate on the causes of fertility decline in late 19th-century Britain see Szreter, S., *Fertility, Class and Gender in Britain, 1860-1940* (1996).

### Figure 7.5    Total deaths, 1831-1911

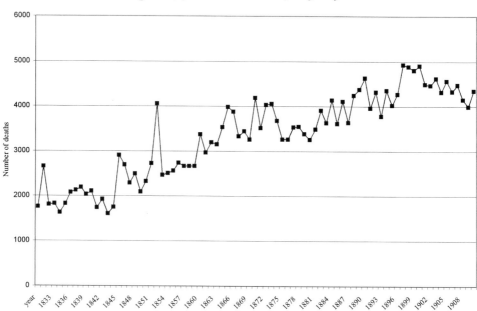

### Figure 7.6    Crude death rate, 1831-1911

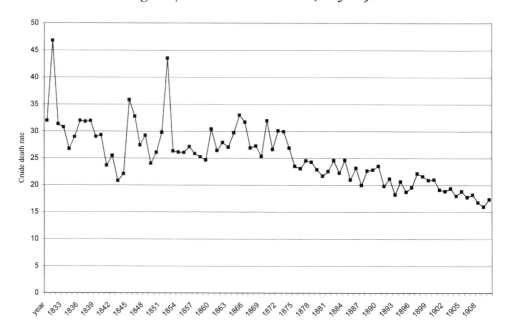

legislation on child labour, played some part in reducing the late Victorian birth rate. But, in order to comprehend fully the changes in fertility we must also consider the changes in mortality as it will be argued here that of particular significance was the increased probability of the survival of offspring who had survived the first year of life.

Figures 7.5 and 7.6 show the number of deaths and crude death rate over the period of civil registration. Up to the 1870s the pattern of death rates is a highly volatile one. Not surprisingly the three major peaks of 'crisis mortality' 1832, 1848-9 and 1853, coincide with cholera epidemics, of which the last 'was the deadliest'.[33] However, other diseases were prevalent and, if less spectacular and less feared, probably more important killers. For example, before the advent of vaccination, almost one quarter of the smallpox admissions to the Newcastle Dispensary in the 1777-1802 period died.[34] Although vaccination reduced the probability, resistance to it remained high, especially amongst the poorer sections of society. Periodic outbreaks caused large numbers of deaths. Between June 1824 and February 1825 over 200 deaths resulted from a smallpox epidemic affecting 1,100 individuals.[35] Dr. Reid noted that for one or two years preceding 1845 'fever' affected 772 people per annum and caused 38 deaths, not in itself a cause for much contemporary concern but the average number of cases had been only 112 per annum in the first quarter of the 19th century.[36] It has been argued that the second quarter of the century was decidedly worse than the first in terms of working-class life chances, 'the worst period being the ten years of the Chartist troubles'.[37] Figure 7.6 does suggest that it is not possible to agree with Woods's statement that 'continuous, albeit slow, improvement in mortality conditions' was experienced by urban Britain from the beginning of the 19th century onwards.[38] Newcastle experienced broad improvement after the 1870s but, prior to this, the pattern is one of considerable variation.

Changes in crude death rates provide a useful long-term summary of mortality but they are strongly influenced by the age structure of the population. Expectation of life at birth ($e_0$ in demographic notation) provides a precise indication of the trend of mortality but requires sophisticated data on the age structure of a total population and ages of death within a specific period. Such data is not obtainable

---

[33] Middlebrook, *Newcastle upon Tyne*, pp.204-5.
[34] Parliamentary Papers, cmnd. 6192, *Third Report of the Royal Commission on Vaccination*, London (1890).
[35] Mackenzie, E., *A Descriptive and Historical Account of the Town and County of Newcastle upon Tyne* (1827), pp.514-15.
[36] Reid, D.B., *Second Report of Commissioners of Inquiry into the State of Large Towns and Populous Districts, Appendix* (1845).
[37] Middlebrook, *Newcastle upon Tyne*, p.204.
[38] Woods, R.I., 'The effects of population redistribution on the level of mortality in 19th-century England and Wales', *Journal of Economic History*, vol. XLV (1985).

for the whole of the century but Table IV compares Newcastle's $e_0$ with a selection of English industrial towns for the time period where appropriate data is available.[39]

### Table IV
### Life Expectancy at birth for English Industrial Cities, 1851-1901

|  | *1851-1860* | *1861-1870* | *1871-1880* | *1881-1890* | *1891-1900* |
|---|---|---|---|---|---|
| Newcastle | 34 | 34 | 37 | 40 | 42 |
| Bristol | 35 | 36 | 37 | 39 | 43 |
| Sheffield | 34 | 33 | 35 | 38 | 39 |
| Leeds | 34 | 34 | 37 | 39 | 41 |
| Bradford | 37 | 36 | 38 | 42 | 44 |
| Birmingham | 35 | 35 | 37 | 39 | 38 |
| Manchester | 30 | 29 | 32 | 35 | 36 |
| Liverpool | 27 | 25 | 28 | 29 | 30 |
| London | 38 | 38 | 40 | 43 | 44 |
| England & Wales | 41 | 41 | 43 | 45 | 46 |

This table presents a grim picture of life chances in 19th-century English towns. All nine places show levels of life expectancy well below the average for England and Wales. Manchester and, especially, Liverpool show the worst decennial figures and the least improvement over the century. Although the experience of Newcastle was not the worst, the combined evidence of Table IV and Figure 7.6 suggests a non-linear pattern of life-chance trends prior to the 1870s. The significance of this in Newcastle's case is that improvement took place precisely when the city was growing to a more significant size and growing most rapidly. Although the data still makes depressing reading, it does seem that Newcastle began to cope with its phase of major growth better than some other large cities. However, earlier in the century when the city was smaller and growing more slowly the picture is one of considerable inconsistency.

A fuller picture of the life chances of the people of Newcastle can be given by examining how the chances of dying varied by age. Information on age-specific death rates and how these changed in the course of the century is shown in Table V. Infant mortality (deaths of children under one year of age), although beginning to decline in the last third of the century, remained high throughout the period. Figure 7.7 shows that the crude infant mortality rate started to decline from a peak in 1871. Did this mean that 'the dangers which beset the path of infant life'[40] started to recede in late 19th-century Newcastle? The answer is only a qualified affirmative –

---

[39] Szreter, S. and Mooney, G., 'Urbanization, mortality, and the standard of living debate: new estimates of the expectation of life at birth in 19th-century British cities', *Economic History Review*, Vol. li (1998).

[40] Armstrong, H., *Medical Officer of Health, Annual Report* (1873), p.6.

## Table V   Age-specific death rates, 1851-1910

*Age-specific death rates (per 1,000)*

| Age group | By year | | | | By decade | | | | | |
|---|---|---|---|---|---|---|---|---|---|---|
| | *1851* | *1861* | *1871* | *1881* | *1851 -60* | *1861 -70* | *1871 -80* | *1881 -90* | *1891 -1900* | *1901 -10* |
| Under 1 | 220 | 189 | 223 | 170 | - | 231 | 223 | 162 | 173 | 143 |
| 1-4 | 52 | 71 | 56 | 40 | 91(*) | 87 | 41 | 33 | 30 | 26 |
| 5-9 | 7 | 14 | 15 | 8 | 11 | 12 | 9 | 7 | 5 | 5 |
| 10-14 | 4 | 7 | 8 | 5 | 5 | 5 | 5 | 4 | 3 | 3 |
| 15-19 | | 7 | 10 | 6 | 8 | 8 | 7 | 5 | 5 | 4 |
| 20-24 | 7 | 9 | 16 | 7 | 9 | 9 | 9 | 7 | 6 | 5 |
| 25-34 | 11 | 12 | 15 | 9 | 12 | 12 | 11 | 10 | 8 | 7 |
| 35-44 | 14 | 17 | 19 | 14 | 18 | 17 | 17 | 15 | 14 | 12 |
| 45-54 | 24 | 24 | 25 | 20 | 23 | 24 | 23 | 22 | 22 | 20 |
| 55-64 | 39 | 42 | 42 | 36 | 41 | 42 | 42 | 40 | 39 | 37 |
| 65-74 | 74 | 82 | 82 | 85 | 81 | 80 | 80 | 79 | 77 | 75 |
| 75 + | 219 | 196 | 198 | 164 | 291 | 191 | 183 | 164 | 166 | 158 |

(*) Deaths of children under 5 only

## Figure 7.7   Infant mortality rate, 1831-1911

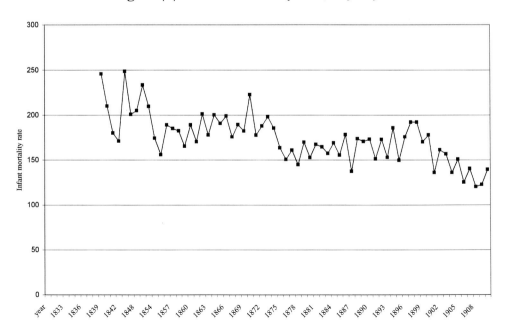

(a)

(b)

qualified by the fact that virtually each year from 1840 to 1906 over 25 per cent of all deaths in the Newcastle registration district were of children under one year of age. The main exception was 1853, when cholera was rife and carrying off people of all ages, but, even in this year, deaths of children under one amounted to 18 per cent of all deaths. But infant mortality also increased somewhat in the 1890s (Figure 7.7), a phenomenon that has been noted in other large urban areas and largely attributed to 'climatic conditions, especially during the third quarter of the year [which] interacted with poor urban sanitary environments which resulted in high levels of diarrhoea and dysentery among infants'.[41] Child mortality (children under five) started to improve substantially in the 1870s, and as the probability of survival of children grew (once having negotiated the perilous first year of life), their potential contribution to the household income declined and their relative 'cost' increased.[42] The desire to limit the number of children, therefore, by one means or another, was likely to increase. In this way, mortality trends were intimately linked to the decline in fertility discussed earlier.

Under the influence of Henry Armstrong, Newcastle's first appointed Medical Officer of Health, 'sanitary reform' proceeded more rapidly in the last quarter of

[41] Woods, R.I., Watterson, P.A. and Woodward, J.H., 'The causes of rapid infant mortality decline in England and Wales, 1861-1921, Part 1', *Population Studies*, vol. xxxii (1988), p.360.
[42] Tranter, N., *Population Since the Industrial Revolution: The Case of England and Wales* (1973).

(c)

**7.1**  From Henry Armstrong, Medical Officer of Health,
Photographs Relating to Public Health 1894-1912:
  (a)  'A convenience', Prudhoe Place.
  (b)  Typical shared convenience at entrance to
        tenement block, Waller's Yard, Forth Banks.
  (c)  Ballast discharging into back of Leighton's yard,
        jerry-built housing at bottom of Byker Bank.
  (d)  Ouseburn tip.
  (e)  Addy's Entry, Sellar's Entry, Sandgate.

(d)

(e)

the century and determined attempts were at last made to ensure that 'a vast amount of misery, disease, poverty, and death … be prevented by the introduction of suitable sanatory [*sic*] regulation'.[43] Reid's report of 1845 noted the lack of regulations for drainage, street cleansing and sewage disposal and observed that over thirty Newcastle streets, some of them new and in quite salubrious parts of the town, were lacking in drainage and sewerage, despite all paying rates. However, it was the poorer and more low-lying parts of the town where conditions were worst: 'some of these, as Sandgate, comprise … the most densely populated portions of the town, with a large excess of impurities beyond those produced in it'.[44] Only nine per cent of households were directly supplied with water[45] and, dangerously, the main supply was from the River Tyne, a factor which the 1854 cholera inquiry demonstrated was responsible for the severity of the outbreak.[46]

There was, therefore, substantial room for improvement from this appalling sanitary (or insanitary) base. Yet it was not until 1865 that the Town Improvement Act provided the Corporation with the necessary powers to control building, sewerage and street cleansing.[47] By the 1880s it appears that substantial progress had been made and Daunton noted that, by 1914, it was a rare Newcastle house that did not have a piped water supply.[48] This factor, more than any other, allowed a major change in the system of sewage disposal, with water closets replacing other methods. The steady and, in the 1890s, rapidly increasing annual expenditure on the provision of sewers reflects this determined assault on the sanitary condition of the city. The length of sewers increased from 122.3 miles in 1889 (1.149 yards per capita) to 275.4 miles in 1913 (1.932 yards per capita).[49]

Although Armstrong and others linked the improvement in death rates with sanitary improvements,[50] these changes were spatially and socially differentiated. Improvement took place but it was not uniform across the city. Table VI shows change in death rates and some associated phenomena for the last two decades of the century. Even new house building, with at least the possibility of providing modern sanitary conveniences, did not necessarily lead to improvement. Byker grew significantly between 1881 and 1901 but its death rate actually increased between those two dates. Westgate, on the other hand, also experienced substantial new

[43]   Reid, *Second Report of Commissioners*, p.124.
[44]   Reid, *Second Report of Commissioners*, p.157.
[45]   *Ibid.*, p.162.
[46]   *Report of the Commissioners Appointed to Inquire into the causes which have led to, or have aggravated the late outbreak of Cholera in the Towns of Newcastle-upon-Tyne, Gateshead and Tynemouth* (1854); Callcott, M., 'The challenge of cholera: the last epidemic at Newcastle upon Tyne', *Northern History*, vol. xx (1984).
[47]   Smith, J., 'Public health on Tyneside, 1850-80', pp.25-46 in McCord, *Essays in Tyneside Labour History*.
[48]   Daunton, M.J., *House and Home in the Victorian City: Working Class Housing, 1850-1914* (1983).
[49]   City Engineer, Annual Reports, 1889-1913.
[50]   Daunton, *House and Home*.

**Table VI Death rates by Registration Sub-Districts, 1881-1901**[51]

|  | Death rate (per 1,000) | | Population per acre | | Inhabitants per tap |
|---|---|---|---|---|---|
|  | *1881* | *1901* | *1881* | *1901* | *1883-85* |
| Westgate | 21.8 | 16.6 | 59.5 | 88.3 | 109.0 |
| St Andrews | 18.0 | 17.7 | 12.7 | 12.2 | 85.0 |
| St Nicholas | 27.1 (*) | 45.6 (*) | 76.6 | 44.4 | 84.5 |
| All Saints | 22.2 | 22.2 | 116.3 | 91.3 | 71.6 |
| Byker | 17.1 | 17.6 | 12.0 | 34.3 | 49.8 |
| City | 21.7 | 21.2 | 21.1 | 32.0 |  |

(*) Excluding deaths in hospital

construction and its death rate fell by over five percentage points. In more central locations, both All Saints and St Nicholas sub-districts declined substantially in population and housing densities but, mainly due to an ageing population, their death rates either remained static, as in the case of the former, or increased, as in the case of the latter. Across substantial parts of the city overcrowding remained a huge problem.[52] At the level of the registration sub-districts, therefore, it is difficult to discern any direct relationship between housing and population densities, between likely sanitary conditions (as reflected in 'modern' housing construction) and mortality trends.

It is possible that the pattern of mortality from some important diseases reflected more local conditions (Figure 7.8). Deaths from three diseases only (typhoid, scarlet fever and diphtheria) are mapped here but their significance was considerable and over the period 1870 to 1901 deaths from these three diseases correlated positively with deaths from other causes. However, as other authors have found,[53] the patterns (of the three diseases separately and in combination) fail to correlate significantly with social and sanitary indicators such as housing and population density, households per dwelling, mean household size, proportion of migrants, proportion of Irish-born and the sex ratio. It appears that socio-environmental conditions do not fully explain disease trends and patterns. As well as considerable sanitary improvement, changes in the overall standard of living were also a major explanation for improved life chances for many, especially for children under five (having survived their first year of life) and older people. Improvements in nutrition especially would be likely to increase resistance to a number of infectious diseases.

[51] Medical Officer of Health Annual Reports, 1881-1901.
[52] Barke, M., 'Newcastle/Tyneside 1890-1980', in Gordon, G. (ed.), *Regional Cities in the UK, 1890-1980* (1986).
[53] Pooley, M.E. and Pooley, C.G., 'Health, society and environment in Victorian Manchester', pp.148-75 in Woods, R.I and Woodward, J. (eds.), *Urban Disease and Mortality in Nineteenth Century England* (1984); Woods, R.I., 'Mortality and sanitary conditions in the "Best governed city in the world" – Birmingham, 1870-1910', *Journal of Historical Geography*, vol. iv (1978).

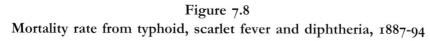

Figure 7.8
Mortality rate from typhoid, scarlet fever and diphtheria, 1887-94

Throughout the period 1850 to 1914 the north east region was generally characterised by high wages.[54] However, high wages could easily be offset by a higher cost of living and the lack of alternative sources of family income. Most obvious amongst the latter was the lack of female employment opportunities. In 1891, for example, the average proportion of females occupied in Newcastle was 28.7 per cent compared with a national average of 34.4 per cent[55] and much of this female employment was in extremely lowly paid sectors such as domestic service, various forms of retailing, dressmaking and laundering. Of the various components of the cost of living it is clear that, as one would expect given the shortage of accommodation, rents were comparatively high,[56] but it seems likely that the cost of food and other necessities of life were lower than in many locations. Coal, for example, cost between 8d. to 1s. per cwt. compared with 1s. to 2s. 2d. in London.[57] General trends in the costs of distribution worked to favour urban areas in the 19th century[58] and, as a port and a major cattle market from 1836, Newcastle benefited from these trends.

The 1908 Board of Trade Enquiry noted: 'The shopping facilities in Newcastle appear to be good, and to allow the customer a very wide range of choice ... the strength of the co-operative society, which has numerous branches throughout the

[54] Hunt, E.H., *Regional Wage Variations in Britain* (1973).
[55] *Ibid.*, p.123.
[56] *Report of an Enquiry by the Board of Trade into Working Class Rents, Housing and Retail Prices*, cmnd. 3864 (1908), pp.321-2.
[57] *Ibid.*, p.324.
[58] Hunt, *Regional Wage Variations*, p.96.

city, must be specially mentioned.'[59] CWS membership in 1905 was 20,000, probably representing an equivalent number of households, implying that over a third of the city's households were members and stood to benefit from guaranteed supplies, good quality, and fair prices, with the accompanying improvements in diet.[60] Also, the traditional source of working-class food distribution – street markets – continued to thrive: 'In the centre of the city also are the large and important covered markets, where, on Saturdays, a big *and almost exclusively working-class trade* [my emphasis] is carried on in meat, vegetables, groceries, provisions, and an indescribable variety of small articles'.[61] However, as Scola[62] has demonstrated, fixed shops also played an important role in the distribution of foodstuffs from early in the century. Table VII shows the trend of change in Newcastle's food shops throughout the 19th century.

The ratio of shops to population and the rate of growth fall away towards the end of the century (although the latter does increase in the last decade), mainly because shops became larger units carrying more stock. This was especially the case in the grocery trade, partly due to the growth of the Co-operative Societies. However,

### Table VII  Growth in food shops in Newcastle, 1827-1901
(population per shop in brackets)

|  | 1827 | 1838 | 1855 | 1869/70 | 1881/2 | 1890 | 1900 |
|---|---|---|---|---|---|---|---|
| Bakers & confectioners | 43 (1,255.8) | 54 (1,236.1) | 67 (1,431.5) | 123 (1,027.7) | 139 (1,080.9) | 200 (960.0) | 309 (743.6) |
| Butchers, tripe dealers, poulterers | 153 (352.9) | 181 (368.8) | 227 (422.5) | 292 (432.9) | 311 (483.1) | 347 (553.3) | 408 (563.2) |
| Fruiterers & greengrocers | 11 (4,909.1) | 26 (2,567.4) | 61 (1,572.3) | 96 (1,316.7) | 146 (1,029.1) | 197 (974.6) | 237 (969.5) |
| Fishmongers | - | - | 15 (6,393.9) | 21 (6,019.4) | 27 (5,564.9) | 29 (6,620.6) | 59 (3,894.6) |
| Grocers & provision dealers | 192 (281.3) | 238 (280.5) | 619 (154.9) | 752 (168.1) | 773 (194.4) | 716 (268.2) | 703 (326.9) |
| Total | 399 (135.3) | 499 (137.3) | 989 (97.0) | 1,284 (98.5) | 1,396 (107.6) | 1,489 (128.9) | 1,716 (133.9) |

% change per annum in shop numbers over the previous year

|  | 1827 | 1838 | 1855 | 1869/70 | 1881/2 | 1890 | 1900 |
|---|---|---|---|---|---|---|---|
|  |  | + 2.3 | + 5.8 | + 2.0 | +0.8 | +0.7 | +1.5 |

Source: Directories of Newcastle upon Tyne

[59] *Report of an Enquiry* (1908), *op. cit.*, p.323.
[60] *Newcastle upon Tyne: A Handbook of the 41st Annual Co-operative Congress* (1909).
[61] *Report of an Enquiry* (1908).
[62] Scola, R., *Feeding the Victorian City: the Food Supply of Manchester, 1770-1870* (1992), p.55.

outlets selling fish, fresh fruit, vegetables and bread, commodities that were likely to have been significant in relation to health, improved their population per shop ratio over the period. Food inspection also led to improvements in the quality of produce on sale,[63] especially compared with the third quarter of the century when problems of adulteration were especially severe.[64] Evidence from local authority inspections of food suppliers suggests that Newcastle was likely to share in this overall improvement towards the end of the century. Retail bakehouses were systematically inspected every six months from the 1880s and samples of butchers' meat, fish and milk were tested for adulteration.[65] Therefore, whilst various sanitary improvements played some role in reducing the mortality levels of late 19th-century Newcastle, this took place against an overall improvement in the standard of living and the availability of better produce, features which must have increased resistance to disease and illness.

## Migration

The study of 19th-century migration from published census volumes is handicapped by four major general problems. First, data is only available from 1841 onwards. Second, because the data relates to place of birth it is only possible from this source to comment on 'lifetime' migration rather than the total moves made by any individual. Third, apart from 1911, the birthplace data itself relates to county of birth rather than actual place of birth. Fourth, the spatial units for which figures are given are not consistent throughout the century, sometimes relating to parishes (1841), sometimes to registration districts (1851 and 1861), sometimes to urban sanitary districts (1881, 1891), sometimes to municipal and parliamentary districts (1871) and, later, county boroughs (1901 and 1911). Some of these defects can be rectified through painstaking analysis of census enumeration books yet, despite the difficulties, it is possible to give a broad indication of trends in migration in Newcastle (Table VIII).

This is a picture of apparent remarkable stability with a consistent proportion of Newcastle's population – about one third or just over – being born in a county other than Northumberland. A further major specific problem with using county of birth stems from Newcastle's location on the north bank of the river that provides the geographic boundary between Northumberland and Durham. In comparison with other places this could serve to 'exaggerate' the apparent proportion of migrants in Newcastle – a short distance move from Gateshead to Newcastle (highly likely)

[63] Scola, R., *Feeding the Victorian City: the Food Supply of Manchester, 1770-1870* (1992), p. 267.
[64] Burnett, J., *Plenty and Want: A Social History of Diet in England from 1815 to the Present Day* (1979).
[65] Medical Officer of Health, Annual reports, 1881/2 –1912/13.

### Table VIII    Birthplaces of Newcastle residents, 1841-1911

| Date | Number not born in county of residence | % not born in county of residence |
|---|---|---|
| 1841(*) | 23,099 | 32.2 |
| 1851(*) | 33,167 | 37.2 |
| 1861(*) | 40,938 | 36.9 |
| 1871($) | 46,149 | 35.9 |
| 1881(#) | 49,304 | 33.9 |
| 1891(#) | 65,741 | 35.3 |
| 1901(+) | 75,290 | 35.0 |
| 1911(+) | 89,427 | 33.5 |

(*) Registration District of Newcastle ($) Municipal and Parliamentary District
(#) Urban Sanitary District      (+) County Borough

being recorded, whilst moves of similar distance within the county boundary not being so recorded. Nevertheless, Table VIII tells us that approximately two-thirds of the population of Newcastle were born within Northumberland with a further significant proportion likely to have been born in County Durham. Availability of more detailed birth-place data for 1911, and sample data from the 1851 and 1891 census enumeration books, allows us to shed more light on this crude picture. In 1911, 57.7 per cent of Newcastle's population were born within the city. In 1851, 44 per cent of the sample were born in Newcastle and in 1891, 54 per cent. Whilst at mid-century migrants from elsewhere outnumbered those born in the town,[66] this situation was not the norm for Newcastle.

County Durham was, of course, the major source area, but it should be noted that it received more migrants from Northumberland than *vice versa*. Contrary to the received wisdom that male migration was the more significant, a factor usually explained in labour-market terms, female migrants from Durham to Newcastle consistently outnumbered male migrants. Despite overall generally low female activity rates in Newcastle, job opportunities were even fewer in County Durham and it seems likely that, in this case, female migration may also be explained by labour market forces. Once again, the overall impression conveyed by Table IX is consistency. The origins of movements to Newcastle remained largely unchanged with the possible exception of the decline in the proportion of Irish-born and a significant increase in County Durham-born people in the first decade of the 20th century. Three further observations are noteworthy. First, distance appears to have been a major factor in the geographical pattern of movement. There was very little long-distance movement into Newcastle. Secondly, although the proportions born in

[66]  Anderson, M., *Family Structure in Nineteenth Century Lancashire* (1971).

### Table IX   Some birthplaces of Newcastle (*) residents

| Date | % of population born in | | | | | | |
|---|---|---|---|---|---|---|---|
| | Northumberland (Newcastle in 1911) | | Cumberland & Westmorland | | Ireland | | Overseas |
| | | Durham | | Scotland | | London | |
| 1851 | 62.8 | 11.1 | 3.1 | 6.5 | 8.0 | 1.3 | 0.7 |
| 1861 | 63.1 | 11.1 | 3.1 | 5.5 | 6.8 | 1.3 | 1.9 |
| 1871 | 64.1 | 10.5 | 3.1 | 6.9 | 5.4 | 1.4 | 1.2 |
| 1881 | 66.1 | 10.6 | 2.6 | 6.0 | 3.8 | 1.4 | 1.2 |
| 1891 | 64.7 | 12.0 | 2.4 | 4.9 | 2.6 | 1.3 | 1.4 |
| 1901 | 65.0 | 12.4 | 2.3 | 5.7 | 1.8 | 1.3 | 1.8 |
| 1911 | 66.5 (57.7) | 15.5 | 2.2 | 4.5 | 1.5 | 1.1 | 1.4 |

(*) 'Newcastle' is defined as for the same years in Table VIII

Cumberland and Westmorland appear to be small, they do represent a substantial relative flow when one remembers the overall low populations of those source counties. Third, it is clear that Newcastle was not a particularly 'cosmopolitan' city as the proportion of foreign-born remained low (with larger populations, Leeds, Liverpool and Manchester all recorded over 2 per cent overseas born in 1911, and London 4.7 per cent). The fact that it could be claimed in 1863 that 'in Newcastle … a Negro is treated as a man and a brother'[67] probably owed much to the extreme rarity of coloured people in the city. Therefore, whilst migration clearly made a substantial contribution to overall population growth, most of that migration was very short range. In this sense, then, the Moore family, introduced at the beginning of the chapter, was quite typical, one parent being born in Walker and the other in Gateshead.

Most studies of migration simply concern themselves with the area of destination but we should not forget either that a significant number of Newcastle people were living elsewhere: 87,328 or 33 per cent of the 1911 population to be precise. Table X shows some of the main destinations of these 'exiled' Novocastrians. In every case apart from Middlesbrough the number of females exceeds the number of males. However, although a large number of Newcastle-born individuals may have been living elsewhere, it does not necessarily follow that they would have stayed there. Figure 7.9 shows the pattern of return migration. We can trace these patterns of movement through the places of birth of their children: 4.8 per cent of the sampled households in 1851 and 6.3 per cent in 1891 fell into this category of return migrants.

[67]   Quoted in Todd, N., 'Black on Tyne: the black presence on Tyneside in the 1860s', *North East Labour History*, vol. xxi (1987).

### Table x  Places of residence of Newcastle-born, 1911

| | *Numbers of Newcastle-born* | | |
| | *Male* | *Female* | *Total* |
| --- | --- | --- | --- |
| Northumberland (*) | 10,300 | 11,433 | 21,733 |
| Cumberland (*) | 1,073 | 1,279 | 2352 |
| Durham (*) | 7,946 | 8,105 | 16,051 |
| Yorkshire (*) | 1,321 | 1,578 | 2,899 |
| Gateshead | 5,747 | 6,229 | 11,976 |
| South Shields | 1,164 | 1,478 | 2,642 |
| Sunderland | 1,036 | 1,260 | 2,296 |
| Liverpool | 338 | 387 | 725 |
| Manchester | 386 | 472 | 858 |
| Leeds | 414 | 543 | 957 |
| Middlesbrough | 455 | 395 | 850 |
| London | 1,985 | 2,253 | 4,238 |

(*) County figures exclude numbers for County Boroughs

### Figure 7.9  Return migrants to Newcastle, 1851-91

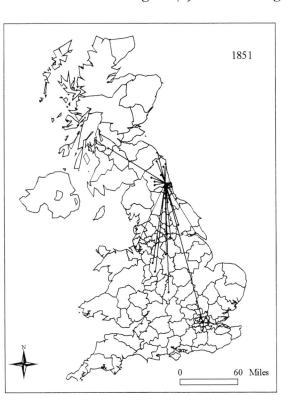
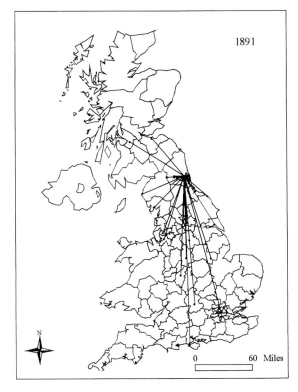

The received wisdom is that migration was a major, often destabilising influence, mainly involving younger males, focused largely on a limited number of 'magnet' locations, principally the growing industrial cities. The Newcastle analysis suggests that migration to and from Newcastle was much more fluid than this. In general terms the pattern appears to be one of short-term fluctuations (Table III) against a background of overall stability (Table VIII). These short-term fluctuations reflect stresses in local labour markets and the migratory response to these represents, not a mindless coming and going, but a quite sophisticated pattern of labour market behaviour. The evidence on return migration and extremely local movement from and within 'industrial Tyneside' points in the same direction. Frequent, short-range, movement may have owed something to the nature of labour recruitment in some industries, especially shipbuilding, where only 'royals' or key workers tended to stay with one firm but 'other men move about the river a great deal', and 'there are large numbers of men very irregularly employed, even in moderately good years'.[68] Improved public transport and the availability of cheap 'workmen's tickets' by the end of the century facilitated local moving about,[69] but it is still likely that changes in place of residence would often follow relocation of employment.

Darroch has argued that, far from the individualistic (usually male), rootless drift into the cities, 'migration was very often undertaken within family and kinship networks, or by whole families'.[70] Similarly, Schurer[71] has demonstrated the role of the whole family in migration patterns and Anderson has provided evidence that 'Migrants were … quite likely … to have living in their households kin who must either have preceded them, come with them *as kin*, or come to join them in the town.'[72] Table XI shows the range of kin-folk in Newcastle in 1851 and 1891 sharing accommodation with households whose head was born in Newcastle and those who were migrants. In 1851, 16.8 per cent of all households had kin living with them and for households with a non-Newcastle-born head the proportion is 16.4 per cent. In 1891 the corresponding figures are 18.2 per cent and 17.9 per cent. In addition, a further 7.7 per cent of households had 'visitors' staying with them at the time of the census of 1851 and 9.7 per cent had resident lodgers. By 1891 the proportion of households with 'visitors' had declined to only 3.7 per cent but 12.7 per cent of households had lodgers staying with them. The evidence is in accord

[68] Mess, H.A., *Industrial Tyneside: A Social Survey* (1928).

[69] Barke, M., 'The development of public transport in Newcastle upon Tyne and Tyneside, 1850-1914', *Journal of Regional and Local Studies*, vol. xii (1992).

[70] Darroch, A.G., 'Migrants in the 19th century: Fugitives or families in motion?', *Journal of Family History* (1981), p.257.

[71] Schurer, K., 'The role of the family in the process of migration', pp.106-42 in Pooley, C.G. and Whyte, I.D. (eds.), *Migrants, Emigrants and Immigrants: A Social History of Migration* (1991).

[72] Anderson, *Family Structure*, p.152.

## Table XI
## Co-residing kin-folk; relationship to Household Head, 1851 and 1891

| | 1851 | | 1891 | |
|---|---|---|---|---|
| Relationship to household head | Head of household Newcastle-born | Head non-Newcastle-born | Head of household Newcastle-born | Head non-Newcastle-born |
| Aunt/uncle | 2 | 6 | 1 | 5 |
| Brother/brother in law | 19 | 42 | 31 | 39 |
| Sister/sister in law | 36 | 61 | 41 | 53 |
| Mother/mother in law | 13 | 32 | 31 | 43 |
| Father/father in law | 5 | 12 | 8 | 11 |
| Grandson/daughter | 30 | 66 | 46 | 97 |
| Niece/nephew | 26 | 68 | 46 | 58 |
| Son/daughter in law | 7 | 25 | 9 | 28 |
| Stepson/daughter | 4 | 7 | 22 | 21 |
| Grandparent | 0 | 1 | 0 | 4 |
| Cousin | 2 | 6 | 4 | 11 |
| 'relative' | 0 | 5 | 3 | 5 |
| Orphan | 1 | 1 | 0 | 0 |
| Total | 145 | 332 | 242 | 375 |

with Anderson's conclusion that a 'considerable attempt [was] made by migrants to maintain relationships with kin',[73] although Newcastle-born households also had a high proportion of resident kin-folk, reflecting the overall shortage of housing accommodation in the city.

The pattern of birth of children for two migrant groups – the Scots and the Irish – is also of interest in this investigation of the role of the family in migration. For example, in 1851, of the 82 households with both parents born in Ireland, 55 per cent had children born in Ireland. That is, they had migrated as a family. Of the 67 households with just one parent born in Ireland, 45 per cent had children born in Ireland. The corresponding figures for Scottish households were 76 per cent (45 households with both parents born in Scotland) and 18 per cent (136 households with just one parent born in Scotland). These figures tend to undermine the stereotype of the single, male migrant and suggest that whole families were migrating together.[74]

Figures 7.10 and 7.11 show the distribution of non-Newcastle-born, Irish-born and Scottish-born by enumeration district for 1851 and 1891. The strongest concentrations of non-Newcastle-born in 1851 were in districts around the Central

[73] *Ibid.*, p.160.
[74] Byrne, D., 'Immigrants and the formation of the North Eastern industrial working class: another venue for the "wild west show"', *North East Labour History*, vol. xxx (1996).

**7.2** Tyneside Scottish, 1915.

Station and St Nicholas church, for example in Forth Street, Orchard Street, Hanover
Street and Square, Clavering Place, Westgate Street, Denton Chare, St Nicholas
Square and King Street. Although the Irish presence was significant in some of
these streets, their strongest concentration was nearer the river in All Saints district,
particularly in Sandgate, Wall Knoll, Pandon Bank, St Ann's Street, New Road,
Silver Street, and the bottom of Pilgrim Street. Scottish-born migrants in 1851 were
more widely distributed but particular concentrations existed in the inner part of
Westgate district, in Wellington Street, Spring Garden Terrace, Pitt Street (many
were neighbours of the Moore family), Blenheim Street, Churchill Street,
Marlborough Crescent and Street, Sunderland Street, Blandford Street, George Street
and Back George Street. Further out from the city centre but still in the western
sector, small concentrations of Scots were present in New Mills and Todd's Nook.
Within the central and older parts of Newcastle in 1851, therefore, there existed
three distinct clusters of non-local-born migrants, living relatively separately from
each other *and* from indigenous residents. This is not to say that other forms of
contact would not take place, for example at workplaces or in leisure pursuits, but
this residential concentration does suggest a strong degree of segmentation in mid-
19th-century Newcastle.

To what extent did this characteristic persist prior to 1891? The strongest
concentrations of non-local-born were quite clearly further away from the city core,
especially in parts of Elswick, Benwell and Scotswood in the west and Ouseburn,

**Figure 7.10**

(a) Percentage of population non-Newcastle born, 1851 (excluding Irish and Scottish born)

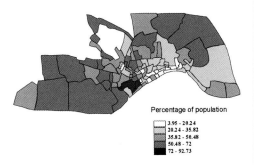

**Figure 7.11**

(a) Percentage of population non-Newcastle born, 1891 (excluding Irish and Scottish born)

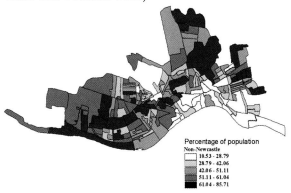

(b) Percentage of population born in Ireland, 1851

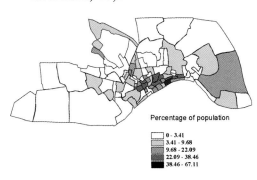

(b) Percentage of population born in Ireland, 1891

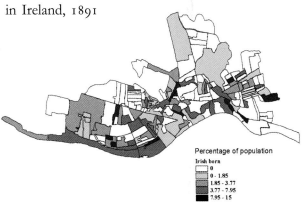

(c) Percentage of population born in Scotland, 1851

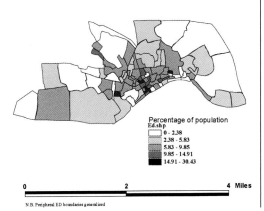

(c) Percentage of population born in Scotland, 1891

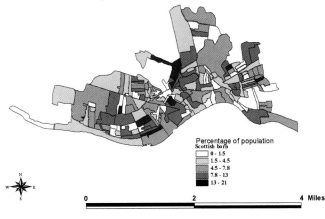

N.B. Peripheral ED boundaries generalised

Byker Bank and Byker village in the east. Industrial expansion along the river produced a decentralisation of workers out of the city, many of whom were not born in Newcastle. However, local migrants from adjacent areas, some rural but the majority from other parts of 'industrial Tyneside', also augmented the populations of these areas. The Irish-born were fewer and clearly much more dispersed than 40 years earlier, as were the Scots. However, the latter were still mainly living in the western sector of the city, in the newer 'respectable' working-class housing developed from the 1870s onwards.[75]

To a large extent, these residential distribution patterns relate closely to the labour market characteristics of the different groups. The occupational structures of the Irish and Scottish immigrants to Newcastle are compared in Table XII for the 1851 and 1891 household samples.

### Table XII   Occupational classes of Irish- and Scottish-born residents of Newcastle, 1851 and 1891 (%)

|  | Irish-born | | Scottish-born | |
|---|---|---|---|---|
|  | *1851* | *1891* | *1851* | *1891* |
| A. *Labouring class:* | | | | |
| Labourers | 57.9 | 47.7 | 14.1 | 13.8 |
| Domestic service, laundresses, dressmakers | 7.2 | 4.7 | 4.1 | 2.7 |
| Coal miners & quarrymen | - | 2.3 | 1.2 | 0 |
| Transport workers | 2.6 | 1.2 | 7.6 | 3.7 |
| B. *Artisan class:* | | | | |
| Skilled manual, factory based | 3.9 | 8.1 | 14.1 | 17.0 |
| Other skilled manual | 7.2 | 9.3 | 14.7 | 19.7 |
| C. *Retail trade:* | | | | |
| Hawkers, assistants | 5.3 | 1.2 | 2.9 | 3.7 |
| Fixed shopkeepers | 13.2 | 9.3 | 26.5 | 16.0 |
| D. *Clerical workers* | 0.7 | 4.7 | 2.9 | 4.3 |
| E. *Managerial, professional and employers* | 2.0 | 9.3 | 11.2 | 16.5 |
| *Living on own means* | - | 2.3 | 0.6 | 2.7 |

Although some detailed changes took place over the 40-year period – for example, the increase in skilled manual Irish workers – the contrast between the two groups is obvious. Labouring and related occupations dominated the Irish employment structure; whilst the Scots were also represented in this category, their modes of occupation were much more varied, being strongly present in the skilled artisan category at both dates and also in retailing and middle-class occupations.

---

[75] Benwell Community Project, 'Private housing and the working class', *Final Report Series*, No. 3 (1978).

Links between the city's social structure and the origins of its population have rarely been considered. It is to this issue that we shall now turn by examining the changing nature of households and families.

## Households and Families

In the section on marriage we examined the broad trends in propensity to marry but the question of who was marrying whom was not dealt with. Of particular interest to the history of modern Newcastle is the issue of inter-marriage of people from different origins. Table XIII provides information on this by places of origin of spouses for 1851 and 1891. What is striking is the relatively low proportion of 'Newcastle only' marriages at both dates and the relatively high degree of inter-marriage of people from different origins.

**Table XIII   Inter-marriage between various groups, 1851 and 1891**

|  | *1851* | | *1891* | |
|---|---|---|---|---|
|  | *No.* | *%* | *No.* | *%* |
| Husband & wife born in Newcastle | 212 | 11.1 | 348 | 16.1 |
| Husband and wife born in Ireland | 98 | 5.1 | 35 | 1.6 |
| Husband and wife born in Scotland | 63 | 3.3 | 70 | 3.2 |
| Husband & wife born elsewhere (1) | 816 | 42.5 | 859 | 39.6 |
| One spouse born in Newcastle, the other elsewhere(2) | 483 | 25.2 | 586 | 27.0 |
| One spouse born in Ireland, the other elsewhere (3) | 72 | 3.8 | 77 | 3.6 |
| One spouse born in Scotland, the other elsewhere (4) | 162 | 8.4 | 181 | 8.4 |
| One spouse born in Scotland, the other in Ireland | 12 | 0.6 | 11 | 0.5 |

(1) excluding those born in Newcastle, Ireland and Scotland (2) excluding those born in Ireland or Scotland (3) excluding those born in Scotland (4) excluding those born in Ireland

One of the most persistent generalisations about the course of 19th-century industrialisation and urbanisation is that these processes disrupted former kinship structures. Some mid-20th-century sociology stressed the disorganisation of the city and the alleged replacement of intimate, 'primary' relationships with superficial, 'secondary' ones.[76] Similarly, the authors of the Royal Commission on Population observed in 1949 that the industrial revolution broke up 'The old settled ways of life, in which ties of family and community were strong ... They were ... succeeded by an intense, competitive struggle in which the emphasis was increasingly placed on the individual rather than the community.'[77] Contemporary views of

[76] Wirth, L., 'Urbanism as a way of life', *American Journal of Sociology*, vol. xliv (1938).
[77] Royal Commission on Population, *Report* (1949).

industrialisation went so far as to suggest that the working-class family was breaking down,[78] but more recently, economic historians have suggested instead that industrial urbanism destroyed 'the extended family/domestic mode of production' only to replace it by the nuclear family.[79] The work of Smelser on the growth of the Lancashire cotton industry is particularly associated with this interpretation.[80] The Moore family introduced above were clearly a strong and large nuclear family: our question is, to what extent were they typical of 19th-century Newcastle?

## Table XIV
### Some types of household and family structure in Newcastle, 1851 and 1891

|  | 1851 | | 1891 | |
|---|---|---|---|---|
|  | No. | % | No. | % |
| 1 person households | 90 | 4.7 | 63 | 2.9 |
| 2 person households; not related | 71 | 3.7 | 56 | 2.6 |
| 2 person households; related | 294 | 15.3 | 163 | 7.5 |
| Childless married couples | 286 | 14.9 | 315 | 14.5 |
| Married couples with children | 1177 | 61.4 | 1570 | 72.5 |
| Total | 1918 | 100.0 | 2167 | 100.0 |

Although Table XIV does not give a complete picture of household and family structure it is clear that the conventional nuclear family dominated and, despite the rapid growth of Newcastle, this changed only a little in the later part of the century. With 11 members, the Moore family was unusually large, as the mean nuclear family size grew from 3.58 to 4.18 between 1851 and 1891. Mean *household* size was, of course, larger at both dates, at 4.32 and 4.94 respectively. As we have seen (Table XI), unlike the Moores, many families would also have other people – often kinfolk – living with them. But, in terms of nuclear families only, Table XV indicates that, although large families were not uncommon and had increased as a proportion by 1891, they still remained a minority.

To what extent did these patterns of family size vary by social and occupational groups? As shown in Table XVI, mean family sizes increased for all occupational groups in the 1851-91 period, with coal mining families the largest. Of particular interest is the broadly similar family size of labourers, clerical employees and managerial and professional workers alike.

---

[78] Engels, F., *The Condition of the Working Class in England*, Henderson, W.O. and Chaloner, W.H. (trans. and eds.) (1958), pp.162-4.
[79] Harris, C.C., *The Family and Industrial Society* (1983), p.126.
[80] Smelser, N.J., *Social Change in the Industrial Revolution* (1959).

### Table XV  Nuclear family sizes, 1851 and 1891

|  | 1851 | | 1891 | |
|---|---|---|---|---|
|  | No | % | No | % |
| Childless married couples | 286 | 17.1 | 315 | 15.9 |
| Married couples or widowed persons with 1 child | 439 | 26.2 | 360 | 18.1 |
| Married couples or widowed persons with 2-3 children | 588 | 35.1 | 704 | 35.6 |
| Married couples or widowed persons with 4-6 children | 331 | 19.8 | 500 | 25.3 |
| Married couples or widowed persons with 7+ children | 31 | 1.9 | 101 | 5.1 |

### Table XVI  Mean nuclear family size by occupation class

| Occupational class of household head | 1851 | 1891 |
|---|---|---|
| Labourers | 3.69 | 4.32 |
| Domestic service etc. | 2.38 | 2.77 |
| Coal miners etc. | 4.29 | 4.94 |
| Transport workers | 4.07 | 4.59 |
| Skilled manual factory workers | 4.12 | 4.73 |
| Other skilled manual | 3.77 | 4.49 |
| Hawkers, shop assistants etc. | 3.70 | 4.29 |
| Fixed shop keepers | 3.55 | 3.89 |
| Clerical | 3.52 | 4.42 |
| Managerial and professional | 3.38 | 4.22 |
| Living on own means | 1.86 | 2.75 |

Rapid urban growth, partially fuelled as it was by substantial in-migration, does not appear to have been inimical to the formation and continuation of the 'traditional' nuclear family in 19th-century Newcastle. If anything, these families grew in significance as the century progressed, a trend that is all the more remarkable because of the severe shortage of accommodation and the notorious overcrowding of a significant proportion of Newcastle's housing stock. It is apparent that a large number of households did not have a house to themselves and, furthermore, a significant proportion quite deliberately shared their dwellings with kinfolk. Whether this was a consequence of housing shortage or a deliberate strategy to achieve economies is a matter for further research. The nuclear family structure appeared to flourish despite the constraints of limited housing supply.

## Conclusion

For most of the 19th century there was a high rate of marriage in Newcastle and this was related to a high birth rate. The latter, however, declined in the latter part of the century but this decline appears to have been closely related to the improved survival chances of young children and increases in the relative 'costs' of a large family. Improvements in the standard of living provide a substantial part of the explanation for this positive change in life-chances. Inward migration made an important but proportionally declining contribution to population growth but most of this migration was short range. Outward migration also took place. Within the city, migrants often had a variety of kinfolk, other than their immediate family, living with them. Overall, however, the family unit as a component of Newcastle's social structure appears to have grown in importance during the century with not much variation in family size by socio-economic group. Some of these features had important implications for Newcastle's population in the 20th century. The dominance of local migration streams, along with a particular and narrow economic base, helped the creation of a distinctive urban-industrial culture. But, despite improved life-chances, late 19th-century Newcastle could, in many ways, be regarded as over-populated. The limited quantity and quality of housing was to prove a massive problem in the mid-20th century and, combined with economic decline, was a major stimulus to out-migration from the city. As 20th-century Newcastle gradually converged towards national norms of marriage and birth rates, this migration loss, usually of younger and more active people, was not compensated for by natural increase.

The author would like to thank Brian Williams for construction of the maps and Nina Chowdry and Sarah Ledger for their expert help in coding and analysing the samples of census enumeration data for 1851 and 1891.

8

# Drink in Newcastle

BRIAN BENNISON

In 1983 the *Adelaide* public house in Newcastle was refurbished and renamed *Joe Wilson's* after the music-hall performer and composer of 'Keep Your Feet Still, Geordie Hinny'. Wilson had been landlord of the hostelry in 1871 and the owner sought to pay tribute to his memory, but whilst much money was expended on renovation, little time was spent on research. Wilson found life as a publican unbearable and left the *Adelaide* after 12 months. From then until his early death he used his songs and recitations to promote the doctrines of the Good Templars.[1]

In its haste to fuse together alcohol and romanticised, Geordie heritage, the brewery christened its premises after someone who had died a sworn enemy of drink. Quite unwittingly two aspects of Newcastle's long relationship with Bacchus had been merged: the passionate, unswerving attachment to drink in some quarters linked to a resolute disapproval in others. Newcastle's deeply rooted devotion to drink amongst some has regularly captured the most attention and continues to this day as an integral part of the city's cultural image, promoted in its sanitised form as the 'Party City'. The brewer's re-creation of *Joe Wilson's* illustrated the drink trade's determination to sustain and reinforce alcohol's traditional role at the heart of local leisure, whilst making every effort to shape the circumstances under which it is consumed.

## Drinking: how and where? 1830-1900

Identifying the strength of a city's bond with drink is a difficult task. National consumption statistics available from the early 19th century merely disclose the yearly intake of that rarest of beasts – the statistically correct average drinker – who dwelt within a much larger population that included children, the adult abstainer and the absolute soak. In the average, age and gender variations are obscured, and regional and class differences are concealed. We can reasonably assume, for instance, that Tynesiders consumed less spirits than whisky-drinking Scots and Cockneys

[1] *Newcastle Evening Chronicle*, 14 December 1983; *Newcastle Weekly Chronicle*, 24 March 1914.

surrounded by gin shops. The poor, no doubt, drank little wine and yet Newcastle's wine merchants found it worthwhile to import directly from Oporto, sending coal in exchange. But whilst the gentlemen of Newcastle drank wine, they did not reject beer entirely; after dinner a party would often adjourn to a public house to 'clear out with beer'.[2]

Beer remained the tipple of most inhabitants. In 1830 Newcastle's 28 breweries and 138 publicans pursued their business, with almost 70 per cent of the beer categorised as 'strong'. Whilst we can't be sure about quantities consumed, the general impression was that Novocastrians were enthusiastic drinkers. One old resident, recalling the situation around 1810, thought that later generations could have 'no idea of the heads and stomachs of men in those days ... prodigious was the quantity they drank'.[3]

The 'drink question' was essentially an anxiety about excessive consumption by the working class. In 1834 a parliamentary select committee found 'the vice of intoxication' in decline amongst the 'higher and middle ranks' but rising among the 'humbler classes'. This inherent class distinction was apparent in a 1804 pamphlet on drunkenness written by Thomas Trotter, member of Newcastle's Literary and Philosophical Society. Conceding that 'the cultivated mind' was occasionally drunk, it was not a concern because it 'commits no outrage, provokes no quarrel'. It was with 'the ignorant and illiterate ... human nature in its vilest yard, and madness in its worst form' that the problem lay.[4]

Those most hostile to drink depicted it not merely as a social menace but the root of sundry evils: 'poverty, crime, prostitution, lunacy, disease and death'. The cause of intemperance was the temptation placed in the workingman's way and increased by an explosion of retail outlets. Calls for liberalisation of the drink trade, plus the belief that wider access to beer would challenge the easy availability of spirits, led to the Beer Act of 1830. From then until 1869 any ratepayer could sell beer on his own premises without the need for a magistrate's licence. The beerhouse was thus created and became the target of much anti-drink propaganda.[5]

Newcastle, where magistrates had not been overly restrictive in the past, did not experience the same spectacular eruption of beerhouses felt in other cities. Indeed, there was debate locally as to whether beerhouses or public houses were the more undesirable. The *Northern Temperance Advocate* thought

[2] Bruce, J.C., *Lectures on Old Newcastle* (1904), p.80.

[3] *Account of Quantity of Beer Exported and Brewed Great Britain and the Number of Brewers, 1830* (1831), PP 60, XVII.67; Bruce, J.C., *Handbook to Newcastle upon Tyne* (1863), p.89.

[4] *Select Committee on Inquiry into Drunkenness among Labouring Classes of UK* (1834), PP 559, VIII.315, p.iii: *An Essay, Medical, Philosophical and Chemical on Drunkenness* (1804), p.23.

[5] Gourvish, T.R. and Wilson, R.G., *The British Brewing Industry 1830-1990* (1994), p.27; Webb, S. and B., *The History of Liquor Licensing in England* (1903), pp.116-26.

public houses exercise worse influence, and present greater enticements to the poor than common beerhouses. Music and cards, and skittles and other games, are suffered. Females of loose character are too often not only permitted, but encouraged to resort to them; there is no precise time named for their closing …

City councillors meanwhile queued up to condemn beerhouses – 'the greatest curse to the borough' – and 'low public houses, covers for all kinds of pickpockets, prostitutes and thieves'. Newcastle gaol's chaplain thought that with one exception every prisoner attributed their offence to a 'connection with low public houses'.[6]

Beerhouses carried a seedier image because of location and appearance, the result of cheap conversions from houses and shops. Newcastle's beershops, selling beer and cider for consumption off the premises, were also regarded with suspicion, a real enticement in the 1840s, 'standing in any out-of-the-way place, to which labourers can resort, quietly and unseen'. Public drinking was at its most blatant at sporting events. Race Week of 1847 meant Newcastle 'thronged with the scum of the surrounding neighbourhood, in the shape of blacklegs, pickpockets, thimble and garter men, strolling players … 135 drinking booths erected on the Moor … a great deal of drunkenness, fighting and swearing'.[7]

Visits to Newcastle by celebrated temperance lecturers – Joseph Livesey in 1835 and Thomas Whittaker in 1836, who spoke at the Spital and Garth Heads 'surrounded by a dense population of the lowest and most disreputable' – gave impetus to the teetotal cause. Splitting from their anti-spirit brethren, Newcastle's abstentionists formed their own group and in 1840 supplied nearly every family in the city with a four-page monthly tract. Teetotalism could claim its converts: at Walker, for example, a number of the watermen became staunch teetotallers, a majority of workers at the tile factory had foresworn drink and all at the brickworks embraced abstinence, ensuring 'the first teetotal brickyard in the north of England'. But generally during the period the consumption of alcohol was thought to be rising.[8]

Who precisely drank what remains unknown, although estimates were made. The working class, it was postulated in 1882, consumed two-thirds of all alcoholic drink, made up of three-quarters beer and spirits and only one-tenth wines. Other investigators, taking into account the proportion of children in the population, the number of abstainers and assumptions about female drinking, computed the average intake of beer-drinking males. On this basis, modern researchers have calculated

[6]  Jennings, P., *The Public House in Bradford 1770-1970* (1995), p.84; *Northern Temperance Advocate*, October 1844; *Proceedings of the Newcastle Council*, 1854, pp.190-2, 1853, p.75.

[7]  *Northern Temperance Advocate*, October 1844; *Northern Counties Journal and Temperance Intelligencer*, August 1847.

[8]  *Temperance Witness*, March 1891, June 1900; *Northern Temperance Record*, May 1858, October 1858; Newcastle Teetotal Society, *Fifth Annual Report* (1840), p.5; Wilson, G.B., *Alcohol and the Nation* (1940), Table 1, pp.331-3.

that in 1876 the average consumption of male beer-drinkers was 16 pints per week, at an annual cost of £7 12s. Drinking was clearly widespread amongst those least able to afford it.[9]

Sound reasons existed for consuming alcoholic drinks. Beer was thirst-quenching when water was not always safe to drink; in Newcastle, reservoir water was supplemented with that from the river and in 1870 samples were described as 'quite unfit for domestic purposes'. For some industries beer was regarded as indispensable for providing energy; in Tyneside's iron and puddling trades it was said to be impossible 'to make men who are daily before hot fires work without beer'. Licensed premises offered warmth and comforts not available in overcrowded homes but the temperance movement reversed this causal relationship between squalor and drink. A doctor wrote of a Newcastle man earning 25s. per week and his wife 7s.: in their home there was 'a fireplace, but no bed; not a table, not a chair. There are four children in rags and misery. Where does the money go? To the public house.'[10]

'By the 1850s', wrote one historian, 'no respectable Englishman entered an ordinary public house.' But not all activities found there were dishonourable and over time public houses moved closer to respectability. Primarily places for drinking, Newcastle's licensed houses performed other functions. Trade unionists congregated there: at the *Victoria* 'initial steps to promote unionism amongst the miners were to some extent decided within its walls' and the *Royal Station Hotel* in Byker officially changed its title to the *Dues Bar* in 1956, formally recognising a nickname originating from the 1870s when its upstairs room was the venue of union meetings and the weekly collection of subscriptions. Local intelligence about employment opportunities was traded in pubs and friendly societies, funeral and sickness clubs, and other forms of working-class mutual benefit operated out of licensed premises. Soup kitchens were common in the east end of the city; on New Year's Day 1903, for example, 350 children were fed at the *Grace Inn*, Byker.[11]

In the second half of the 19th century enterprising landlords encouraged amusements and diversions to complement drinking and compete with other houses. Informal musical entertainments – 'free and easies' – were introduced, a practice replicated later by the workingmen's clubs. The public house also played its part in the evolution of sports. Football clubs were organised from licensed houses, the

---

[9] Rowntree, J. and Sherwell, A., *The Temperance Problem and Social Reform* (1899), pp.10-20; Gourvish and Wilson, *British Brewing Industry*, p.35.

[10] *Newcastle Corporation Minutes*, 1870, pp.339, 353, 385; *Newcastle Daily Chronicle*, 27 September 1890; *Temperance Witness*, March 1890.

[11] Harrison, B., *Drink and the Victorians. The Temperance Question in England 1815-1872* (1971), p.46; Bennison, B., *Heady Days* (1996), p.17; *Newcastle Magistrates Court* (hereafter NMC), *Publicans' Licences and Beer, Wine and Spirit Registers*, 1870-1965, Tyne & Wear Archives Service (hereafter TWAS), MG/9/1-4 & 10/1-3; *Northern Gossip*, 10 January 1903.

**8.1**  *The Stack Hotel*, Walker, 1910. Raising bread and money for hungry children.

*Lord Hill* having the distinction of being the first changing rooms for St James' Park. Some premises had 'clay ends' for quoits and billiards also grew in popularity as many of the larger properties fitted out rooms, with the *Argyle House* of the 1890s, for example, 'a favourite rendezvous for habitués of the cue'. One activity that had caused disquiet was gambling but by the end of the century the Chief Constable of Newcastle thought that betting was a rare occurrence, even though it continued in 'a few less respectable houses' where 'games called puff and dart, tippet ... simple instruments of gaming' often led to 'disputes, consequent disorders and bloodshed'.[12]

Free-licensing had its influential critics from the outset. Publicans felt threatened by the proliferating beershops and magistrates were against the burgeoning of licensed premises. The focus of temperance agitation shifted from the consumers to all-out attack on the producers and traders. In 1858 the North of England Temperance League was founded to work for 'Total Abstinence for the Individual and Prohibition for the Nation' and energetically canvassed magistrates for support. Restrictive pre-1830 conditions were re-imposed when the 1869 Wine & Beerhouse Act gave justices

[12]  Gibson, J., *The Newcastle United Story* (1985), p.14; Bennison, B., *Heavy Nights* (1997), p.29; *Northern Gossip*, 28 August 1897; N.M.C. *Special Licensing Session Minutes and Orders*, 1870-1917, T.W.A.S. MG/7/3.

powers to refuse to grant or renew licences for all types of outlet, powers that many had waited eagerly to exercise. Brewster sessions following the Act were said by the *Newcastle Chronicle* to be notable for the way magistrates dealt with beerhouses ('determined to severely restrict this class of house') and 'the determined hostility of large employers … for any further extension of public houses'.[13]

The abundance of licensed premises – in 1899 Newcastle's 691 licensed premises meant there was one for every 43 dwellings and every 307 of the population – had a magnetic effect on surrounding areas. Forty per cent of all drunkenness proceedings in Newcastle were against non-residents. And it was the drunkenness statistics that the temperance movement seized upon to prove that Newcastle – 'the most drunken town in England' – had a severe problem. Late 19th-century drunkenness proceedings, expressed in terms of the number per 10,000 persons, averaged 62 across England but stood at 207 for Newcastle. In 1901, when the average rate for ten similar 'seaports' was 88, Newcastle's equivalent rate was 225; and by 1908, when Newcastle had reduced its rate to 116, it was the sixth worst amongst the 75 county boroughs that together averaged only 67. The enthusiasm with which the constabulary and justices pursued their task may have influenced the number of charges brought, but Newcastle's unenviable record on drunkenness was more likely a reflection of the citizens' greater propensity to drink and drink immoderately.[14]

A report of 1896 revealed that one third of all miscreants were labourers, although the absolute number of charges cannot be an infallible measure of each occupation's propensity to get drunk. For example, three charges were taken out against veterinary surgeons; insignificant in the context of the total convictions that year, but perhaps of some note in the city's veterinary circles. Equally, the absence of some professions in the drunkenness returns is not necessarily evidence of sobriety. The statistics offer only positive evidence of over-indulgence in public places; intemperance of a more discreet nature presumably went on, but unnoticed and unpunished.[15]

Police reports also disclosed the relationship between prostitution and drink. Prostitutes accounted for half the drunkenness charges against females. Anti-drink propagandists were also quick to couple drink with death. In Newcastle in 1901, for instance, 19 died from 'acute chronic alcoholism and delirium tremens' and 50 from 'cirrhosis of the liver', but drink's precise contribution to patterns of ill-health and mortality was a matter of conjecture. There was no shortage of medical opinion and

[13] Winskill, P.T., *The Comprehensive History of the Rise and Progress of the Temperance Reformation* (1881), p.88; Taylder, T.W.P., *History of the Rise and Progress of Teetotalism in Newcastle upon Tyne* (1886), p.11; *Temperance Witness*, June 1900; *Newcastle Daily Chronicle*, 29 August 1870.

[14] Rowntree & Sherwell, *The Temperance Problem*, p.401: *Report of Chief Constable of Newcastle*, 1898-1906; Shadwell, A., *Drink, Temperance and Legislation* (1902), p.256; Wilson, *Alcohol and the Nation*, pp.430-9; *Statistics as to the Operation and Administration of the Laws relating to the Sale of Intoxicating Liquors, 1908*, Cmnd 4612 (1909).

[15] *Reports of Chief Constable of Newcastle*, 1897-1906.

**8.2** *The New Hawk*, Byker, 1930: landlord oarsman Bob Gray. The next landlord was 'Seaman' Tommy Watson, boxer and challenger for the world title.

**8.3** *The Portland*, Mill Lane, 1912: national brewers in Newcastle.

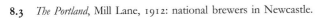

remedies were on offer. A Blackett Street shop advertised *Dr Haine's Golden Specific* which was undetectable in tea, coffee or food and, although harmless, produced 'a permanent and speedy cure' for everyone, be they 'moderate drinker or alcoholic wreck'.[16]

## Competition in the drink market, 1900-1960

As Newcastle brewers prospered, the rail network began to make the Tyneside market a target for big producers of superior beers from outside the region. Consuming more than ever, Newcastle drinkers had become more demanding of quality: by 1852 beer made in Newcastle was estimated at one third of that brought in from outside and within two decades there were almost fifty brewers from other parts of the British Isles with agencies in the city. By 1890 brewers were striving to make beer 'less in gravity, less intoxicating and less narcotising' and ten years later it was reported that the traditional, local speciality, Newcastle Mild Ale, 'is hardly to be had now'. The quality of Tyneside beers improved as the trade became concentrated in the hands of fewer wholesale brewers with better facilities. Licensed victuallers who brewed their own beer – almost 150 in the city in 1850 – dropped to less than 50 in 1870 and had disappeared completely by the opening of the 20th century.[17]

The 1869 Act had put a premium on the ownership of retail outlets, awakening brewers to their power to command the drinking market. They set about purchasing freeholds or buying up leaseholds. Between 1872 and 1902 brewer-ownership of Newcastle's public houses grew from 16 to 39 per cent. Prices rose rapidly, owners of 'free houses' cashed in and the effect in Newcastle was to 'wipe out almost entirely the old fashioned publican'.[18]

The brewers' position was strengthened when the early 20th-century reduction in the number of licences hit the independent owners hardest. Legislation of 1904 gave magistrates discretion to close houses on the grounds of redundancy and they were keen to flex such newly acquired muscle. In 1905 Newcastle magistrates closed 16 licensed houses, a further 21 in 1906 and another 18 in 1907. Closure was damaging for individual licensed victuallers, but worked to the long-term competitive advantage

[16] *City and County of Newcastle upon Tyne, Annual Report of the Medical Officer of Health, 1896-1905*; Mitchell, K., *The Drink Question* (1876), pp.115-16, 209-10; *Newcastle Daily Chronicle*, 20 July 1889.

[17] Bruce, *Handbook to Newcastle upon Tyne*, p.277; *Christie's Newcastle & Gateshead Directory*, 1870; Monckton, H.A., *A History of the English Public House* (1969), p.94; *Newcastle Daily Journal*, 22 December 1900; *Account of Number of Persons in UK Licensed as Brewers and Victuallers* (1851), PP 174, LIII.25 (1871), PP 335, LXII.1.

[18] Bennison, B., 'The Scramble for Licensed Houses: Some Evidence from Newcastle', *Journal of Regional and Local Studies*, 15, Winter 1995, pp.1-13; *Royal Commission on Liquor Licensing Laws, First Report, 1897* (Cmnd 8693/4), p.303.

**8.4** Town Moor temperance festival 1895 – forerunner of 'The Hoppings'.

of brewers. Justices closed houses which were 'badly adapted', so brewers both with the funds and the inclination to ensure premises were well-kept had a better chance of avoiding closure, and when they did lose licences they often had better-appointed houses nearby. Newcastle's licensed houses were undoubtedly improving and the disreputable beershops were much less significant: unlike Leeds, Manchester, Bradford and other boroughs in 1906, Newcastle had fewer beerhouses than full-licences.[19]

Brewers did not have it all their own way, however. Opponents confronted the drink trade and magistrates alike when new public houses were under consideration. In Heaton, for example, resistance was orchestrated by church people, temperance activists and others under the umbrella of the 'Heaton Anti-licensing Council'. Other anti-drink initiatives – attempts to provide alternative, drink-free public houses – were of limited success and hardly worried the brewers. The British Workmen

[19] *Newcastle Daily Journal*, 20 March 1906, 8 May 1907, 15 May 1907, 23 February 1907; Simpson, J., *Should the Beerhouse be Abolished?* (1907), Table I p.5, Table II p.9.

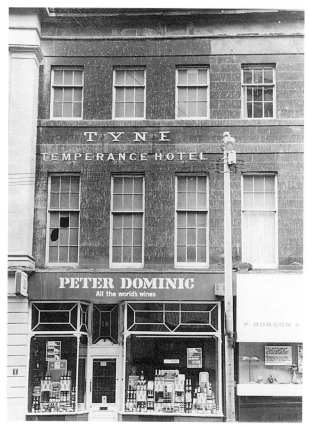

**8.5** *Tyne Temperance Hotel* in 1971.

movement reached Newcastle in 1871 when three houses opened 'on teetotal principles', including the *Nursery Cottage* on Scotswood Road where in 1874 Joe Wilson first performed with temperance slides for his newly acquired magic lantern. In 1902 Earl Grey's Northumberland Public House Trust built the *Delaval Arms* on Scotswood Road with a canteen and temperance bars in addition to a conventional bar. The handful of dry or semi-dry public house ventures carried on for sometime but had little appeal.[20]

By the first decade of the 20th century Newcastle's licensed trade had shed a deal of its vulgarity and achieved a measure of respectability. Some imposing and lavishly fitted hotels and public houses had been constructed, and their owners took every opportunity to remind the authorities and public about the worthiness of their premises and custom. In 1902 the *Portland* catered 'for every class of society,

[20] Bennison, *Heavy Nights*, pp.13-14; NMC, *Special Licensing Session Minutes and Orders*, 1870-1917, TWAS MG/7/3; *Newcastle Daily Journal*, 29 November 1871, 14 August 1903; *Newcastle Weekly Chronicle*, 18 January 1913; Bennison, B., 'Earl Grey's Public House Reform', *Tyne & Tweed*, No.48, 1994, pp.68-72.

from the pitman who is early for his train at New Bridge Station to the scientific man who finds it a halfway house to Heaton'. The *Addison*, 'one of the most important hotels in the East End', had a staff of eight and 'a superior class of customer'. In the *Raby*'s spacious upper room, 200 people – 'thoroughly representative of all classes, members of the Council Chamber, professional men, tradesmen, and last but not least, the horny-handed sons of toil' – attended smoking concerts. Not everyone, of course, was impressed with what the trade was doing; the *Grand Hotel* was hailed by the press for its distinguished facade and 'noble suite of public rooms', but the *Temperance Witness* thought it an 'insult to the Christian and moral feelings of the citizens'.[21]

Some members of the drink trade used part of their personal fortunes to help the arts and cement the growing acceptance of their line of business. The most obvious and lasting contribution was that of Alexander Laing, who came to Newcastle in 1849 as a salesman for an Edinburgh brewer before setting up on his own account as a bottler, wine merchant and hotel-owner. In 1900 he funded the Laing Art Gallery. A.H. Higginbottom – wine and spirit merchant, cocoa-room proprietor, licensed victualler and pioneer of 'snack lunches for your busy city man' – was a connoisseur of Japanese art and donated his collection to the Laing. Of those who entered public life, none was more outstanding than John Fitzgerald. Arriving from Tipperary in 1878, Fitzgerald began to bottle ales and stouts, manufacture aerated waters and acquire licensed houses in a manner later adjudged to have 'thrown an air of superior respectability into Newcastle hotel life'. Fitzgerald's career away from the trade was equally rewarding: elected to the Board of Guardians in 1888 and the City Council in 1891, he became Sheriff in 1906, an alderman in 1910, Lord Mayor in 1914 and a knight in 1920.[22]

The real threat to the drink trade's dominance came not from temperance but from the workingmen's clubs. The city's first, the Newcastle Working Men's Club and Institute, had been set up in 1863. Joe Wilson had written a rhyming appeal for support. The original prospectus of the Working Men's Club & Institute Union (CIU) had promised 'recreation and refreshment, free from intoxicating drinks', reflecting its founder's aim to help 'the hard-working industrial classes … throw off the wretched and degrading bondage to the public house'. But in 1875 the CIU accepted that clubs 'should be free from all vexatious infantile restrictions on the consumption of intoxicating drinks'. As clubs became established the CIU talked

[21] *Northern Gossip*, 1 February 1902, 6 September, 29 November 1902; *Newcastle Weekly Chronicle*, 27 September 1890; *Temperance Witness*, September 1890.
[22] *Newcastle Journal*, 28 May 1915, 11 August 1917, 25 April 1918, 6 October 1927, 3 June 1929, 3 November 1930; Conte-Helme, M., *Japan and the North East of England* (1989), pp.68-73; *Northern Gossip*, 6 June 1896, 2 April 1898; *Brewing Trade Review*, 1 July 1896.

up their superiority, stressing their inherent civility, unlike the public house and beershop which attracted 'the loafer, the blackleg and the rowdy'. Brewers, licensed victuallers and temperance advocates were united in condemning clubs for operating outside the control of justices and police and encouraging unrestrained drinking. Clubs, in fact, had their own codes of discipline and were generally quick to deal with drunkenness.[23]

By 1914 there were almost sixty clubs in Newcastle. Many were workingmen's clubs in the conventional sense, formed under the auspices of the CIU and having the standard objective of affording 'members means of social intercourse, mutual helpfulness, mental and moral improvement, and rational recreation'. Some had evolved from occupational groupings, like the Elswick Collieries Workingmen's Social Club, the National Union of Gasworkers & General Labourers Club and the Tramway & Vehicle Workers Social Club. A handful of other clubs – for instance, the Elswick Conservative Workingmen's Club – affiliated to the Association of Conservative Clubs and ruled that 'persons professing Conservative or Unionist principles are alone admissible as members'. The political social clubs included the Irish Literary Institute, with 250 members in the early years of the century and registered to 'promote the diffusion of political information and the fostering of Irish national principles'. Also on the club register were a score of individual masonic lodges which shared bar facilities at the local temple; work-based associations, for example, the Elswick Shipyard Officials Dining Club, the Walker Shipyard Messroom and the Post Office Dining Club; and sports groups wishing to serve alcohol in their clubhouses. Unique amongst Newcastle's licensed premises of the time was the St Dominic's Catholic Recreative Club, having been blessed by His Holiness, Pope Leo XIII in October 1902.[24]

Newcastle also had its long-standing gentlemen's clubs with more exclusive membership, although attempts to open similar clubs were less successful. The Bentinck Club launched 'on acknowledged principles of London West End clubs' closed in 1911 and a similar venture, the Blackett Club, suffered the ignominy of being closed because of 'frequent drunkenness'. Clubs were also struck off for not being 'conducted in good faith as a club', a euphemism covering such matters as supplying alcoholic drink to non-members and tolerating misbehaviour. Ironically, in the middle of the First World War the United Services Club received its marching orders.[25]

[23] Hall, B.T., *Our Fifty Years. The Story of the Working Men's Club and Institute Union* (1912), pp.51, 138-9; Tremlett, G., *Clubman. The History of the Workingmen's Club and Institute Union* (1987), p.12; Hall, B.T., *Working Men's Clubs: Why and How to Establish Them* (1908), p.6.
[24] NMC, *Register of Clubs*, 1870-1965, TWAS MG/Nc/12/1-8.
[25] *Ibid.*

The drinking environment was radically altered by wartime governmental regulation. The temperance movement predictably pronounced on the issue but others entered the debate, including the Shipbuilding Employers' Federation which pressed for a total ban on the sale of alcoholic drink. The government, however, doubled spirit duty, quadrupled wine duty, introduced two-tier beer duties and raised the maximum limit on dilution of spirits. Direct intervention was secured by the creation of the Central Control Board, whose chairman visited Newcastle to spell out his intentions to restrict alcohol sales to two principal mealtimes, to put an end to treating and credit, and to curtail off-sales. The Board subsequently reported that in Newcastle the restrictions had markedly affected drinking habits, resulting in 'better order in the streets, more comfortable homes, better cared for children, and better timekeeping at work'.[26]

Limitations on brewing meant Tyneside firms ceased producing some beers, reduced the gravity of others and generally cut back on the supply to the free trade and the clubs. Drinkers were naturally aggrieved: after meeting in Newcastle, the Workmen's Protection League took up the slogan 'Give Us Beer and Regular Hours' and an inquiry into industrial unrest in the region found resentment fuelled by shortages of supply and exorbitant prices. With the trade looking after its own tied houses and poorer terms being offered to clubs, the *CIU Journal* declared the brewers to be 'as light fingered as their ales are light'. One drinker equated Newcastle's bars with 'high prices, inferior quality', and in the correspondence columns of the *Newcastle Weekly Chronicle* brewers were berated for producing 'flat, stale and profitable sloppy beer not fit for hogwash'. Prices tripled between 1914 and 1919, and by 1918 the consumption of beer of standard gravity was a third of its pre-war level, although the consumption of spirits at proof strength was up 40 per cent.[27]

A short-lived boom in consumption after the Armistice was followed by a long-term decline, and by 1929 the trade reluctantly acknowledged that 'the public house had lost its social importance'. High prices, low earnings and restricted opening hours played their part, but changing social attitudes were being uncovered in the region in 1930. For example, 'an increasing interest taken by fathers in their families … and the ambition of girls, fostered by better education and the cinema, to obtain better homes … impelling them to bring their influence to bear on the young men'. New working practices – machinery which meant less heavy labour and hot and arduous shifts – and a week's paid leave prompting saving for holidays, all served

---

[26] *Newcastle Daily Journal*, 30 March 1915, 23 November 1916; Carter, H., *The Control of the Drink Trade: A Contribution to National Efficiency, 1915-17* (1918), p.267.

[27] *Club and Institute Journal*, April 1917; *Newcastle Daily Journal*, 31 March 1915, 8 July 1918, 27 May 1919; *Commission of Inquiry into Industrial Unrest. Report of Commissioners for North East Coast Area* (1917), p.3; *Newcastle Weekly Chronicle*, 2 August 1919; *Brewing Trade Review*, 1 December 1918.

**8.6** Newburn Club, 1925.

to modify the traditional hard drinking associated with some occupations. Mass spectator sports and the cinema were identified as the chief counter-attractions. The success of league football had encouraged clubs to increase ground capacities and lift standards of comfort. Luxurious 'picture palaces' came into their own after the arrival of sound (15 new cinemas were opened in Newcastle between 1931 and 1939). By the mid-1930s additional threats to the public house came from within the home: the wireless meant more free time spent by the fireside, library books became accessible to almost all and participation in a range of hobbies and crafts blossomed.[28]

[28] Wilson, *Alcohol and the Nation*, p.335; Gourvish & Wilson, *British Brewing Industry*, p.339; *Statist*, 14 December 1929; Buckmaster Group, *The Social and Economic Aspects of the Drink Problem* (1931), pp.47-95; *Newcastle Daily Chronicle*, 12 February 1930, 24 February 1930; Walvin, J., *Leisure and Society 1830-1950* (1978), pp.137-43; Walton, J.K. and Walvin, J., *Leisure in Britain, 1780-1939* (1983), pp.31-52; Manders, F., *Cinemas of Newcastle* (1991), p.17; Hawkins, A. and Lowerson, J., *Leisure, 1919-1939* (1979); Cunningham, H., 'Leisure and Culture' in Thompson, F.M. (ed.), *Cambridge Social History of Britain, 1750-1950, Vol. 2, People and Their Environment* (1990), pp.279-340.

**8.7** Benwell Club, 1930.

There remained, however, a demand for simple socialising and for alcoholic drink, and in this context it was the licensed clubs which emerged in a strong position. Between 1920 and 1938 the number of Newcastle clubs rose by 60 per cent, as public houses fell by 16 per cent and beerhouses by over 50 per cent. An additional concern for brewers was the establishment in 1921 of the Northern Clubs Federation Brewery which provided clubs with cheaper beer. To challenge the clubs in the market for drink and to resist the competition from counter-attractions, public houses had to absorb some of the respectability and family-centredness of recreation in the home, and also emulate the cinemas and football clubs in improving facilities for their patrons.[29]

The public house was in danger of being seen as an increasingly inferior product and running a profitable one became more difficult. In 1924 it was estimated that half the houses in Newcastle failed to pay their way. By the late 1920s more publicans were leaving the licensed trade than there were those aspiring to enter it, although some brewers were tempted into the market by the possibility of buying a particularly prestigious property. In the 1920s James Deuchar bought two of Newcastle's biggest hotels, the *County* and the *Royal Turk's Head*, in order to add to the firm's ownership of the *Grand*.[30]

[29] *Statistics as to the Operation and Administration of the Laws relating to the Sale of Intoxicating Liquors, 1920,1930* (Cmnd 1386 & 6145); *North Mail*, 25 August 1939.
[30] *Brewing Trade Review*, 1 April 1924; *Newcastle Daily Journal*, 4 May 1920, 20 October 1927.

Closure on redundancy grounds was pursued in a systematic way with police, magistrates and temperance bodies all relying on simple arithmetic to make their case. In 1925, for instance, figures for Shieldfield showed a licensed house for every 244 residents while the city-wide ratio was one for every 503, and the annual per capita spending in the district's licensed premises was £11 9s. while the national average was £7 2s. Consequently, the licensing bench specifically targeted the Shieldfield and Jesmond Vale areas and referred 12 houses for compensation. In 1933 the justices reported eight premises in Scotswood Road after learning that there were 25 licensed houses in a mile-and-a-half stretch.[31]

Licensed victuallers owning single properties were the most vulnerable as a loss of licence meant loss of livelihood. For brewers with extensive portfolios of property it was less damaging; they were not immune from closure – given that brewers owned 41 per cent of Newcastle's public houses in 1920 they were bound to lose some licences – but they rarely objected to closure on grounds of redundancy. They were more interested in the prospects of constructing new houses in the developing residential estates and extending or rebuilding the busier of their existing properties. By the early 1930s magistrates, generally ill-disposed towards most licensed premises, were prepared to grant permission to rebuild on the basis of the inadequacy of the existing building. When, for example, in 1936 Newcastle Breweries told magistrates of up to 200 customers crowding the passages, yard and outhouses of the *Green Tree*, Benwell, because of a five-fold increase in trade due to housing developments, the bench readily agreed to a new building with a floor space of 4,610 square feet compared with the 924 square feet of the old premises.[32]

When it came to entirely new pubs in new localities, magistrates insisted on the trade-in of a number of existing licences and left the leading brewers, as holders of extensive estates, with a distinct advantage. In 1937 the Newcastle bench was praised by the teetotal United Kingdom Alliance for making it difficult for brewers; nevertheless, between 1921 and 1939 over 30 permissions to build or rebuild public houses had been granted in the city. There was, however, consistent and co-ordinated outside opposition to any proposal, most strikingly against the grander projects in

[31] NMC, *Special Licensing Session Minutes and Orders*, 1917-1935, TWAS MG/Nc/7/4; *Newcastle Daily Journal*, 26 May 1933. Under legislation of 1904 magistrates could close licensed premises on grounds of 'redundancy', after an annual report and recommendations made by the police. The criteria used in Newcastle to determine 'redundancy' included the density of houses in the vicinity, the state of trade, the size of the local population and the level of business for a particular house. The instincts of the police were to refer a large number of houses for closure. The pattern that emerged at annual brewster sessions was one of deliberation on a long list of referrals and renewal of a proportion on stringent conditions about improvement. The owners of premises closed on redundancy grounds (rather than some breach of licensing laws) were entitled to compensation and the authorities were therefore ultimately constrained by the amount of funds available. In 1928, for example, 20 houses qualifying as redundant remained open because the city's 'compensation fund' had been exhausted.

[32] NMC, *Special Licensing Session Minutes and Orders*, 1917-35, TWAS MG/Nc/7/4; *Newcastle Daily Journal*, 14 October 1936; NMC, *Publicans' Licences, and Beer, Wine and Spirit Register*, 1870-1965, TWAS MG/9/1 & 10/1-3.

the more suburban locations. On the old battle-ground of Heaton, when the *Corner House* proposal went before magistrates, clergy and barristers asked the bench to visualise its effect on the minds of schoolchildren, but their case was undermined by the vicar of St Gabriel's who said his congregation 'certainly desired' the proposed hotel, and a petition in favour signed by 300 voters and a local total abstainer who acknowledged that most residents desired licensed premises. On the other side of the city, claims and counter-claims were put before the brewster sessions in 1936: an objection by 738 residents, 623 of them living within a quarter-mile radius of the site, was challenged by a brewery's canvass which uncovered 753 persons within the same quarter-mile radius in favour. The *Denton Hotel* was built but magistrates insisted it be positioned so that its main entrances did not face a Methodist chapel.[33]

Smaller brewers and private individuals were unable to build houses with all the amenities – car parks, concert halls, dance halls, bowling greens, quoit grounds and so on – which the more discerning customer now expected. So the better, more profitable houses were concentrated in the hands of the bigger firms, which had a particular advantage with regard to 'roadhouses' (newly built houses on important roads on the outskirts of conurbations or rebuilt or enlarged wayside inns). In 1935 the *Wheatsheaf Hotel* at Woolsington replaced a small roadside inn and offered a bar, buffet and lounge which accommodated 200 people. Within two years, however, the hotel felt handicapped by not having a catering service, and a dining hall was added. Similarly, a public house in Heaton with a car park, veranda, lawns and wine shop originally seated 263 people, but was found to be 'hopelessly inadequate' and an extension was built.[34]

As the overall number of licensed houses fell and spatial redistribution better matched the location of their custom, brewers strengthened their hold on the licensed house sector. By 1939 over 60 per cent of Newcastle's public houses were owned by brewers, although leaseholding undoubtedly increased the extent of brewer control. The public house still appealed to the traditional clientele of working-class men but, as its physical appearance was enhanced and facilities expanded, more women and middle-class drinkers were sampling the pleasure of a visit to licensed premises. One local brewer later reflected upon the way the public house of the inter-war period became an 'altogether larger, cleaner and brighter establishment'.[35]

But the success of clubs continued to bother the brewers. Newcastle had a greater incidence of clubs than in most districts, growing from 72 in 1920 to 115

[33] *Newcastle Daily Journal*, 4 May 1937; *Builder*, 1921-1939; Bennison, *Heavy Nights*, pp.13-14; Bennison, B., *Lost Weekends* (1998), pp.31-2; NMC Special Licensing Sessions, TWAS MG/7/4&5; *North Mail*, 29 February 1936, 31 March 1936.
[34] *Newcastle Daily Journal*, 18 October 1935, 6 May 1936, 14 December 1937.
[35] NMC, *Publicans' Licences, and Beer, Wine and Spirit Register*, 1870-1965, TWAS MG/9/1 & 10/1-3.

in 1938 and constituting a quarter of the city's drinking places compared with a national proportion of under one fifth. A feature of the inter-war years had been the formation of social clubs for ex-servicemen with most, like the Walker British Legion Club founded in 1920, adopting standard CIU objectives but adding a subsidiary clause 'to also advance the comradeship which sprang up whilst serving their country'. But clubs, just like public houses, were not immune from the effects of growing unemployment and falling consumption. The Gladstone Social Club in Shieldfield closed indefinitely in 1932 'owing to the present state of trade depression', and the Westgate and St John's Conservative Club also shut up shop. Another closure was the William Morris Club which had a membership of over 200 on the outbreak of the First World War. Set up to 'promote the interests of labour and the Socialist Movement in Newcastle', it closed in the symbolic year of 1926 when saddled with rent arrears. Perhaps the most remarkable of all ventures into the Newcastle licensed trade was that by the British Union of Fascists which opened two clubs in 1933, one in the west end of the city having as its stated objective 'the promotion of Fascism in Benwell'. The clubs closed after only two years but at one stage had a membership of 400.[36]

One consequence of the First World War had been the development of 'trade defence' – brewers and licensees coming together to act in their own collective interests – and this cooperation continued after the war, running alongside normal competitive instincts and putting increasing emphasis on non-price competition. Rivalry found expression in widening the range of services and improving the quality of products and premises, all reinforced by more advertising and promotion. Competition was most evident in bottled beers as local brewers promoted well-conditioned, good-looking products able to compete in public houses and the 'take-home' trade. In 1927 Newcastle Brown Ale went on to the market at 9d. per imperial pint. Consumption patterns were changing in other ways too. In the mid-1920s members of the Newcastle trade argued that excessive taxation 'was drawing those who wished for alcoholic refreshment to wines', and by the end of the 1930s the local brewers' association was attacking 'this largely advertised, cheap and highly alcoholic' drink. There were also concerns about the increasing popularity of cider.[37]

During the inter-war period, drunkenness – once 'half admired as a sign of virility ... now regarded as, on the whole, rather squalid and ridiculous' – fell. But Newcastle maintained its high ranking in the insobriety league. In 1920 the city's 2,357 prosecutions represented a rate of 80 per 10,000 inhabitants when the national

[36] *Statistics as to the Operation and Administration of the Laws relating to the Sale of Intoxicating Liquors, 1920, 1930* (Cmnd 1386 & 6145); NMC, *Register of Clubs, 1870-1965*, TWAS MG/Nc/12/1-8.
[37] *Brewing Trade Review*, 1 September 1924, 1 January 1926, 1 November 1927; Northumberland & Durham Brewers' Association, *Annual Reports*, 1920-39.

**8.8** Brown Ale in *The Green Tree*, Scotswood Road, 1958. Photograph by Jimmy Forsyth.

average was just 52. The city rate fell to just below 40 in 1930 and stayed at that level until the outbreak of the Second World War when 1,148 drunkards were charged. Newcastle was always in the top five of the drunkenness table and comparatively its problem was getting worse: whereas its 1920 level was about 1.5 times the national rate, throughout the 1930s it was 2.5 times as bad.[38]

In 1939, in Lord Woolton's view, the British were 'a sober and temperate nation' and the war brought no restrictions on drink production and opening hours escaped almost unscathed. Taxation, however, reached unprecedented heights, shortages of labour and materials limited output, and draught beer rose in price from 5d. to 12d. per pint. With a population 'bent upon relieving its sorrows and privations in the welcome atmosphere of the public house', beer-drinking regained some popularity and in all but one of the war years beer output, albeit of a weaker kind, rose while the consumption of spirits fell. A more responsible attitude was detectable in the drunkenness statistics: Newcastle, which averaged in excess of 1,000 cases per annum in the late 1930s, had only 257 prosecutions in 1946.[39]

[38] Nicholson, B.D., 'Drink' in *New Survey of London Life and Labour* (1935), Vol. 9, pp.243-69; *Statistics as to the Operation and Administration of the Laws relating to the Sale of Intoxicating Liquors, 1920, 1938* (Cmnd 1386 & 6145).

[39] Jennings, *Public House in Bradford*, p.250; Monckton, *English Public House*, p.119; Gourvish & Wilson, *British Brewing Industry*, p.359; *Report of Chief Constable of Newcastle*, 1964.

With peace came an escalation in demand for beer as Newcastle victuallers appealed to drinkers to 'leave a little for the other fellow'. A temporary four-hour day for city pubs was introduced and brewers instructed landlords to be more polite to customers when beer ran out. Normality took some time to return, especially with regard to the poor fabric and condition of pubs. When restrictions on materials and construction were finally lifted, the brewers watched beer consumption fall into what would become a long-term decline and set about trying to rescue the status of the public house. By the late 1950s the brewers' efforts were having some effect; public houses were perceived as more agreeable places and the clientele had widened to include more moderate drinkers and their families.[40]

For a decade or so following the Second World War public houses remained much as they had during the pre-war days: 'places to which ordinary people with ordinary incomes can come without formality, ... meet strangers and talk about anything'. Other attractions, such as cinemas or sporting events, meant admission charges and an experience of relatively passive on-looking. In pub and club, basic facilities were provided but the customer largely determined its nature. Licensing authorities published returns on the physical state of licensed premises and the trade and its critics produced statistics on consumption, but such documentation veiled the social aspect. The essence of the pub and club was its human dimension: participation in an unpolished democracy of mutual support and beery argument. It was also to licensed premises that people gravitated during life's significant moments: christenings, weddings and funerals, job offers and retirement, celebrating achievements and drowning sorrows. The 'local', for all its rudimentary amenities, was transformed into a social institution by the vigour of its customers. By the 1960s, however, brewers and landlords were beginning to take a keener interest in governing the environment in which drinkers passed their time.[41]

## The 'social package deal', 1960-2000

Newcastle's reputation for irresponsible heavy drinking surfaced from time to time. Annual convictions for drunkenness (338 in 1945) were almost 1,900 in the early 1960s, increasing numbers were prosecuted for being under the influence of drink whilst driving and other incidents of drunkenness were merged with more serious offences. The city's Housing Committee was told in 1961 that some who paid only 7s. a week in rent spent £4 on beer and the *Financial Times* could describe pubs of the time as being 'for serious drinkers' and those in Scotswood 'a byword for

[40] *Newcastle Daily Journal*, 2 August 1945, 25 July 1945, 3 September 1945.
[41] Mass Observation, *The Pub and the People* (1943), p.17.

**8.9** *Freemasons Arms* on Scotswood Road, 1961. Cruddas Flats behind. Photograph by Jimmy Forsyth.

violence'. But the brewers and authorities, echoing policies pursued between the wars, saw to it that licensed estates were rationalised, existing properties thinned out, the remainder improved and new premises constructed in accordance with rehousing schemes. The process was seen at its most dramatic in the Newcastle of the 1960s when many public houses were cleared away in the great wave of renewal that swamped working-class residential areas and the city centre. The 'mark of masculinity, adulthood and membership of a social group associated with a particular neighbourhood' – identified by one researcher as the essence of traditional drinking in Newcastle – was progressively erased as scores of street corner pubs were demolished. The symbolic dissociation of the public house with working people could be observed in the disappearing sign-boards: gone were the *Ordnance*, the *Gun*, the *Rifle*, the *Hydraulic Crane*, the *Moulders*, the *Shipwrights* and the *Mechanics*, and in came names indicative perhaps of a more refined past, the *Runnymede*, the *Turnpike* and *Howlett Hall*.[42]

[42] *Report of Chief Constable of Newcastle*, 1964; *Newcastle Evening Chronicle*, 14 April 1961; *Financial Times*, 11 November 1969; Gofton, L., 'On the Town. Drink and the New Lawlessness', *Youth & Policy*, No 29, April 1990, pp.33-9; Bennison, *Lost Weekends*, pp.19-24, 44-6.

In the immediate post-war period the enduring success of social clubs continued to rankle the trade itself and those most antagonistic towards it. A 1940s study found that two-thirds of drinkers who frequented both clubs and public houses preferred the 'stability, conviviality and good recreational facilities offered by the club'. In 1945 Ald Angus Watson complained, in a familiar refrain, that for every three public house or beerhouse licences taken away since 1903, 'a club licence, beyond the control of anybody, has been granted'. At the beginning of the century there had been 15 public houses for every club in the country; by the mid-1960s there were only three and in Newcastle the ratio was less than 2:1.[43]

In 1960 the 'Party City' of the future closed down at 10.30p.m. but in the decade that followed, while pub numbers fell by one quarter the nightclub arrived. By 1971 Newcastle had 20 clubs offering late-night drinking, gambling and entertainment. The working men's clubs were themselves moving with the times and their own idiosyncratic form of cabaret – 'a much celebrated mixture of song and alcohol, domino cards, twisted handkerchiefs and indifferent acoustic engineering they call a go-as-you-please' – was being overhauled. As clubs accepted generous loans from the Federation brewery to improve and extend, professional entertainers were booked. In 1965, for instance, the Walker Jubilee Club, only 30 years after its birth in the lamp cabin of the shut-down Jane Ann Pit, opened a concert hall seating 400 with accommodation for a further 170 on its horseshoe balcony. The region's *Clubman* magazine could claim, without any hint of bashfulness, that the workingmen's club was 'one of the most swinging and scintillating places in the Britain of the Sixties', having taken on a 'new look of gloss and glamour, style and sophistication'. Now, where 'once mostly husbands used to go, it is husband and wife'.[44]

The increased attendance of women at clubs came gradually and grudgingly, progressing through initial guest nights confined to 'the singing end' and bingo until, eventually, in about one third of the region's clubs by 1995, full membership. For some men this was the great betrayal. Others formulated their own rationale as to why male-only attendance was actually in the ladies' interest. When the *Clubman* was claiming their movement to be in tune with a new, liberal mood, it was also publishing letters explaining how 'women tend to forget they like a bit of chit chat with the women neighbours next door, and the fact that once the old man's out of the way, dress patterns can be laid out in front of the kitchen fire'.[45]

In their efforts to modernise, public houses and clubs were facing up to a developing post-war trend: the practice of going out for a drink being partially

[43]   Gourvish & Wilson, *British Brewing Industry*, p.417; *Newcastle Daily Journal*, 20 September 1945; Monckton, *English Public House*, pp.123-53.

[44]   *Newcastle Evening Chronicle*, 22 April 1971; Bean, D., *Tyneside: A Biography* (1971), p.193; *Clubman*, June 1967, October 1967.

[45]   Bean, *Tyneside*, p.197; *Newcastle Evening Chronicle*, 9 March 1995; *Clubman*, March 1964.

replaced by staying in for a drink. Better housing and widespread television ownership proved a potent counter-attraction to licensed premises. Other factors – for example, the more convenient packaging of drink (exemplified by the 1962 debut of Newcastle Brown Ale in cans) and licensing legislation making alcohol freely available in supermarkets – contributed to the declining share of alcohol bought and consumed on the premises. A feature of many new public houses was an integral off-sales shop. It is still the case, however, that more drink is consumed outside the home than in it and surveys point to the most dedicated on-trade drinkers being in the North East.[46]

The changing nature of the pub was put succinctly by a spokesman for the local brewers' association in 1971:

> Today [it] is more of a social package deal than a place to drink. Before the war, drinking was the thing … generally confined to one sex and one class. Nowadays people expect to go to the pub for relaxation in a pleasant comfortable atmosphere often with a bit of food thrown in and entertainment of some kind.

Catering has been the most remarkable recent development. In the mid-1960s a journalist found it 'nearly impossible' to obtain a pub lunch in the region. In 1964 food sales in Scottish & Newcastle's 1,000 houses totalled £5,000, but within five years had risen to £270,000. Brewers included restaurants in new premises and built them onto existing ones; a nondescript public house built on the Chapel House Estate in 1966 was promoted as 'a luxurious and well-appointed wining and dining centre' and a roadhouse extension of the period became 'an attractive drive-to-and-eat place'. A city centre public house, the *Empress*, was transformed into a 'modern eating house and cocktail bar' with monkey gland steaks on the menu. In 1998, 90 per cent of public houses served meals and made up two-thirds of all catering outlets.[47]

At the same time, remodelling of public houses was vigorously pursued and designs which initially looked confidently forward were very soon re-designed to look fondly back. In the late 1960s many substantial, traditional Newcastle public houses – the sort the *Guardian* could describe as 'a gorgeous, huge, Victorian men-only place of mirrors, mahogany and plush comforts' – were replaced by ones with 'bold and exciting decor' and 'modern simplicity of line'. The circle of pub design turned quickly and fully. The 1970s open-plan *Northumberland Arms*, for example,

[46]  *Newcastle Evening Chronicle*, 7 December 1962; Barr, A., *Drink. A Social History* (1998), p.186; Wilson, *Alcohol and the Nation*, p.446; Mintel, *Leisure Intelligence*, March 1998.

[47]  *Newcastle Evening Chronicle*, 23 November 1964, 22 April 1971; *Financial Times*, 11 November 1969; Bennison, *Lost Weekends*, pp.31, 46; Barr, *Drink*, p.186.

**8.10** Westerhope Club
concert room, 1960s.

was soon altered to create a 'more traditional English pub interior' by erecting
screens. Remodelling revealed identity crises amongst the brewers. The Edwardian
*North British* became 'a new, modernised, Victorian age, London-style pub'. Themes
emerged, particularly the uniformly distressed 'spit and sawdust' chains (with every
decorative cliché but the spit and sawdust) and the standard, mock-Irish pubs with
equally bogus names. A nod to the globalisation of culture came when the old
*Crow's Nest* was transformed into an Australian bar.[48]

As the brewers indulged in an orgy of renovation and redesign, workingmen's
clubs were running into problems. By the mid-1980s the large concert rooms,
financed by borrowing and filled so easily in earlier decades, were, along with soaring
rate bills and falling takings, a drain on resources. The secretary of the ClU's
Northumberland Branch rallied members by reminding them, in a statement jarringly
out of tune with the Thatcherite times, that 'whatever we do, whenever we do it,
we remain committed to uphold the principles of caring for each other and
collectively working to overcome intolerance and so defeat prejudice … we as a
movement exist to give rather than take.' Some clubs closed but most continue to
function, to organise leek shows, dart competitions, trips to race meetings, outings
for old people, treats for pensioners and to assist charities. Yet, as genuinely
democratic and well-supported as such activities are, they are unlikely to seduce the
young away from the expensively-appointed city centre bars and clubs.[49]

[48] *Guardian*, 1 May 1971; Monckton, *Public House in Bradford*, p.125; Bennison, *Heady Days*, pp.10, 33; *Newcastle Evening Chronicle*, 21 December 1983.
[49] *Newcastle Evening Chronicle*, 21 February 1987, 30 September 1992.

In the last two decades of the 20th century licensed premises became more diverse. The old distinction between pub and social club was blurred in a profusion of late-licensed clubs, continental style bistros and wine bars (never solely confined to wine). Newcastle citizens now consume a wider range of drinks in a variety of establishments, over longer opening hours, often accompanied by food and frequently in the company of children. Marketing experts now talk of 'repertoire drinkers'; people whose preferences vary with the occasion and location. Until relatively recently all Tynesiders took alcoholic refreshment in the form of beer or a narrow range of spirits, but many now consume pints of beer or lager in a workingmen's club or neighbourhood pub, then drink from bottles of premium lager in a city-centre bar or club, before going to sip wine in a restaurant. In 1995 a group of American travel agents decided Newcastle rated eighth in the world as a 'place to party', thus bestowing some quasi-official approval on the city's ability to gratify drinkers. The notion of 'Party City' was born.[50]

But beneath the public relations veneer, the old problems persist. As the Bigg Market and Quayside emerged as the locus of nightlife and moved towards an unlikely ranking with Rio, unease was once more being expressed about Newcastle's troubled relationship with drink. One study suggested that a quarter of all hospital beds in the region were occupied by patients with drink-related complaints. The local press focused on surveys highlighting the amount of drink 'downed by the unemployed' and the growing consumption of relatively cheap and accessible wines, a trend more pronounced in the North East than elsewhere in the country. In particular, just as drunkenness statistics had once seized the attention of the temperance movement, those alarmed by alcohol abuse fastened upon figures for drinking and public disorder amongst the younger generation. 'Nine out of ten Newcastle youngsters', it was reported, 'say they need alcohol to put a fizz in their life.'[51]

One of the trans-Atlantic tourists who praised the 'Party City' thought 'the entire economy of Newcastle revolves around the almighty pub'; a guileless, sweeping statement which would nonetheless accord with the impressions of others. Media attention lingered on one self-promoting aspect of Newcastle social life which concentrated on the activities of one age group with a more extrovert attitude to the consumption of alcohol. For some observers there is an enviable gusto about such hedonism: it is carnival. For others it is the revival of a local identity in 'the playing out of what it means to be a Geordie'. For the less enthusiastic, however, it merely teeters on the edge of rowdyism and disorder. A hundred and twenty-five

[50] *Observer*, 17 September 1995.
[51] *Newcastle Evening Chronicle*, 25 February 1985, 16 October 1984, 8 August 1986, 24 January 1987.

years ago, Joe Wilson sang about those who drunk 'till they can hardly stand, then stagger through the streets, an' loss all self-command' then 'bawl an' shoot, an' rowl aboot'. He could have been describing scenes commonplace today.[52]

The most far-reaching change since Wilson's day has been in the attitude of the city authorities who for so long loaned their support to the censorious voices of the temperance movement. This gradually gave way to the more constructive policy, wherein magistrates and police worked closer with the trade to ensure less, but better equipped and better conducted premises in more appropriate settings. In more recent years, however, there has been a striking switch in policy, particularly from elected representatives. From a position of accommodating, often reluctantly, some of the wishes of the trade, the council has moved to one of outright encouragement. In 1999 the chairman of the city's Development Committee called for magistrates who were 'forward thinking enough to be bold and allow new and innovatory outlets'. The new, liberal approach was founded not on some reconsideration of the social or medical consequences of drink, but in hard economic reality. On post-industrial Tyneside the 'evening economy' is one of the few sectors with export potential. Equally, in the process of 'regeneration' it is the brewers and public house chains which offer the most visible evidence of investment in empty or under-utilised buildings.[53]

As 'Party City' prepared to celebrate the millennium, some sobering facts prevailed: a greater percentage of North East household expenditure went on drink than in any other region, almost one third of males consumed higher than recommended sensible levels of alcohol and only one person in ten knew how much could be drunk without endangering health. A chief superintendent of police argued that Newcastle was distinct from the northern cities of Manchester and Leeds because 'people go out much earlier in the evening and behave differently'. So whilst a majority of the citizenry display a responsible, if un-newsworthy attitude to drink, a sizeable minority ensure Newcastle's reputation for heavy drinking persists.[54]

[52] *Newcastle Journal*, 13 September 1995; Hollands R.G., *Friday Night, Saturday Night. Youth Cultural Identificaton in the Post-industrial City* (1995), p.20; Wilson, J., 'The Sober Real Injoyment Feel', *Tyneside Songs and Droleries* (1890), pp.369-70.
[53] *Newcastle Journal*, 2 July 1999.
[54] *Regional Trends*, no.31, 1996; *Newcastle Journal*, 14 May 1998, 24 March 1998.

# 9

## Sport on Tyneside

### RICHARD HOLT & RAY PHYSICK

Tyneside's most famous sporting event was a wash-out. The Blaydon Races were first held in 1861 – the year before Geordie Ridley wrote the song – and stopped in 1864. The races at Blaydon were not important in themselves but Ridley's song became the Geordie anthem. The song celebrated more than a forgotten horse race. It conjured up the special place of sport in the festive life of the city whether it was racing or rowing, running or football. The song says as much about the spectators as the performers, as much about the crowds 'gannin' along the Scotswood Road as the horses or jockeys they were going to see. It contains a simple truth about sport as urban entertainment: that crowds are as important as performers. It is the quality of the relationship between the two which encapsulates the spirit of a place and its sense of itself. To understand sport on Tyneside is to see how the connections between athletic contests and popular culture were made and changed. It is to see how different sports at different times expressed a sense of belonging both to the city and to the wider community of the Tyne.

Before the late 19th century, sports mainly took place on the Town Moor and on the river. Racing was the first organised spectator sport to be properly recorded. In the early 17th century races were held on Killingworth Moor by local gentry families such as the Delavals and Fenwicks, who roped off the finish and even put up a makeshift stand near what is now Benton Church. Racing began on the Town Moor in the 18th century and from 1751 a 'race week' was held.[1] This became the focus of great midsummer festivities including cockfighting – a thousand birds were said to be matched during the week – with dozens of side shows, trinket stalls, beer tents, pie sellers, entertainments and, of course, bookmakers. The great horses went down in popular legend: Squire Riddell's Dr. Syntax, who won 38 of his 48 races and sired Beeswing, whose 51 wins in 64 starts from 1836 to 1842 were celebrated in popular song and ballad. Horses were amongst the first Geordie sporting heroes.

In 1800 a committee of local gentry put up a permanent grandstand on the Town Moor which was surrounded by tents and marquees when the races were on.

---

[1] Moffat, F.C., *For a purse of gold: northern racing* (Newcastle, n.d.), p.2.

**9.1** 'Pedestrianism', 1912.

In keeping with the national move towards enclosed racing and entry charges, in 1880 the Grandstand Committee decided on a move to a private site. The former Brandling estate at High Gosforth was bought and transformed into a race course. Gosforth Park races have been a part of Newcastle's sporting calendar ever since. From 1904 a tram line running to the park gates brought Geordie punters in their tens of thousands to see the Northumberland Plate and the other big races. For many years something of the old hurly-burly of the Town Moor tradition lived on in the more genteel surroundings of Gosforth Park, though the earlier excesses and petty crimes of racing were gradually stamped out.

Contests of speed or stamina on the Town Moor were not just for horses. Tyneside was famous for its 'peds' (or 'pedestrians' as those who walked or ran competitively for money were called). The first to win national renown was George Wilson, a small slightly-built man who took part in many challenges against the clock of fifty miles or more, cleverly promoting himself in the process and travelling widely. In 1822 at the age of 56 he went to the Town Moor on Easter Monday to walk 90 miles in 24 hours. A half-mile stretch of the Moor was roped off. 'Though the night was most gloomy and tempestuous, through wind, rain, snow and large hailstones ... resolute and steady to his purpose, he pursued his way', refreshing himself with a few small mutton chops, tea, bread and a glass of warm gin.[2] Wilson managed the feat with 14 minutes to spare in front of a crowd of 40,000 to whom he addressed an impromptu speech before appealing for donations from the gentry and the crowd. Here was a hero for all Tyneside, who was duly carried off in style to the *Queen's Head* whilst the bells of his parish of All Saints peeled out in triumph.

As the century wore on, the Moor became the main focus for sport amongst the miners of the south Northumberland coalfield, whose population had grown dramatically to over 90,000 in the 1880s. 'Potshare' bowling required men to compete over a course of 875 yards laid out on the eastern edge of the Moor. These bowling matches were far removed from the finesse of green bowls. 'Road bowling', of which 'potshare' bowling was a variant, required a strong and a skilled arm. Heaving a heavy bowling ball was nothing to men whose lives were spent wielding a pick at a coal seam. Bowling had taken place on the Town Moor from the early 19th century and all the great champions had played there: Davy Bell in the 1820s, Harry Brown in the 1830s and 1840s, Thomas Saint in the 1850s and 1860s. The sport was still thriving in the early 20th century with 69 different bowling handicaps played on the Moor in 1906 alone.[3] Change, however, was afoot. The press even suggested that the 1906 match between Tommy Thompson of Newbiggin and James Nicholson of Burradon – two of the greatest champions – should be postponed because of a clash with the Newcastle and Sunderland football derby at St James's Park. Durham and Northumberland miners were starting to find new sporting enthusiasms and 'potshare' bowling went into decline.

The Tyne was a site for sport. As shipbuilding and river commerce grew rapidly, there were thousands of watermen ferrying goods back and forth and acquiring skill as oarsmen in the process. The best of them were the sporting heroes of Victorian Tyneside. They drew vast crowds to the river banks to bet and to cheer on their 'Geordie lads', especially when the challenge came from the watermen of the Thames. As Harvey Taylor has remarked in a valuable essay, 'connections of work and trade between the Tyne and the Thames served to fuel the competitive jealousy, producing a continuous sporting rivalry and creating the first regional sporting heroes with whom the people could identify'.[4]

[2] *An account of the wonderful walking match performed by Geo. Wilson, the celebrated Newcastle Pedestrian*, printed by J. Marshall (Newcastle, 1822); see also *The Book of British Sporting Heroes* (The National Portrait Gallery, 1998), p.231.

[3] Metcalfe, Alan, 'Potshare Bowling in the mining communities of South Northumberland', in Holt, R. (ed.), *Sport and the Working Class in Modern Britain* (1990), pp.29-30; Alan Metcalfe has made a unique scholarly contribution to the region's sporting and social history.

[4] Taylor, Harvey, 'Sporting Heroes' in Colls, Robert and Lancaster, Bill (eds.), *Geordies: Roots of Regionalism* (1992), p.115.

Professional rowing was bound up with the career of one man: Harry Clasper from Dunston, a ferryman who became not only the Tyne's greatest oarsman but also an innovative boat designer and a gifted trainer of new talent. On 16 July 1842 the Tyne was the scene of a match between the young Clasper's crew and a Thames boat:

> Take if you will a bird's eye view of the river's banks, and you will find every available elevation clad with living forms. Men of all cliques, classes and colours are there – Radical and Tory – Quayside merchant and slouching loafer – master and servant – the great white-washed and 'the great unwashed' are there, nay even women and children.[5]

On that day Clasper's crew lost and he resolved to build a new boat to beat the Londoners. He lightened the structure, changed the keel, fitted outriggers to improve the pull of the oars and took the new boat named the *Five Brothers* – for this was a family venture – to London, where on 26 June 1845 they won a famous victory. Clasper rowed his last race 22 years later in 1867, at the age of fifty-seven. He was an honest, friendly and a justly famous man. He owned eight public houses when he died in 1870. Crowds estimated at over 100,000 lined the route from the town to his grave at St Mary's Church, Whickham.

Harry Clasper brought on the talent of younger men, the most famous of whom was Robert Chambers, from the parish of St Antony's. He won the national sculling championship in 1859 by five lengths after falling behind when his oar was caught in a barge rope. Joe Wilson finished a hastily composed ballad on the race with a burst of local patriotism: 'For TYNESIDE PLUCK had gained the day, an noo it is wor pride / Ti say we can defy the world wive a CHAMPION frae Tyneside.'[6] 'Honest' Bob, who won four more national titles before dying young of tuberculosis in 1868, was soon followed by another exceptional talent, James Renforth, of Gateshead, whose sporting career was even shorter and more tragic. Between his debut in 1868 until he collapsed and died over his oars in Canada in 1871, he won 39 of his 45 races. There were rumours of drug taking and it seems Chambers was also epileptic. The Tyne never saw their like again. From the 1850s the river was gradually dredged and improved so that big ships could discharge their cargoes directly onto the quayside without the aid of watermen.

In their place came the new 'amateur' clubs. The amateurs were determined to break the link between money and sport, to outlaw gambling and to promote

[5] Lawson, William D., *Lawson's Tyneside Celebrities, sketches of the lives and labours of famous men of the North* (Newcastle 1873, pub. by the author), p.316.

[6] Halladay, E., *Rowing in England: a social history* (1990), p. 96; Halladay's excellent history is especially good on the Tyne, for which he had a particular knowledge and affection.

sportsmanship – and social exclusivity – on the river. The Newcastle Amateur Rowing Club broke away from the pre-eminent Northern Club, which mixed amateurs with professionals, and soon recruited 180 members at half a guinea subscription and twenty shillings entrance fee. The Tynemouth Rowing Club, formed in 1867, claimed 140 members and South Shields Amateur Rowing Club was also well supported. The amateur rowing tradition prospered on Tyneside but the working-class oarsman was effectively excluded. Of 64 new members joining the Tyne Amateur Rowing Club between May 1920 and May 1923, 54 were traceable. Almost half were from commerce and the liberal professions with the remainder made up mainly of clerks and draughtsmen. There was only one manual worker – a stevedore – among them.[7]

Just as rowing emerged as a more organised contest in the age of Clasper, so running shifted from wagers against time to races between individuals over set distances. In the 1870s the 'penny farthing' bicycle suddenly became important and George Waller, a professional cyclist from Tyneside, won the long distance world championship in 1879, riding 1,400 miles in six days round an indoor circuit of the Agricultural Hall in Islington. He was 22 at the time and returned to Newcastle in triumph, setting up a cinder track at Dalton Street in Byker with his brothers Tom and Henry. He acquired a huge tent, 200 yards in length, and a portable wooden track, touring the North East with a cycling 'circus' which mixed racing with trick cycling acts and brass bands. But in 1883 his tent was destroyed in a storm. The following year his track shut down and he went back to work as a stone mason. Cycle racing, however, survived and prospered in the late 19th century with tracks in Wallsend, Jarrow and Gateshead.

This was all part of a growing demand for more regular sporting entertainment for an industrial labour force enjoying rising real wages and shorter hours of work. Professional athletics was popular and new enclosed running grounds were built, beginning with *The Grapes* on Westgate Road, which could hold races of 200 yards or less. These were the notorious 'ped' sprints where handicappers would all too often cheat to lengthen the odds in favour of their man. Soon the 'Victoria Grounds' were built in the West End, with a full sized track and covered stands, for 'sporting gentlemen associated with the turf and the ring as well as leading lights of the entertainment industry'.[8]

The Victoria Grounds were the scene of some famous races, notably between two Tyneside champions James Rowan and Jack White ('The Gateshead Clipper'). Matches were organised in taverns and the most important races were advertised

---

7 Halladay, *Rowing in England*, p.96.

8 Watson, Don, '"Champion Peds": road running on Victorian Tyneside', *North East Labour History*, 25, p.44.

in *Bell's Life*, the London sporting paper, with Newcastle runners now able to use the train to go to London and Londoners able to compete in Newcastle. William Bell of Felling, for example, defeated Eric Mills from London at the Victoria track in 1861. In the same year Rowan ran several times against James Pudney of Mile End as the Tyne-Thames rivalry reached its height on the river and the track. When the Victoria Grounds were bought up for railway development in 1863, the Fenham Park Grounds on Ponteland Road were quickly laid out as a replacement. Here pedestrianism, dog racing and rabbit coursing – the trio of miners' gambling sports – had their heyday until the Victorian moral conscience, armed with a new Betting Act, led the police to close the Fenham track in 1875. Pedestrianism, of course, still flourished in the mining villages where small-scale gambling was beyond police control. Professional footballers such as Jackie Milburn made a few bob this way in the 1940s – but it was no longer a major sport in the city.

New amateur athletics clubs were formed in the 1880s at Elswick, Felling, Saltwell and Gateshead and in 1890 a club was formed in Heaton. The inaugural club run of the Heaton Harriers took them along Heaton Road and across Armstrong Bridge; 'nearing Jesmond Road they came upon another pack, and on sounding their war cry "good old Heaton", met with the response "gan on Wallsend"'. They raced each other down Jesmond Road and returned via Jesmond Dene, tearing around the side of a frozen pond to the shouts of the skaters, and home to Stannington Avenue.[9] The Heaton club, which was composed of skilled artisans, clerks and small businessmen, was one of many which combined city runs with cross-country runs, getting men out of the 'great indoors' of factory, shop and office and into the fresh air. They were also forging new kinds of 'parish' loyalty as the city spread into the suburbs. This increasingly co-existed with a sense of belonging to a wider industrial region which the athletes spontaneously marked out in their races from Newcastle to Whitley Bay, from Gateshead to South Shields and up the Tyne Valley.

Of all these races the New Year Morpeth to Newcastle road race, officially started in 1902, attracted the largest field and was the most important. Bert Helmsley of Gosforth Harriers won his first 'Morpeth' in 1937, his second in 1948 and his third at the age of 42 in 1951. Here was an athletic achievement to set alongside the feats of a George Wilson or a Jack White. In 1953 the status of the race reached new heights with the victory of Jim Peters, a world-class athlete, who knocked four minutes off the record in what was one of the greatest sporting performances ever seen in the North East. The warmth and democracy of the Tyneside running tradition live on in the continued success of the 'Morpeth' and the 'Great North Run'. The

[9] Allen, Don, *The Eastenders: Heaton Harriers 1890-1990* (Newcastle, 1990s), p.2; author Richard Holt's father, Jim Holt, was a member in the early 1920s and his uncle Jack Scott was a prominent Harrier in the 1930s. The author has drawn on his memory of their recollections.

stranglehold of men on the sport has been broken with top-class runners such as Jill Hunter leading a new generation of women emancipated from the restrictions of the past. Coming out of this running tradition with Jim Alder, Maurice Benn, Brendan Foster, Mike McLeod and Steve Cram, the North East as a whole has been very successful. Gateshead has established itself as a nationally important venue, giving the town an extra edge in its traditional rivalry with Newcastle across the river.

Running clubs were not just places where young men met to run. There were socials and dances, too, and brothers brought their sisters, who brought their friends. But 'community' was not something unique to the working class. The city's strong and well-rooted middle class also saw sport both as a form of exercise and a social opportunity. Here the expanding ranks of the educated and affluent could meet and perhaps marry. This was a central feature of the new sport of lawn tennis, which was designed for the back gardens of large suburban villas. In the 1880s it quickly established a unique position as a sport for men and women alike. The first star of Wimbledon, in fact, was a girl, Lottie Dod, the daughter of a wealthy Liverpool merchant, who won the ladies' singles title in 1887 at the age of 15 and was unbeaten thereafter. Not that the matrons of Jesmond would have wanted 'The Little Wonder' for a daughter. Destroying a young man on the tennis court was not the best recipe for making a good marriage.

The social geography of tennis said it all. The Portland Park Tennis Club was founded in Jesmond in 1878 and soon had five courts and a croquet lawn.[10] A close-knit group comprising 11 families and 19 single members, a revealing question is recorded in the club minutes for 1884: should a single member who marries *outside* the club be allowed family membership? The decision was left to the discretion of the committee. There was certainly no shortage of young hopefuls. Three vacancies for single members in 1885 attracted 17 candidates and the committee expressed its disapproval of those who actively canvassed for election. Membership was fairly stable up to the First World War. There were 20-25 family memberships at three guineas (increased to four in 1912) and 45-55 single members at two guineas. Fees were high enough to deter the lower middle classes without putting the game beyond the reach of an aspiring solicitor or accountant.[11] Another tennis club was set up on the Grainger estate in 1884 and more clubs in Jesmond, Fenham and Forrest Hall followed. The South Northumberland Cricket Club in Gosforth changed its name to incorporate 'tennis' in 1927, and there were regular inter-club matches.[12]

In England tennis and golf tended to go together as recreational sports for the middle-aged suburban middle class. There was a golf boom in the 1890s with

[10] Minutes of the Portland Park Tennis Club, Tyne and Wear Archives, SX18 1/1.
[11] Minutes of the Portland Park Tennis Club, SX18/4/1.
[12] Patterson, Norman H., *Lawn Tennis by Tyne and Wear* (Newcastle, 1921).

**9.2**   Third Northumberland Lawn Tennis Championships, 1931.

hundreds of new courses laid out. Casual games of golf may have been played for centuries over the Town Moor but a golf course was not laid out until 1891. This arose from a petition by 79 merchants, doctors, lawyers and academics who persuaded the Freemen of the City to lease out a part of the Moor for golf.[13] The petitioners had to create their own course, which became the City of Newcastle Golf Club. It soon had a membership of 300, used an old windmill as a clubhouse and employed as its professional Tom Fernie, who was provided with a shop and house on Claremont Road. But sharing space with the sheep and the strollers, the bowlers and the footballers who frequented the Moor was not in keeping with bourgeois standards of privacy and comfort. Nor was sharing the course with an artisan golf club formed in 1892 at Lockhart's Cocoa Rooms in Clayton Street. This club continued to play over the Moor until 1975.

The middle classes soon left this rudimentary public course for a new one laid out around the Gosforth Park race course. The Northumberland Golf Club was formed with 130 members in 1898. The Chairman of the Race Committee, Charles Perkins, became the first President of the golf club, a custom that continued until

[13] Sleight, J., *The City of Newcastle Golf Club: The City Centenary 1891-1991* (Newcastle, 1991), p.4.

1972. With the extension of the tram service to the gates of Gosforth Park, a clubhouse was built near the terminus. The entry fee for new members was raised to ten guineas plus an annual subscription. Membership was restricted to 300 in 1910 with 150 on the waiting list. The liberal professions and business elite established their networks of influence and the waiting list grew. Membership of such a club was a source of pleasure and prestige and as often as not would more than pay for itself. Meanwhile, in 1906 the remainder of the City of Newcastle Golf Club removed themselves from the Moor to land opposite the *Three Mile Inn* in north Gosforth, where Harry Vardon, the leading player of the day, had laid out a course. Members paid a five-guinea entrance fee and the same sum in annual subscriptions. This new associational life was more accessible and less dangerous than hunting with the 'county set' and yet conveniently removed from contact with the mass of working people. Golf was a haven of bourgeois sociability. Women were an important part of the club but only by virtue of their relationship to a male. The club was very traditional, refusing to have a 'Ladies Section', though wives and daughters of members could play without charge but were not allowed in the dining room.[14]

Middle-class girls were expected to play hockey and tennis at private schools. State elementary schools, however, had poor facilities and few resources, though some athletic sports were introduced to supplement the gymnastic drill that was taught as part of the Edwardian curriculum. Hockey was played by girls at some elementary schools on Tyneside between the wars and some inter-school games were organised for Saturdays, though it has not been possible to determine the precise extent of this. The Newcastle Schools Athletic Association was re-constituted in 1923 and was responsible for athletic competition in elementary schools. 'Girls are usually well represented in the annual school sports', wrote the author of a *Handbook for Newcastle upon Tyne Education Week* in 1925. However, 'their games appear to be limited to netball, and to the minor team games such as end-ball and cornerball' whilst 'the playing of hockey does not seem to have been fostered'. The provision of better facilities improved girls' school games post-war with secondary girls' state schools such as Middle Street Technical High playing hockey and netball within the school whilst a visiting American teacher caused a thrill by introducing basketball and volleyball. Competition between state school sides was weak, and in 1967 the Newcastle upon Tyne Schools Sports Association had only two schools in the regional senior netball league, nine in the intermediate and five in the junior.

Tyneside resembled the rest of industrial England when it came to women's sport. Not much seems to have survived the transition from school to work and

---

[14] Minutes of the Northumberland Golf Club, Tyne and Wear Archives, SX 22, 11 October 1905, 30 April 1906, 1 March 1909.

**9.3** Whorlton School girls games, 1900.

family life, after which women were tied to the home and children. The development of girls' and women's sport outside school has been restricted until recent years. However, since the 1970s aerobics and keep-fit have become far more popular in the network of leisure and sports centres set up since the 1970s. Swimming, however, was always significant, especially for girls who were often taught to swim at elementary school. This was important in a city with a great river and near the sea. Drowning was all too common and organisations such as the Humane Society agitated to cut death rates by compulsory swimming lessons. This, combined with Victorian concerns for cleanliness and public health, meant that proper facilities were provided, the grandest of which was the Northumberland Baths in the city centre. The Newcastle and District Amateur Swimming Association organised a girls' competition from 1898 and there were ladies' sections in all the major swimming clubs such as Newcastle, Jarrow, Westoe and South Shields. These clubs could compete with others like Sunderland, Middlesbrough and Darlington in the North Eastern Counties Amateur Swimming Association, which was founded in 1901.

Sport for women, however, was a predominantly middle-class phenomenon, assisted by servants and by a greater tolerance from the men, some of whom were attracted by the idea of shared recreation. Cricket was a sport where women were welcome as spectators and where wives took some part in the social life of the club, even if it was only making the teas. Genteel Gosforth had a remarkable concentration of such sporting facilities. Alongside tennis and golf, there was cricket and rugby. Gosforth Cricket Club began when a number of players, including Henry George Carr, the son of the 'squire of Gosforth', and William Wookey, the Chief Constable, decided to rent land for matches in 1864-5 near Gosforth Villas. This became the South Northumberland Cricket Club, which had around 200 members at a guinea each in the 1870s and hired the services of a professional bowler. There were, of course, other less exclusive clubs such as the 'Mechanics', the 'Claremont', the 'Newcastle' and the 'Press', either with their own grounds or playing inside the race course on the Town Moor.[15] Cricket was also popular amongst manual workers where church and chapel clubs were important. Newcastle United, as we shall see, had its origins in a cricket club formed in 1881, which played on vacant land near Stanley Street in south Byker. A survey of match results in the Newcastle press in 1900 revealed 143 clubs in the Northumberland cricket league of which around a dozen came from Newcastle itself, including Walker, Heaton, Newcastle Victoria, Gosforth Percy, Blaydon, Newcastle St Phillip's, Westgate, Jesmond, Rutherford College and, of course, South Northumberland.

Although cricket did not have the same central role in defining regional identity as it did in the Roses counties, the game went back at least to the 1820s when there were two clubs. One of these was the Northumberland Cricket Club, which played near Ridley Place. In 1847 the Northumberland CC took on the might of William Clarke's famous 'All England XI'. The local team was allowed to field 20 players, including two Yorkshire professionals and several leading Scots, against the stronger All England.[16] The club had their own band as did another side, Newcastle Clayton. Northumberland's band 'played during the progress of matches which greatly enlivened the scene' and attracted quite large numbers of spectators.[17] Northumberland CC moved to Heaton in 1881 with the help of the armaments magnate Sir William Armstrong, and in the same year a county association was formed which used the Heaton ground. In 1897, with cricket in its 'golden age', the county side bought the Constabulary Ground at Osborne Avenue and it was here that minor counties games were held and more prestigious visitors were entertained, including the occasional visiting Test side.

Rugby union was another sport with a strong middle-class and Gosforth base. Gosforth RUFC was formed by former Durham University students at 1 Gosforth

[15] Lawson, *Tyneside Celebrities*, pp.304-5.
[16] Jude, J.H., *Northumberland, a History of County Cricket* (Newcastle, n.d.), p.2.
[17] Harbottle, G., *A Century of Cricket in South Northumberland* (Newcastle, 1969), p.76.

Villas in 1877 playing their first match against Northern, which had been founded two years before at Elswick.[18] There was strong competition between the two clubs, though socially they both drew on the fee-paying schools of the city, especially the Royal Grammar School which began to play the game around 1877 and made it compulsory in 1893. These clubs supplied many of the best players for the Northumberland side. Rugby clubs had a wider county identity and county games, especially against Durham, were considered very important. Northern had an imposing entrance and a comfortable clubhouse with 'all mod cons'. These two sides dominated rugby in Newcastle for most of the 20th century but there were some important exceptions, such as the team formed by Newcastle College of Commerce in 1928, which went on to win the Northumberland Senior Shield in 1935-6.

Gosforth finally established itself alongside its great rival in 1955, complete with a club house, three pitches and a cantilever stand which cost £30,000. Gosforth were an up-and-coming club in the 1970s, winning the newly created John Player Cup in 1975-6. They sold their ground for housing development for £1.75 million in 1988 and moved to a magnificent new home nearby. By this time money was flooding into the top level of the game from television, and rugby went professional in 1995. The club was bought by Sir John Hall and duly won the national championship by buying in top players such as Rob Andrew. But this almost bankrupted the club and alienated some of the old established members, who departed. They re-established Gosforth in the amateur tradition, run by enthusiasts who graduated from the juniors up through the ranks and then slowly descended again, retiring to run the club – and prop up the bar. Not all rugby, of course, was socially exclusive. South Shields, for example, had a rugby union club which changed to play rugby league in 1902, though the travel costs forced them to give up in 1904. A Newcastle rugby league side was formed in the 1930s but gates were poor and it soon closed down.[19] In 1967 there were only ten schools in the rugby section of the Newcastle upon Tyne Schools' Sports Association against 103 football teams which played 700 games.

The passion for football was such that working-class rugby was bound to fail. If there is a single image that conjures up Newcastle to the outside world it is St James's Park with the Geordie crowd crammed into the vast terraces of the Gallowgate and the Leazes ends. Newcastle United was the best supported football club in England in the first half of the 20th century. The Edwardian team averaged

[18] Gosforth RUFC, records 1877-81, Tyne and Wear Archives, S/RFC4/13/2; also Northern RUFC, Tyne and Wear Archives, DX635; the authors are grateful to Fred Briggs, who played for North Durham in the 1940s, for his recollections of the time.
[19] Tony Collins provided the references to rugby league.

home gates of around 25,000. Crowds got even bigger between the wars. When Newcastle won the League in 1926-7 they had an average home crowd of over 36,000 with big games attracting 50,000 or more – a substantial share of the male industrial work force. And, of course, these were only the spectators who went through the turnstiles and were officially recorded.[20] As Joe Hind, born in Shieldfield in 1924, recalled:

> Whether we had the money or not, we would never pay to enter the grounds … it was simply a matter of jumping over the turnstiles – or ducking underneath them. … It was not just the kids who dodged into the match; lots of grown ups could not afford the gate money but would not be denied the pleasure of watching their beloved Black and Whites.[21]

Newcastle broke the Football League attendance record in 1947-8 with an average home crowd of over 56,283. Almost 1.2 million tickets were sold that season for St James's Park as Newcastle United won promotion to the First Division. Before the 1990s only Manchester United ever sold more, and then only once, when they won the European Cup in 1968.

How did this extraordinary passion for football take hold? Although games of folk football where youths would fight for a ball must have been played from ancient times, association football only arrived in 1877 via ex-public schoolboys from among rugby players working as engineers and managers at Elswick. They founded Tyne Association which played its early games at Northumberland Cricket Club, entering the FA Cup in 1879 and losing to the powerful Blackburn side 5-1 in front of a crowd of 300.[22] From these elite beginnings football spread very quickly, with around 50 to 60 clubs in Northumberland and Durham by 1882. One of these was a team from Stanley Street in south Byker, formed from players in the local cricket team and appropriately first named Stanley FC. Another local club, Rosewood, merged with Stanley FC to become Newcastle East End, playing near Heaton railway junction. Meanwhile West End cricket club also formed a football team and with the help of an affluent resident of Leazes Terrace, William Nesham, rented the ground that was to become St James's Park.

As their rivalry grew, both East End and West End began to advertise for players, especially in Scotland. Both clubs won the Northumberland Cup and East

---

[20] Tabner, B., *Through the Turnstiles* (Harefield, 1992), p.186.

[21] Hind, Joe, *A Shieldfield Childhood* (Newcastle City Libraries, 1994), p.116.

[22] For the history of Newcastle United see Joannou, Paul, *United: The First 100: The Official History of Newcastle United FC 1882-1995* (1995); the club and the city are fortunate to have so detailed a work, which is far superior to most club histories; there are also fine things in Arthur Appleton's *Hotbed of Soccer: the story of football in the North East* (1960); see also R. Hutchinson, *The Toon: a complete history of Newcastle United FC* (1997).

End issued shares in 1890 which were taken up by 83 individuals, mostly small shopkeepers, clerks and skilled artisans. East End was becoming much stronger than West End, whose officials invited the Eastenders to take over the lease for the Leazes ground and merge the clubs. On Friday 9 December 1892 Newcastle United was formed. The following year they applied to join the Second Divison of the Football League along with Liverpool and Arsenal. At first, results were poor and crowds were thin. The East End fans were angry at the move from Byker and the West Enders felt they had been supplanted. However, a shrewd appointment in the shape of Frank Watt from Edinburgh as 'secretary' saw results improve. Crowds grew quickly to an average of around 6,000 by 1900. Watt stayed with Newcastle for nearly forty years. If anyone made the club, he did.

This was a critical moment. The Geordie public overcame their parish factionalism and started to identify with the club as a force binding the city together. Beating top sides such as Burnley in the Cup at St James's Park, which was turned into a major stadium in the course of the 1890s, was important in the process of building a football community that extended across the city. The pitch was levelled, new stands were built and 20,000 turned up to see the first home match against Wolves. On Christmas Eve 1898 Newcastle played their first fixture with Sunderland at the newly opened Roker Park and so began one of the most famous rivalries in football. The *Northern Mail* described the desperation of fans locked out of the capacity crowd at the derby game of 1905:

> Thousands of disappointed people crowded into the streets and open spaces adjoining the ground, and listened with envy to the great noise that uprose. Any sort of eminence that afforded the tiniest glimpse of the field was strenuously secured. An empty house in the neighbourhood was literally raided, dozens of men hanging out of the windows at right angled positions to the walls. They lay on top of each other, packed like flies … Thousands who never saw a glimpse of the game or the players, braved the wild afternoon and stood by for the result. They knew how to interpret the cheers and the groans, and were correspondingly elevated or depressed. Nothing to approach it has been known at a Newcastle football match.[23]

Honours went first to Sunderland's 'team of all the talents', which was the top side of the 1890s. Newcastle did not beat Sunderland at St James's until 1903, which stung the pride of the larger and older city. But then came a remarkable Edwardian spell under the influence of the Scottish internationals Andy Aitken and Bob McColl,

[23] Cited in Hutchins, P., 'Sport and Regional pride: Association Football and the North East of England, 1919-1961', unpublished PhD thesis, Sussex University, 1990.

supported by Colin Veitch, a versatile player and an influential figure in socialist politics and culture on Tyneside. Along with the brilliant international winger Jackie Rutherford, the 'Newcastle Flier' from Percy Main, there was the famous Ulsterman Bill McCracken – the inventor of the off-side trap – who, with his other full back Frank Hudspeth, played for a record 19 seasons. From 1904 to 1922 the Scottish international Jimmy Lawrence played 496 games as goalkeeper for a team which dominated Edwardian football, winning the League three times between 1904 and 1909 and featuring in five FA Cup Finals.

In just ten years Newcastle United had gone from a makeshift and reluctant merger of two local teams to winning the Football League and becoming the best supported team in England. The Newcastle-Sunderland rivalry ran through the communities of South Tyneside, dividing 'border' towns such as South Shields. Though closer geographically to Sunderland and Roker Park, there was a strong loyalty to the community of the Tyne and to the Tyneside dialect in South Shields. Football was a team game that blended players from far and wide, especially Ireland and Scotland, with the northern English. As such it mirrored the actual process of migration and demographic change in Newcastle. Supporting the same club was a powerful tool of social integration on Tyneside just as it was in the valleys of south Wales through rugby or in the cities of the United States with baseball.

Success in football created self-confidence in a region far removed from London, the seat of parliament and monarchy and the traditional bastion of culture, wealth and authority. In this sense Newcastle's battles with Arsenal, Chelsea or Spurs gave a fresh lease of life to the north-south divide, which had for so long been a feature of professional rowing and running. Newcastle's reputation for football gave the city a congenial masculine image of virility, camaraderie and success. The Edwardians who filled St James's Park adapted a new sport to a traditional purpose; they transferred the devotion of their forefathers for men like Clasper to new heroes, especially centre forwards.[24]

Of these figures – and there have been several – two stand out above the rest. The first was Newcastle's greatest player; the second its finest son. On 3 September 1930 a club record of 68,039 fans crammed into St James's Park – not counting all those who 'dodged in' – to see the match with Chelsea. But it was not the team they had come to see. It was Hughie Gallacher, who had led Newcastle United to the League Championship in 1926-7, and had been sold against his will and the wishes of the fans. Standing only five feet five he was sturdy, two footed, good in the air and as hard as nails. From 1925 for five seasons, in Gallacher Newcastle had the best all-round attacking player in Britain and arguably in the world. The crowd

---

[24]  See Taylor, 'Sporting Heroes', in Colls and Lancaster, *Geordies*, pp.121-3.

gasped and fell silent when he ran out for his first home match against Everton. He was so small. But in that match he scored the first two of his 143 goals in 174 appearances for Newcastle. Gallacher's career total of 463 goals in 624 appearances included the 5-1 thrashing of England in 1928 by the 'Wembley Wizards' which won him a permanent place in Scottish football legend. But he was a hard and a difficult man, a drinker and a brawler. In a classic tale of decline he drifted down the leagues and back to Tyneside, eventually throwing himself under a train in 1957 before he was due to appear in court for child neglect.[25]

Gallacher was a great player but he was not a good husband or father. Tyneside needed someone who 'represented all the finest features of a working class life in the north-east'.[26] In Jackie Milburn

**9.4**  Jackie Milburn, 1951.

they found a brilliant player with an exemplary life. His nickname said it all. He was 'ours': 'Wor Jackie'. He was born in 1924, the son of an Ashington miner whose family had a long footballing tradition; his great grandfather ('Warhorse') had played in goal for Northumberland in 1886 and he had four cousins who played professionally and a fifth, Cissie, who was the mother of Jack and Bobby Charlton. Boys in Ashington went down the mines or played professional football – Milburn once counted 47 local boys who had played in the First Division – and 'Wor Jackie' did both, working as an apprentice fitter in the pit and famously scoring six goals in his war-time trial for Newcastle.

He signed for Newcastle in 1943 and retired in 1957 scoring 238 goals in a record 492 appearances. Starting as winger because of his exceptional pace – his first nickname was 'Jet' and he once ran 100 yards in 9.7 seconds – Jackie switched to centre forward in 1947-8 as Newcastle won promotion back into the First Division.

[25]  Joannou, *United: The First 100 Years*, pp.142-3.
[26]  Cited on the back cover of Kirkup, Mike, *Jackie Milburn in Black and White: a biography* (1990); Kirkup has a deep understanding of his subject's character and origins whereas John Gibson's *Wor Jackie: the Jackie Milburn Story* (1990) is a more conventional sports biography. Milburn's autobiography, *Golden Goals* (1957), was ghosted but has useful insights into his childhood and family life.

He was capped for England and went on to score Newcastle's two goals in their Cup Final victory over Blackpool in 1951. They were both exceptional goals, one a run from the half-way line and the other a classic Milburn long range drive from a cheeky back heel from Ernie Taylor. 'It was the sort of goal you dream about', as Stanley Matthews generously admitted.[27] The following year Newcastle beat Arsenal in the Cup Final, which was especially satisfying though the game was poor. When the FA Cup was still considered more important than the League, Newcastle were the first team to win the Cup in consecutive years since 1891. In 1955 Jackie scored the fastest goal ever seen in a Wembley final with a long range header from a corner inside the first minute. Newcastle went on to win. 'Wor Jackie' had brought the FA Cup home to Tyneside three times in five years.

This alone would have given him legendary status. Newcastle is still waiting for another domestic trophy. But there was more to the Milburn myth than this. Post-war regulations meant he was not allowed to leave his job at Ashington Colliery until 1948. He did not have a car and took the bus with other miners who were going to see him play. He played in the era of the maximum wage and never earned a lot more than many miners. Modest to a fault, friendly and decent, a family man who married and settled back in Newcastle after a few years away, Jackie Milburn's fame seemed to grow rather than to fade with the passage of time as poor teams and hooligans dragged the club's reputation down. He seemed to stand for a vanishing age when there had been honest jobs for men who had worked hard and taken care of their families. Jackie Milburn became an unselfconscious focus of community nostalgia. In 1980 he was made a Freeman of the City along with Cardinal Hume, who said Jackie 'was not only a footballer, but a great gentleman, and a person who won instant respect. There was a quality of goodness about him which inspired others'.[28] His death in 1988 produced a spasm of grief. Crowds gathered in their thousands to see the funeral pass and mourn not just the death of 'Wor Jackie' but what he stood for. *The Newcastle Evening Chronicle* opened a public subscription for a statue. A second was put up in Ashington. Streets, buses and trains were named after him and a successful musical and video of his life were produced.[29]

The great cup days of the '50s have never been repeated. Charlie Crowe, an apprentice pattern maker from Walker and a tenacious half back, recently produced a fascinating insider's memoir of the post-war club.[30] The likes of Frank Brennan,

[27] Joannou, *United: The First 100 Years*, p.194.
[28] Kirkup, *Jackie Milburn in Black and White*, p.172.
[29] Holt, R., 'The legend of Jackie Milburn' in Gerhmann, S., *Football and Regional Identity in Europe* (Germany, 1997); for a summary see 'No more heroes anymore?', *Times Higher Education Supplement*, 15 May 1998, pp.15-16.
[30] Crowe, Charlie, *A Crowe Amongst the Magpies* (ed. Mike Kirkup, TUPS, Newcastle, 1998).

the great Scottish centre half, Joe Harvey, the captain, and Bobby Cowell, the popular and long-serving local full back, have cast a long shadow over Tyneside football. Like Tyneside itself, the team seemed to go into a decline. Crowds fell and Newcastle were relegated three times between 1960 and 1990 but fought their way back. Even so, no more domestic honours have followed the Milburn years despite three Cup Final appearances and a wonderful League run under Kevin Keegan in the 1990s. Newcastle won its only European trophy in 1969, defeating such big names as Feyenoord, Sporting Lisbon and Glasgow Rangers to win the Inter-Cities Fairs Cup (forerunner of the UEFA Cup). There was Bryan 'Pop' Robson, Wyn 'The Leap' Davies and, of course, Malcolm Macdonald, 'Supermac', who caught the city's imagination. Paul Gascoigne, 'Gazza', however, has been too wayward both as a player and as a person to be a true Tyneside hero whilst Alan Shearer, whose values are in some ways similar to those of Milburn, has yet to win anything and has nothing in common with the fans in material terms.

Newcastle fans indeed have become more famous than the team, famous for their loyalty, their passion and their patience, though marred like so many other big city sides in the 1970s and 1980s by hooliganism. Famous, too, for the 'new football' of the 1990s as Sir John Hall, self-made property millionaire, forced out the old board, re-built the stadium and financed a team which gave Tyneside back its place at the top of English football. But there was a price to pay – a financial price which in turn denied access to many of the club's most loyal fans. Yet identification with the team was never stronger. It didn't seem to matter to the Geordie public that their players were not local. It never had done. Half of the great Edwardian side, after all, were Scots. What mattered was that 'their' men were better than the rest and that post-industrial Tyneside could look the world in the eye as it had done when coal was king and the Tyne built big ships.

The great days of Newcastle United from the Edwardian years to the '50s were also the heyday of boxing. Bare knuckle fights had long been part of popular tradition, especially at race meetings. From the 1880s they were replaced by gloved contests under the Queensberry rules. From 1909 there was boxing in the St James's Hall, conveniently sited beside the football ground, which could accommodate 3,000 and was rebuilt in 1930 to take 5,000. The hall was filled on Friday and Saturday nights to see the likes of 'Seaman' Tommy Watson, a Byker lad who narrowly lost a world title fight in New York. He joined the navy, buying himself out and winning the British title in 1930. Big crowds greeted his return on an open-topped bus holding his Londsale belt. He had 120 fights – too many as it turned out. Like his contemporary 'Cast Iron' Casey, a Sunderland middleweight who fought 220 bouts and was never knocked out, Watson paid the price and died 'punch drunk'. Recession in the 1980s brought a revival to boxing with men such as Billy Hardy who won a European featherweight title and Glen McCrory, a cruiser-weight with a pub in Consett.[31]

But the days of the 'small halls', the smoky, floodlit rings and thudding, blood-spattered gloves had gone. Like the professional oarsmen before them, boxers seemed out of place in a Tyneside of wine bars and fitness centres. Running, however, took on a new lease of life, adapting itself to the 'aerobic revolution', which saw men and women, especially in the younger and more affluent groups, flocking to take up healthy sports as part of a fashionable new life style. Apart from middle-class tennis clubs and school games, sport for women was very new. Historically, sport on Tyneside was a male space from which women were excluded. There were women's football teams during the First World War to amuse the munitions girls' and women's football during the miners' strike of 1921 when Lillian Ritchie emerged from obscurity to score 45 goals.[32] But the FA banned its clubs from allowing their grounds to be used for women's football and Lillian was reduced to kicking a turnip across the floor of the Co-op. Until recently the female half of Tyneside was excluded from playing the game which made it famous.

Playing football was a normal part of growing up for most boys on Tyneside, which produced a higher proportion of professional footballers than any other region of England. As early as 1900 there were 106 Saturday amateur football teams whose results were published in the *Newcastle Evening Chronicle*; around two in five of these came from Newcastle itself with the remainder divided between the shipyard communities of the Tyne like Jarrow or Hebburn and the pit villages or smaller ports like Blyth. This was just the tip of an iceberg, which included school teams, park sides and, of course, the back lane football that was played throughout the working-class districts of the city and beyond. Colin Veitch captained the first Newcastle Boys team to play Sunderland on Easter Tuesday in 1896. In 1903 the Newcastle and District Schools' Association was formed with two divisions including Burradon, Gateshead, Swalwell and Dunston. Boys started playing in back lane games, coats for goal posts, the youngest with the girls in the back yards, the older ones too big or too hard for the nine- and ten-year-olds; then came informal park games, maybe against the next back lane. Jackie Milburn learned to play this way, before and after school and all weekend. He recalled getting his first pair of new

[31] Potts, Archie, 'Northern Boxing', unpublished paper, 'Sporting heroes of the North', conference organised by the Centre for Northern Studies, 5 September 1998.
[32] Mason, Tony, 'Women's football in North East England', unpublished paper, Sporting Heroes of the North, 5 September 1998. We regret being able to say relatively little about female sport, for which few records survive and there is no oral history. We would like to thank Olive Scott for her memories of girls' state school sport in the 1920s and Hilary Briggs for her recollections of Middle Street Technical High School in the late 1950s. We would also like to thank Robert Colls for his suggestions for improvement in the style and content of this chapter.

boots for Christmas and going straight out to play at the crack of dawn only to find the other kids were already there and had made up the teams in the dark, lit by the flares from the nearby pits.

It was through this passionate love of football that a great industrial city and its surrounding region found a way of communicating with the outside world and with each other. Indigenous Geordies, along with Scots, Irish and other immigrant groups, joined together in their tens of thousands to watch Newcastle United and to bask in its glory. Between the wars improved bus services broke down the relative isolation of the mining villages. Milburn's post-war success forged the final links in the chain that bound the city to the coalfield. A pattern was set. Support for Newcastle United survived the closing of the pits and shipyards. But it survived in a new form. St James's Park looms like a fortress over the city. The days of 'dodging in' are long gone. Watching satellite television is the closest most supporters get to seeing their team. Yet regional identity remains as strong as ever and is seemingly impervious to economic and social change. The 'Americanising' of sport in recent years, the hype, the merchandise, the media, the share deals and the growing internationalism have not diminished the local and the regional. Global corporate football co-exists with a fierce affinity to 'the toon' and the conceit that no-one quite knows their football like a Geordie. The love of sport as an expression of the love of place – industrial or post-industrial – seems to burn as brightly today as it did in the century that spanned Harry Clasper, Hughie Gallacher and 'Wor Jackie'.

10

# *Architecture in Newcastle*

## THOMAS FAULKNER

The purpose of this chapter is to provide an overview of architecture and, to some extent, planning in Newcastle from the late 18th century to the 1960s, and to convey some sense of the city's architectural character. It concentrates on what are seen as the most significant developments during the period under review. It highlights the work of major, and especially local architects, as well as that of the legendary speculative builder and entrepreneur Richard Grainger (1797-1861), and will briefly examine the ways in which the legacy of Grainger and other Georgian and Victorian contributors has been utilised and re-invented in more recent times.

In his *English Journey* (1934) J.B. Priestley famously popularised the enduring image of Newcastle upon Tyne as a grimy, workaday place. He disliked both the city and the district as a whole, which seemed 'so ugly that it made the West Riding towns look like inland resorts'.[1] Even he, however, conceded that Newcastle itself had 'a certain sombre dignity'[2] and in fact, though for centuries financially dependent on coal mining and surrounded by linked industrial developments, the city has always had the character – at least until recently – of a residential and commercial capital. By 1700 Newcastle's merchants, many of whom had friends and relatives in London, expected their town houses to be on a par with those in the metropolis. Around the margin of James Corbridge's *Map of Newcastle upon Tyne* of 1723 are numerous illustrations of recently built houses in fashionable classical styles; also illustrated are modern public buildings including the Mansion House (1691), one of the earliest provincial structures of this type.[3]

From the point of view of planning, Newcastle presents an interesting case study in having Georgian and early Victorian developments grafted on to and partly replacing a medieval, walled core which had evolved northwards from the riverside. This development includes a coherently planned central area of classical streets and public buildings unique in England for its date, for which Richard Grainger was

[1] Priestley, J.B., *English Journey* (1994 edn.), p.290.
[2] *Ibid.*, p.291.
[3] The Mansion House was sold in 1837 and destroyed by fire in 1895. See Faulkner, T.E. and Lowery, P.A.S., *Lost Houses of Newcastle and Northumberland* (1996), p.26.

largely responsible during the 1820s and '30s. Later, the main focus of commercial and administrative activity moved northwards once again. (Indeed, the city's sloping, constricted site has always prevented concentric expansion around a natural centre.) During the 1960s and '70s, Newcastle was subject to a major if ultimately unfinished programme of comprehensive redevelopment involving the removal of large areas of Georgian and Victorian townscape; this resulted in a loss of population to suburban high-rise estates and to satellite new towns such as Cramlington, Killingworth and Washington. This phase was ultimately followed by a major facelift from the late 1980s onwards, mainly in the old riverside area ('Quayside'), involving a fashionable post-modernist mix of converted industrial buildings and innovative new architecture.

A prevailing sense of incomplete integration in much of the urban fabric which remains seems to be exacerbated by the rapid reduction in commercial activity associated with the decline of the former manufacturing and extractive industries, and the consequent move to an economy based on the public (especially education and local government) and service sectors. Also symptomatic, perhaps, of Newcastle's reduced importance has been the recent loss of its regional Assay Office, Royal Mint and branch Bank of England. Meanwhile, out-of-town retail palaces such as the 'MetroCentre', near Gateshead, south of the Tyne, threaten the prosperity of city centre shops. Comparisons are instructive. Bath, for example, has some resemblance to Newcastle in having Georgian development added on to a medieval nucleus – also walled and adjacent to a river, albeit a smaller river than the Tyne. However, it has been a centre of leisure, tourism and entertainment since the mid-18th century and largely remains so. Edinburgh, also vastly extended during Georgian times, has, of course, retained its importance as a national capital and indeed has recently increased it with the opening of the Scottish Parliament. Among major English cities, Birmingham and Manchester have to some extent retained their commercial and industrial bases, as has Leeds, which is becoming an increasingly important financial centre; all these are now competing to host international events. But Newcastle is fighting back, largely through its reputation as the nightlife centre of the North East. Redundant Victorian buildings, both public and commercial, are being converted into restaurants, clubs and bars, especially in and around the historic and now fashionable 'Bigg Market', just north of the Cathedral. Moreover, 'history', 'heritage' and 'conservation' are now marketable commodities. Throughout the city, once-expendable 18th- and 19th-century structures are being 'conserved' (although nowadays this can mean no more than retaining their facades), while 'historicist' rather than Modernist designs are favoured for the most sensitive sites.[4]

[4] A good example is 'Monument Mall' (1990-2) at the top of Grey Street.

Newcastle originated around a Roman fort. By the early Middle Ages its strategic position as a bastion against the Scots was recognised with the rebuilding of its Castle keep by Richard I. Later, in the 14th century, its prosperity founded largely on the coal and to a lesser extent the wool trades, Newcastle was ranked third in wealth amongst English towns.[5] In the early 17th century the antiquarian Camden commented that Newcastle 'makes a glorious appearance, as the very eye of all the towns in this part of the kingdom'.[6] Strategically placed and an important centre of consumption and trade, Newcastle by 1700 was the fourth largest English town.[7] Around this time it was further described as 'a spacious, extended, infinitely populous place'.[8] Elegant structures were being built (mostly by local architects) and its surprisingly large number of newspapers provided information about the latest London commodities and events. More than is often realised, the coal trade actually mitigated Newcastle's geographical remoteness by facilitating contact with London; the 18th century saw Newcastle become increasingly sophisticated both architecturally and in terms of 'polite' culture generally.

By this time a well-educated local architectural profession had begun to emerge. William Newton (1730-98), the son of a shipwright turned builder and surveyor, was a highly competent Palladian who probably did more than anyone to reinforce the evolving classical tradition in the North East. Thus it was Newton to whom the town elite turned in 1774 for the design of Newcastle's still-existing Assembly Rooms (Plate 10.1). This Newcastle elite, incidentally, included several minor aristocrats who employed Newton to design their country houses, as did other Northumbrian landowners; the more major grandees brought in national figures such as Adam, Paine and Vanbrugh. Meanwhile, Newton also designed Charlotte Square, Newcastle's first completed Georgian square (begun 1770)[9] and, before that, between 1764 and 1768, the compact and elegant church of St Anne's, City Road, to serve the growing population living eastwards, along the riverside. At the same time he occasionally turned his hand to 'Gothick' design. A 1780 example is his remodelling of the now-demolished Heaton Hall, Newcastle, the nearer country seat of Sir Matthew White Ridley, also of Blagdon, Northumberland.[10] In this context it should be noted that Heaton, as well as other present-day suburbs such as Benton, Benwell,

[5]  Musgrove, F., *The North of England: a History from Roman Times to the Present* (1990), p.147.
[6]  Camden, W., *Britannia, or, a chorographical description of England, Scotland and Ireland* (1586, first English edn. 1610), quoted in Hutchinson, W., *A View of Northumberland, etc* (1778), vol. 2, pp.366-7.
[7]  Musgrove, *North of England*, p.255.
[8]  Defoe, D., *A Tour through the Whole Island of Great Britain* (1724-6, edn. with an introduction by Cole, G.D.H., 1927), vol.2, p.659. Similarly, Miege's *The Present State of Great Britain and Ireland* (10th edn., 1755) referred to Newcastle as a 'a large, rich trading town, and very populous' (p.59).
[9]  In *c.*1720 work had commenced on Hanover Square, Newcastle, centering on a Dissenting chapel built by voluntary subscription, but was never finished; only a very few houses were completed.
[10]  Sir Matthew had also been a prime mover in the formation of the new Assembly Rooms.

10.1　The Assembly Rooms, Westgate Road, by William Newton, 1774-6.

Elswick, Fenham, Gosforth and Jesmond, were then rural villages encircling the still compact town of Newcastle itself. Other mansions of the local gentry, all also now lost, included Benton Hall (*c.*1760, architect unknown), the seat of the prominent coal-owning Bigge family, and the late 18th-century Benton Park, possibly by Newton, which was home to the interconnected Dixon and later Clark families. There was also Elswick Hall, in the then fashionable 'west end', designed by the prominent local architects William and (his son) John Stokoe in 1803.[11] This was the residence of the industrialist John Hodgson and later, briefly, as we shall see, of Richard Grainger.

Links with national trends are further exemplified in the work of David Stephenson (1757-1819), the first Newcastle architect to study at the Royal Academy.[12] In 1786 he designed the noble and elegant church of All Saints, high above the quayside. It has some fashionable neo-classical details typical of its period although its unusual oval plan, less orthodox than that of Newton's rectangular St Anne's, recalls the early 18th century – and was adapted from an unexecuted design

[11] For more details and illustrations of all these 'lost' houses see Faulkner and Lowery, *Lost Houses*.
[12] Little has so far been published on this important architect. Stephenson was admitted to the Academy in 1782, returning to set up practice in Newcastle the following year. In 1805 he became Surveyor-Architect to the Duke of Northumberland, designing estate buildings in the county and from 1806 the important New Quay, North Shields (never completed, now partially demolished); he may also have been responsible for some surviving terraces in the vicinity.

of 1720 by James Gibbs for his church of St Martin's-in-the-Fields, London.[13] Later, Stephenson's pupil John Dobson (1787-1865), also partly London trained, from his base in Newcastle became a neo-classicist of considerable national renown. Like Newton before him, Dobson designed many country houses in the North East. He was much influenced by the early 19th-century idea, promulgated above all by Sir John Soane and other Royal Academicians, of the architect as academic professional. Consequently he was at pains, perhaps rather ungenerously, to distance himself from the builder-architect tradition from which he emerged.[14]

Dobson, the most eminent architect to be born and have worked in the North East, produced over four hundred works of virtually every type.[15] He may be compared with the slightly earlier John Foster of Liverpool or Thomas Harrison of Chester and Manchester, or with his contemporary R.D. Chantrell of Leeds, as a major provincial figure who achieved national status as well. One of Dobson's most important works is of course the Central Station, Newcastle (1846-50, first phase), an example of nationally significant monumental classicism. In the ecclesiastical field, Dobson was a pioneer of the Gothic Revival in the region, being responsible for the first church in Newcastle of this type, St Thomas's, Barras Bridge (1827-30), built on a northwards site hitherto occupied by the ruins of St Mary Magdalen's Hospital. St Thomas's (Plate 10.2) still retains much of the flavour of the 'Commissioners' Gothic'[16] or even the Georgian 'Gothick' when compared with Dobson's later, more archaeologically correct designs such as Jesmond parish church (1858-61). Even so, it must have made a considerable impression in its day, complemented as it is by the same architect's appropriate if unusual 'Tudor-Gothic' elevations for the adjacent street of St Mary's Place (begun 1829).

In 1800 Newcastle was now only the ninth largest English town,[17] largely because new industrial growth came comparatively late and then peripherally so, mainly along the river bank. Even so, it had by the early to mid-19th century a larger number of architects and architectural practices than most other provincial cities (Ward's *Directory* of 1850 lists 17, a figure which, incidentally, rose to nearly 70 by 1900).[18] Both in terms of its architectural profession and its leaning towards classicism for its public buildings and streets, Newcastle can perhaps be best compared at this

---

[13] See Little, B., *The Life and Work of James Gibbs, 1682-1754* (1955), pp.70-2.

[14] See Faulkner, T.E. and Greg, A., *John Dobson: Newcastle Architect, 1787-1865* (1987), pp.11 and 94-5.

[15] *Ibid.*, pp.98-109.

[16] So-called from the rather standardised and simplified neo-Gothic churches being built in urban areas under the auspices of Commissioners appointed by Act of Parliament in 1818. In fact, although of this type, St Thomas's was funded not by the Commissioners but by the Newcastle Corporation as a replacement for the old St Thomas's Chapel near the river bridge.

[17] Musgrove, *North of England*, p.255.

[18] See Ward's *Northumberland and Durham Directory* (1850), p.130, and Ward's *Directory of Newcastle-on-Tyne, etc.* (1899-1900), pp.560-1.

**10.2** St Thomas's, Barras Bridge, by John Dobson, 1827-30.

time with Edinburgh, where such architects as Gillespie Graham, Thomas Hamilton and W.H. Playfair practised so successfully. Earlier trends in Newcastle now culminated in the work of Dobson and other talented local architects contributing substantially to Grainger's building developments in the second quarter of the century. In turn, these 'improvements' introduced a new monumentalism and created a new city centre which substantially enhanced Newcastle's status, as well as underlining the affinity of its architecture with the 'national' London-based 'mainstream' – a factor which has perhaps been underestimated. Late 19th-century and early 20th-century developments reinforced the city's now essentially neo-classical character, the city Priestley nevertheless saw as an unattractive place in 1934.

It seems also that, in matters of architecture (and perhaps in other matters too), members of Newcastle's ruling elite tended to be happier with the people they knew. Dobson, and David Stephenson before him, had semi-official positions as 'attached' architects to the town. Late in his career, Dobson was even accused of jobbery, such was his monopoly of public commissions.[19] Almost until the mid-20th century nearly all the work in Newcastle – although not, as indicated earlier, in the county of Northumberland – was reserved for local men,[20] albeit almost invariably working in nationally accepted styles. This was not the case with comparable cities such as, for example, Manchester and Liverpool. Thus it is significant that a classical building as major as Newcastle's town hall (1858-63, demolished c.1969) was designed not by a prominent national figure but by the local architect John Johnstone.[21] Subsequently, we find that as late as the 1920s and '30s the design of several major new public and commercial buildings in Newcastle's city centre was entrusted to Robert Burns Dick (1868-1954), probably the most talented local exponent of the then fashionable 'Beaux-Arts' classical style. It is true that Sir John Burnet and Partners were brought in to collaborate with the Newcastle firm of L.J. Couves in the design of Carliol House (1924-8), the prestigious new headquarters of the North East Electricity Supply Company (a steel-framed, Portland stone-faced 'stripped classical' building on the corner of Market Street and Pilgrim Street which, incidentally, accords well with the nearby 'Grainger/Dobson' architecture). Similarly, L.G. Ekins, chief architect to the London C.W.S., was responsible for the stylish, rather 'Art Deco' Co-operative department store in Newgate Street of 1931-2.[22] Even so, the local spell was only finally broken when an open competition for the design of a new Civic Centre, approximately on the site of the present building, was organised in 1939 after the rejection of several earlier proposals by Burns Dick. A little-known firm of Bournemouth architects, Collins and Geens, won it although the proposal was ultimately abandoned because of the war.[23] Later, prominent national and international figures began to be employed during the period of post-1945 comprehensive redevelopment as Newcastle's leaders were increasingly prepared to sacrifice much of the city's Georgian and Victorian

[19] Faulkner and Greg, *John Dobson*, p.86.

[20] The most important exception which proves the rule was probably St Mary's Cathedral (RC), Clayton Street, Newcastle (1842-4), by A.W.N. Pugin in his favourite 'Decorated' style. The tower was completed by Dunn & Hansom (see main text, below), who also added the spire in 1872.

[21] The 'old' Town Hall, built when the historic Guildhall became inadequate for modern needs, actually incorporated at ground-floor level the Corn Exchange of 1838-9 by the local architects John and his son Benjamin Green (see also note 51, below). The Town Hall stood opposite St Nicholas's Cathedral before being replaced by the present undistinguished office block.

[22] It should be noted, however, that even Ekins was not a total 'outsider'. He had been Chief Architect to the Newcastle C.W.S., 1905-16, before taking up his London appointment.

[23] For the record, their winning design was a symmetrical exercise in 'stripped classicism' with central tower.

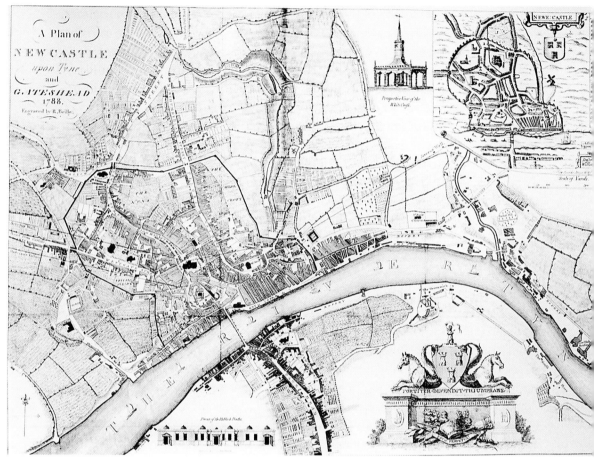

**10.3**   R. Beilby's *Plan of Newcastle upon Tyne and Gateshead* (1788); inset: Speed's map, 1610.

heritage in their search for a new image based on their view of international modernism.

The 18th-century trend in Newcastle towards classicism and fashionability, as reflected in the illustrations appended to Corbridge's map and later developed, as we have seen, by architects such as Newton and Stephenson, was reinforced by a limited number of late Georgian municipal 'improvements'. These included the construction by Stephenson of Mosley Street (1784-6, soon to contain his elegant new Theatre Royal of 1788), and then Dean Street (*c.*1787-8) which gave better access from the quayside (Plate 10.3). Collingwood Street, linking Mosley Street with Westgate Street (now Road), was constructed in 1810. Together, Newton and Stephenson were employed by the Corporation in 1796 to remodel the north front of the ancient Guildhall. John Stokoe designed the 'Moot Hall', an early example of neo-classicism in Newcastle, in 1810. Meanwhile, as the middle classes migrated from the quayside area, good quality residential streets were being built outside the walls. Saville Row, begun in the 1770s to run eastwards from the 'wide and well-built'[24] Northumberland Street, was followed by Brandling Place, Claremont Place, Eldon Place, Eldon Row, Ellison Place, Higham Place (see below), Lovaine Place, Summerhill, Swinburne Place and Victoria Square. These Georgian terraces were invariably of brick, with sash windows and classical doorcases. Meanwhile, a portion of the 'town wall' between the Pilgrim Street Gate and the Carliol Tower was removed in 1811 to make way for New Bridge Street. This latter street was similar to those cited above for much of its length, except that its western end, towards the bridge itself, and its continuation beyond the bridge, Picton Place, boasted an impressive series of detached and semi-detached neo-classical villas, some to early 1820s designs by Dobson.[25]

However, communication routes were still generally inadequate. Although Newcastle's single medieval bridge was replaced on the same site after 1771 with an elegant Georgian structure,[26] later widened by Stephenson, it still made a tortuous entrance into the city, slightly west of the Guildhall and almost blocked by the medieval St Thomas's Chapel (demolished 1827). Moreover, even in the early 19th century, the period of Richard Grainger's youth, Newcastle was still dominated by the Castle and St Nicholas's church (now Cathedral). Other surviving medieval buildings included the churches of St John, Westgate Street, and St Andrew, Newgate Street, as well as the former monastery of Black Friars, and the Hospital and Chapel of St Mary the Virgin in Westgate Street, then occupied by the Grammar School and later demolished for the widening of Neville Street in 1845. There also still existed many houses of the type earlier described by the local historian Henry Bourne as 'very ancient and mean'.[27] Commercial activity centred on the old quayside, from which led narrow alleys and dark, unlit stairs. Newcastle's expansion remained inhibited by its medieval street pattern and largely surviving encircling walls. Within these walls was also the curious survival of about thirteen acres of neglected ground to the west of Pilgrim Street[28] comprising the 'Nuns' Field', from the original nunnery

[24]   Brand, J., *The History and Antiquities of Newcastle upon Tyne* (1789), p.424.

[25]   See Faulkner and Greg, *John Dobson*, p.38, and Faulkner and Lowery, *Lost Houses*, p.27. The only survivors of this development of villas are what was Dobson's own house, dating from 1823 (now a night club, near the Laing Art Gallery) and some houses ('Ridley Villas') east of the present Falconar Street; similarly, little more than the terraced houses opposite 'Ridley Villas' survive of the original main development of New Bridge Street.

[26]   By, again unusually for Newcastle, a London-based architect, Robert Mylne.

[27]   Bourne, H., *The History of Newcastle upon Tyne, or, the Ancient and Present State of that Town* (1736), p.53.

[28]   Richard Grainger referred to it as having been 'in a most terrible condition'. See *Report of the Commissioners Appointed to Inquire into the late Outbreak of Cholera in the Towns of Newcastle upon Tyne, Gateshead, and Tynemouth* (1854, hereafter *Report of the Cholera Inquiry Commissioners*), p.308.

of St Bartholomew, and the historic manor and gardens of Anderson Place[29] (see Plate 10.3). There had been Improvement Acts for Newcastle of 1747 and 1786, the latter resulting in the construction of Dean Street,[30] but progress was generally slow and as late as 1827 another local historian, Eneas Mackenzie, was able to complain that 'no master mind conceives and directs the public works'.[31]

Before long Grainger had, unofficially at least, taken on this role. At the age of 12 Grainger had been apprenticed to a builder. He set up on his own account in 1816 and was soon building an attractive terrace for the prominent Methodist, Alderman William Batson, in Higham Place (c.1819-20), followed by houses in such recent streets as New Bridge Street and Carliol Street. At about this time Grainger purchased his first property.[32] His first major developments were necessarily peripheral to the 'Nuns' Field'/Anderson Place site. Blackett Street (1824) was just to the north, financed by a dowry from his recent marriage and jointly planned by John Dobson and Thomas Oliver (1791-1857), another local architect, to lie on the site of a northern section of the old town wall.

Then came the monumental Eldon Square of 1825-31, designed on the northern side of Blackett Street by Dobson, and, to the west, Leazes Terrace (1829-34), by Oliver, their novel 'polished stone' ashlar facades dramatically aggrandising the established classical tradition of Newcastle street architecture (see Plates 10.4 and 10.5). In a similar style was the Royal Arcade, a commercial building at the foot of Pilgrim Street (by Dobson, 1831-2); this further reinforced the fashionable air which Grainger was bringing to the town. Significantly, the entrepreneur's careful division of commissions between architects such as Dobson and Oliver may have reflected not only a desire for control but also his awareness that both were evolving development plans of their own. Blackett Street in its original form, the Royal Arcade, and most of Eldon Square were demolished for redevelopment during the 1960s and '70s, but Grainger's new commercial and residential city centre, constructed on the 'Nuns' Field'/Anderson Place site and adjacent ground, remains largely intact. This development is bounded by the ancient routes of Pilgrim and Newgate Streets to the east and west respectively, and to the north by Blackett Street. The acquisition of what had been a largely vacant site, the removal of Anderson Place and the purchase and demolition of adjoining property to the south enabled the area to be developed as an architecturally coherent entity. Essential, too, had been the support

[29] Anderson Place was built in the 1580s, extended in the late 17th century and demolished as part of Grainger's central redevelopment in 1834. See also Faulkner and Lowery, *Lost Houses*, p.8.

[30] The Act of 1786 was, rather momentously, 'for widening, enlarging, and cleansing the streets, lanes, and other public places, and for opening new streets, markets, and passages'. See Abstract of an Act (26 Geo. III) (1786), p.7.

[31] Mackenzie, E., *A Descriptive and Historical Account of Newcastle upon Tyne* (1827), p.197.

[32] In Percy Street at the foot of Leazes Lane. For more on Grainger's life and work see Wilkes, L. and Dodds, G., *Tyneside Classical* (1964) and Ayris, I., *A City of Palaces: Richard Grainger and the making of Newcastle upon Tyne* (1997).

10.4    Eldon Square, by John Dobson, 1825-31, largely demolished early 1970s; photographed in 1949.

10.5    Leazes Terrace, by Thomas Oliver, 1829-34.

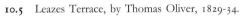

of the Council, which saw self-advantage in the scheme, and in particular that of John Clayton, the Town Clerk, who lent money himself, arranged other loans and supervised Grainger's usual system of purchase by deferred payment and continual mortgaging of newly built property in order to finance further developments.

Grainger was able to acquire Anderson Place for £50,000 in July 1834,[33] having already presented to the Council a scheme 'for opening new streets in the Nun's Fields';[34] this is indicated on a *Plan* which he published almost immediately afterwards, showing the dramatic innovation of a major new street (now Grey Street) running from Dean Street through the area then occupied by the Butcher Market, opened as recently as 1808, to the eastern end of Blackett Street. The major new street, which also necessitated the removal of Stephenson's comparatively modern Theatre Royal,[35] was to have four lateral streets linking eastwards with Pilgrim Street and westwards to what is now upper Grainger Street, the last-named being one of a quadrilateral of streets containing a new Market planned by Grainger. The most northerly of these was to become Clayton Street, connecting with Grainger's earlier Eldon Square development.

This arrangement was essentially the scheme as carried out (see Plate 10.6).[36] Council approval for the scheme was given in June 1834 – before Grainger had even formally completed the purchase of Anderson Place – and work started immediately. Astonishingly, the new Market, designed by Dobson, opened as early as October 1835 and nearly all the other streets and buildings by 1840, in spite of the great amount of levelling required. Grainger himself planned all or most of the layout,[37] which contained not only what later became known as the 'Grainger' Market but also the new Theatre Royal (by the father-and-son local architects John and Benjamin Green, 1837) and the Central Exchange (by Grainger's then salaried architects John Wardle and George Walker, 1838). The stately, neo-classical Grey and upper Grainger Streets, with their intersections, the two further streets linking Grey Street with Pilgrim Street, and the plainer but still dignified Clayton Street were also largely the work of Wardle and Walker, except for the lower east side of Grey Street, which was done by Dobson. Within the unifying discipline of Grainger's classical facades, faced in fine ashlar (rather than metropolitan stucco) are judicious points of emphasis such as public buildings and the junctions between streets. This

[33] Taylor, C.C., 'Development of Central Newcastle', in Barke, M. and Buswell, R.J. (eds.), *Historical Atlas of Newcastle upon Tyne* (1980), p.25.

[34] Minutes of the Newcastle Common Council, 22 May 1834.

[35] Crucial, of course, to obtaining Council support had been Grainger's ingenious offer to replace both the Market and the Theatre with newer and bigger alternatives.

[36] Some proposals for subsidiary streets were quickly abandoned, probably because of difficulties in acquiring property. These included one of the streets linking Grey and Pilgrim Streets and a small diagonal street between Grey Street and High Bridge Street.

[37] *The Newcastle Courant*, 31 October 1835.

**10.6** Reprinted from the *Newcastle Journal*, 24 October 1835.

is a system fully displayed in Grey Street, with its sweeping curve up to the junction with Blackett Street.

In this massive central reconstruction Grainger is said to have been inspired by the Edinburgh New Town development,[38] although any direct influence of Georgian Edinburgh on his essentially commercial scheme was surely limited to street facades. The New Town's more formal arrangement, involving for example parallel squares, was not adopted. In his planning, Grainger was more probably influenced by the recent 'Metropolitan Improvements' in London undertaken for the Prince Regent by his architect John Nash between 1811 and 1827. These involved a series of 'Picturesquely' sited terraces in and around London's new Regent's Park and, crucially, a north-south route from this to St James's Park via Portland Place, Oxford Circus and Regent Street. This latter route involved a series of slight curves, largely necessitated by the exigencies of property acquisition. However, Nash turned the situation to his advantage, as Grainger later did, by creating strategically placed vistas. Thus, for example, there is a distinct resemblance between Grey Street, Newcastle, and London's Regent Street, even in the latter's now redeveloped form.

[38] *The Newcastle Daily Journal*, 5 July 1861.

Closer to home, Grainger must also have been aware of two well-publicised schemes for the improvement of Newcastle produced earlier in his career, the first by Dobson (c.1824), and the second by Oliver (1830). Both, needless to say, remained unrealised. Dobson's scheme would have used the 'Nuns' Field'/Anderson Place area to create a grand central square, containing a market and other public buildings including a 'civic palace' of his own design on the site of Anderson Place itself.[39] Also proposed by Dobson was a continuation of Blackett Street via two classical squares westward to the West (Carlisle) Road. Had it been implemented, Dobson's scheme would have given Newcastle a stately, formal quality, more definitively reminiscent of the Edinburgh New Town or even of many continental cities with their central squares. Importantly, it would have re-defined and consolidated Newcastle's centre around the upper part of what is now Grey Street, towards Pilgrim Street, and would almost certainly have lessened later northwards drift. It would also have obviated the later need for the construction of major civic headquarters in both the mid-19th and mid-20th centuries.[40]

Oliver, by contrast, was much less concerned with the 'Nuns' Field'/Anderson Place site, merely borrowing one of Dobson's ideas for this: a street to run from Newgate Street into Blackett Street opposite Eldon Square, though extended to open up an additional east-west link to the Westgate (West) Road. His main focus was on the much needed improvement of communication routes; thus he not only retained Dobson's notion of extending Blackett Street (minus the classical squares) but also proposed a new lateral route eastwards via Collingwood Street to the New Road and thence to the industrial areas towards the coast. Another of Oliver's new streets would have connected the east quayside to Lovaine Place, near the site of the present Civic Centre, foreshadowing rather remarkably the line of the present inner-city motorway (east) and linking also with his own Leazes Terrace via Northumberland and Percy Streets.[41]

In many ways it is a pity that Oliver's far-seeing proposals found so little favour with the Council of the day. If carried out, even in part, they would have done much to alleviate traffic congestion, with attendant economic benefits, and to prevent

[39] The main features of Dobson's scheme are indicated on John Wood's *Plan of Newcastle-upon-Tyne* (1827) and described by Mackenzie, *Descriptive and Historical Account*, pp.200-2; see also Faulkner and Greg, *John Dobson*, ch. 4 n. 22.

[40] In fairness to Grainger it should be noted that in 1838 he did make a (belated) proposal to build new Law Courts and Civic Offices on a site between Grey and Pilgrim Streets. This would have been based on a typically Graingerite exchange deal involving property such as the old Guildhall and Mansion House, the failure of which, incidentally, may have been a sign that the newly reformed Town Council was becoming less sympathetic to Grainger. In the event the prepared design was modified to become the present Lloyds Bank building.

[41] Thomas Oliver was a former pupil of Dobson who was also a surveyor and cartographer. His ambitious proposals were shown on his own 1830 *Plan of Newcastle upon Tyne* and unsuccessfully presented to the Corporation in the same year. They were further explained in his *A New Picture of Newcastle upon Tyne* (1831).

some of the infamous demolitions of more recent years. Moreover, the schemes of Dobson and Oliver could actually have been combined; it is possible that Oliver intended this. Had this happened, Newcastle's new formal centre would have been much more effectively integrated with the rest of the town, thus avoiding the still slightly apart and enclosed quality of Grainger's central redevelopment. Indeed, a similar result might also have occurred had Grainger himself taken a less commercial and more philanthropic view, building second- and third-rate (in the Georgian sense) housing around the periphery of his new centre. The delightful Leazes Crescent of 1829-30, by Oliver, near the same architect's more grandiose Leazes Terrace and, unusually for Newcastle, stucco-fronted, shows what Grainger could do on a rare excursion into two-storey artisans' or lower-middle-class housing.

In any event, Dobson's proposed monumental square may have suggested to Grainger the more commercial idea of a central market bounded by a quadrilateral of intersecting streets. Also Dobsonian is the street connecting Eldon Square with Newgate Street (i.e. Clayton Street, which originally extended to Blackett Street), while the idea of extending it westward may have derived from Oliver. However, Grainger avoided the formality of Dobson's classical grid and, unlike Oliver, concentrated only upon what was financially and politically possible. Grainger's was the more practical, informal development, utilising the site more profitably than earlier proposals would have done, connecting only with already existing routes, and centering not on a grand square of the type Dobson had proposed, but solely on a market. Its principal street, Grey Street, provided an important link between the upper and the lower town which previous schemes would not have achieved.[42] This street was also intended to attract what Grainger called the 'most opulent consumers',[43] who now lived in the upper town. In addition, development took place only on the limited zone of land acquired by Grainger. Here an effect of grandeur could be achieved in a relatively short time, contrasting with the still-existing older areas of town which contained numerous run-down and, in many cases, squalid buildings.

Grainger's pragmatism is reflected in almost every aspect of his central redevelopment. He exploited his good fortune in being able to employ talented local architects, both independent and salaried, with whom he, as the developer,

[42]   On what is thought to be Grainger's own copy of his 1834 *Plan* (now in the Northumberland Record Office) are sketches of two proposed alternative routes extending Grey Street northwards to Barras Bridge and the Great North Road. Had either of these been carried out, Grey Street would have become established once and for all as the city's principal north-south route.

[43]   *The Newcastle Chronicle*, 7 June 1834.

[44]   More than a century earlier, for example, the traveller Celia Fiennes had been impressed by the quality and variety of Newcastle's specialist shops (see Morris, C. (ed.), *The Journeys of Celia Fiennes*, 1949, pp.209-11). Similarly, Miege, *The Present State* (p.59) commented 'Here are plenty of all things, and provisions cheap'.

had an unusually dominant relationship. He kept control by carefully using their services for different portions of his scheme. What Grainger also did was to develop further Newcastle's long established retail and commercial tradition.[44] Had he not done this it is most unlikely that he would have attracted backing for his enterprises. Accordingly, his new commercial streets were what he described as 'places of business; shops below and dwelling houses or warehouses, above'.[45] Some of the houses in Grey Street were occupied exclusively as offices, while in others the prosperous shopkeepers Grainger was anxious to attract resided above the shop.[46] By the mid-1850s his prestigious new centre was well established, having not only the new Market but also public buildings, banks, offices, showrooms, marts, hotels and inns and three or four hundred fashionable specialist shops.[47]

Admittedly, Grainger's new centre was not without the potential for its later dilapidation and neglect. The layout disregarded the importance of peripheral communication routes. Grey and Grainger Streets, particularly to the north, were not major thoroughfares. Grey Street still presented a considerable gradient. Grainger Street is slightly less steep but was extended southwards only much later, in 1868, and then not as Grainger had proposed. In addition, Grainger failed to take sufficient account of the imminent coming of the railway and with it an important new road link, over the High Level Bridge, in 1847-9. His own earlier proposal for an elevated bridge of 1843 would have linked directly to the east rather than the west end of Mosley Street, and so into Grey Street, but included no provision for a railway and therefore stood no chance of being built.[48] These factors indicate an increasing failure of judgement on Grainger's part and, more specifically, helped to prevent Grey Street from ever becoming the major north-south axis he had desired. By the 1880s Grey Street was no longer Newcastle's principal street, and before long, also, Northumberland Street as the city's major retail area was supplanting Grainger Street.[49] Even so, as a result of Grainger's central redevelopment, Newcastle has been described as the best-designed city in England.[50]

Probably as a result of the strong classical tradition promoted by Grainger and evident in the work of the local architects discussed above, the Gothic Revival only

---

[45] *Report of the Cholera Inquiry Commissioners*, p.303.

[46] *Ibid*.

[47] These included milliners, drapers, hosiers, haberdashers, bootmakers as well as wine and spirit merchants, chemists, opticians and jewellers; see for example Ward's *Northumberland and Durham Directory* (1850).

[48] See Wilkes and Dodds, *Tyneside Classical*, p.142. Grainger's earlier scheme for a railway terminus at Elswick had been equally impractical, in this case because of the remoteness of the site. By contrast, as early as 1830 Thomas Oliver had sought to develop an earlier concept of Dobson, a street northward to the Groat Market from the Castle Garth, through an additional connection with a proposed high-level road and railway bridge across the Tyne approximately on the site of the present High Level Bridge.

[49] Ayris, *City of Palaces*, pp.77-8.

[50] Pevsner, N., *The Buildings of England: Northumberland* (1957 edn.), p.56.

really established itself in Newcastle in the field of church architecture. Here, an impressive neo-Gothic tradition initiated, as we have seen, by Dobson, was developed during the later 19th and early 20th centuries by eminent local practitioners such as Thomas Austin (1822-67), a pupil of Dobson, his partner R.J. Johnson (1832-92), the latter's pupil W.S. Hicks (1849-1902), and A.M. Dunn (1832-1917). By the late 19th century, also, the national model of architectural practice increasingly applied in that Newcastle architects were now specialising in work for a single religious denomination rather than working for all of them, as Dobson had done. Thus Johnson and Hicks worked almost exclusively for local Anglicans. By contrast, Dunn, whose 'Neville Hall', Westgate Road (1870-2), with its Ruskinian emphasis on the use of polychromatic contrasting stone, is one of the few High Victorian Gothic secular buildings in Newcastle, became the favourite architect of North East Roman Catholicism.[51]

This pattern of employment invariably reflected the often deeply held personal affiliations of these men. One of them, R.J. Johnson, like Dobson before him, achieved a considerable measure of both regional and national renown. At the time of his death, Johnson had become one of the most respected architects working outside London. He was important in anticipating some of the ideals of the Arts and Crafts movement through his careful use of materials and concern for craftsmanship and was also an early and influential pioneer of a more reverent, conservative approach to restoration work. His architecture reflects not only a continued affinity with mainstream developments but also a typically late Victorian desire to create a range of appropriate and identifiable building types. Although primarily a neo-Gothic specialist, he designed a number of major public and commercial buildings in Newcastle in a variety of mainly classical styles (see below).[52]

At this point it is also interesting to note that a line of succession – almost a 'family tree' – can now be traced within Newcastle architecture from the late 18th to the mid-20th centuries; this via the architect and/or pupil or partner relationship existing successively through Stephenson, Dobson, Austin, Johnson (Austin & Johnson succeeded to the practice of Dobson) and Hicks (the latter's practice, Hicks & Charlewood, survived in the hands of his successors until the 1940s and, with different personnel, later still).

[51] Archibald Matthias Dunn set up in Newcastle c.1855 and was later in partnership with E. J. Hansom (1842-1900) 1871-93; from 1887 to 1893, when A.M. Dunn retired from full-time practice, the firm was Dunn, Hansom & Dunn (jnr.), later Dunn, Hansom & Fenwicke (W. Ellison Fenwicke), 1895-1914. 'Neville Hall', home to the North of England Institute of Mining and Mechanical Engineers, makes a splendid and probably deliberate contrast with its much more typical neo-classical neighbour, the Literary and Philosophical Society building of 1822. The latter was designed by another highly competent member of the Newcastle 'school' of classical architects, John Green (1787-1852) (see also note 21, and the reference to the Theatre Royal, Grey Street, in the main text, above).

[52] For more on Johnson see Faulkner, T.E., 'Robert James Johnson, Architect and Antiquary', in *The Durham University Journal*, new series vol. lxi, no. 1 (January 1995).

**10.7** Bank, formerly of Hodgkin, Barnett, Spence, Pease & Co., Collingwood Street, by R.J. Johnson, 1888-91.

During the late 19th century Newcastle's business district began to re-centre just to the north of the Central Station, between the old Quayside and the area of Northumberland Street and the Civic Centre (St Mary's Place and Sandyford Road). Of particular importance were Mosley Street and especially Collingwood Street, both being rebuilt with massive Renaissance-style banks and offices designed by distinguished local architects such as R.J. Johnson, Oliver Leeson & Wood, and F.W. Rich. A good example is the Bank, formerly of Hodgkin, Barnett, Spence, Pease & Co., in Collingwood Street, by Johnson, of 1888-91 (Plate 10.7). These massive classical structures, as well as the monumental and resplendent neo-Gothic churches of the same period, such as Johnson's own St Matthew's, Summerhill (begun 1878, tower by Hicks, 1895) and All Saints', Gosforth (1887), and Dunn, Hansom & Dunn's church of St Michael and All Angels, Westmorland Road, of

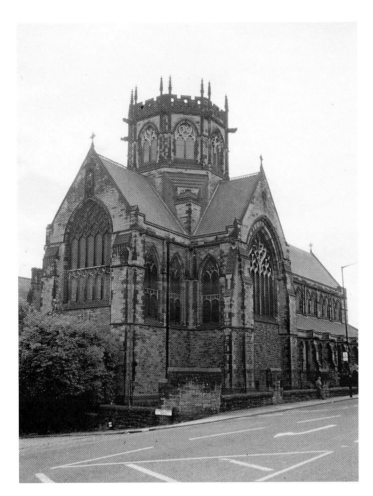

**10.8**   Church of St
Michael and All Angels,
Westmorland Road, by
Dunn, Hansom &
Dunn, 1889-91.

1889-91 (Plate 10.8) continue Dobson's legacy: architecture possessing 'a certain
distinctive heaviness and strength'[53] furthered by the use of the hard and durable
local stone. This is what constitutes the defining quality of Newcastle's public
architecture.

However, only one other local architect can be described as a 'visionary' in the
tradition of Dobson, Grainger and Oliver. This was Robert Burns Dick, mentioned
earlier, whose flair for the 'stripped classical' style fashionable after the First World
War powerfully developed the 19th-century tradition of monumentalist architecture
in Newcastle adumbrated above, and might have done so even more had not so
many of his projects, like those of Dobson before him, remained unexecuted. Burns
Dick did design a number of substantial, if unconnected, buildings in the central

[53]   Faulkner and Greg, *John Dobson*, p.95.

area of Newcastle between the wars, such as the magistrates' courts, police and fire stations (1931-2) in Pilgrim Street, then being redeveloped following the construction of the Tyne Bridge, and the Northumberland County Council Offices, completed in 1934. The latter is an 11-storey stepped block, steel-framed and clad in stone[54] (it is now, in somewhat altered form, the *Vermont Hotel*). These later works by Burns Dick show his earlier monumental classicism being effectively abstracted, and simplified, under the influence of 'Modern Movement' design. This process culminates in his church of the Divine Unity, Ellison Place (1938-40), with its block-like forms based on reinforced concrete construction with cladding of very plain brick and, internally, an arrangement of intersecting planes reminiscent of the work of Frank Lloyd Wright.[55] Other noteworthy modern churches in Newcastle of this period include those of the Holy Cross, Fenham (1935-6), by H.L. Hicks,[56] and the Venerable Bede, Benwell (1936-7), by W.B. Edwards.[57] Both, again, are finished in severe, unadorned brick.

Meanwhile, Burns Dick was also responsible for the architectural treatment of the Tyne Bridge (1924-8; engineers: Mott, Hay and Anderson). Indeed, his original scheme for this, involving enlarged pylons and a gigantic Beaux-Arts style arch, would have provided the city with a truly magnificent approach. The Bridge, necessitated by the growth of motor traffic in the 1920s, and built partly as a make-work scheme, consolidated Pilgrim Street and Northumberland Street as the main north-south axis. In so doing, it foreshadowed the demise of Grainger's Royal Arcade and accelerated the drift north. Northumberland Street, rather than Grainger Street, became the city's main shopping street.

In 1924 Burns Dick had also evolved an unexecuted *Plan for Newcastle* which proposed an intersection from the Tyne Bridge, placed further south than the present Pilgrim Street roundabout, and feeding a new road to the quayside. There would also have been a major new axial route from the Tyne Bridge to Barras Bridge running east of Northumberland Street (its northward section anticipating the present John Dobson Street), and another new north-south route parallel to this placed to the west of Pilgrim Street. Visually the most impressive feature of the 1924 *Plan*

[54] It was actually a comprehensive enlargement of an earlier building of 1910 by J.A. Bain.

[55] This church was built on the site of an earlier church by Dobson, that of St Peter, a Gothic design of 1840-3. Burns Dick was in partnership firstly, from *c.*1898, with J.T. Cackett (1860-1928), who specialised mainly in industrial work, and then, additionally, from 1920, with R. Norman Mackellar, who may well have helped to push him in a slightly more Modernist direction. The practice of Cackett, Burns Dick & Mackellar continues to this day as the Mackellar Schwerdt Partnership (having been R.N. Mackellar & Partners, 1963-91); another remarkable example of continuity.

[56] H.L. Hicks (1883-1947) was the son of W.S. Hicks and continued his father's practice, working largely in the neo-Gothic tradition. This church is therefore a rather uncharacteristic work for this architect.

[57] W.B. Edwards (1898-1964) was Head (later Professor) of Architecture at King's College (later Newcastle University) 1943-61. He was responsible for the master plan of the University's campus immediately after the Second World War (with Sir Howard Robertson) and later for several of its major buildings.

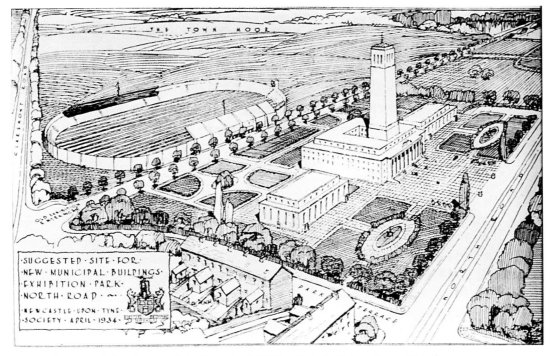

**10.9**  Proposed design for new Civic Centre in Exhibition Park, by Robert Burns Dick; from *Report* of the Northumberland and Newcastle Society, 1934.

would have been a Parisian-style boulevard leading further northwards from Barras Bridge to a projected civic centre in what is now Exhibition Park, the latter taking the form of public buildings grouped symmetrically around a square. Burns Dick submitted a modified version of this latter proposal, involving a monumental central block with side pavilions, to the Council in 1934 (see Plate 10.9). The project, although unsuccessful, may at least have influenced the subsequent choice for a new civic and education centre on the present site near Barras Bridge.

At this point it may be useful to turn our attention to the more utilitarian, 'functional' aspect of Newcastle's architecture. Grainger for one does not seem to have been very interested in this field.[58] However, it should be noted that his purchase of Elswick Hall in 1839 (by which time his career was beginning to go downhill amid accusations of financial impropriety[59]) had been with the intention of redeveloping its huge estate, between the river and the West Road, with a novel

[58]  Thus, for example, he tended to disclaim any involvement in the provision of working-class housing, indeed conceding that his central redevelopment had actually reduced such provision; see Faulkner, T.E., 'The Early Nineteenth Century Planning of Newcastle upon Tyne', in *Planning Perspectives*, v (1990), p.157.

[59]  He was only saved from bankruptcy and humiliation by Clayton's manoeuvrings behind the scenes; see Wilkes and Dodds, *Tyneside Classical*, pp.105-21.

mixed development of houses, factories, a shipping quay and even a railway terminus. Although the development largely failed to happen,[60] some areas of housing were actually laid out and included some brick-built streets of artisans' dwellings.[61] Another developer of the period, who sought to cater more for the needs of the 'respectable' working classes, was the solicitor George Tallantire Gibson, who was responsible for 'Gibson Town', a coherently planned, almost self-contained area of terraced streets and commercial buildings laid out between New Bridge Street and the City Road between 1836 and 1848.[62]

During the period of great population growth *c.*1850-1914, large numbers of grid-like terraced streets, built of brick and slate, sprang up around the older central zone. These were almost invariably laid out by industrialists for their workers or by other private developers. Thus Byker, Heaton and Walker, in the east, and Benwell, Elswick and Fenham in the west, still have extensive areas of 'artisan' housing while larger terraced houses, with typically Victorian bay windows, were built mostly in Jesmond and Gosforth. Everywhere, many 'houses' of this period are in fact flats and the distinctive 'Tyneside Flat' is an ingenious two-storey terraced arrangement whereby one household lived above another, each having its own individual front and back door.[63] There are many variations. Good surviving examples of the cheaper, flat-fronted type can be found in Walker Road, east Newcastle, and more elaborate versions, with bays, in the streets around West Jesmond Metro Station, such as Lavender Gardens, Sunbury Avenue or Glenthorn Road. Later, during the 1920s and 1930s, Newcastle saw numerous developments of speculatively built semi-detached houses, typical of their period, along main roads or sometimes on the former estates of demolished suburban mansions.[64]

By this time, too, the Council itself had made a vigorous if belated entry into the field of municipal housing.[65] As a result of the Housing Town Planning Act of

[60] For a discussion of Grainger's Elswick scheme see *ibid.*, and Ayris, *City of Palaces*, pp.63-6.

[61] These were named after Grainger's 13 children. However, one of the few surviving fragments of Grainger's abortive Elswick scheme, the monumental, stone-fronted terrace known as 'Graingerville South', along (upper) Westgate Road, is from one of the more expensive areas of the Elswick development.

[62] The architect of 'Gibson Town' was no less a figure than Thomas Oliver. The development was largely demolished, 1962-8. See Giddings, R.D., 'Thomas Oliver, 1791-1857' (unpublished dissertation for the degree of B.Arch., University of Newcastle upon Tyne, 1981), pp.43-5.

[63] The origins of this form of design are obscure. The best account is Pearce, K., 'Newcastle's Tyneside Flats 1850-1900: By-Law Housing or Cultural Phenomenon?', in Lancaster, B. (ed.), *Working Class Housing on Tyneside 1850-1939* (1994).

[64] For examples of this see Faulkner and Lowery, *Lost Houses*.

[65] The 1890 Housing of the Working Classes Act was not invoked in Newcastle for more than a decade. In the early 1900s a few experiments in municipal housing were carried out, designed either by private architects or by the Corporation Property Surveyor (at that time F.H. Holford); these included a series of one-, two- and three-room working-class dwellings in Albion Row and Walker Road (see *Proceedings of the Newcastle Council*, 1901-2, p.601) and 'Newton Dwellings' (by Holford), which were in effect Tyneside Flats, at St Lawrence's, of 1906. For more background information see Barke, M. and Callcott, M., 'Municipal Intervention in Housing: Constraints and Developments in Newcastle upon Tyne 1835-1914', in Lancaster, *Working Class Housing*.

1919 it immediately purchased five areas of land for housing schemes, circling the central area, in addition to land already possessed and partially developed at Walker. These were at or near Fenham, North Elswick, the former Pendower Estate (West Road), Heaton, and Kenton Road. Additional land at Cowgate was purchased in 1924.[66] Thus became established the locations of Newcastle's main council housing estates.[67] Furthermore, in 1919 the highly capable R.G. Roberts was appointed City Housing Architect, initially in the City Property Surveyor's Department, with a small staff of draughtsmen and assistants. Roberts was given his own department the following year and, by 1935, 11,000 houses had been erected under his charge. By now his responsibilities had widened and he was appointed Newcastle's first official City Architect in 1936.[68]

The estates designed by Roberts and his team are clearly influenced by the general ethos of the early 20th-century Arts and Crafts and Garden City movements. Given limited budgets, they are remarkably well built, using friendly red brick and tile (not slate),[69] with much care and variety in the detailing. Although in some instances visually much altered,[70] they have stood the test of time. With gardens, there is a seemingly endless variety of two-storey dwelling types. These include: semi-detached cottages, in several versions; 'double semis', i.e., a form of 'Tyneside Flat', with projecting gables at each end or with an arched entrance to the rear below a central gable, in both cases with sets of main entrances at the front and at the side; and horizontal, terrace-like blocks of six or even eight flats, their design punctuated by various dispositions of gables, 'front' entrances, and arched entrances to the rear. The Pendower estate, begun in 1919, is a rare example of the employment of private architects for municipal housing, within an overall plan. Here no less a figure than Burns Dick, with his then partner Cackett,[71] later introduced a slight change of style with a series of plainer, more block-like semi-detached houses in Pendower Way (in brick and pebble-dash or faced entirely in pebble-dash), perhaps reflecting a slight Modern Movement influence.

These municipal estates also break away from the grid-like arrangements of earlier, speculatively built working-class housing. Instead, we have diagonals, crescents and cul-de-sacs, and sometimes even 'enclaves' of dwellings built around or radiating

[66] See *Proceedings of the Newcastle Council*, 1918-19, p.675 and *ibid.*, 1924-5, pp.486-7.

[67] These estates included the Cowgate, the Delaval Road, the Fenham Nurseries, the Fenham Hall, the High Heaton, the Montague, the Pendower, and the Walker (including the Morton Street).

[68] See for example *Proceedings of the Newcastle Council*, 1918-19, p.671; 1919-20, pp.691-5; 1935-6, pp.142 and 345. An example of Roberts's non-housing work is the Branch Public Library, Fenham Hall Drive (*c.*1925).

[69] During the 1920s several short-lived experiments were also made with 'model' houses of concrete, steel and even wood. See for example *Proceedings of the Newcastle Council*, 1925-6, pp.196 and 765 *et seq.*, and 1926-7, pp.204 *et seq.*

[70] As a result of 'privatisation', this is probably most in evidence at the High Heaton estate.

[71] See *Proceedings of the Newcastle Council*, 1920-1, p.788. The other local practices of Marshall & Tweedy and Charles Errington were also involved in designing for this estate.

from a small communal green. Everywhere there is a pleasant informality. But at the same time a reassuring sense of organisation is derived from geometric patterns, visually unobtrusive but often quite complex, which can be traced in the planning and layout of these estates. That at High Heaton, for example, is based on a series of concentric crescents with radiating streets.

Meanwhile, a similar municipal effort was being made in school architecture. Hitherto, this had been the domain of local private architects, with distinguished figures such as A.M. Dunn, R.J. Johnson and F.W. Rich working in the field. Examples of their work, in what might be termed an institutional 'Queen Anne' style favoured in Newcastle as elsewhere by the School Boards, include R.J. Johnson's Mitford Street School, Scotswood Road (designed 1881, now demolished), the Westgate Hill School (1896-9) by Dunn, Hansom & Fenwicke, built to house no fewer than 1,520 pupils, and F.W. Rich's exuberant Ouseburn Schools, Albion Row (1891-3, now a depository), with its remarkable variety of gables, and Japanese pagoda-like roof forms.[72] Now the talented F.W. Harvey, the City's first Education Architect, 1927-56,[73] proved more than worthy of this inheritance. His first major design, the Middle Street Central Schools (1932-3, now Walker Comprehensive), is a well-crafted example of municipal neo-Georgian said to be the first elementary school in the country with a gymnasium separate from the hall. More adventurous is his former Whickham View Schools, in the west end (1936-8, now the John Morley Centre), an eye-catching Moderne, even Art Deco design having horizontal wings spreading from a stepped, central block. It was one of the first schools in the country to have a swimming pool. His Rutherford Grammar School on the West Road, also now a community centre, dates from the early 1950s and is a confident exercise in Modernism. Like all his designs it is executed in brick, and again incorporates a swimming pool. This building has been subsequently much altered and enlarged.

Of industrial architecture in Newcastle, most earlier examples have disappeared. However, the surviving bonded warehouses between Hanover Street and the Side (1841-4), massive and stern, their cliff-like facades looking towards the Tyne, provide a clue as to the probable appearance of Dobson's now-demolished Quayside warehouse for the tobacco importer Benjamin Sorsbie of 1818-19 (and that of his even larger warehouse for the Newcastle, Berwick and North Shields Railway of 1847-50 on the present Manors Station site). Still in existence, as a complex of craft workshops, is the same architect's former Plummer's Flax Mill by the Ouse Burn at

[72] As late as 1934 Cackett, Burns Dick & Mackellar designed the Dame Allan Schools, Fenham.
[73] Harvey also designed the furniture and fittings for his schools. For more on him see, for example, *Proceedings of the Newcastle Council*, 1932-3, pp.104-5, 1935-6, p.334 and *The Shields Gazette*, 12 April 1956.

**10.10** Former Wills (Imperial Tobacco Co.) Factory, Coast Road, by Cecil Hockin 1946-50, photographed in 1978.

Byker (1847-8). Stone-built with bold classical detailing, it reflects the desire, typical of its period, that functional structures should be monumental. Another good example of this late Georgian and Victorian functional tradition is the enormous two-staged stone railway arch at the lower end of Dean Street;[74] Piranesian in scale, it helps to create one of the most 'sublime' views in Newcastle. Also noteworthy in this context are two closely matching viaducts by John Green of 1837-9, the Ouseburn, at Byker, and the Willington, at Wallsend (in both cases in 1869 iron replaced the original laminated timber construction, the original design allowing for this). The later 19th century is probably best represented by the former C.W.S. Warehouse on the east Quayside, an early example of exposed, reinforced concrete construction,[75] now being incorporated into the 'post-modern' redevelopment of the area.

One of the most prominent 20th-century industrial structures in Newcastle is the former Wills Tobacco Factory – on the coast road, just east of Benton Road – by Cecil Hockin, the then architect to the Imperial Tobacco Co. (Plate 10.10). Steel-framed, with cladding of brick, in continuous bands, and Portland stone, its horizontal emphasis is effectively balanced by a massive central entrance tower, conveying unity and monumentality; this effect has largely survived the recent demolition of all except the front block (which has been converted into flats). Originally, the factory itself was integrated with offices, administrative headquarters, staff restaurant and other facilities, reflecting Wills's personnel policy and the ethos of the new, 'clean', suburban industries generally. Though built 1946-50, the design

[74] Robert Stephenson, 1847-9, built the first arch; a second, identical arch was added on the north side in 1894.
[75] By T.G. Gueritte and F.E.L. Harris, using the Hennebique method (1899-1900).

has a strong 1930s feel which may derive from the fact that Wills had first decided to build then but were delayed by the war. Other expressions of post-war optimism, more contemporary in style, are Richard Sheppard's offices and associated buildings for Swan Hunter's shipyard at Wallsend (mainly *c*.1948-52), in an advanced Modernist idiom so admired by Pevsner,[76] and the C.A. Parsons (now Siemens) works at the junction of Depot Road and Shields Road (originally, the Research and Design Building) of 1951-3.[77] The latter is a taut, precise design, by the firm's own Construction Department (consulting architect: Stanley Milburn), which makes much use of brick, polished granite and other facing materials while frankly and effectively exposing its framed structure.

We have already noted the non-implementation of Robert Burns Dick's ingenious 'Beaux-Arts' schemes. A later 'vision' which, perhaps more fortunately, also remained unexecuted was the curious 'Proposed Civic-Academic and Central Business Area' from the municipal *Plan for Newcastle* of 1945 – an extreme modernist scenario in which hardly an existing building seems to be retained. To be fair, the *Plan*[78] as a whole also tried to address the more practical problem of Newcastle's notorious traffic congestion. Therefore it proposed a major new central ring road, linking the High Level Bridge and the Tyne Bridge, and joining the Great North Road at approximately the southern boundary of Brandling Park. The *Plan* also extended the earlier scheme for a civic centre and academic precinct, based on an expanded University, around Barras Bridge and envisaged the city's main shopping centre developing in the then comparatively run down area bounded by Blackett Street, Percy Street and Northumberland Street.

Next came the city's *Development Plan* of 1951,[79] generated by the requirements of the 1947 Town and Country Planning Act. This also remained a paper exercise, largely because of the economic stringency of the time. For the record, it repeated most of the proposals of 1945, apart from a re-alignment westwards of a suggested western inner ring road and some detailed modifications to the projected shopping area between Blackett Street, Percy Street and Northumberland Street. It advocated also the demolition of the Royal Arcade and the Holy Jesus Hospital, a historic 17th-century building, for a new Pilgrim Street traffic intersection north of the Tyne Bridge.

These and other elements were retained in modified form in the much more comprehensive *Development Plan* of 1963. In any event, the comparative lack of movement during this period and absence of substantial wartime bomb damage

[76] Pevsner, *Buildings of England*, pp.309-10. These buildings survive but have been spoilt by later additions.

[77] The building replaced the original Parsons Works of 1889. See Hutchinson, J.C., 'New Research and Design Building, Heaton Works', in *Heaton Works Journal*, Christmas 1953.

[78] *Plan Newcastle upon Tyne 1945: Report of the Town Planning Sub-Committee* (1945).

[79] Outlined in *Proceedings of the Newcastle Council*, 1950-1, pp.1187-1206.

meant that Newcastle's city centre, as a coherent expression of Georgian and Victorian classicism, survived almost unchanged until the mid-1960s. Unfortunately, far from being valued as an outstanding example of north English heritage, it was now, as outlined in David Byrne's chapter in this volume, perceived as an area 'ripe for development'.[80]

The 1963 *Development Plan*, the main proposals of which were first evolved in 1961, went much further than its predecessors in upgrading the earlier scheme for an inner ring road (east) to motorway status. This central motorway was to link with a new street aligned further east of Northumberland Street than had been previously suggested (the present John Dobson Street). In addition, the proposed Pilgrim Street intersection was completely redesigned to incorporate not only an underpass, but also an office block. Also proposed was a new central motorway (west) from the Redheugh Bridge to the Great North Road via the Haymarket.[81] This was to be linked to the eastern motorway by two major east-west routes, one parallel to the Quayside, the other passing underground from the New Bridge Street intersection to the Haymarket, while pedestrian and traffic routes were to be segregated wherever possible, in grand Le Corbusian manner. Other significant innovations were proposals for the regeneration of the Quayside, to include an office development surrounding All Saints' Church, and the comprehensive redevelopment of Eldon Square, which was to be retained as an open space surrounded by a prestigious shopping complex with a high-rise hotel on one side. Similarly, a cultural plaza with a new central library and museum overlooked by a residential tower spanning the road was to occupy the area adjacent to the junction of New Bridge Street and John Dobson Street. Architects of international fame and status were commissioned for many of these proposals: Sir Robert Matthew for the office block, now known as 'Swan House', occupying the Pilgrim Street intersection; Sir Basil Spence for both the new central library and the All Saints' development;[82] and the Danish modernist Arne Jacobsen for the Eldon Square hotel.

At the same time, perhaps surprisingly, the 1963 *Plan* placed emphasis on conserving and improving Grey, Grainger and Clayton Streets.[83] However, the *Plan*'s

[80] Galley, K., 'Newcastle upon Tyne', in Holliday, J. (ed.), *City Centre Redevelopment: a Study of British City Centre Planning* (1973), p.207. See also Chapter 15 of this volume.

[81] Only in recent years has this been (partially) implemented.

[82] Here only two of the intended concrete blocks surrounding the church were built (from 1969, designed in conjunction with T.P. Bennett & Partners), and then not linked to the lower Quayside as originally proposed.

[83] Perhaps because it had been systematically built on an open or cleared site, the planners of the 1960s seem to have felt a curious affinity with this central area – 'the first major comprehensive planning and redevelopment scheme', according to *The Development Plan Review* for Newcastle of 1963, p.4 – and were impressed with what was described as the 'unified conception' of Grainger's central redevelopment (Burns, W., *Newcastle: a Study in Replanning at Newcastle upon Tyne*, 1967, pp.4-6). Thus they concentrated their depradations upon Grainger's more peripheral monuments, such as Eldon Square and the Royal Arcade.

main mistakes are catastrophic in their obviousness. These included the demolition not only of Eldon Square and the Royal Arcade but also of many other less prominent but still valuable Georgian and Victorian buildings, and the alignment of the central motorway (east) too close to the historic central area. In addition, 'Swan House', seen in the rhetoric of the time as one of the major gateways to the 'modern city wall'[84] of the central motorway, had the detrimental effect of severing the northern exit of the Tyne Bridge from its original and natural outlet, Pilgrim Street. The general situation was made worse by the only partial completion of projects such as the proposed Quayside regeneration scheme and the redevelopment of Eldon Square. In the latter case the intended hotel was not built, and the survival by default of the eastern wing of the original square only serves as a further reminder of a particularly tragic and unnecessary loss. Similarly, in the case of the proposed cultural centre near John Dobson Street, the new central library (by Basil Spence, opened in 1970) and the high-rise block of flats – both buildings executed in the variously-textured forms of concrete of 1960s 'Brutalism' – were served by an equally bleak concrete walkway spanning the street. Always little used, this walkway was largely demolished in the mid-1990s, leaving one of the entrances to the library at the present moment opening into thin air.

Most damagingly of all, the failure of the 1963 *Plan* to achieve its aim of integrating the modern with the historic led to harsh juxtapositions of old and new architecture, either by default, or intentionally so, based on the modernist principle of 'dynamic contrast'. Examples of this include such insertions as that of 'MEA House' (1974), assertively cutting through and across Ellison Place, a Georgian terrace, or of the block opposite St Nicholas's Cathedral (1975) which replaced the 'old' (Victorian) town hall and was originally designed to be part of an even larger scheme.[85] Similarly inappropriate is the overwhelming size, scale and character of such grey high-rise slabs as the Commercial Union office in Pilgrim Street (1971) and the Norwich Union office in Westgate Road (second phase, completed 1975), both built right across their respective streets. Sir Robert Matthew's flagship 'Swan House' of 1963-9 has also been much maligned, but in this case the most relevant factor may be that it sits on the site of Grainger and Dobson's much admired Royal Arcade. Furthermore, it was obliged to incorporate at ground-floor level an absurd seven-bay facsimile of the Arcade's original eight-bay interior. Viewed dispassionately, the building itself is far from being monolithic. Indeed, it can be seen to integrate an ingenious variety of contrasting forms, textures and levels within a complex (if now unfashionable and little-used) system of pedestrian walkways, underpasses and decks

[84] Smith, (T.) D., *An Autobiography* (1970), p.51.
[85] Illustrated in *Planning Progress and Policy 1973 Newcastle upon Tyne*, p.24.

10.11   'Swan House', by Sir Robert Matthew & Partners, constructed 1963-9.

(see Plate 10.11). The design had to be adapted to a difficult and isolated site and was subject to many enforced modifications.[86]

Interestingly, however, the most prominent modern building in Newcastle, the Civic Centre (Plate 10.12), although completed in 1969, was not part of the programme of redevelopment based on the 1963 *Plan* outlined above. Indeed, the idea for such a building goes back at least to the 1930s, as we have seen, and the design for the present structure by the then City Architect George Kenyon was commenced as early as 1950. Certainly, the Civic Centre cannot be accused of failing to make a grand statement. Its expensive facing materials, its internal marble and rich wood veneers, its external varying forms of Portland stone and Norwegian Otta slate, enhance this effect. The general emphasis is on the expression of distinct elements, in complete contrast to the greater unity of the superseded 1930s designs by Burns Dick and others, referred to earlier. What stands out is the relationship between the strongly differentiated blocks along St Mary's Place, and Sandyford

[86]   For a detailed account of the demolition of the Royal Arcade and the construction of Swan House see Faulkner, T.E., 'Conservation and Renewal in Newcastle upon Tyne', in Faulkner, T.E. (ed.), *Northumbrian Panorama: Studies in the History and Culture of North East England* (1996), pp.142-4.

**10.12**  The Civic Centre, by George Kenyon, City Architect, constructed 1958-69.

Road (the Rates Hall), these dating from 1958-9, then the 12-storey main office block with tower (completed 1963), these elements forming a 'cloister' or 'garth', and finally the circular, chapter-house-like council chamber and almost baronial banqueting hall (1965-9). Historical references abound, yet, apart from the familiar 1950s mannerism of grids of small square windows set within large expanses of blank wall, the building is strangely like no other in Britain and by the time it was finally completed it must have appeared curiously old-fashioned. The closest comparisons seem to be with the Stockholm City Hall (by R. Ostberg, 1911-23) and even more with the Oslo City Hall (by A. Arneberg and M. Poulsson); design work for the latter began in 1920, but after many modifications construction did not begin until 1931 and the building was only inaugurated, perhaps significantly, in 1950. The Newcastle Civic Centre's Norwegian connection is further emphasised by the fact that King Olav V officially opened it in November 1968.

At the present time, as Newcastle enters a 'post-industrial' phase, efforts are being made to re-invent this once great mercantile city as a tourist venue complete with the paraphernalia of 'heritage trails', plaques and the cast-iron signposts associated with established holiday destinations such as Edinburgh, York and Bath. Crucial to this policy is the current insistence on re-naming certain central areas, such as 'Chinatown', 'Theatre Village' and now 'Grainger Town'[87] – all part of a regenerative strategy intended to attract business and tourism to what remains of the city's historic core. The title 'Grainger Town' is being applied both to the city centre streets which Grainger laid out, and, inauthentically, to parts of the surrounding area as well.[88] Even now, such is his mythical status, Grainger's name appears to be almost synonymous with the city's development. However, as we have seen, his legacy is complex and concepts such as 'Grainger Town' are based on a serious misrepresentation of the past. Grainger himself, though not without an element of egotism, generally avoided any acts of self-commemoration in his central redevelopment.[89] This was never intended to be a town within a town but an integral part of a larger whole. His purpose, however commercial, was to achieve a metropolitan effect which could be understood nationally through the use of mainstream and culturally dominant rather than through local and particular forms of architecture. By contrast, the description 'Grainger Town' is not only personal but also essentially local.

Grainger thrived in the hectic, entrepreneurial atmosphere following the Napoleonic Wars, when construction was fuelled by surplus capital and low interest rates. There may be some affinity between this situation and the business-minded encouragement of market forces characteristic of 'Thatcherism' in the 1980s and even, perhaps, of 'New Labour' today. The ruthlessness of Grainger's attitude to the city's historic environment has evoked comparisons with the recent, though ultimately unsuccessful, attempts by the Newcastle businessman Sir John Hall – creator of the 'Metrocentre' and at the time Chairman of Newcastle United FC – to build a new stadium on part of Newcastle's ancient Town Moor and much of the centrally placed 19th-century Leazes Park.

There are also parallels with another Tyneside 'visionary', T. Dan Smith (1915-93). Smith was the council leader who in the 1960s rushed through much of the redevelopment of Newcastle alluded to above. Smith and his associates – principally, his Chief Planning Officer, Wilfred Burns – were seeking what they saw as a clean, new, international image which, they believed, would dispel unfavourable industrial myths and attract new business.[90] To publicise his schemes Smith used exhibitions of plans and models and the services of a sympathetic press in a manner pioneered

[87]   As also in Ayris, *City of Palaces*, pp.75-83 and Lovie, D., *The Buildings of Grainger Town* (1997).

[88]   Some of the material in this chapter on Grainger and his legacy is adapted from a paper 'From Grainger to Grainger Town: Visions and Visionaries of Newcastle upon Tyne', given by the author at the Lectures de la Ville/ The City as Text Colloquium, University of Northumbria at Newcastle, in conjunction with the University of Nice, September 1999.

[89]   Other than the naming of Grainger Street.

[90]   For a discussion of the impact of the policies of Smith and his associates see Faulkner, 'Conservation and Renewal', *Northumbrian Panorama*, pp.138-41.

by Grainger more than a century before. Both men dreamed of glorifying their native city. Smith, in his desire to create what he called the 'Brasilia of the North', employed big-name architects to build it, as indicated earlier, and even dreamed of employing Le Corbusier.[91] He also promoted the lavish incorporation of contemporary art into the finished design of the Civic Centre, seeing the building as a kind of peoples' art gallery.[92] Grainger, as we have seen, chose his architects carefully from a local pool of talent and expended large sums of his own – and his backers' – money on extra embellishment. His insistence on superlative new design, 'taste for art'[93] and natural flair for planning were such that he was frequently described as an architect in his own right, a title which he was happy to accept even though his approach was essentially that of a businessman.[94] In or near the central area Grainger was careful to restrict himself to prestige developments. By contrast Smith was propelled by the kind of 'progressive' ideology which underpinned the policies of comprehensive urban redevelopment fashionable at the time. He was an enthusiastic promoter of tower blocks and other Utopian housing schemes.

Grainger enormously reinforced Newcastle's status as an English regional capital. But for all of the 20th century Grainger's name (and Dobson's) has been repeatedly invoked to support almost any piece of replanning and redevelopment in Newcastle upon Tyne.[95] At the present time we feel profound relief that the core, literally and metaphorically, of Grainger's achievement has survived so many vicissitudes.

[91] Smith, *Autobiography*, p.55.

[92] Smith, *Autobiography*, pp.140-1. The Civic Centre has, for example, sculpture by David Wynne and A.B. Reid, a John Piper tapestry and murals by Elizabeth Wise and (in the Rates Hall) by Victor Pasmore.

[93] *Report of the Cholera Inquiry Commissioners*, p.309.

[94] He is referred to as an architect in, for example, *The Dictionary of National Biography*. See also Wilkes and Dodds, *Tyneside Classical*, pp.142-3. In addition, see the *Report of the Cholera Inquiry Commissioners*, p.302. Here, giving evidence to the Commission, Grainger was asked, 'Are you a builder and an architect?' He replied, 'Yes'. He is also listed as an architect in the Directories of the period.

[95] As with Burns Dick's *Suggested Plan* for Newcastle of 1924 which contained much which would have further marginalised the central area, and even with Wilfred Burns's *Development Plan* of 1961-3. See Faulkner, 'Conservation and Renewal', *Northumbrian Panorama*, pp.138-44.

# II

# *Art on the Margins*
## *from Bewick to Baltic*

### PAUL USHERWOOD

## *The old man and the soldiers*

Is it possible to talk of a 'Newcastle art'? Have the forces of metropolitan imperialism, always strong in matters of culture, ever allowed the emergence and survival of a distinctive local art? One of the Laing Art Gallery's most often reproduced pictures, *The Bard* (1817) by the locally-born but London-based painter of theatrical blockbusters, John Martin, perhaps gives the answer. It depicts what purports to be an episode in medieval history during the final stages of Edward I's conquest of Wales. From a lofty, isolated crag in Snowdonia (it actually looks more like the Alps) the semi-naked, white-haired figure of the last Welsh bard, harp in hand, hurls down abuse at the English army as it streams out of a huge and brutal-looking castle. The soldiers look chillingly anonymous; he on the other hand, representative provincial artist that he is, looks appealingly individual and authentic, in a rugged kind of way. Yet clearly there is little hope for him. Read the 1757 poem by Thomas Gray on which Martin's picture is based and this is confirmed. Moments later he throws himself to his death into the cataract below.

It is certainly the case that Newcastle artists, and arts officials and arts commentators with them, have often boasted they have nothing to learn from London.

11.1 John Martin, *The Bard*, 1817.

Bout Lunnen then div'nt ye mak' sich a rout,
There's nouse ma winker to dazzle;
For a' the fine things ye ate gobbin about,
We can marra in canny Newcastle.[1]

Nevertheless this is probably whistling in the dark. In their heart of hearts those who say such things must surely know that the relationship between provincial and metropolitan art is always likely to be more or less what John Martin's picture implies. Thus the argument running through this chapter is that, whilst there has been much art produced in Newcastle in the last two centuries, much of it about Newcastle, there has so far been only one moment when the town (later city) could claim a genuine art of its own and this was at the start of the 19th century, during the age of Bewick.

## *'Metropolis of the north of England'[2]*

'I was now in the land of Bewick' announced the Rev. Thomas Frognall Dibdin, travel-writer and chaplain in ordinary to the Queen, on arriving on Tyneside at the end of the 1830s.[3] Dibdin took it for granted that the engraver Thomas Bewick was Newcastle's main claim to significance as far as visual art was concerned. Quite rightly. 'Our own great engraver and moralist', as Ruskin was later to call him, had

**11.2** A vignette with St Nicholas in the background by Thomas Bewick.

taken on the previously neglected art of wood-engraving and demonstrated its artistic and commercial potential.[4] For his three great best-selling books in particular, *A General History of Quadrapeds* (1790), *A History of British Birds* (1797, 1804) and *Fables of Aesop* (1818), he developed a slightly sentimentalised, sometimes overtly moralising, way of representing animals and birds in familiar surroundings which exactly suited an emerging middle-class taste for natural history and scenes of provincial rural life. Thus, although the first edition

[1] Allan, Thomas, 'Canny Newcastle' (*c*.1800), *Tyneside Songs* (1972 edn.), p.47. (I have very slightly revised Allan's spelling.)
[2] Sopwith, Thomas, *The Stranger's Pocket-Guide to Newcastle-upon-Tyne and its Environs* (1838), p.12.
[3] Dibdin, Thomas, *A Bibliographical, Antiquarian and Picturesque Tour in the Northern Counties of England and in Scotland*, vol.1 (1838), p.335.
[4] Ruskin, John, 'Ariadne Florentina: Six Lectures on Wood and Metal Engraving', Cook, E.T. and Wedderburn, Alexander (eds.), *The Works of John Ruskin*, vol.22 (1906), p.456.

of *Quadrapeds* (published, significantly, a year after Gilbert White's *Natural History and Antiquities of Selborne*) was sold only in the North, later editions, of which there were soon many, appeared in booksellers throughout Britain and abroad. Indeed, Bewick's tiny illustrations and tail-pieces have never lost their appeal for readers everywhere, whether it be for the way they demonstrate 'the magnificent artistic power, the flawless virtue, veracity, tenderness – the infinite humour of the man', as Ruskin contended, or their cosy nostalgic view of the English countryside.[5] The writer Charles Kingsley, for instance, claimed he had been 'brought up on Bewick's Birds'.[6]

Such was the achievement of Bewick and his workshop that the turn of the 19th century must be counted the one moment in the last two centuries when it can be said that the town had a 'school' in the art historical sense.[7] It is not that there were suddenly more resident artists; trade directories (admittedly not an entirely reliable source) list just three engravers and plate-makers in 1790 and five engravers in 1822.[8] Numbers are not what matters here; after all, the number of artists in Florence in the 15th century and in Siena in the 14th century was relatively small. What matters is that the engravers in the Bewick workshop produced a distinct, recognisable type of work and were confident enough of its merits not to feel that they had to look to other centres, especially London, for patronage and critical validation.

Thus in his *Memoir* one finds Bewick keen to emphasise that London held no appeal for him. As a young man he had been there on a Society of Arts premium but quickly wearied of its delights. 'Notwithstanding ... my being so much gratified in seeing such a variety of performances in every Art & science – Painting, statuary, Engraving carving &c were to be seen every day, yet I did not like London ... I tired of it and determined to return home – the scenery of Tyneside, seemed altogether to form a paradise for me & I longed to see it again.'[9] It might perhaps be objected that the countryside for which he pined was around his birthplace near Ovingham rather than Newcastle. However, his images suggest that this was not a distinction he particularly wished to make. Newcastle he looked upon as the focal point of his native heath, its capital in all but name. It is noticeable, for instance, how frequently the square Norman keep of the Castle and the 15th-century lantern of St Nicholas's are to be found in the background of his tiny images.[10]

---

[5] *Ibid.*, p.366.

[6] Kingsley, Charles, *Letters and Memorials of His Life*, vol.2 (1877), p.222.

[7] Bewick's workshop, it should be pointed out, was neither the first nor the only engraving workshop in Newcastle. Joseph Barber set up an engraver's in the town as early as the 1740s and Ralph Beilby, Bewick's master, established himself with his brothers and sisters around 1760. See Tattersfield, Norman, *Bookplates by Beilby and Bewick* (1999), pp.2-4.

[8] Whitehead's *Directory of Newcastle and Northumberland* (1790) and Pigot's *Directory for Northumberland* (1822).

[9] Bewick, Thomas, *A Memoir* (1979 edn.), p.75.

[10] Bain, Iain (ed.), *Thomas Bewick Vignettes* (1970), pp.2, 42, 53 and Tattersfield, *Bookplates*, pp.43, 91, 101, 126, 131, 161, 167, 190, 220, 224, 234 are good examples.

In presenting Newcastle as this kind of self-sustaining, independent metropolis, Bewick's work can be seen as similar to a number of paintings and prints produced by other locally based artists at the time, for example, Thomas Miles Richardson's magnum opus, *Newcastle from Gateshead Fell*, commissioned by Newcastle Corporation in 1816.[11] This duly depicts Newcastle as a dynamic, expanding town which has long since burst its medieval walls and is now beginning to thrust its way north and west, along Westgate Hill and up Northumberland Street. However, significantly, much of the canvas is devoted not to Newcastle itself but to miscellaneous rural goings-on in the foreground and to hills and fields stretching away to Simonside and the Cheviot on the horizon. It is as if, despite all the changes it is undergoing at the time, the town is still to be thought of as having a balanced, mutually beneficial relationship with its environs.

On the strength of his work organising art exhibitions in the town, Richardson came to be dubbed 'Father of the Fine Arts in Newcastle'.[12] However, his efforts to persuade the local gentry and wealthy middle class to patronise Newcastle artists rather than their London counterparts met with little success. From 1822 to 1843, the period during which the exhibitions were held, a small number of local artists in the town did manage to make a living of sorts either by selling work or by giving drawing lessons, and this encouraged artists from elsewhere in Britain to take up residence in Newcastle. Henry Perlee Parker, for instance, a genre painter who had come to Newcastle from the West Country in 1815, stayed on until 1841. However, the art which Parker and Richardson and their fellow artists exhibited never displayed the same sense of self-worth and independence as the products of Bewick's workshop. Although their subject-matter was often local, what one might call a distinctive Newcastle style never emerged. Furthermore, press reviews always tended to judge the success of any individual exhibition by whether or not stars of the metropolitan art world had been persuaded to participate. For instance, it was regarded as a great achievement when for the final exhibition in 1843 two works by London stars of the day, Augustus Wall Callcott's *A Dead Calm on the Medway* and John Martin's *Seventh Plague of Egypt*, were secured from a local collection.

Indeed, after Bewick died in 1828 art life in Newcastle generally languished, especially once it became clear that sales at the exhibitions were never likely to be

[11] For the reasons for believing that this dates from 1816 rather than the 1830s, as is sometimes claimed, see Usherwood, Paul, *Art for Newcastle. Thomas Miles Richardson and the Newcastle Exhibitions, 1822-1843* (1984), p.54.

[12] *Durham Chronicle*, 10 July 1835. For the history of the exhibitions run by the Northumberland Institution for the Promotion of the Fine Arts in the North of England and the equally grandly named institutions which followed in its wake, see Usherwood, *Art for Newcastle*, pp.11-33. It should be noted that these exhibitions included several likenesses of the then elderly engraver by the London-born artist James Ramsay as well as Ramsay's now most celebrated painting, *The Lost Child* (1823), which shows Newcastle worthies gathered in the Corn Market outside St Nicholas's with Bewick prominent among them. However, they did not include engravings either by Bewick or anyone else – a common policy towards engravings at the time.

11.3    T.M. Richardson Snr, *Grey Street, 1838.*

anything but poor. After 1828, most of the key artists began to leave, either for other provincial centres, or, more often, for London. Parker, for instance, went to Sheffield. The sculptor David Dunbar and the painters John Wilson Carmichael, Thomas Carrick, and Richardson's son, Thomas, all went to the capital.[13]

Yet while it was hard for an artist to make a living in Newcastle in these years, the image of the town that art projected was of a buoyant, forward-looking northern metropolis, rich in ancestry. This is particularly true of the various watercolours and engravings which Richardson himself produced, among them scenes of shipping on the Tyne and views of the various new-fangled marvels in the area such as the extraordinary railway viaducts over the Ouseburn and Willington Dene as designed by John and Benjamin Green and the streets and terraces of central Newcastle currently being planned or constructed by the developer Richard Grainger.[14] A good example of the latter is the view of Grey Street with the still-to-be-completed Grey's Monument at its head which serves as the frontispiece to the first volume of Dibdin's *Tour of the Northern Counties* (1838). The subject was impressive enough on its own account – 'our finest street' was how Gladstone described it on his

[13]   It should be noted that Martin went down to London in 1805 long before the Newcastle exhibitions began.
[14]   See plates 91-4 in Usherwood, *Art for Newcastle.*

[ 249 ]

triumphal visit to Newcastle in 1862. Typically, however, Richardson felt obliged to make it more impressive still: by levelling out the slope to the river, by making 'Earl Grey's Pillar' slightly taller, and by depicting Newcastle shoppers as without exception dedicated followers of fashion!

Nor was it only depictions of Newcastle itself which presented the town as this kind of civilised, bourgeois metropolis. In their way so did Richardson's watercolours and drawings of antiquities and scenery in Northumberland and Durham, such as the Lion Bridge at Alnwick, the new spa at Shotley Bridge and the fishing village of Cullercoats. For these implied that Newcastle was the centre of a picturesque and historically interesting area.[15]

Richardson's depictions of Newcastle's medieval heritage, some of which, interestingly, show the walls and gates actually in the process of being demolished, probably served a rather different role: they announced how far the town had progressed in the modern era. As the publisher and historian M.A. Richardson in his introduction to Thomas Miles Richardson's *Castles of the English and Scottish Borders* (1834) put it, they testified to the fact that 'The days of chivalry', for all their glamour, were 'days of war … deadly feuds and predatory inroads and burnings' and had been replaced by something altogether better.

More generally, Richardson's watercolours and engravings helped to anaesthetise and naturalise the tumultuous changes which the rapidly expanding and industrialising town was undergoing at the time. This they did by mobilising various standard devices of picturesque landscape: broad sweeps of light and shade, benign puffy clouds, artfully arranged clumps of foliage, boat tackle and rubbish, and figures who always seem relaxed and never likely to spill out into the viewer's space.

Overall, then, it is a strangely contradictory idea of the town that emerges from art in the second quarter of the 19th century. Newcastle is made to seem at once both a centre of technological excellence *and* a place of backward-looking picturesqueness. Look at Richardson's view of Willington Dene viaduct and compare this with *Rain, Speed and Steam* (1844), Turner's almost contemporary painting of Brunel's Great Western Railway crossing the Thames at Maidenhead. The two images have certain features in common, for example the diminutive figure of a farm labourer who continues with his ploughing seemingly unaware of the iron monster passing nearby. Yet the Richardson, in sharp contrast to the Turner, is ultimately a benign and reassuring image. It pays tribute to the astonishing feats of engineering that the construction of the railways represented while at the same managing to ignore the profound effect that these were actually having on so many aspects of people's lives.

---

[15] Usherwood, *Art for Newcastle*, plates 90, 95 and 96.

**11.4**   T.M. Richardson Snr, *Willington Dene*, 1838.

## Iron and Coal

Human toil seldom appears in pictures produced in Newcastle before the mid-19th century. Parker, it is true, painted miners with blackened faces playing quoits with their wives and children, but these can be seen as really only variants of his stock-in-trade scenes of Cullercoats fisherfolk. It was at the start of the 1860s that the heroic worker makes his appearance. With the success of Newcastle's industries, a statue to a suitable 'founding-father', the locally born George Stephenson by John Graham Lough, was erected in 1862 and this incorporates four emblematic workers lounging at the base, one of whom is a miner with a Stephenson safety-lamp in his hand (see Plate 12.4, p.284). In his muscular physique, erect head and benign expression obviously indebted to figures on the Parthenon, this man embodies the dignity of labour in a way which makes him entirely different from Parker's diminutive, almost jokey figures.[16]

[16]   See Usherwood, Paul, Beach, Jeremy and Morris, Catherine, *Public Sculpture of North-East England* (2000), pp.149-52. The other founding-father figure in Newcastle to be honoured in this way was the armaments and engineering magnate, William Armstrong. His statue did not appear until 1906. Interestingly, it has none of the formality and classical overtones of Stephenson but instead shows its subject standing casually in what seems to be Armstrong's study with a pet dog at his feet. References to public achievements are confined to two relatively small base-relief depictions of Armstrong's career as a manufacturer on the screen wall on either side of the main statue, one of which shows a 12-inch gun being lowered onto a battleship at Elswick, the other a battleship passing through the Amstrong-designed Swing Bridge.

**11.5**  William Bell Scott, *Iron and Coal*, 1861.

William Bell Scott's painting, *Iron and Coal*, first exhibited a year earlier, can be seen as the pictorial counterpart of Lough's statue. A rare painting of what has come to be known as the 'Industrial Revolution', it tends to be discussed nowadays as if it offers more or less a straightforward naturalistic depiction of work going on at the time in a particular place, Robert Stephenson's engineering works in South Street, behind the Central Station. To contemporary viewers in Newcastle, however (the picture was shown in Grey Street before being put on display in Pall Mall), it must have been readily apparent that it is no such thing. There is a plethora of painstakingly rendered objects and incidents but very few are correctly located in topographical terms. The painting has to be seen therefore as an allegory.[17] Hammering workmen, the barrel and shell of one of Armstrong's new breech-loading guns, a ship's anchor and marine engine, telegraph wires, a varnished technical drawing of a locomotive, a pitboy with a Davy (or perhaps a Geordie) Lamp, a local newspaper, all these bits and pieces are piled together in order to proclaim that Newcastle's moment as one of the most dynamic, technologically advanced industrial centres in the world has suddenly and most gloriously arrived.

---

[17]  See Usherwood, Paul, 'William Bell Scott's *Iron and Coal*: northern readings', in Tyne and Wear Museums Service, *Pre-Raphaelites: Painters and Patrons in the North East* (1984), pp.39-56.

Proclaim to whom? It might be assumed that since the identity of each local element would only have been apparent to local viewers, *Iron and Coal* was primarily intended for a local audience; that is, it is a Newcastle artwork in the same sense as, say, Richardson's *Newcastle from Gateshead Fell* (1816), mentioned earlier. However, Richardson's painting contains only a few signs of industrial activity, for example the shot tower at Elswick whereas *Iron and Coal* contains little else. This is because by the 1860s it was assumed that industry is what makes Newcastle interesting and distinctive to outsiders. The 1860s is the moment, in other words, when Newcastle begins to see itself through others' eyes; when it begins to be self-conscious about its place in the world.[18]

## Art School Art

There was another reason for the outsider viewpoint inscribed in *Iron and Coal*: the fact that the artist did not think of himself as a Newcastle artist. William Bell Scott came to Newcastle from London only reluctantly, in order to take up a post as an art teacher. Revealingly, in his autobiography he makes a point of recording how on the evening before he left for Newcastle a friend warned him against moving north: '… in the country one may preserve one's natural form. But you will cease to do your best: you won't be always stunning, trying to do your damn'dest …'.[19] Nevertheless, move north he did, because in 1844 he felt there was no alternative. Unsuccessful in the competition for decorations for the new Houses of Parliament, he was in no position to turn down the post of master of the new government School of Design in Newcastle when this was offered to him.

Once settled in the town his attitude towards his new job was ambivalent. Like many who taught in art schools after him, he was disdainful towards those who (as he did) relied on teaching for a living, criticising 'Old Richardson' for teaching 'more or less every day of his life'. He was also scathing towards Richardson's method of teaching: 'Like that of all the craft throughout the provinces of England at the time [Richardson's pedagogical approach was] exclusively landscape, exclusively by successive tints: first lesson, sketching the picture in, and laying on a wash of bistre or Paine's gray; second lesson, doing the sky, and so on. It was partly to revolutionise this false position of both teacher and pupil that the Schools of Design were established: the two systems could not very well coexist.'[20]

---

[18]  It should also be noted that whilst *Newcastle from Gateshead Fell* was commissioned from a local artist by Newcastle Corporation, *Iron and Coal* was painted by an artist who came to Newcastle from London and was commissioned by a member of the landed gentry, Sir Walter Trevelyan of Wallington Hall, who had spent much of his life outside the region.

[19]  Minto, W. (ed.), *Autobiographical Notes of the Life of William Bell Scott* (1892), vol.1, p.175.

[20]  *Ibid.*, vol.1, p.208.

Yet, truth be told, Scott's own classes were not without problems of their own. As their name suggests, the schools of design had been set up across Britain chiefly in order to train designers and draughtsmen for local industry. In practice, however, they tended to promote art rather than design, partly because this was what most of the students they attracted wanted to do. As an 1845 report makes clear, although a few of the students at Scott's school were workers on day release, most were not; indeed, half were women, either governesses or women without other occupation.[21]

We find something rather similar if we leap forward a hundred years to the 1950s and '60s and Newcastle's most notable contribution to art education, the King's College basic design course set up by two more London artists, Victor Pasmore and Richard Hamilton.[22] Derived from the preliminary course at the Bauhaus established by Johannes Itten in 1919, the King's course was intended to be a series of first-year exercises concerned with line, tone, colour, form and space which would break down barriers between art, design and architecture. In practice, however, as the critic and historian John A. Walker, a student at King's at the time, recalls, there was precious little contact between the art school and the school of architecture next door.[23] Students tended to assume, rather, that the logical outcome of their time at King's was not so much design in the real world as abstract paintings and constructions in the approved Victor Pasmore manner. It is true that a number of them – the playwright David Storey, the actor Jack Shepherd and the singer Brian Ferry, among others – did go on to find success *outside* the domain of fine art. However, this was probably more a consequence of the college's social mix and the open, enquiring attitude it engendered than of anything they learned from their tutors about art.

Nor was there any real connection between the kind of art that students at King's produced, or aspired to produce, and art produced outside the college. In fact the latter – 'local art', the kind of 'amateur art' which each year crowded the walls of the Federation of Northern Art Societies' exhibitions at the Laing – tended to be shunned by students at King's. Reputable art, art worthy of being emulated, was assumed to be necessarily metropolitan in outlook and appearance. When, for instance, in 1967 the work of the locally born painter Ian Stephenson, a long-standing teacher at King's, was featured in the definitive swinging London film of the time, Antonioni's *Blow Up*, this was regarded as a singular achievement.

After Pasmore left in 1961 the character of art at King's changed somewhat as Hamilton's interest in such developments as Cinemascope, cinerama and the Polaroid camera began to have an influence. This did not mean it was any more in touch

[21] See Tyne and Wear Museums Service, *Pre-Raphaelites: Painters and Patrons in the North East* (1984), p.101.
[22] King's College was still at this time part of Durham University.
[23] I am grateful to John A. Walker for providing me with his unpublished account of his student days.

**11.6**  Victor Pasmore, Apollo Pavilion, Peterlee, 1960s.

with what was happening outside in the city, for although Hamilton later gained a huge and lasting reputation as a 'Pop' artist, few in Newcastle outside the college at this date knew of his work either as teacher or practitioner. Hence, in the late 1950s, as John Walker confirms, the prevailing house style in the college remained the austere constructivism of Pasmore. And even in the late 1960s, as another King's graduate, Hilary Fawcett, recalls, abstraction still reigned supreme.[24]

It is true that a number of artworks by these art school artists did manage to find a wider local audience simply by dint of their being sited outside the gallery. The most notable of these were the houses and landscaping for the new town of Peterlee, Co. Durham, for which Pasmore acted as artistic adviser from 1955. However, it should be noted that, despite being acclaimed in metropolitan art circles, the brave new world of Peterlee was never much appreciated by the town's residents. Indeed, at the time of writing, Peterlee's showpiece, Pasmore's severely modernist 'Apollo Pavilion', is threatened with demolition by Easington District Council.

Such lack of appreciation, even hostility, on the part of local people is of course hardly surprising. After all, the reason why Scott, Hamilton, Pasmore and others were appointed to their Newcastle teaching posts was their association with, and

---

[24]  By then it was more likely to be the American-inspired and equally arcane seeming abstraction of the subsequently renowned New York painter, Sean Scully, a student and then teacher at King's.

understanding of, metropolitan rather than local art. Similarly, the reason why students applied to King's was that at the time the college had a national reputation for being one of the best in which to be initiated into the mysteries of officially authorised 'modern', which is to say, 'metropolitan' art. Furthermore, when these same students graduated, they tended always to think of going to London (or possibly New York) rather than staying put in Newcastle. Staying put in Newcastle they regarded as some kind of opting-out from the responsibility of being a serious artist.[25]

Another factor reinforcing the non-local focus of art school art in this period was the increasing availability of magazines and books about contemporary art in Europe and North America. John Walker recalls that in the 1950s magazines such as *Studio*, *Art International* and *Art News* were available in King's.[26] Students did not have to travel down to London to see the latest shows. It was possible to keep abreast of developments in the capital and abroad simply by paying occasional visits to the college library.

## Local Colour

Since Bewick's time officially accredited, professional art in Newcastle has not completely turned its back on local life. There has always been a strand which has celebrated the people, events and scenery of the North East – for example, the 1820s genre scenes of Henry Perlee 'Smuggler' Parker with their amusing 'characters' in local settings. Indeed it was these works by Parker which effectively established the little fishing village of Cullercoats, nine miles east of Newcastle, as a favourite spot for locally based painters seeking subjects conveniently close-by but apparently blessedly untouched by modernity.

As with so much painting in this vein, Parker's Cullercoats scenes give only a very partial account of what life was like at the time. That is, anything upsetting or even dramatic is always rigorously excluded. Typically, what is shown are fishermen and smugglers (hence Parker's soubriquet) amidst a picturesque assortment of fish and tackle, enjoying the kind of ease and contentment which bourgeois visitors out for the day from Newcastle might want to find for themselves.

Later in the 19th century the formula changed slightly. In the 1880s William Lionel Wyllie and the American artist Winslow Homer presented Cullercoats as the scene of a daily struggle with the elements fought by noble men and women, whose

[25] Many did go to either London or New York and enjoyed considerable critical success. The roll call of distinguished artists who graduated from King's, or from the fine art course at what eventually became the University of Northumbria, is impressive. It includes Sean Scully, Stephen Buckley, Louise Hopkins, Tania Kovats, Matthew Higgs, Stefan Gec, Eric Bainbridge and Jane Wilson.

[26] Walker, *op.cit.* also says that such material was only rarely available at this date at the local bookshop, Thorne's in Barras Bridge.

statuesque forms are derived from the peasants of Millet and Bastien-Lepage. However, even though such work might be considered more 'realistic' than Parker's scenes of almost child-like idlers, its appeal was probably largely the same: that of a fairy-tale world at once remote from the lives of the picture-buying public and at the same time unaffected by modern technological and social developments.

Much of William Bell Scott's work can be described in these terms. In his autobiography, the painter of *Iron and Coal* talks of the fascinating contrast of old and new which Newcastle presented when he first came to the town in the mid-1840s:

> Half-timber mullioned-windowed old houses and the family mansions of county magnates were brow-beaten and jostled by great stone-built streets and detached buildings in the 'Italian style' … And this change, which has taken place everywhere, was in Newcastle going on with accelerated speed by the extension of trade and the centralising tendency of railway travelling.[27]

However, significantly, it was never the new streets or the new market 'as yet only half inhabited, under long arcades of iron and glass, with walks appropriated to all classes of goods' which he actually chose to paint. Instead, it was the Castle, the approach to the Black Gate, the spire of St Nicholas's, and the almost medieval confusion of the Bigg Market.

This taste for the old and quaint became entrenched in the mid-century. Slightly earlier than this, the new aspects of Newcastle had still held some appeal. The travel writer, Dibdin, for example, was enthralled by the 'march of improvement' in Newcastle with Richard Grainger, 'the Northumbrian Vitruvius', at its head. Nevertheless, even Dibdin, it seems, was mostly drawn to old Newcastle. His first act on arriving in the town was to ask Emmerson Charnley, 'the veteran-emperor of Northumbrian booksellers', to show him 'everything … old, close, strange, dark, dingy, and out of the ordinary course of domestic and street scenery'.[28]

Ralph Hedley's best-known pictures, *The Newsboy* (1892), *Sandgate Market* (1892) and *Seeking Situations* (1904), might seem to mark a departure in that they show the poor in grimy but up-to-date settings; the latter, for instance, is a scene of unemployed men looking through job advertisements at Newcastle Free Public Library. However, it can be argued that in truth there is nothing about these works which the picture-buying public at the time would have found in the slightest degree disturbing. The plight of the poor is presented as sad but inevitable; the poor, such works seem to say, are always with us.

---

[27]  Minto, *Autobiographical Notes*, vol.1, p.182.
[28]  Dibdin, *Tour in the Northern Counties*, vol.1, p.359.

This could also be said of much late 20th-century documentary photography, notably the Finnish-born Sirkka-Liisa Konttinen's series of photographs of Byker which appeared in 1983 to considerable acclaim in both Newcastle and London. These were publicised at the time as a reliable record of a particular close-knit working-class community in east Newcastle before it fell before the developers' bulldozers in the 1970s. Nevertheless, what chiefly comes across from Konttinen's scenes of terraced houses, little girls dressed up in their mother's clothes, old ladies gossiping, tomatoes growing in the window of a funeral parlour and the like, is chiefly an amused fascination with a seemingly exotic way of life, something which, incidentally, makes them entirely different in feel to Jimmy Forsyth's wonderfully unsentimental 'snaps' of the people he was living amongst on the Scotswood Road.

What about the paintings of the Ashington Group set up in 1934 in the big pit village of Ashington in Northumberland, 15 miles north of Newcastle? Are these not different in that they present the world of miners and mining from a miner's rather than from a tourist's point of view? Certainly that is how they have often been described. For instance, one of their first metropolitan champions, Janet Adam Smith, Arts Editor of *The Listener*, claimed in 1938 that

> All the men [and all of them were men] insist that this work is a special affair, done to please themselves. They are shy of outsiders seeing it and criticising it as they would criticise the work of full-time artists. They don't want to become full-time painters. They don't want to send work to the Royal Academy or the London Group. They don't want to be looked on as curiosities, publicised by dealers as 'Miner Painters' and made a collector's fashion.[29]

And yet, once they were taken up by the art world and exhibited at the Laing or the Hatton galleries in Newcastle, or in London, it could be said that 'curiosities' is exactly what the Ashington Group became. Their work took on the same appeal as that of Parker or Hedley. Annexed by the authorised art sytem, it came to offer a neatly bracketed-off, alternative world where nothing untoward seems to occur, where everyone seems content and where history and politics supposedly do not impinge.

That of course might equally be said of Bewick's tail-pieces, book-plates and illustrations and it is no accident that, like the members of the Ashington Group, Bewick was lauded in his own day and beyond as an untaught genius whose art was steeped in the local and the particular. But is there not an important difference? The Ashington Group did not consciously present themselves as naive northerners.

[29] *The Listener*, 28 April 1937, quoted in Feaver, William, *Pitmen Painters: The Ashington Group 1934-1984* (1988), p.69.

**11.7** 'Tally men': Jimmy Forsyth, *Scotswood Road*.

That was a gloss put on them by others, for instance, by Robert Lyon, Master of Painting at Armstrong College, Newcastle, who set up the group in the first place as a Workers' Educational Association class, and by metropolitan intellectuals such as Tom Harrisson, Julian Trevelyan and Charles Madge, who publicised their work nationally. Bewick, on the other hand, recognised that potential purchasers wanted to believe that his seemingly simple scenes in the seemingly humble medium of wood engraving (formerly mostly associated with children's book illustration) were the work of a naturally gifted countryman responding straightforwardly and directly to his immediate surroundings. He therefore deliberately developed an appropriate public persona.[30] Hence the many accounts one comes across of the 'fine old fellow, this jolly old Cock o'the North' who liked nothing better than to talk to dogs, ducks and pigs in the inn-yard and the few accounts, by contrast, of the hard-nosed businessman who would demand the money his apprentices were paid for work they had done in their spare time on the grounds that apprentices' drawings were always legally a master's property.[31]

[30] Ruskin, for instance, was typical in seeing the fact that Bewick had been brought up on 'Northumbrian hills' and had never been near an academy as crucial to his greatness as an artist in later life. See Ruskin, 'Ariadne Florentina'.
[31] See Williams, Gordon (ed.), *Bewick to Dovaston: Letters 1824-1828* (1968), pp.13 and 16.

## Selling the Quayside

In the last two decades there has been much talk of the universalist claims of Modernism losing their authority and of a position on the margins being the most productive place for an artist to work. 'Perhaps one of the positive results of the 1980s', suggested the New York-based, Australian-born critic, Robert Hughes, 'will be finally to clear our minds of the cant of cultural empire. Under the present circumstances, a great artist can just as easily emerge in Hungary or Australia as in New York.'[32] And indeed the curator Lewis Biggs coined the term 'local international' to describe what he saw as the phenomenon of a new breed of British artists who were deliberately choosing to live outside London.[33] They were doing this, he said, because they realised it allowed them to draw

> on a deep and personal experience to provide the emotional impetus for [their] art. 'Local' describes a position in the cultural, not the geographical, sense – the notion of purposes and values held, of conviction … But this sense of intimacy, of something known and felt from the inside out, is balanced by the artist's awareness of other cultures, of the many interpretations that will be brought to his or her art by people ignorant of its original source.

In the Newcastle context 'local international' is probably most usefully applied to the videos, banners, mixed media installations and performances of artists such as Mona Hatoum, Stefan Gec, Richard Wilson, Pat Naldi and Wendy Kirkup commissioned for non-gallery sites by Jon Bewley and Simon Herbert of the energetic Newcastle-based agency, Locus +. For although, or perhaps because, these were often unashamedly 'difficult' works, and hence seen by only the smallest of audiences, nevertheless they won a formidable reputation in the metropolitan art world. *Natural History*, for instance, a 1995 banner piece by Gec about the heroic role played by Ukrainian firemen after the nuclear disaster at Chernobyl which appeared on the top of the fire station in Pilgrim Street, Newcastle, was hailed as much outside the region as it was within it.

However, challenging, critically acclaimed art like this was unusual in the 1990s. More commonly, art was asked to fulfil the role of publicising and legitimising property developments on the Quayside, an area of Newcastle which, following the example of cities elsewhere such as Baltimore and Liverpool, was being earmarked for regeneration. I am referring here not only to pieces by Andre Wallace, Andrew

---

[32] Quoted by Suchin, Peter in 'Somewhere near the Northern Edge: The Sense and Nonsense of the Centre', Hatton Gallery, Newcastle upon Tyne, *Artlanta: 32 artists from the North of England* (1996), p.29.
[33] Laing Art Gallery, Newcastle upon Tyne, *New North. New Art from the North of Britain* (1990), p.9.

**11.8**  Stefan Gec, *Natural History*, 1995.

Burton, Neil Talbot and Raf Fulcher on the Newcastle East Quayside but also to works by Richard Deacon, Richard Harris and Colin Rose in the area of reclaimed land between between the Swing Bridge and the Redheugh Bridge now known as the Gateshead Riverside Sculpture Park.

From time to time temporarily sited works also played the developers' game – for instance, the artworks commissioned for the second 'Tyneside International' (1993) and installed at the Sallyport Tower, the Castle keep, the area behind the new Law Courts and various sites in and around the Quayside. The centrepiece of this particular event was a mini-retrospective by the New York performance and video artist, Vito Acconci, in the then semi-derelict 1897 CWS warehouse owned by the Tyne and Wear Development Corporation (TWDC), the quango responsible for promoting the development of the area. At the time this seemed a flop in that it attracted hardly any visitors, even though the CWS warehouse was only a few metres away from where thousands gathered that summer to watch the Tall Ships Race. Nevertheless, in the long run, from a property developer's perspective, it probably can be counted a success for, whilst an initial notion of turning the CWS warehouse into a permanent contemporary art space when the exhibition closed came to nothing (the former grain silos of the Baltic Flour Mills on the other side of the river were favoured instead), the building a few years later became one of Newcastle's most expensive hotels, needless to say minus most of its original trappings.

It was a similar story with 'Edge 90'. A series of installations by non-local artists such as Richard Wilson, Rosie Leventon and Mark Thompson were staged in the dark, dingy rooms of an empty 19th-century warehouse in Hanover Street on the West Quayside. The hope was, presumably, that, once the exhibition closed, the building would be converted into a set of up-market riverside apartments. Yet for one reason or another this transformation never occurred. In fact the building was destroyed soon after in a mysterious fire.

In the long run, however, even 'Edge 90' probably served the developers' interests. By being commonly referred to as 'public art', the exhibits helped to suggest that the changes occurring along the Quayside were for the good of the wider community. 'Edge 90' also helped to forge the link in people's minds between the Quayside as a space, and what is thought of as the highly desirable, socially exclusive world of 'Art'. This was particularly important in the early 1990s because the Quayside was then still a largely neglected area which possessed none of the expensive apartments, offices, restaurants and wine bars it boasts today.

Yet there was a price to pay for this type of regeneration. Formerly, the Quayside had been an area which was shabby but heterogeneous in character, as a series of elegiac black and white photographs by the photographers and film-makers' co-operative, Amber Associates, published in 1979, make clear. Despite the emphasis given to the word 'community' in early 1990s Development Corporation publicity, the Quayside was in effect being re-branded as a high-earning luxury enclave, a place of consumption, cappuccino and culture for the comfortably-off.

Just occasionally, genuine public artworks were commissioned in the 1990s, genuine in the sense that they did not merely provide ornaments for new buildings but raised questions about the social and political implications of the way the Quayside was being re-developed. One such was a piece for the first 'Tyne International' in 1990 by the Polish-American artist Krzysztof Wodiczko, a projection on the side of the Tuxedo Royale, a ferry-turned-night club moored beneath the Tyne Road Bridge. This showed skeleton hands paddling their way through piles of coins, an image which seems to have been intended as an indictment of the money then being made out of the Quayside by various private concerns. Another genuine public artwork was *True North* by Paul Bradley for the same exhibition, which consisted simply of the words 'TRUE NORTH' in shiny steel letters on the wall of a disused railway shed on the Gateshead side of the river beside the High Level Bridge. Described like that, it probably sounds neither stimulating nor thought-

**11.9** Paul Bradley, *True North*, 1990.

provoking but in fact it was both. This was because the letters were located in such a way that they could really only be seen from the Newcastle side of river, looking southward. It seemed, therefore, to be saying: don't expect the north to be in charge of its own destiny any more; True North is where money and power are, and that's in the South.

However, it is questionable whether these pieces ruffled many feathers. In the case of the Wodiczko, the projected image was mysteriously switched off on Guy Fawkes Night, the one time of the year when it might have been viewed by a substantial audience. More generally, few viewers were ever likely to try to fathom the possible meanings of such a work. Which is why perhaps the Tyne and Wear Development Corporation, the body supervising the Quayside regeneration programme, saw fit to provide some of the funding. The sad truth with 'cutting-edge' public art is that, since it is regarded as inscrutable by most of the population, sponsors feel they can safely support it, however critical it may seem, because they can be sure it will be largely ignored.

## The Soldiers Return

Since Bewick's day art in Newcastle has always been dogged by a sense of being dependent upon, and inferior to, art in London. But maybe no longer. Maybe the situation is about to change. When it is finished in the spring of 2002, the £45.7 million Baltic, the converted former grain silo on the Gateshead East Quayside mentioned earlier, will provide vast tracts of space for contemporary art; in fact it will be the largest exhibition space for contemporary art outside London. It will also, at least initially, have the advantage of ample money to stage exhibitions without the burden and expense of having to look after a permanent collection at the same time.[34]

One can imagine, therefore, the opening of Baltic marking the dawn of a new era for art in Newcastle. It has been predicted that 400,000 people a year will visit it.[35] And maybe that is so. Figures for Visual Arts UK, a region-wide, year-long £15m series of exhibitions, events, commissions and conferences in 1996, suggest that, where contemporary art is concerned, supply can create its own demand.[36] That is to say, if enough exciting shows are put on and suitable publicity provided, as large a proportion of the total population can be expected to turn out to see them on Tyneside as anywhere else, even London. Affluent Tynesiders may soon therefore be wanting to go to Baltic if only for the roof-top restaurant which will afford fabulous views of Newcastle across the river. Likewise, an army of art tourists from outside the region, like a new version of the soldiers in John Martin's *The Bard*, may soon be wending its way northwards. And if they do, this could well have an invigorating effect on local art practice.

But one should be cautious. In the past Newcastle has had its share of one-off, large-scale, expensive projects which in the long run have had little lasting impact on art practice in the city – projects where a famous metropolitan artist was selected, fulfilled a brief, and then promptly disappeared, probably never to return, if indeed he ever came to the city in person in the first place. This, for example, is what happened when Edward Hodges Baily sculpted his *Earl Grey* for Benjamin Green's column at the end of Grey Street (1838) and Hamo Thornycroft, John Tweed, Alfred Gilbert and George Frampton produced their statues of Lord Armstrong (1906), Joseph Cowen (1906) and Queen Victoria (outside St Nicholas's, 1903, and outside the RVI, 1906).[37] Likewise, this is the story of the two main Great War memorials in the city, Goscombe John's *The Response.1914* at Barras Bridge (1923) and C.L.

---

[34] Sune Nordgren, the director of Baltic, has explained that Baltic will generate artworks and exhibits through commissions and residencies which 'might be kept as temporary or even permanent works for public spaces as well as in collections. With the agreement of their creators, these works will be taken care of by different institutions, of which BALTIC could be one.' (Nordgren, Sune, 'To Collect or not to Collect? – That is the question', *Baltic Newsletter*, no.7, March 2000.)

[35] Gateshead Council, *Baltic News Release*, 24 March 1999.

[36] Harris Research Centre for Northern Arts/Arts Council, *Visual Arts UK: Public attitudes towards an awareness of the Year of Visual Arts in the North of England* (1997).

[37] John Graham Lough might seem to be the exception here in that he was born locally, near Shotley Bridge. However, at the time that he produced the Stephenson Monument in Newcastle (1862) and the Collingwood Monument at Tynemouth (1843) he was very much a London-based sculptor. See Usherwood, Beach and Morris, *Public Sculpture*, pp.149-50, 207-9.

Hartwell's *St George and the Dragon* at Eldon Square (1923). In fact the only instances of major sculpture commissions in Newcastle which were awarded to local sculptors rather than to London 'stars' are Thomas Eyre Macklin's South African War Memorial in the Haymarket (1908) and John Reid's 6th Northumberland Fusiliers' Memorial outside St Thomas's (1924). Even 'Visual Arts UK' in 1996 was dominated by what is referred to nowadays as 'parachute art' dropped in, as it were, from outside: Antony Gormley's *Field for the British Isles* in Gateshead, Velasquez's *The Rokeby Venus* at the Bowes Museum, Bill Viola's video *The Messenger* in Durham Cathedral, and an exhibition of recent British work from the Tate at the Laing – 'Tate on Tyne'.[38]

Furthermore, experience in recent years suggests that large new showpiece galleries like Baltic have a tendency to display the kind of art which can circulate benignly within a set of global institutional expectations and values, regardless of, and outside, any determining local conditions. In other words, one can all too easily imagine a scenario in which the soldiers in John Martin's painting return, this time as art tourists, only to find much the same art as they would find were they to visit contemporary art galleries in, say, Bilbao or Malmo.

Which is not to say that there is not a need for a distinctive Newcastle art. With the opening in May 2000 of Tate Modern at Bankside (London's version of Baltic) the metropolitan bias of the British art world has undoubtedly been hugely reinforced and so also has the monopolistic power of the major metropolitan art institution.[39] And in the long run that is something which cannot be healthy for London or for the rest of the country, however outward-looking and enlightened the Tate as an institution might endeavour to be. It must be in the interests of everyone that a distinctive and vigorous contemporary provincial art scene should emerge.

But is it likely to happen? The omens are not good. Only 16,000 went to see the sculptor Anish Kapoor's *Taratantara*, a highly ambitious and hugely expensive temporary installation filling the vast hollowed-out interior of Baltic in the summer of 1999, though that may have been because it was poorly publicised.[40] And the experience of cities elsewhere is not encouraging either. For sure, there was considerable talk in the late 1980s and early 1990s of a Glasgow renaissance.[41] But

[38] The tendency mentioned earlier in connection with T.M. Richardson's exhibitions for exhibitions in Newcastle to be judged by whether or not they include star attractions from London has if anything grown more pronounced in our own day.

[39] It should be noted that, even before Tate Modern opened at Bankside, there were already annexes of the Tate at Liverpool and St Ives.

[40] Figures given in *Baltic Newsletter*, no.7, March 2000. *Taratantara* comprised a deep-red PVC membrane looking like a trumpet or something more gynaecological stretched from one side wall to the other.

[41] 'New Image Glasgow', Third Eye Centre, Glasgow (1985) and 'The Vigorous Imagination – New Scottish Art', National Galleries of Scotland, Edinburgh (1987) especially focused on four young graduates from Glasgow School of Art, Steven Campbell, Peter Howson, Ken Currie and Adrian Wiszniewski, whose work seemd to tie in with a commercially driven, international art-world interest in promoting a revival of figurative painting. They were dubbed the new 'Glasgow Boys'.

sadly not only did this soon peter out but also the kind of art which became dominant in Britain in the Nineties, 'BritArt', was always very much associated with London. It is also questionable whether the 'New Glasgow Art' was ever particularly distinctive or homogeneous. With hindsight it is probably more accurate to see it as something developed by and for the London art world which, like a colonial plantation, languished the moment the metropolitan world ceased to have need of it.[42] And maybe that is how it has always been with art on the margins. Art on the margins flourishes only so long as it happens to meet the needs of the metropolis.

Nor is the situation necessarily any different because there has been a remarkable increase recently in the amount of information and discussion about art in the British media. It may be that it is no longer altogether true that the art metropolis is somewhere geographically distant. That is to say, thanks to all the talk about art in London, it may be that London no longer seems the faraway Babylon it did in Bewick's day, or in the late 1950s when the young John Walker hitch-hiked down the A1 to see Jackson Pollock's drip paintings at the Tate.[43] Sadly though, this does not mean that a provincial city like Newcastle is more likely to emerge as a distinct, viable artistic centre in its own right. Far from it. The truth is, the greater Newcastle's awareness of artistic developments in London, the less the chance of its own artistic renaissance at home.

---

[42] Despite the fact that some 2,000 artists now live and work in Glasgow, these artists, significantly, are not recognised in the international art world, or if they are (as for instance is the case with the Turner Prize-winning Douglas Gordon), not as 'Glasgow artists'.

[43] A story in John Walker's unpublished account of his time at King's, *op.cit.*

12

# Remembering George Stephenson
## Genius and Modern Memory

ROBERT COLLS

## Site of Memory

On Thursday 2 October 1862, Newcastle upon Tyne remembered George Stephenson. Ten thousand people marched in his memory, and it was estimated that a further 100,000 watched them do so. So many wanted to see that ladies and gentlemen perched on building-tops while those who lived along the route rented out their upper-storey windows. It was observed that 'lamp posts sustained a burden that no lamp post was intended to bear'. Crowds thronged all the way from the Haymarket down to St Nicholas Square where the workmen's procession met up with business and political leaders who, together with Mr. Lough the sculptor and Mr. Stephenson the nephew, took their places at the front. Led by the band of the 41st Regiment, on they went as one rising tide out of the narrow town and up into Neville Street bottom of Westgate Road where, at two o' clock in the afternoon, they inaugurated Stephenson's monument.

Only 35 years before it had been said that Newcastle was not a manufacturing town, but on this day the town was proclaiming not only its manufacturing but also its modernity.[1] Indeed, it might be said that on 2 October 1862 Newcastle's modern sense of self began. The men who marched that day – pattern makers, moulders and millwrights, joiners, boilermakers and smiths, brass founders and finishers, fitters and turners – from Stephenson's, from the North Eastern Railway, from Hawks, Crawshay, and Hawthorns', Thompson's, Armstrong's and Abbot's, carried in their hands the skills that would sustain their sons, grandsons and great-grandsons for a hundred years. Two lads from the Stephenson frame shop carried a blue flag saying: 'He was one of us'.[2]

---

[1] Mackenzie, E., *A descriptive and historical account of the town and county of Newcastle upon Tyne including the borough of Gateshead*, vol. 2 (1827), p.731.

[2] *Newcastle Daily Chronicle*, 3 October 1862, and see reports in this newspaper for the following week concerning the visit of the Chancellor of the Exchequer to the Tyne. Mr. Gladstone amply confirmed both Newcastle's manufacturing and its modernity. For a full description of the monument: Usherwood, P., Beach, J., Morris, C., *Public Sculpture of North-East England* (2000), pp.149-50.

After the monument had been opened and Lord Ravensworth had orated on it, and the Vicar of Newcastle had blessed the proceedings, the gentlemen retired to drink wine. The workmen, or at any rate 700 of them, departed to take tea with Newcastle's finest moderns – Mr. Bruce the schoolmaster, Mr. Clephan the newspaper editor, Mr. Cowen the well-known Radical, and Mr. Armstrong, of Elswick, gun maker.

## 'He was one of us'

This chapter is about how Newcastle has chosen to remember, and forget, George Stephenson. In 1862, there was no doubt that he had come to stand for Newcastle, for all it had achieved and all it was about to achieve. On the face of it, to build a public statue appears to be a very simple way of remembering. But there are many ways of conceiving a statue and, of course, it didn't have to be a statue at all. It could have been something else; something perhaps more fitting to the man. As this chapter will show, a statue had been a very contentious matter because it involved taking Tyneside's greatest son – a man of very poor origins – and making him look like a gentleman. To some, co-opting Stephenson into the ranks of the gentry seemed like a compliment. To others, it seemed like a betrayal of the man as he was – a man who in his lifetime was never really accepted by the gentry and probably never wanted to be. As for Newcastle itself, was the building of a classical statue an appropriate way of celebrating its modernity, its technological brilliance, its democratic airs? Or was it the last gasp of an older patrician élite trying to hold on? How do we remember the past? How does the past try to present itself for remembering? Who was the real George Stephenson and what was the real Newcastle? Is history equipped to answer such questions? As well as telling something of the story of George Stephenson, which is a good story, and the making of modern Newcastle, which is the subject of this book, it is hoped that the chapter will also raise some interesting questions about the writing of history.

When Stephenson died in 1848 he was not yet a full national hero. He was only a newly rich and famous engineer, and what is more he had had business links with George Hudson, a man whose financial empire was about to unravel in scandal and shame.[3] However, by the time of the publication in 1857 of Samuel Smiles' celebrated biography of Stephenson, the bad odour of his association with Hudson had begun to clear. Smiles had taken the trouble to count the railway achievement to date: £308,000,000 capital expended, 8,635 miles of public track laid, 129,000,000 passengers

---

[3] Hunter Davies enters the tricky ground of his unseemly association with Hudson, particularly the latter's patronising of 'Old George': *George Stephenson* (1975), p.231.

moved, half of them at a cost of less than a penny a mile.[4] Smiles made famous the way-marks of Stephenson's life: 1781, born in a pitman's cottage; 1814, successful experiments in steam locomotion at Killingworth; 1815, invention of the miners' safety lamp; 1819-23, completion of the Hetton colliery line; 1825, the Stockton and Darlington first public railway, and *Locomotion*; 1829, the Rainhill trials, and *Rocket*; 1830, the Liverpool-Manchester railway and all the other lines that followed – the Birmingham and Derby, the Manchester and Leeds, the North Midland, and the York and North Midland. For a brief period in the 1840s, his son Robert and other young railway captains such as Brunel and Hudson overtook him, in fame at least. But in the longer term 'The Father of Railways' became the world's most famous engineer and his fame grew in proportion to the length of track laid. By the time of the Stockton-Darlington Jubilee in 1875, the whole capitalist world was criss-crossing itself with railways and believing in their magic. Stephenson was seen as the originator of a transport system which had turned that world into a market and its territories into nations by subduing 'time and space', and compressing 'the march of twenty centuries … into a few prolific years'.[5] Newcastle had been slow to honour its greatest son but when it finally did so, in 1862, it did not stint itself.

It is important to know George Stephenson's precise achievements because his friends did not always get it right. First, he did not build, still less did he 'invent', the first working locomotive. The Cornishman Richard Trevithick probably did that, at Penydarran, Merthyr Tydfil, in or around 1804. Nor did Stephenson build the first powerful working locomotive. John Blenkinsop (born Walker) did that, with Matthew Murray (born near Newcastle), at Middleton Colliery, Leeds, in 1812. George Stephenson did not build even the North East's first powerful working locomotive nor even the first locomotive in his home village of Wylam. Honours here go to Blenkinsop and William Chapman at Coxlodge Colliery, and William Hedley (born Newburn) with prototypes for *Puffing Billy* and *Wylam Dilly*, in 1813.[6]

Stephenson's *Blucher* first raised steam on Killingworth moor the year after that. It went at only three miles per hour but that didn't matter because Stephenson knew it could go faster and in every respect – design, construction, traction, transmission – it was a superior engine. Time and again, the Stephensons produced

---

[4]  Smiles, S., *The Life of George Stephenson* (1857), *Preface* and 'the grandest organization of capital and labour that the world has yet seen' (p.507); for more details, Railway Investment 1830-1973, and Route Miles of open line in Great Britain, see Simmons, J. and Biddle, G. (eds.), *The Oxford Companion to British Railway History from 1603 to the 1990s* (1997), pp.229, 492.

[5]  *Newcastle Daily Chronicle*, 28 September 1875; *Daily Telegraph*, 22 September 1875. The Italian nationalist Giuseppe Mazzini came from Piedmont where the term 'railway' was censored (along with others such as 'nation' and 'constitutional liberties') as subversive to the state: Boruma, I., *Voltaire's Coconuts* (1999), p.131.

[6]  Tomlinson says that Trevithick left developments 'to be carried out by men of less genius but more persistent character': Tomlinson, W.W., *The North East Railway. Its Rise and Development* (1914), p.19.

12.1    George Stephenson: working-class hero, 1859.

engines that went better, faster, cheaper, longer.[7] Of the two engineering breakthroughs that mattered – the realisation that smooth rails and smooth wheels produced sufficient friction, and that sharp intakes of steam exhaust into bigger boilers produced more power – there was no clear first innovator. Instead, there was a cluster of schools of building and design, all near to each other in theoretical advances but less so in practical performance.[8] Chief rival to the Stephensons at the Rainhill time trials of October 1829 was Timothy Hackworth's *Sans Pareil*. But weighing in at just over four tons and riding in yellow and black, the Stephensons' *Rocket* averaged 29m.p.h. on its final run to beat Hackworth and the rest out of sight. So rapid were the engineering advances of the time, within weeks of this famous victory the Stephensons' Forth works in Newcastle had produced *Planet*, an entirely superior class of engine over *Rocket* and a modern steam loco in every regard.[9] Up to this time, for well over a hundred years the northern coalfield had been serviced with lines of various degrees of length and sophistication. Horses, inclined planes and stationary engines hauled coals along these 'waggon ways', up hill and down dale, to the rivers, where they were shipped for export. As the coal industry grew in size and importance so did this vast network of track and the burdens it had to bear. Under the circumstances, it could be said that the steam locomotive was an invention waiting to happen. Edward Pease hired Stephenson at two guineas a day to survey a line to Stockton telling him it was 'for a great public way, to last so long as the coal continues'.[10]

Stephenson's other great national achievement was topographical. When in 1836 the essayist 'Agricola' warned the gentlemen of County Durham that 'Mr Pease and his friends have fixed upon a line' which would change the whole county, he was right and not just for Durham.[11] By surveying its first main railway arteries, George and Robert completely re-shaped the pattern of British economic and social development. Stephenson always saw one line in connection with another, and another, and another. He surveyed new lines according to this talent for connection and a preference for big loads, easy gradients and long straight stretches.[12] When

---

[7] Rolt, L.T.C., *George and Robert Stephenson. The Railway Revolution* (1960), chs.3 to 8. Rolt gives the best account of the engineering battle. The contributor to *The Oxford Companion* estimates George as 'actually a very conservative engineer' and Robert and his apprentice Joseph Locke as much better engineers – along with Brunel, best in the century: Simmons and Biddle, *Railway History*, p.477.

[8] Hedley's 1858 account is a polemic against Stephenson (and Smiles' account of him) but nevertheless he made clear that which Stephenson and his friends often did not make clear – that there was a squadron of practical mechanics getting very close to the same breakthroughs: Hedley, O.D., *Who Invented the Locomotive Engine?* (1858), pp.7-9.

[9] 'There has been little fundamental development since': Beckett, D., *Stephenson's Britain* (1984), p.22. Hackworth had been born at Wylam and apprenticed to the Stephensons.

[10] Edward Pease to George Stephenson, 28 June 1821, draft copy R.S. Watson Collection, Newcastle Central Library, vol.1.

[11] Agricola, *To the Inhabitants of The County of Durham* (1836).

[12] Rolt, *Railway Revolution*, p.251; Wood, N., *Address on The Two Late Eminent Engineers* (1860), pp.38-9.

the Newcastle-Carlisle Railway Company bought land west of Newcastle looking for a crossing at Redheugh[13] (bridge built 1839), the Stephensons and Hudson saw this as an aggressive act which could swing a line west then north to cross centrally into Scotland. Stephenson 'regarded the integrity of the East Coast route as a matter of national importance' and acted as he always acted, practically.[14] On 18 June 1844 a specially prepared locomotive left Euston at 5.30a.m. and, after averaging 37m.p.h. on route allowing for a stop at York to pick up Hudson and his cronies, steamed into Gateshead some eight hours later, at 2.24p.m. exactly. That settled it. London to Scotland would be York-Newcastle-Berwick. After a complicated manoeuvre involving three lines in mid-Durham, the Newcastle and Darlington Junction railway would link with the Newcastle and Berwick in the north and the York and Newcastle to the south. In order to secure the final link to Edinburgh, Hudson, meanwhile, was involving himself in the affairs of the North British Railway (bill passed 1844, line completed 1846). Hudson also made sure that Newcastle's Town Improvement Committee would grant permission for a railway crossing from the south over the Tyne gorge into Newcastle where a grand Central Station would be built. The template of modern Britain was in the making. When the Forth Bridge was finished in 1890, its eastern side was complete.

From humble cottage to great engineer, the story seems like a life of unbroken achievement. But crossing land meant crossing landowners too, and that quartet of influence so beloved of 19th-century pamphleteers – the 'Nobility, Gentry, Clergy, Freeholders &c' – had to be appeased, usually in rents.[15] Stephenson made more than his fair share of landed enemies and when he was a landowner himself he made fun of their arrogance. But it has to be said that, from very early on, Stephenson had as many rich men with him as against him. His deepest and most protracted conflicts were not with landowners such as Lord Howick but with technical and professional men who tried to censure him. Foremost among these was Sir Humphrey Davy, who never forgave Stephenson for inventing the safety lamp before he did. This Fellow of the Royal Society called the colliery engineman a thief and an impostor, though not to his face.[16] Then there were the engineers who challenged Stephenson's work, not always maliciously and not always wrongly but always with deep resentment on Stephenson's part. Messrs. Stevenson, Jessop,

[13] Richard Grainger had proposed such a crossing: Grainger, R., *A Proposal for concentrating the termini … submitted to the respective companies* (1836).

[14] Tomlinson, *North East Railway*, p.447.

[15] From part of the lobbying for a Newcastle-Carlisle railway – *Additional Supplement to a Letter from Mr Chapman to Sir James Graham of Kirkstall* (1824). As was often the case, anxiety was hierarchical: 'The chief anxiety, at present, is as to the opinion of his Grace the Duke of Northumberland.'

[16] By the committee appointed, *Report upon The Claims of Mr George Stephenson, relative to the invention of His Safety Lamp* (1817); Stephenson, G., *A Description of the Safety Lamp…now in use in Killingworth Colliery* (1817); Hunter Davies, *George Stephenson*, pp.24-30.

Vignoles, Telford and both Rennies were all put, or put themselves, in this position. The *Mechanics Magazine* doubted Stephenson's victory at Rainhill, while his own former apprentice Joseph Locke replaced him as engineer on the Grand Junction in 1835. In 1836 Joshua Richardson published his *Animadversions on the Report of George Stephenson*. The sons of his early rivals, Trevithick, Hedley and Hackworth, challenged his reputation and dogged him all his days.[17]

In the later years, happy in his Derbyshire garden, Stephenson often declined to mix with the gentlemen. Even the Prime Minister had his invitations turned down. It might have been that Stephenson remembered the slights. He said he did, and he most certainly recalled his humiliation at the hands of those barristers who, in 1825, were hired to oppose the first Liverpool-Manchester railway bill. After four days in the witness box Stephenson was, we are told, 'near collapse'.[18] On the first day, he held his own on engineering matters to do with weight, velocity and mechanical traction. Over the next three days, interrogated on lines and bridges, according to Smiles, by 'an extraordinary array of legal talent', he was torn apart. Summing up against the bill on 2 May 1825, Mr. Harrison referred to Stephenson's 'ignorance almost inconceivable' in the 'trash and confusion' of his evidence, while Mr. Giles the civil engineer wondered if he was in his right senses. Mr. Alderson KC called him stupid, credulous: 'He makes schemes without seeing the difficulties, and when the difficulties are pointed out, then he starts other schemes.'[19] The bill fell. Stephenson was removed and new men were hired to make new surveys where Lord Sefton's and Lord Derby's lands got skirted round, and where absurd promises were made about how slow the locos would go (not to frighten the cows). It was said that the line would be mainly horse-drawn anyway.[20] Accordingly, the second bill passed. The cotton lords of Manchester and Liverpool got their railway but Stephenson, the up and coming Tynesider with the grating accent, had been humiliated.

Part of the Stephenson myth was to make a lot of his early defeats in order to make more of his later victories.[21] In a speech at the Newcastle Assembly Rooms on 18 June 1844, the 63-year-old Stephenson told how he had had to put up with every rebuff from a class of rich men who had been wrong on almost every practical point. 'I was however a poor man' was his refrain, a poor man who, in the end, was

---

[17] On the Newcastle, Edinburgh and Glasgow railway, 'I am at a loss to conceive how he could possibly have been induced to write such a Report': Richardson, *Animadversions*. A good deal of Rolt's account is taken up with attacks on the Stephensons' engineering reputations: *Railway Revolution*.

[18] Carlson, R.E., *The Liverpool & Manchester Railway Project 1821-31* (1969), p.121.

[19] Smiles, *Life*, pp.226-9; Rolt, *Railway Revolution*, pp.110-12.

[20] Parliamentary Debates, House of Commons, 6 April 1826 (1827), vol. 15.

[21] As well as Smiles, Stephenson himself and his supporters and colleagues could be adroit in this regard. See extracts from his speeches in Newcastle in 1844 and Tamworth in 1847 reproduced in the *Gateshead Observer*, 19 August 1848; Welford, R., *Men of Mark 'Twixt Tyne and Tweed*, vol.3 (1895), p.443.

vindicated. Some of this refrain was true. In committee in 1825 Alderson the barrister had savaged Stephenson over his proposal to run part of the line over Chat Moss, a 12-square-mile peat bog to the west of Manchester. Nothing could be more stupid than this, opined Alderson. Five years later Stephenson's *Northumbria* ran straight across Chat Moss at more than 30m.p.h. in full public display, vindicating his engine, the speed and his construction of the line.[22] So he had his vindications, but how much of 'a poor man' was he? While it is true that Stephenson had been born poor and was illiterate up to age 18,[23] it is *also* true that he had been a well-paid engineman from his twenties and a businessman from his thirties. In 1821, aged 40 and still used to getting his hands dirty, he already had a number of consultancies, a partnership in a colliery, and was a five per cent creditor on a £1,300 loan.[24] George Stephenson never tired of saying he was a plain man born poor, but both he and Robert were Tories – and not even radical Tories at that. In their wills, neither of them left a penny to workers' associations. The young station conductor who was rebuked after he'd asked George for his ticket clearly misunderstood the Stephenson notion of 'plainness'. It had nothing to do with equality. The obituaries may have talked of Stephenson's plain tastes and 'crowdie' breakfasts, the engravings and popular songs may have made him a genial working-class hero, and the two lads from the frame shop might have carried a flag saying he was one of them, but this was not self evident from the life he lived.[25] There were those who wanted to remember him as a mechanic and there were those who wanted to remember him as a gentleman, and both sides had a case.

[22] On the triumph of Chat Moss, Rowland, J., *George Stephenson* (1954), pp.188-92. Stephenson would have to do the full speed ride again on the public opening of the line, 15 September 1830. This time he was carrying the terminally injured William Huskisson MP, member for Liverpool, to medical attention in Eccles. Huskisson had been hit by *Rocket* while strolling on the track.

[23] He was never happily literate: 'Where such letters are quoted elsewhere in this book, the phrase "George Stephenson writes" should not be taken literally' – Rolt, *Railway Revolution*, p.14.

[24] He'd been earning £100 a year as a coal company enginewright in 1812, with wage rises and plenty of freelancing thereafter, including a consultancy for the massive Hetton Coal Company from 1819.

[25] *Gateshead Observer*, 19 August 1848 and *London Journal*, 30 September 1848; *Civil Engineer and Architect's Journal*, 11 December 1848; *Eliza Cook's Journal*, 2 June 1849; *Newcastle Daily Chronicle*, 3 October 1862. George left £140,000, nearly all to Robert (Davies, *Stephenson*, p.276), and Robert left most of his cash fortune, plus the locomotive works, the Snibston collieries in Leicestershire and all lands, profits, shares and household effects to his cousin George Robert Stephenson, of Wimbledon, himself an up and coming engineer. Sums of between £1,000 and £10,000 were left to friends and the families of friends. £10,000 was left to Newcastle Infirmary and £2,000 sums to Newcastle Lit. & Phil., the North of England Institute of Mining Engineers and some Anglican societies. He left £100 a year for life to Margaret Tomlinson, his servant: Last will and testament, 13 August 1859 (Plate 12.1, p.272), Tyne & Wear Archives DT/SC/319. On folksy representations see *The British Workman*, no.49, January 1859, and Geordie Ridley's song 'The Stephenson Monument', 1862, in Allan, T., *Allan's Tyneside Songs* (1862) (7th edn. 1972), p.462. The most famous painting is John Lucas' dramatically northern portrait, first used by Smiles and then in possession of Robert. For plainstocking memories 'by TS who knew him when he was poor', Summerside, T., *Anecdotes, Reminiscences etc* (1878). A flood of mugs, plates, engravings and other commemorative ware appeared on the centenary of his birth: Duncan, W., *The Stephenson Centenary* (1881).

## Gentleman George?

Stephenson's was not the first public statue in Newcastle. Earl Grey had been hoisted onto his column at the top of Grey Street in 1838. Although the noble lord did not have the benefit of a parade,[26] there never was any doubt that his 134ft. erection marked the centre of the new Newcastle. The town's MP had first suggested a Stephenson memorial in 1851, with the backing of the *Gateshead Observer*.[27] The plan fizzled out only to revive after Smiles' best-selling biography of 1857.[28] Mr. Fairbairn raised the matter again at a dinner of the Institute of Mechanical Engineers in August 1858, and Mr. Armstrong the gun maker and Mr. Lothian Bell the iron master walked round from the *Queen's Head* to the *Turf* to suggest it to the Institute of Civil Engineers, who were also meeting that evening and who also agreed. Two months later a public meeting was held in the Council Chambers to decide on how to proceed.[29]

Apologies for absence were received both from Armstrong (who did the fund raising)[30] and from the Duke of Northumberland (in bed with gout), but there were plenty of other gentlemen willing to take the lead. What is more, they knew what they wanted. What they wanted was a public statue of Stephenson, erected in Newcastle, and sculpted by Mr. John Graham Lough RA. And they did not want any other suggestions. The meeting started at 2pm, convenient for gentlemen but nobody else, and when the Vicar dared say he thought perhaps that some educational scholarships might be a good thing, given Stephenson's struggle for knowledge, he was slapped down by the chairman for time wasting.

So George Stephenson got John Graham Lough and Newcastle got its second public statue. Among those responsible for this decision were the chairman, Henry Thomas Liddell, First Earl Ravensworth – Eton, Cambridge, JP and MP, classical scholar and President of the Society of Antiquaries; Henry George Liddell – Eton, Oxford, JP and MP, crack shot, good cricketer and Colonel in the Northumberland Hussars Yeomanry; Matthew Bell – gentleman, former MP, and officer in the Northumberland Hussars Yeomanry; Matthew White Ridley – Oxford, MP, High Sheriff, Agriculturalist, Master of the Hunt, Lt. Colonel in the Northumberland

[26] Brett, P., 'The Grey Monument. The Making of a Regional Landmark', unpublished paper, 1999.
[27] *Gateshead Observer*, 20 December 1851; handbill, *National Monument to George Stephenson*, 29 August 1850.
[28] *Newcastle Courant*, 6 February 1852. A humbler, more liberal-minded group of memorialists persevered for Stephenson Memorial schools at Willington Quay, where George had lived in his younger life. Work started 1852, stone laid 1858, opened with soiree 1860, Joseph Cowen jnr. in the chair: *Gateshead Observer*, 6 November 1852 and 11 February 1860.
[29] *Northern Daily Express*, 27 October 1858; *Newcastle Daily Chronicle*, 3 October 1862.
[30] Armstrong himself donated £100; Newcastle Corporation £105; top whack came from the Duke of Northumberland at £250. Donations, like anxieties (fn.15) and the order they came in, were strictly hierarchical: Monument to George Stephenson, Committee for Promoting the Object, *List of Subscribers* (1859?).

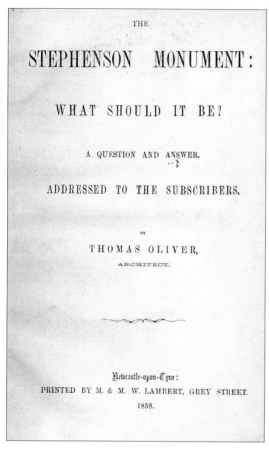

THE

## STEPHENSON MONUMENT:

WHAT SHOULD IT BE?

A QUESTION AND ANSWER.

ADDRESSED TO THE SUBSCRIBERS.

BY

THOMAS OLIVER,

ARCHITECT.

Newcastle-upon-Tyne:
PRINTED BY M. & M. W. LAMBERT, GREY STREET.
1858.

**12.2**    Thomas Oliver, *What Should It Be?*, 1858.

Hussars Yeomanry and patron of John Graham Lough.[31] There were others, such as Nicholas Wood the coal owner and John Hodgson Hinde of Elswick Hall, but the point is they got their (largely Tory) way. It seems likely that the meeting had been orchestrated. On the death of Robert Stephenson a year later they turned out to do it again but, this time, the opposition had rallied their forces.

Who were the opposition? First there was the architect Thomas Oliver. Soon after the 1858 meeting Oliver published his remonstrance *The Stephenson Monument. What should it be? A question and answer addressed to the subscribers.*[32] As Thomas Faulkner's chapter in this volume shows, Oliver stood in a line of outstanding Newcastle architects. John Dobson had been apprenticed to David Stephenson RA, and Oliver to Dobson. In 1823, while still a young man, Oliver had designed what was probably Newcastle's first domestic classical building, 37-39 Northumberland Street. In 1829 he did the highly regarded Leazes Terrace and in 1831 he had suggested a high-bridge rail crossing 'level with the Castle Garth' as part of a comprehensive development plan. During the 1830s and 1840s, in a town in the midst of re-building itself, Oliver had not been short of work. His case against the monument decision of 1858 was quite simple: a self-elected clique had got control of the meeting to block out subscribers' wishes and other architects' designs. Moreover, he didn't like classical statues of the sort Lough was known for and he proposed instead something more like the Waverley memorial to Sir Walter Scott in Edinburgh.[33]

A second opposition group gathered across the river in Gateshead – described by Pearson in 1838 as a town notable for its 'dirt, smoke and Radicals'.[34] They were

[31]    Information from Welford, *Men of Mark*, 3 vols.
[32]    Oliver, T., *The Stephenson Monument. What should it be? A question and answer addressed to the subscribers* (1858).
[33]    Oliver, T., *A New Picture of Newcastle Upon Tyne* (1831), p.131. He wasn't the first to draw parallels between Scott and Stephenson.
[34]    Pearson, W. and Atkinson, R., *A Journal of an Excursion to the North of England*, ms diary (1838), p.163.

led by W.H. Brockett, his *Gateshead Observer* and its mercurial editor, James Clephan. Clephan was a radical of the type who 'loved to look at the greatest problems in the clear white light of reason'. He believed in free trade, free thought and a free press. As an energetic member of the Press Club, the Gateshead Mechanics' Institute and Newcastle's Literary & Philosophic Society, Clephan was devoted to reason and to learning. To him, Stephenson stood for both these things. When the great man died, Clephan devoted the *Observer's* front page to him – an extraordinary act given 19th-century newspaper conventions. Three years later, in 1851, Clephan's columns had been quick to back the memorial proposal, but not for a statue. The *Gateshead Observer* called instead for a Stephenson Institute as a sort of cross between a mechanics' institute and a working-class university. This was an old idea, first floated as an alternative to Grey's monument by the radical *Tyne Mercury*, way back in 1838, but in Stephenson's case it had real merit. He had been involved in the founding of the Newcastle Mechanics' Institute in 1824 and the value of education to poor men like him had been one of his favourite themes. In campaigning mode, Clephan published Stephenson's letter to a friend telling how proud he was to be president of Birmingham Mechanics' Institute but would stay with his decision not to be an FRS nor a member of the Institute of Civil Engineers: 'I ... objected to those empty additions to my name', 'I have no flourishes to my name, either before it or after'. 'We must have no "classical statue"' thundered the *Observer*: no 'old thing' no 'Roman habit'. 'We must have some more appropriate monument.'[35]

William Newton, surgeon and councillor for All Saints, Newcastle's poorest ward, also came out against the statue. Newton was one of those eminent Victorians who could win five silver medals at university and still devote his life to the poor. In 1853, as a doctor he had fought the cholera on the ground, thickest in his ward. Like Clephan, Newton was a public-good radical – anti-vested interest, pro-Reform and in favour of free libraries, open parks, clean water, state education and public health. Both men believed in the reform of the criminal justice system and Newton

---

[35] *Newcastle Daily Chronicle*, 27 February 1888; *Gateshead Observer*, 19 August 1848; *Tyne Mercury*, 11 September 1838; *Gateshead Observer*, 27 December 1851. Stephenson had presided over a meeting in Fletcher's long room, Bigg Market, in February 1824, calling for a library for mechanics intent on the 'useful arts': unidentified newspaper cutting, Newcastle Central Library, vol. 1848-81 L920/S836. A Mechanics' Institute was opened the following month. In 1836 it was claimed that it had few working-class members: Liddell, D., *Suggestions relative to the Best Means for Diffusing Useful Knowledge* (1836). For a cool attitude to working-class education from one of the statue faction: Matthew White Ridley, 'The Education of the Agricultural Labourer', pamphlet read to Morpeth Chamber of Commerce, 2 February 1870. The owner of the *Gateshead Observer*, W.H. Brockett, backed his editor's campaign and, much to the disgust of the controlling faction (see Hodgson Hinde in *Northern Daily Express*, 27 October 1858), stubbornly persisted with a one guinea subscription to the memorial to make his point about all subscribers having (or in this case not having) an equal say in what sort of memorial it should be. On Brockett, see Manders, F.W.D., *A History of Gateshead* (1973), pp.263-4. On Newcastle's rather haughty attitude to radical Gateshead and Clephan in particular – 'a Triton among the Gateshead minnows' – see: *Club Portraitures of the Authors* (1850s?).

was against capital punishment.[36] At the 1859 meeting for Robert Stephenson, Newton had lined up with Dr. Collingwood Bruce, Mr. T.E. Harrison of the North Eastern Railway, and Mr. Rapier, workers' delegate from Stephensons' workshops who called for 'a comprehensive educational institution' with 'free library and evening classes'. Newton had a very clear sense of the opposing sides. He said he thought the Stephensons were not the only ones worthy of a memorial and suggested perhaps that the 'shoal of blue sharks' who had followed Robert for his money might like to pay now for his statue. Statues were 'a huge mistake' anyway, he said, cold and lifeless and backward looking. In his penny pamphlet brought out after the meeting, Newton drew attention to the chairman's 'intensely classical address'. He tried to show his learning by matching Lord Ravensworth in classical allusion and analogy.[37]

## The True and Beautiful

Classical allusion and analogy was, of course, the *motif* of Richard Grainger's new, upper Newcastle. Born the son of a quayside docker in a room only five feet high, Grainger had married well and speculated better. After making a bit of money building fashionable houses, he turned a £5,000 wifely inheritance into a vast and energetic fortune. Between 1834 and 1839 he added a local property boom to the coal and railway boom already underway. Building in four-storey slabs, he achieved not a genuinely beautiful city in the manner of Renaissance Italy with its squares and palazzos and gardens, but more a 'metropolitan effect' *in the manner* of a great city.[38] Those who did not realise how great it all was could have it explained in the handbooks. Was not Green's Theatre Royal 'from the Pantheon'? Was not Wardle and Walker's Central Exchange 'after the temple of Vesta at Tivoli'? Was not Green's monument to Grey in the manner of Trajan, of Rome? John Dobson was not the only architect involved in Grainger's rebuilding of Newcastle, but he got most of the credit. It was to his 'fine perception of the true and beautiful', remarked Welford in 1895, that Newcastle owed so much.[39] Achieving the true and beautiful in a town

---

[36] Welford, *Men of Mark*, vol. 1, 2. The Sunday School movement also saw itself as in these progressive ranks, see: Walters, Rev. W., *The History of the Newcastle-On-Tyne Sunday School Union* (1869).

[37] *Gateshead Observer*, 26 November 1859; Newton, W., *A Letter on the Stephenson Monument, and the education of the district, addressed to the Right Hon Lord Ravensworth* (1859). Newton wanted named scholarships (after great Novocastrians) invested in the new Royal Grammar School. A scholarship scheme, recently set up in connection with Bath Lane Church, is mentioned in Duncan, *Stephenson Centenary*.

[38] Faulkner, T.E., 'The early 19th century planning of Newcastle upon Tyne', *Planning Perspectives*, vol. 5 (1990), p.163.

[39] Collard, W. and Ross, M., *Architectural and Picturesque Views in Newcastle Upon Tyne* (1841), pp.76-80; Collingwood Bruce, Rev. J., *A Hand-Book to Newcastle On Tyne* (1863), pp.115-18. "'Great height is the cheapest way … of obtaining sublimity'", John Wilson Croker in 1814, quoted in Yarrington, A., *The Commemoration of the Hero* (1988), p.330. Welford, *Men of Mark*, vol.1, p.83.

recently described as 'the coal hole of the North' was quite an achievement.[40] Believing in its possibility under the dross of the world might be called not so much the metropolitan effect, as the 'Reynolds effect'.

In 1769, in order to fulfil their desire to be seen 'as lovers and judges of the Arts', certain aristocrats had started a Royal Academy in London. They asked Sir Joshua Reynolds to talk at its opening. In his *Discourses*, Reynolds laid down the 'perfect and infallible' Rules of Art as understood since the time of Raffaelle. His *Third Discourse*, given in 1770, charged the classically trained artist to look beyond what he actually saw in the world for the truthful and beautiful form beneath it, or beyond, or, as Reynolds had it, 'above'. In other words, the Art

**12.3**   John Graham Lough, 1828.

of the Academician lay in what was classically, not particularly, true, 'in being able to get above all singular forms, local customs, particularities and details of every kind'. This Art was not to be confused, said Reynolds, with 'the mechanic and ornamental arts', the workings of the 'mere mechanic'. The 'ancient sculptors' were the exemplary ones; 'having but one style', 'grave and austere', 'this science of abstract form' kept to 'exact equipoise'. Being 'indefatigable in the School of Nature', in their sculpture lay all the truth and beauty of the classical form. Lord Elgin's sale of the Parthenon frieze to the nation in 1816 gave tangible new inspiration to these 18th-century classicist ideals. The Academy could now throw out its old casts and work from the originals.[41] The first two professors of sculpture at the Academy were Reynolds' disciples. Flaxman got the chair in 1810, Westmacott in 1825.

In 1824, a young Northumbrian mason, John Graham Lough, went to London to learn how to sculpt. In 1826 he exhibited at the Academy, to no great effect it has to be said, but the following year Benjamin Robert Haydon and his set discovered him. They went to his lodgings to see his Milo – so big that its head poked through the ceiling – and they spread the word that Lough was *a genius*. The Duke of

---

40   Sopwith, T., *The Stranger's Pocket Guide to Newcastle upon Tyne and its environs* (1838), p.88.
41   Reynolds, Sir Joshua, *Discourses delivered to the students of the Royal Academy*, 1769 (1905), Third and Tenth Discourses.

Wellington, Lord Egremont and Mrs. Siddons attended his second Academy exhibition, in 1828. From this point it might be said that young Lough never looked back. He married well, he cultivated contacts, he travelled in Italy (for years) and, once established, he spent the rest of his life trying to live like a gentleman. Among his patrons, as well as Sir Matthew White Ridley whom we have noted already, were the Lords Rothschild, Sudley, Guilford, Hastings, the Dukes of Sutherland and Northumberland, and Prince Albert. But still he lived beyond his means. Ridley's daughter said of Lough that he thought he was a genius who could do great works 'yet he has constantly before his eyes the fear of utter ruin ... His wife, too, makes him worse ... with a great contempt not only for other artists but for everyone who does not appreciate his works'. Of those works, Haydon said: 'Lough is the only man I have ever seen who gave me an idea of what people used to say of me. In short, he is the only man I have ever seen who appears a genius.'[42]

And Lough did not demur, because a good deal of the romantic cult of 'genius' existed as a highly declamatory style which was capable of exciting its participators to higher and higher levels of self-awareness. After Reynolds, the ideal which artists were bound to, both in nature and in themselves, was not necessarily what nature and self offered first. Rather, it was a form existing in nature and in themselves which had to be recognised, sought out, and expounded, through their training and in their commitment. Haydon wore his hair like Raphael and slept under his portrait, and if the artist suffered because of his commitment (Reynolds said the investigation of form 'I grant, is painful', and Haydon and Lough both agreed on how much they had suffered) it was a sign of the 'Art'.[43] Thus, according to Buonarroti writing in 1828 and taking his cue from Reynolds, Lough's figures carried all the 'solemn dignity' and 'perfect beauty' of true classical works yet that beauty was 'in many respects incompatible with what is merely addressed to the senses'. In his Milo, about to be eaten by a wolf, 'there is no distortion of features' (though one might have thought there would have been). True form lies beneath, beyond or, as we have seen, 'above', real sensual life. Robinson in 1886 said that Lough's statue of Stephenson had noble qualities, but we should note that for Robinson as for Lough these were the qualities of any noble man rendered in the classical style. As such, they are nearer to being tautologies than qualities. Nobility, dignity, vigour and

[42] Haydon, B.R., *The Autobiography and Memoirs*, vol.1, 1853 (1926) Taylor, T. (ed.), pp.410-14; Allen, C., 'Sculpture in England. John Graham Lough', BA dissertation, King's College, Newcastle (1958), p.18; Haydon, *Autobiography*, p.413.

[43] Haydon lived in a 'circle of mutual admiration': Brown, D.B., *Benjamin Robert Haydon 1786-1846* (1996), introductory essay. Aldous Huxley wrote an excoriating criticism of Haydon, ungallantly one might think, as an introduction to his *Autobiography and Memoirs*. On pain and tears for Art's sake, Reynolds, *Discourses*, p.55 and Haydon, *Autobiography*, p.412 – 'we excited each other so much by mutual accounts of what we had suffered'. On 19th-century 'genius' as a god-like creativity confined to a few males yet with very powerful female resonance: Christine Battersby, *Gender and Genius* (1994).

massiveness are rendered not because Stephenson signified them but because they signified him.[44] As Reynolds insisted, the true artist had to get beyond 'all singular forms, local customs, and particularities'. He had to eschew mechanics.

So, for those who wanted to remember George Stephenson as he was there were two options. They could have an educational bequest in memory of a poor and illiterate workman who had overcome the odds. Or they could have a statue all could recognise as in the likeness of a singular, local and very particular Tyneside mechanic. Given that it was to be a statue, there was no possibility that Lough could sculpt Stephenson in that way. Lough was *a classicist* and he was *a genius* in the classicist mode.[45] For him to have remembered Stephenson's 'genius' in a non-classical way would have been to deny his own.

Lough's last major northern commission had been in 1842 for Cuthbert, Lord Collingwood. A statue in the grand manner followed the year after, for which Lough was paid a fee of £1,400, or 14 years' wages for a Newcastle mason. Son-in-law to Blackett the mayor, friend and successor to Nelson the chief, Major General of Marines, Baron and Freeman, Commander in Chief Mediterranean and Admiral of the Fleet Red Flag – no one could say that Collingwood did not fit the bill. If his statue did not look like him but like an ideal form of gentlemanly truth and beauty ('make 'em handsome'),[46] few would know. Collingwood had been dead for over three decades and when he died he had died in service, at sea, years after he had last been seen in Newcastle. Few knew him, fewer would be able to remember him and, with his statue high above the mouth of the Tyne, fewer still would be able to check the likeness. In Stephenson's case, the prospect of a gentlemanly statue was entirely different. Not only was he known, but also he had spent his life refusing honours. More to the point, Stephenson's genius, if genius it was, was not the genius of Reynolds' *Discourses*, nor the self induced oratorical 'genius' of the Haydon set, but the patient deductive intelligence of a mechanic. For his mechanisms to work, imitation and repetition was not the despised but the desired end. Fellow mechanics subscribed to his monument but the statue they got was not Stephenson as 'one of us' so much as Stephenson as one of them.[47] He peers down on you on your way to work, as it was intended he should. He is larger than life in bronze, on

---

[44]  Buonarroti, *Statues of John Graham Lough* (1828), pp.10-11, 14; Robinson, J., *Descriptive Catalogue* (1886).

[45]  'Tonight he said to me, as if half afraid he should be laughed at, "Mr Haydon, I fancy myself in the Acropolis sometimes, and hear a roaring noise like the tide"': *Autobiography*, p.412.

[46]  Lord Egremont recommending portraiture as a way of making money. On the Collingwood: Lough, J. and Merson, E., *John Graham Lough 1798-1876. Northumbrian Sculptor* (1987), p.68, and Usherwood *et al.*, *Public Sculpture*, pp.207-9.

[47]  Predictably, the design was too classical for the *Gateshead Observer* (3 September 1859). Robert was reported preferring a globe as a pedestal at the design stage but was apparently happy with the final facial resemblance (*Newcastle Daily Chronicle*, 3 October 1862). The fund-raising committee was always keen to publicise working-class support, as in its publication of a letter and £25 donation from five Newcastle (ex-Stephenson) mechanics out in Hong Kong: Committee, *Letter* (1859) – 'our admiration of one of our own class'.

**12.4** Stephenson's Monument by John Graham Lough, 1862 (3 views).

a plinth taken from Bandinelli and Tacca's Ferdinand I in the Piazza della Darsena, Leghorn.[48] He has a passing likeness to the engineer, but few lines, no eyes, a massive body and a rather strange outfit. As a concession to modernity, the sculptor dispensed with the toga and replaced it with a 'Northumbrian plaid'. Four gentlemen lounge at Stephenson's feet. They're supposed to be workingmen but it's obvious they've never done a day's work in their lives.

## Modern Newcastle

No single construction better expressed Newcastle's entry into the modern age than the High Level Bridge – first pile driven October 1846, opened August 1850. There had been previous proposals for a high level crossing of the Tyne, and the high Ouseburn viaduct running east to North Shields had been opened in 1839, but Robert Stephenson's High Level Bridge completed the vital link bringing Newcastle into the whole north-south trajectory.[49] Before it, you had to get off the train in Gateshead and walk or take a cab to the other side. Newcastle Central Station took its first train from the bridge in January 1851.[50] It had taken the town's middle classes over a hundred years to shuffle away from the riverside and up the hill but the High Level leapt that all in a single stride. Communication was rapid, the view was high and handsome.[51]

By way of contrast, Chatto had defined old riverside Newcastle in 1835 by its dirt and clutter, while Dibdin thought the Black Gate's 'grotesque tenements' and 'dense population, breathing into one another's mouths' beggared everything he had seen, 'even at Rouen'. There are no shortages of travellers' tales as to a dirty and mutinous early 19th-century Newcastle. The cholera came in 1831 and again in 1853, with a *Report* the following year. A more comprehensive public health report was published in 1866 and a Medical Officer of Health was appointed in 1872. When the filthy and overcrowded Sandgate area of the Quayside was destroyed by fire in 1855, it wasn't just the property developers who rubbed their hands.[52]

Mutiny, too, had always lurked down there. Newcastle's mayors habitually went in dread of sailors and keelmen. It was almost their badge of office. In 1839,

---

[48] The design was taken in turn from Lough's failed entry for a Nelson monument in Trafalgar Square.

[49] Before it was built, 'Here, therefore, the Traveller must either walk or make use of the Omnibus': *Reid's Railway Ride from London to Edinburgh* (1849). If the east route couldn't carry Scottish-bound passengers without a break, 'the western lines would command': Collingwood Bruce, *Handbook*, p.116.

[50] But trains heading north still had to reverse. This was solved with the building of the King Edward VII bridge in 1906.

[51] Barke, M. and Buswell, R.J. (eds.), *Newcastle's Changing Map* (1992), chapters 9 and 10 by Michael Sill.

[52] Chatto, W.A., *Rambles in Northumberland and on the Scottish Border* (1835), p.13; Dibdin, T.F., *A Bibliographical, Antiquarian, and Picturesque Tour in the Northern Counties* (1838), p.360; see Callcott's and Barke's chapters in this volume; Rewcastle, J., *A Record of the Great Fire of Newcastle and Gateshead* (1855).

**12.5** High Level Bridge by Robert Stephenson, 1850.

pamphlets on *Street Warfare* were being sold for a penny in the Side, and it would appear also that there was no shortage of powder and shot to go with them. On Saturday mornings, muskets, 'crows' feet' and pikes (2s. 6d. polished, 18d. rough) were all on sale. Lower Newcastle had two serious riots in July 1839. Troops and armed police had patrolled the streets. In his old age, the revolutionary, Devyr, claimed that the area had 65 armed districts ready to rise (even though they didn't). There were strong Chartist links out of town in the collieries and in the industrial suburbs. At a Chartist meeting on the Forth in August 1842 Stephens the superintendent of police sent Hodgson the nervous mayor a public order report every 15 minutes.[13] No wonder that on completion of Grey's monument in August 1838, there was no show of Whiggery to mark the event. In June, sixty thousand had gathered to hear the Chartist leader Feargus O'Connor, while in December thousands met on the Forth to send three delegates to the Convention – all of them

---

[13] See Colls, R., *The Pitmen of the Northern Coalfield* (1987), part 3, and, for example, letter Col. Sir Henry Rofs to Maj. Gen. Bouverie, 6 April 1831, Home Office papers 40/29/1 1831; pamphlets 18 May 1839, HO 40/42; *Monthly Chronicle North Country Lore and Legend*, vol.3 (1889); Harrison, B. and Hollis, P., *Robert Lowery. Radical and Chartist* (1979), p.143; letter Sir John Fife to Russell, 21 July 1839, HO 40/46; Newcastle Spring Assizes 1840, trial for sedition and riot, ASSI/45/65; Devyr, T.A., *Odd Book of the 19th Century* (1882), p.195; out of town links, *Northern Liberator*, 16 February-6 July1839; reports, John Stephens to James Hodgson, 23 August 1842, 13/13/34-48, Tyne & Wear Archives.

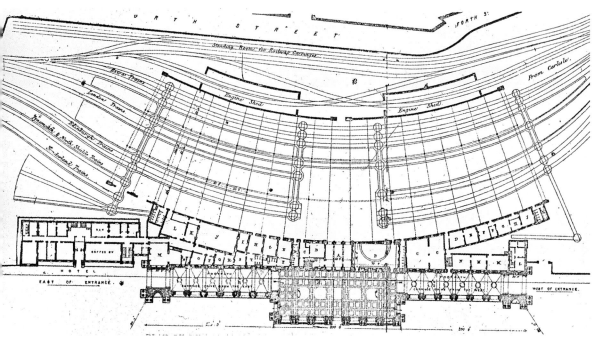

**12.6** Plan of Central Station, 1848.

physical force men. The Chartist high point was a mass meeting on the Town Moor on Whit Monday 20 May 1839, with crowd estimates of between seventy and a hundred thousand. After the summer riots there was talk of arson. Threats to civic order of such a magnitude are not easily forgotten.[54] A lower town that sold itself grenades clearly had no place in an upper town that had built a 600 ft. long glass roof to cover its trains. (There were rumours of Chartist ordnance buried beneath the new station.)

If the High Level Bridge denoted straight linear power, Central Station denoted organised mass dispersal. Designed as a machine for computing large numbers of people on the move, its great front concourse got them in and all aboard while its ten platforms and seven signal cabins got them out and on their way. Travellers found their train simply by walking in the direction they wanted to travel: west to the right, east to the left, and north and south straight on. The information was bold, the lamps electric, the clock 21 hours, the concourse spacious.[55] In the 1820s Grainger's prosperous residents may have fought to keep Eldon Square private, and in the 1850s some of the riff raff may have regretted the fact that they had 'Nee

[54] *Northern Liberator*, 25 May 1839; Devyr, *Odd Book*, p.205.
[55] Rankin, S., Rawlings, K., Woods, M., *Newcastle Central Station* (1986); Hoole, K., *Railway Stations of the North East* (1985) pp.37-41; Bywell, E.M., 'Central Station', *The Railway Magazine*, vol.8 (1901).

Pleyce noo to play' ('Wor canny Forth an' Spital te, eh, man, they've tu'ne away') but this was the old Newcastle talking.[56] Steam railway was definitely on the side of modernity and modernity was on the side of the masses. On Whit Monday 1899, the Station issued over 33,000 tickets and the city hardly noticed the flux.[57]

Along with the railway companies the other great moderniser was the Tyne Improvement Commission, charged with deepening the river, dredging it free of all obstruction and equipping it for world trade and big ships. The Commission not only did these things, it also relieved the Corporation of its ancient and privileged 'conservatorship' of the river. Yet, the Tyne's modern democratic wonders were seen as Newcastle's modern democratic wonders too.[58] With river and rail links unmatched anywhere in the world, this was a city on the move.

At the turn of the century Newcastle upon Tyne could take a commanding view of itself. To enter the old town in 1800 you had to cross the low bridge on foot, or at a trot, and slip into the banked melee of things. To enter the new city in 1900 you could come in from on high, at speed, with swift perspectives turning below you. As the city's historian put it in 1901: 'And so we might sweep round the whole circuit, and meet similar metamorphoses in every line of radiation'.[59] With so much landscape to behold, this was now a city fit for Art as well as engineering.[60]

Stephenson's monument stood in a cluster of modern institutions just over the Bridge and just down from the Station. As Charleton put it, in this 'wide open space', ancient site of hospital and grammar school, 'you forget the dirt and squalor you have left behind in admiration of the view before you'.[61] Across Neville Street was the Station's hotel (1854) and long front portico (1863), while behind the statue was the Assembly Rooms (1776) and the offices of the *Newcastle Chronicle* – homes respectively of Newcastle's greatest modern business, the North Eastern Railway, its first modern association, and its most modern newspaper.[62] Over the road, by the line, were the Lit. & Phil., the Museum of Natural History, the School of Art, the North of England Institute of Mining and Mechanical Engineers and the Wood Memorial Hall – institutions for the combined forces of modern knowledge and

[56] Indenture of Feoffment, 26 September 1826, and Memorial to Town Improvement Committee, 16 May 1839, 374/1/16 &10, Tyne & Wear Archives; *Corvan's Song Book* no.1 (n.d., 1850s?).

[57] Bywell, 'Central Station', p.19. Thomas Cook of Leicester saw the mass opportunities early and coated them in the veneer of modern progress: *Cook's Excursionist and cheap trip advertiser* (1854).

[58] The Russian novelist Yergeni Zamyatin turned these modern wonders into a great dystopian science fiction: Alan Myers, 'Zamyatin in Newcastle', *Slavonic and East European Review*, vol.71 (1993). On the TIC, see the report of its chief engineer, Messent, P.J., *Description ... of Works Completed and in Progress* (1885-6).

[59] Scott, J., *The Ecclesiastical, Political, and Civic Chiefs of Newcastle* (1901), p.14.

[60] Watson, A., 'The Coaly Tyne', *The Magazine of Art*, vol.6 (1883).

[61] Charleton, R.J., *Charleton's History of Newcastle upon Tyne*, 1885 (1950), p.150.

[62] Tomlinson, *North Eastern Railway*, pp.1-5. On the Assembly Rooms and their associations with literacy, civic pride, a sense of inclusiveness and modern histories of the sort written by John Baillie (*An Impartial History*, 1810) see: Sweet, R., *The Writing of Urban Histories in 18th Century England* (1997) pp.159-72. For Cowen and his modern newspaper, see Hugman's chapter in this volume, above.

modern industry. Close up, were Baker's Coffee and Dining Rooms and Temperance Hotel and Family Boarding House. Temperance often saw itself like the railway, as a rational force fuelled by water.[63] The Union Club followed in 1877, built by the Newcastle Club Company for modern businessmen.

Stephenson's monument, then, stood at the centre of modern Newcastle. Or did it? The *Illustrated London News'* engraving of the city for 16 July 1887 shows the monument in full view of trains coming in across the High Level, just as they turn into Central Station. Behind the Stephenson, away in the higher part of town and higher still on its column, is Grey's monument. Those who came out of the station hotel would not see Stephenson because he had his back to them. And if they wanted to shop, they would find themselves walking up Grainger Street (extended 1868) towards the Earl rather than down Neville Street towards the engineer, though if they were on business it is the engineer they would pass on their way to Dean Street and Mosley Street. All in all, it is strange that George is not in front of his station. It is strange that he is down the street rather than up the street meeting passengers as they enter the life of the city. With his back to the station and away from it, Newcastle's most important son is more like a commissionaire than a son. In Pike's 1905 book of Northumbrian worthies, aristocrats continued to lead the rankings; engineers came ninth.[64]

## Public Memory

In public memory, the years 1858-61 were a watershed. In 1858 it was decided that Newcastle should remember George Stephenson. William White had recalled going to his birthplace at around this time and finding not a record of it there, and then to his engine works to find *Rocket* rusting in a corner, 'a thing of no account'. Then, in 1859-60, the three greatest locomotive engineers of the century died and they all died young: Robert Stephenson and Isambard Kingdom Brunel in 1859, and Joseph Locke in 1860; aged 53, 56 and 55 respectively. With Hudson down and the engineers dead, it was the end of an era and the whole nation knew it. In 1861 William Bell Scott painted eight scenes from Northumbrian history at Wallington Hall. Last and best was called *The Nineteenth Century. Iron and Coal*. It marked Stephenson's epoch.[65]

---

[63] Wood, N., *Inaugural Address to the North of England Institute of Mining Engineers* (1852); the northern Jubilee celebrations of the Stockton-Darlington line were in no doubt about the connection between prosperity and science and technology – see, for example, *The Northern Echo*, 7 August 1875, *Stockton & Darlington Times*, 4-18 September 1875. In the region, between 1851 and 1911 coal provided eight well paid jobs for every low paid job lost in agriculture: Hunt, E.H., 'Industrialization and Regional Equality', *Journal of Economic History*, vol.46 (1986), p.956. On modern temperance, *The Northern Temperance & Rechabite Almanack* (1843).

[64] Pike, W.T. (ed.), *Northumberland. At the Opening of the Twentieth Century* (1905).

[65] White, W., *Northumberland and the Border* (2nd edn. 1859), pp.78-9, p.88. Scott's painting was held to depict men from Stephenson's, and Hawks, Crawshay's works, a year before they marched to the monument. See Usherwood's chapter in this volume, above.

**12.7** 'A Northcountry-man with his family of inventions.'

The next 20 years remembered Stephenson as a national hero, master *and* man.[66] In a period when the British began to take stock of what they were learning to call an 'Industrial Revolution', George Stephenson took on the glow of an industrial folk hero – a Northcountryman with his family of inventions living in the shadow of the pit. Here was a man who had industrialised for sure, but had retained his humanity as well. In 1881 *The Graphic* happily recorded how at 12.30 every day Stephenson's own 'greasy and grimy toilers' would break for dinner and stroll in the vicinity of his monument.[67] The 1860s and 1870s were golden years in the

[66] In industrial relations, between 1860 and 1880 the temper eased. It was possible for masters and men to negotiate, and in the North East they did so, particularly in the coalfield: Wedderburn, K.W., *The Worker and the Law* (1966), pp.211-15; Church, R., *History of British Coal Industry*, vol.3, 1830-1913 (1986), pp.652-8. It was said that the distinction between a worker and a gentleman mattered less. Chesterfield's Stephenson Memorial Hall was opened to all classes, groups and associations in 1877.

[67] *The Graphic*, 4 June 1881, but it reported also that the rowers Chambers and Renforth were the workers' 'leading heroes'. See chapter by Holt and Physick in this volume, above. Contemporary engravings of the industrial folk hero shown in Skeat, W.O., *George Stephenson. The Engineer and His Letters* (1973), figs. 2, 7, 54. Arnold Toynbee popularised the phrase 'Industrial Revolution' in the 1880s.

remembering of George Stephenson: England and the world would ne'er see his like again.

By the mid-1880s Stephenson had been replaced as 'monarch of industrial Newcastle' by Sir William Armstrong, a man intensely aware of his own place in history. Armstrong had more workers, more money and more involvement in the city. His largesse was everywhere, whilst Stephenson's was (virtually) nowhere. Armstrong had not avoided honours but had sought them, and in a way he deserved them.[68] Stephenson's memory remained, of course, but it was the gun maker who stood now for modern Newcastle with a statue of his own (1906) at Barras Bridge, gateway to the northern suburbs. Young Wesleyans in 1897 were still being taught about Stephenson as a Smilesian hero, but the truth was that the 'Father of Railways' entered the 20th century as a mid-Victorian cliché.[69] This was still the case at the 1948 Laing centenary exhibition.[70]

In the 1950s Stephenson the cliché was lost in Stephenson the forgotten man. The technology he pioneered was no longer modern. Indeed, there were deep forebodings about a city choking on steam and smoke. The BBC Home Service programme 'Tonight in Newcastle', broadcast in 1956, said not a word about him but a lot about slummy Scotswood Road, bracing itself for the chop ('You know, Newcastle is tremendously built up').[71] British Rail scrapped steam in 1968. At about the same time, an office block blocked off his monument, as well it might. The bicentenaries of his birth were perfunctory and the 1980s city guides the same. He popped up on the £5 bank note in 1990, against the odds and probably with Mrs. Thatcher's blessing. A Smilesian hero again. Still a cliché. Just her type. In spite of this, or because of it, Newcastle didn't seem to care. The *Official Guide* to Newcastle, published in 1996, not only omitted him but showed an urge to bury him, proudly boasting 'Newcastle has no coal mines or steel works'. Its perceptual view of the city left out his monument completely.[72] In a *Guardian* special North East supplement

[68] *Illustrated London News*, 16 July 1887. Armstrong entertained royalty at Cragside and not just British royalty. In August 1884 he had the Prince and Princess of Wales and their children. In the day they swanned round the city, opening things; in the evening it was back to Rothbury. In 1887 as mayor he led the jubilee celebrations with a huge industrial exhibition in the city.

[69] 'George Stephenson. His Life and Works', exercise book read at the Wesleyan Young Men's Institute, 4 February 1897, Newcastle Central Library.

[70] Laing Art Gallery, *George Stephenson Centenary Exhibition*, 12-21 August 1948. In Chesterfield, as well as an exhibition, they held a civic commemoration, Miss Janet Taylor, Britain's Railway Queen, and a grand dance in the evening organised by the rail unions: Borough of Chesterfield, *Centenary Commemoration* (1948).

[71] BBC Home Service, 'Tonight in Newcastle', script, 13 March 1956; and for dinginess, Lloyd, A.L., 'Newcastle upon Tyne: a life story', *History Today* (1951), p.22.

[72] *Official Guide to Newcastle upon Tyne* (1996); Association of City Guides, Walking Tour Notes (1980, 81, 84), Newcastle Central Library. There's a very brief mention of the monument in Pearson, L., *Northern City. An architectural history of Newcastle upon Tyne* (1996), p.66. Series 'A' Stephenson banknotes were chosen by the appropriate committee at the Debden printing works in 1988 but they told me that the choice of illustration could not have been made without agreement at the highest level.

in May 2000, its respected northern correspondent talked about somebody called 'Stevenson'. A low point.[73]

Lough the sculptor was a lot quicker to rise and a lot quicker to fall. He too was a Tynesider, born only a few miles from Stephenson, at Greenhead in 1798, the son of a small farmer. If Royal Academy talent spotters liked their geniuses rough-hewn, then Lough was their man. But after that first treasured moment of discovery, even geniuses have to make a living. When he died in 1876 Lough's overblown classicism was already falling out of favour. His obituarist tried to be kind: 'Few men have lived who will be more regretted by a very large circle'.[74] In terms of pure romantic genius, Lough peaked at the outset.

It didn't take long for the tide of opinion to turn against him and when it did its judgement was final. Of the Stephenson monument *The Builder* said in 1898, 'Not much can be said in [its] favour'. In 1910 the monument still held a position as one of 17 postcard *Views of Newcastle on Tyne* but after the war *The Builder* returned to the attack. Of Lough's works – or more accurately of their plaster casts, first housed and then eventually broken and lost at Elswick Hall, former home of one of his patrons – Professor Hatton said only: 'It is best not to go', 'Enough about Lough can be gathered from his statue…'.[75] And it wasn't just Lough. The 1920s saw a revulsion against public statuary in general, at least among those who claimed to know about such things. Borenius pointed at London's 'interminable' soldiers. Gleichen loathed the bad taste Latin tags and togas. Back in Newcastle, G.R.B. Spain joined in at Lough's expense.[76]

The turn against the sort of sculptures Lough made, and the sort of people he made them for, can be attributed largely to the inspirational criticism of one man. John Ruskin identified 19th-century classicism with the vitiated tastes of industrial England. Ruskin denied there could be any 'metropolitan effect' ('There is no Attic style, but there is a Doric and Corinthian one … There is no London or Edinburgh style, but there is a Kentish and Northumbrian one'). He saw the railways as vile emblems of capitalist greed. He stood against Reynolds and the Raphaelites ('Nothing must come between Nature and the artist's sight'). He thought the art of middle-class England came out of a drain ('the mere effluence of Grosvenor Square and

---

[73] 'Moving Up', *Guardian* supplement, May 2000. A BBC TV Look North 'Millennium Poll' in May 1999 voted Stephenson as the region's greatest inventor, on 42 per cent. Armstrong was second on 25 per cent. We don't know how many votes were cast. There has, of course, been fairly consistent academic interest in the engineering achievements.

[74] *Art Journal*, 1876, quoted in Allen, *Lough*, p.203.

[75] *The Builder* (1898), p.308; Allan, T. and G., *Views of Newcastle on Tyne* (1910); Hatton, R.G., 'The Architectural Visitor to Newcastle', *The Builder* (1925), p.66.

[76] Borenius, T., *Forty London Statues and Public Monuments* (1926), p.28; Gleichen, Lord E., *London's Open Air Statuary* (1928), p.xxxiv; Spain, G.R.B., 'Thoughts in the Street', unidentified newspaper cutting, 1930, L720, Newcastle Central Library.

Clapham Junction'). He detested, or he would have detested if he'd been asked not to, Grainger's and Stephenson's modern Newcastle: 'the mere effluence of Grey Street and Central Station'? And if he'd ever been invited to think of a respectful memory of Stephenson, he'd have surely chosen Turner's *Speed* over Lough's bronze.[77]

In 1928, Osbert Sitwell came to sneer on Ruskin's behalf at industrial statuary and all its classical connotations. In a rush to the head of southern English snobbery and conceit, Sitwell put down Stephenson and Lough and Newcastle all together:

> But to the child of poor parents in a rich provincial town there was nothing to indicate that such things as beauty or the arts had ever existed. No intelligence was visible there save that of Skinflint and Gradgrind. Architecture, sculpture, painting and books lay hidden away out of sight of this wilderness of gaslit houses, in the windows of which an occasional fern, dying for want of air and sunlight, asserted the pathetic claim of its owner to belong to a race bred of open fields and woodlanes. Very seldom a convert, perhaps, might call them to miserable realisation that there might be other gods than iron and industry, other pleasures than football field and whippets … it is possible to estimate the character of this cultured age by the nature of the men it celebrated: never, scarcely, a musician, poet, painter or philosopher, but instead, the inventors of engines and spinning jennies, politicians and contractors, aldermen and plumbers.[78]

In the 1960s, Newcastle's civic leaders declared the end of the industrial era. In order to prove it, they were prepared to demolish the city's entire 19th-century housing stock. Across the region as a whole, there was a strong sense that that which was 'old fashioned' and 'Victorian' had had its day. Both those in favour of a museum at Beamish and those who argued against it, argued from exactly the same position: that the industrial past – dead ferns, whippets, gaslight, all that – had gone forever.[79] Even the meaning of 'modern' had moved on.

When we talk of modern Newcastle remembering George Stephenson we must not think there was still a George Stephenson to remember. Stephenson the man died in 1848. After that there was only his memory. No matter how well informed or professionally devised, memories are inherently unstable. The essence of Stephenson was unstable enough while he lived but after he died it was up for

---

[77] Ruskin, J., 'The Art of England' (1883), in Cook, E.T. and Wedderburn, A., *The Works of John Ruskin*, vol.33 (1908), p.397; Ruskin, J., letters to editor Daily Telegraph 1865-70, in Cook and Wedderburn, *Works*, vol.17 (1908), pp.528-35; Hewison, R., *Ruskin, Turner and the Pre-Raphaelites* (2000), pp.13, 18.

[78] Sitwell, O., *The People's Album of London Statues* (1928), pp.34-5. Robert's life is described as 'a long list of boring events most of which were connected with helping his father on the railways' (p.98).

[79] On demolishing the Victorian: Burns, W., *Newcastle. A Study in Replanning at Newcastle upon Tyne* (1967), p.65; on making a museum of it: 'North of England Open Air Museum', 1960-69, file T132/59, Tyne & Wear Archives.

grabs. The moment of 1862 represented only the victory of a faction. They wanted him remembered their way. His fall into insignificance over the next hundred years was partly to do with the normal way in which the world moves on – particularly the technological world – but it was also to do with the fall into disfavour of the way in which it was decided to remember him. If he had been remembered in other ways, in ways more in line with the ways Newcastle was ready to develop – a world-beating Stephenson Institute of Technology, say – then the Stephenson we remember, and indeed the Newcastle we know, would be very different.

Capturing the true condition of someone's *historical-ness* is as near as we get to holding to their essence, or to what used to be called their soul, and it is the same for places as well as for people. That is why the study of history interacts with all we are and all we claim to be.[80] There are those who say that the past is the past and cannot be changed. But that is not the case. The point is, there is no past that is finished: there is only how we choose to remember it. Tomorrow is easy; it's yesterday that needs some thought.

[80] See Williamson, B., 'Living the Past Differently' in Colls, R. and Lancaster, B., *Geordies. Roots of Regionalism* (1992).

# 13

## Winged Words
### Literature of Newcastle

ALAN MYERS

Though the Roman emperor Hadrian was a middling poet, the settlement he founded on the Tyne had to wait many centuries before it could claim a literary life of its own. The glories of the Golden Age of Northumbria – the first known English prose writer, Bede; the first known English Christian poets; the first English biblical text; the oldest poem in the language, *Widsith*, even perhaps *Beowulf*, the greatest of Old English poems, indeed the first major vernacular poem in any European language – all have their regional associations elsewhere: Jarrow, Lindisfarne, Durham, Hexham and Whitby. Domesday Book may have been, in large part, the work of a scribe attached to the monastery at Durham. In fact, throughout the Middle Ages the North of England produced religious, historical and Arthurian work of national importance and popularity, but none is associated with Newcastle itself. John Duns Scotus (1265-1308), who vies with St Thomas Aquinas for the title of the greatest of all medieval philosophers, is traditionally linked with the Franciscan monastery in the town, but his subsequent career and writings belong to continental Europe, as do those of his disciple, Hugh of Newcastle. Of the town's cycle of mystery plays the only survivor is *Noah's Ark*.

There were certainly eminent literary visitors, among them Jean Froissart, the celebrated chronicler of the Hundred Years War, who visited this country on several occasions and rode the length of Hadrian's Wall in 1361. Harry Percy, called Hotspur for his reckless courage, clashed in single combat with the Earl of Douglas at Barras Bridge under the walls of Newcastle in August 1388, and Froissart vividly describes the ensuing Battle of Otterburn, fought by moonlight, in which Douglas was killed and Hotspur made prisoner. The voluminous writer Aeneas Silvius Piccolomini, later Pope Pius II, was favourably impressed by the town 'founded by Caesar', as he came south from Scotland in 1435. The most influential visitor, however, has turned out to be the mysterious Sir Thomas Malory (d.1471) whose *Morte d'Arthur* is the finest prose romance in English. It has been drawn upon by Tennyson, Swinburne and T.H. White in *The Once and Future King*, among many others –

including, at one remove, T.S. Eliot in *The Waste Land*, one of the greatest poems of the 20th century. Malory appears to have been present at Edwards IV's reduction of the Northumberland fortresses during the Wars of the Roses, and locates Sir Lancelot's castle, Joyous Gard, at either Alnwick or Bamburgh, north of Newcastle; Blaise, Merlin's master, lives in the Northumberland forest, and we also find the extraordinary tale of the Northumbrian knights Balin Le Sauvage (who carried two swords) and his valiant brother Balan.

The fiery religious pamphleteers John Knox and John Udall both spent time in Newcastle in the 16th century, while James Melville, the Scots poet and diarist, passed some years of exile there. Ben Jonson, who was probably of Border descent, trudged through the town in mid-August 1618 on his celebrated walk to Scotland, and returned in January 1619, still wearing the shoes he had bought in Darlington. An indigenous Newcastle literary life is not recorded at this period, however. As England's northern bastion Newcastle was, rather, a place for mustering troops and the venue for fateful royal encounters. Virtually every English monarch from the Conqueror to Cromwell has visited Newcastle on diplomatic and martial business, and two Scots kings have been killed near Newcastle and two taken prisoner. Newcastle must be unique among cities in having held both a Scots and an English king captive. The Border war lasted for centuries and no area of England is more studded with castles or soaked in blood. Shakespeare made Harry Hotspur the glamorous star of the first part of his *Henry IV*, while the Border Ballads, which reflected the thrilling turbulence of the northern frontier, travelled the whole country and were performed in London by northern minstrels. The sophisticated Sir Philip Sidney was more moved by the old song of Percy and Douglas than by the martial trumpet, and Ben Jonson said that he would give all his works to have written 'Chevy Chase', which was still the favourite ballad of the common people a hundred years later. Over the centuries the northern ballads have inspired poets as various as Walter Scott, William Morris, who considered them the finest poems in the language, Swinburne (who knew them all by heart), Auden and Bunting.

The North East coalfield, the 'Black Indies', was also a source of wonder and pride to the Elizabethans, and William Camden summed up the twin importance of Newcastle for his own and later ages when he called it 'Ocellus, the eye of the North, the hearth that warmeth the south parts of this kingdom with fire'. The most popular poet of his time, John Cleveland, may have written 'News from Newcastle' (1651). The beginning is arresting and Newcastle is pronounced with the short 'a' which was polite usage until the 19th century:

> England's a perfect world, has Indies too;
> Correct your maps, Newcastle is Peru!

Then follows a wonderfully convoluted set of conceits in praise of coal, including a strikingly modern enunciation of vehement regional resentment at the centralisation of wealth and power in the capital. The coal staiths on the Tyne are mentioned, along with Blaydon and Stella:

> We shall exhaust their chamber and devour
> Their treasures of Guildhall, the Mint, the Tower.
> Our staiths their mortgaged streets will soon divide,
> Blathon own Cornhill, Stella share Cheapside.

If the author is not Cleveland, this extraordinary work represents the first genuine poetic voice to emerge from Newcastle. In prose that honour may go to the earliest historian of the town, William Grey. Middlebrook describes his *Chorographia* (1649) as having winged words and a touch of high imagination, a 'fascinating and original fragment'.[1]

The lapsing of the Licensing Act in 1695 signalled a remarkable change in the literary life of Newcastle. What was now the fourth largest provincial town in England became the country's most important printing centre after London, Oxford and Cambridge. Periodicals were rare outside London, Dublin and Edinburgh: Newcastle had 10 during the 18th century. Few towns had more than one local newspaper: Newcastle had seven start up before 1760. At least three expensive subscription newsrooms also existed. As Kathleen Wilson writes, London's status and growth as a major publishing centre depended directly on a flourishing provincial trade, and the sharp rise in urban literacy during the 18th century helped to make printed artefacts one of the first mass cultural commodities.[2]

One aspect of these developments was a heightened consciousness of Newcastle's own history and traditions. In 1725, Henry Bourne, curate at All Hallows, published his *Antiquities of the Common People*, and in 1736 his widow brought out his *History of Newcastle upon Tyne*. In 1777, John Brand published his *Popular Antiquities*, based on Bourne's previous work, and left a mass of manuscript collections to add to that work. His *History and Antiquities of the Town and County of Newcastle-upon-Tyne* was published in London in 1789. In the 1770s Newcastle published more children's books than any other town in England outside London, and by 1790 the town could boast 20 printers, 12 booksellers and stationers, 13 bookbinders and three engravers, among them the internationally celebrated Thomas Bewick. There were seven subscription libraries, as well as the St Nicholas parish library with its 5,000 books, and three circulating libraries, including that of William Charnley, set up in 1757, and

---

[1] Middlebrook, S., 'Newcastle upon Tyne: Its Growth and Development', *Newcastle Journal*, 1950, p.116.
[2] Wilson, Kathleen, *The Sense of the People* (1998), pp.30-1.

Joseph Barber's 1746 establishment in Amen Corner, which, with over 5,000 volumes, was one of the largest collections outside London.[3] Print, however, did not displace ballad-singing in the streets, which had been an integral part of the Newcastle scene since the 16th century and continued into the nineteenth.

Visiting writers have often divertingly illuminated the context of Newcastle literary life and may justly be regarded as part of it. Early in the century, two notable travellers recorded their impressions of the town. The redoubtable Celia Fiennes, who rode through England side-saddle, thought Newcastle 'most resembles London of any place in England'. She admired the Newcastle Quayside, the fine shops and the cheap markets. She describes, in her inimitable style, 'little things look black on the outside and soft sower things'. What she means by these curious items of local cuisine we may only conjecture. In his *Tour Thro' the Whole Island of Great Britain* (1724-7), Daniel Defoe also declares himself impressed by Newcastle and its quays. He marvels at the amount of coal shipped from the port and concludes: 'They build ships here to perfection, I mean as to strength and firmness, and to bear the sea'. Under the name of Alexander Goldsmith, Defoe was intermittently active in Newcastle as a secret government agent after September 1706, and was back in 1710 as Claud Guilot, with lodgings in Hillgate, across the river in Gateshead. He published his *British Vision and Family Instructor* through Joseph Button, a bookseller on Newcastle Bridge (built-up, like old London bridge), and may have collaborated with him on the *Newcastle Gazette*.

Mark Akenside (1721-70) was the first Novocastrian to achieve a national literary reputation. Born at 33 Butcher Bank (now Akenside Hill), the son of a butcher, he eventually rose to be Physician to the Queen in 1761. He was touchy about his humble origins, and spiteful remarks that his limp had been caused by an accident with a butcher's cleaver. In fact, he had been born with one leg shorter than the other. Perhaps for this reason, Akenside tended to behave roughly towards the poor, especially women, as he toured his wards in full-bottomed wig and clanking sword. The irascible Scots novelist Tobias Smollett took exception to one of Akenside's remarks about Scotland and satirised him as the conceited and pedantic Doctor in *Peregrine Pickle*. In Newcastle, Akenside wrote a number of minor poems, including 'A Hymn to Science', but it was while visiting relatives in Morpeth that he conceived the plan for *The Pleasures of the Imagination* (1744), his most celebrated work. It is a long, complex, erudite poem and for all its occasional striking passages has many leaden stretches, stuffed with classical allusions. Doctor Johnson, however, tempered his criticism by saying that 'in the general fabrication of his lines, he is perhaps superior to any other writer of blank verse'. As this included Milton, it was

---

[3] Brewer, John, *The Pleasures of the Imagination* (1997), pp.176-7, 504.

**13.1** Mark Akenside, poet and royal physician.

praise indeed. Recalling his youth by the 'dales of Tyne' and the Wansbeck, Akenside finds an appealing immediacy:

> … O ye Northumbrian shades! which overlook
> The rocky pavement and the mossy falls
> Of solitary Wensbeck's limpid stream,
> How gladly I recall your well-known seats,
> Beloved of old.

By sharp contrast with Akenside's well-wrought lines, an extraordinary native talent emerged in the person of Edward Chicken (1698-1746), who lived opposite the *Three Tuns* on the corner of Low Friar Street. His celebrated *Collier's Wedding*, published posthumously in 1764, is a remarkably frank poem (unthinkable in the following century), with fascinating glimpses of marriage observances in the coalfield. Even the church ceremony is somewhat rowdy, few present being acquainted with the place, and the drunken wedding reception is described with startling realism. After lively scenes of eating and dancing, the company begin to tire:

> Dead drunk, some tumble on the floor,
> And swim in what they'd drunk before.
> 'Hiccup', cries one. 'Reach me your hand.'
> 'The house turns round. I cannot stand.'

> So now the drunken senseless crew
> Break pipes, spill drink, piss, shit and spew.

The trepidations of the bride are also addressed and she is prepared for her wedding night with considerable poetic relish.

John Cunningham, an itinerant Irish actor-poet, was the author of the play *Love in a Mist* (1747), something of a popular success in its day. Cunningham's northern headquarters had been Newcastle, a town he had 'originally quitted with regret and to his last breath used emphatically to call his home'. He published *Poems, Chiefly Pastoral* there in 1766. After his death in 1773, his table tomb outside St John's Church was erected by Thomas Slack, the bookseller and publisher of the *Newcastle Chronicle*, who had eventually taken the indigent poet into his house. Thomas Bewick managed to sketch a likeness of the ill-favoured bard clutching a herring in a handkerchief. Cunningham showed enthusiasm enough for his adopted town in 'Newcastle Beer', the beverage then patronised by all classes. The God of Revelry on Olympus celebrates Britain's success in war:

> And freely declared there was choice of good cheer
> > Yet vowed to his thinking,
> > For exquisite drinking,
> Their nectar was nothing to Newcastle beer.

The exhilarating atmosphere of a town on the verge of becoming a major printing centre was not confined to the male sex. Newcastle also produced a number of interesting female writers at this period, and two of the pioneering feminists of England were born near the Quayside. Mary Astell was educated by her uncle in Latin, French, logic, mathematics and natural philosophy. She was writing religious poetry of high quality by 1687, and had settled alone in Chelsea, then near London. In 1694, she published *A Serious Proposal to the Ladies* which put forward the idea of a kind of monastery or university for unmarried women. A Tory in politics, Mary was 'the first respectable female writer' and has been called incalculably influential. In 1700, her tract *Some Reflections upon Marriage* pleads that men should look on women as reasonable creatures and not confine them 'with chain and block to the chimney corner'. The 1706 edition asks: 'If all men are born free, how is it that all women are born slaves?'

Elizabeth Elstob, 'The Saxon Nymph', was proficient in eight languages and, though denied the university education enjoyed by her scholarly brother William, became from 1702 onwards part of the circle of intelligent women around Mary Astell, who helped to find subscribers for her *Rudiments of Grammar for the English-*

*Saxon … with an Apology for the Study of Northern Antiquities* (1715) the first ever such work. Elizabeth, like her mother Jane, was a keen admirer of feminine learning and kept lists of famous women. In middle age, however, a school she ran in Evesham failed because she was inadequate at spinning and knitting. In 1756, she died surrounded by the 'congenial elements of dirt and books'.

While not aspiring to similar heights, Ann Fisher was a notable figure in Newcastle, and applied her intelligence in the field of education. Ann kept her maiden name even after marrying Thomas Slack, then became a partner in his business, and opened a school in 1745. Her extremely popular works include *A New Grammar: Being the Most Easy Guide to Speaking and Writing the English Language Properly and Correctly* (1745). No woman had written anything like it before, and it went through 30 editions before 1800. Remarkably, the book does not downgrade English in relation to classical tongues. Other works followed, ending with *Fisher's Spelling Dictionary* in 1774.

Jane Gomeldon (d.1780) continued this tradition of spirited female writing. Jane Middleton, well educated in languages, science and philosophy, was married at an early age to Captain Francis Gomeldon, a friend of George Bowes, the Newcastle coal magnate. She left him, however, and escaped to France in male dress, where a number of exploits are ascribed to her. She returned to England on Gomeldon's death in 1751. Her book of essays *The Medley*, published in Newcastle in 1766, raised over fifty pounds for the city's lying-in hospital. In the essays, Jane creates a range of lively characters and assumes a male persona to discuss Milton, Homer, the education of daughters, cross-dressing, and the unbroached subject of female adultery – having resolved 'not to play the Prude'. She asserts that gentlemen now need improvement to be fit companions to women.

Eminent male scholars include John Horsley, whose *Britannia Romana* (1745) is the first scientific treatise on Roman Britain, and Richard Dawes, who after being appointed headmaster of the Newcastle Grammar School in 1738 apparently became totally unhinged. His continual disputes with the governors ruined the school before he retired in 1749 to Heworth, where he enjoyed boating on the Tyne. The book on which his fame rests *Miscellanea Critica* (1745) was written in Newcastle and has been described as 'an honourable and enduring monument of English scholarship'. Mark Akenside remembered him with aversion as 'facetious Momion'.

John Brown became vicar of St Nicholas in 1761. He wrote essays and poetry as well as two plays in which the great David Garrick acted. His *Estimate of the Manners and Principles of the Times* (1757-8) was a popular national success and earned him the title of 'Estimate Brown'. His work was of abiding interest in France (Robespierre called his dog 'Brown') and it was doubtless familiar to Jean Paul

Marat. The French revolutionary practised as a vet in Newcastle in the early 1770s, though he would accommodate humans also. His first overtly political work, *Chains of Slavery*, was published in Newcastle in 1774 (in English). By his own lurid account, he had lived on black coffee and slept only two hours a night before completing the 65 chapters in three months – and had then slept for 13 days.

Other notable literary visitors to Newcastle over the century included Oliver Goldsmith, who in 1753 spent two weeks in the Newgate gaol, on suspicion of travelling to join the French army. The ship on which he put into the Tyne has not been traced, however, and it has been suggested that the poet was actually unromantically jailed in Sunderland for debt. Tobias Smollett was in Newcastle in May 1766, and in his best novel, *Humphrey Clinker*, Tabitha Bramble attends a Wesley meeting in the town. Smollett certainly knew his way about: in *Roderick Random*, the hero is recognised by his old friend Strap, who is working in a barber's shop on Pilgrim Street.

In what is now called White Knights in Spital Tongues was a private asylum, where James Boswell used to visit his mentally unstable brother John. Boswell was there in May 1775 and again in March 1776, when John unexpectedly said: 'Take me with you.' Boswell was moved to tears, though he knew John was well looked after and in no anguish of mind. Samuel Johnson himself arrived in Newcastle on 11 August 1773 on his way to join Boswell for their celebrated tour of Scotland, and seems to have stayed several days in the town, presumably with William Scott, the future Lord Stowell, who accompanied him to Edinburgh.

Johnson was a qualified admirer of Elizabeth Montagu, who won praise for her *Essay on Shakespeare* (1769). She was the queen of literary London for fifty years and held a famous salon where she would entertain anyone from kings to chimney-sweeps – but 'no idiots'. Elizabeth was a frequent visitor between 1758-89 to the family manor house at East Denton Hall. At first she evinced some metropolitan disdain for the practical-minded society of Newcastle, but was soon ordering Northumbrian delicacies for her southern houses. Interestingly, the famous cookery writers of the time, Hannah Glasse and her rival Ann Cook, were both Northumbrian ladies, as were Elizabeth David and Jane Grigson, their modern counterparts, one might say. Elizabeth Montagu noted: 'Our pitmen are afraid of being turned off and that fear keeps an order and regularity among them that is very uncommon.' Though she enjoyed hearing them singing in the pit, their dialect was, alas, 'dreadful to the auditor's nerves'.

John Wesley (called a 'tadpole in divinity' by James Murray, Newcastle's turbulent priest-pamphleteer) had been shocked by the drunkenness and swearing 'even from the mouths of little children' when he came to Newcastle, but soon developed a fondness for the town and its people. He preached at the Sandgate on 30 March 1742, and records in his *Journal*: 'I never saw so large a number of people together, either in Moorfields or at Kennington ... after preaching, the poor people were ready to tread me under foot out of pure love and kindness.' Wesley established the Orphan House in Northumberland Street as the northern headquarters of his Methodist movement, and made many visits to the area, all noted in his absorbing *Journal*. It was at the Orphan House that Wesley met Grace Murray, the widow of a Geordie seafarer, who nursed him in his illness of 1746. He thought he had met his help-meet at last, but his relations with women were constantly bedevilled by misunderstanding, and Grace wed another. Wesley thereupon impulsively married the widow of a London merchant, who tormented him for thirty years. She was even seen to haul the diminutive Wesley across the room by his hair. In 1778, we find Johnson and Boswell discussing Wesley's encounter with a Newcastle girl who had seen a ghost. Boswell later taxed Wesley about it in Edinburgh, but reports: 'His state of the evidence as to the ghost did not satisfy me.' Those inclined to complain about the local weather might consider the opinion of Wesley, a man who travelled some 250,000 miles around England: 'Certainly if I did not believe there was another world, I would spend all my summers here, as I know no place in Great Britain comparable to it for pleasantness.'

As we have seen, it is remarkable how many Newcastle natives felt confident enough to essay original fields of literary and scholarly endeavour. Charles Avison, who began his subscription concerts in the town in 1736, is described in *New Grove* as the most important English concerto composer of the 18th century. He is mentioned in Sterne's *Tristram Shandy* and is the subject of one of Browning's better late poems. His *Essay on Musical Expression* (1752) was the first English treatise on musical criticism. In it, moreover, he dared to accord the revered Handel no more than faint praise, and then proceeded to defend himself spiritedly against attacks from Oxford and elsewhere. Despite offers from York, Dublin and London, Avison preferred to remain in Newcastle. Nor did 'Estimate' Brown, James Murray (in his *Sermons to Asses*) or his friend, the utopian thinker Thomas Spence find it in any way incongruous to address all England from her northernmost city. This civic self-confidence, outwardly reflected in elegant buildings by local architects, such as David Newton's Assembly Rooms of 1774 and David Stephenson's great elliptical All Saints' Church (1786), found perhaps its most important symbol in the Literary and Philosophical Society, founded in 1793 by the Reverend William Turner and others. The library (still in existence) contained works in French, Spanish, German and Latin; its contacts were international, and its members debated such issues as American science and Scottish political economy.

The Newcastle citizen of greatest renown at the turn of the century was the celebrated wood engraver Thomas Bewick, addressed enviously in verse by Wordsworth as: 'The poet who lives on the banks of the Tyne'. Bewick too had rejected a career in London and joined the Newcastle Lit. and Phil. in 1799. His *Memoir* is a vivid record of his Tyne valley childhood and his life as a craftsman, but also includes much sensible meditation on politics, education and religion, no doubt reflecting the talk at favourite Newcastle haunts such as the *Fox and Lamb* and Swarley's Club in Groat Market – 'Newcastle's House of Lords'. He also records a fight with his friend Thomas Spence, for whose phonetic alphabet he had cut the punches. Bewick's pupils included Ebenezer Landells, who moved to London in 1829, where he established a high reputation as an engraver. It was Landells who suggested the idea for the humorous magazine *Punch*, which first appeared on 17 July 1841.

Civic self-confidence also prompted an increasing interest in the cultural heritage of Newcastle and its environs. John Bell, who opened a second-hand bookshop on the Quayside in 1803, published his extensive *Rhymes of the Northern Bards* in 1812, and it is to him that we are indebted for some of the best-known North East pieces like 'Buy Broom Buzzems' and 'Bonny at Morn'. Among his papers is the earliest known copy of the familiar and controversial 'Foggy Dew'. *Archaeologia Aeliana* was first published in 1822 by the Newcastle Society of Antiquaries, and in 1825 John Trotter Brockett brought out his *Glossary of North-Country Words in Use*. 'Chare' is defined as: 'A narrow street, lane or alley ... peculiar to Newcastle, where there are several, especially on the Quayside ... from the Saxon cyrran, to turn; a chare being a turning from some superior street'.

Thomas Dibdin, the noted bibliographer and librarian to Lord Spencer at Althorp, visited Newcastle and describes his encounter with the society luminaries in his lively *Picturesque Tour in the Northern Counties of England* (1838):

> We were lighted up by gas; and warmed in addition, by the choicest viands and wines which a neighbouring tavern could supply. My friends, John Clayton Esq. and John Adamson Esq. took the top and bottom of the table; supported by Messrs. Brockett, Leadbitter, Fenwick, Hodgson, Charnley and two other gentlemen whose names have escaped me ... Toasts, speeches, puns and social happiness ensued. It were difficult, I think, to have enjoyed a more rational, as well as splendid, symposium: concluding with coffee and tea ... in a small adjoining room, pretty well choked up with Egyptian mummies, chain armour and Esquimaux canoes.

John Adamson, a Portuguese scholar and author of a life of Camoens, showed Dibdin round the new Grainger covered market (still in existence), then the largest in Europe. The opening of the premises, according to him, had been marked by a ceremony the like of which had not been seen since the days of Belshazzar.

The great coaching inns on Pilgrim Street saw a continuing traffic in visiting literati. Walter Scott was a frequent transient and Shelley had passed through in 1811, on the way to his first marriage in Edinburgh (Mary Shelley travelled both ways in 1812 and 1814). William Wordsworth was in Newcastle in January 1795, visiting his sister Dorothy, then staying with the Miss Griffiths: 'Very chearful pleasant companions and excellent women', as she records. He was there again in 1832 when he was shown 'the magnificent buildings which adorn our town' by John Hernaman, editor of the *Newcastle Journal*. William Cobbett, moved by the deputation and address he had received in September of the same year, on his first visit to Newcastle, called it 'this fine, opulent, solid, beautiful and important town'.

A native poet who carried on the vernacular tradition of Edward Chicken was Thomas Wilson (1773-1858). Born in Gateshead, the self-educated Wilson published his chief literary work *The Pitman's Pay* between 1826 and 1830. It is a metrical description, much of it in mining language, of the incidents and conversations of colliers on their fortnightly pay nights. Other Wilson poems show the influence of Burns, and some consider that in the 'Tippling Dominie', Wilson is perhaps seen at his best. Another local poet was Joseph Robson. His *Blossoms of Poesy* came out in Newcastle in 1831 and many other volumes followed, including *Summer Excursions in the North of England* (1851). Robson translated the 'Song of Solomon' into Newcastle dialect for Prince Lucien Bonaparte in 1861, and also wrote songs of topical thrust, like that commemorating the fire in Mrs. Trotter's pawnshop (1849), 'The Paanshop Bleezin', with its stirring ending: 'I wish they aal wor bleezin!' Robson's work gained him more than local fame, and Queen Victoria sent him twenty pounds 'as a slight recognition of his talents as a poet'.

Robson stands at the sententious end of a rich spectrum of popular writing and performance which underpinned Newcastle literary life throughout the 19th century, and lasted well into the next. The North East was the last area of England to have its own music halls, for example, and it always retained an independent tradition, quite different from towns in the rest of the country.

Few authors remained untouched by the unique atmosphere and language of Newcastle. Mrs. Gaskell (then Elizabeth Stevenson), high-spirited and handsome, passed the winters of 1829 and 1830 with the Reverend William Turner in Clavering Place. Her relative, the eminent physician and travel writer, Sir Henry Holland, had spent four happy years of schooling with the family (1799-1803), then at 248 Westgate Road. Turner's social, practical Christianity appealed to Elizabeth's compassion and sense of justice as evinced in novels such as *Mary Barton* and the controversial *Ruth*,

**13.2** Elizabeth Stevenson (later Mrs. Gaskell) in 1832.

her 'Newcastle novel' as she called it. It is probable that Turner's daughter, Ann, was the model for Faith Benson in that book, and the Reverend Thurston Benson may well be based on Turner. Like him, he is a Unitarian pastor, a man of rare goodness, charm and active charity during the Hungry Forties. The great North East cholera epidemic of the early '30s forms the climax of *Ruth*.

Mrs. Gaskell writes to Miss Fox in 1849: 'I picked up quantities of charming expressive words in canny New Castle.' Elizabeth enjoyed the town and had many friends there with whom she went dancing. The well-known bust of Elizabeth by the younger David Dunbar was probably executed in Newcastle at this time. The dashing harpooner, Charley Kinraid, in her novel *Sylvia's Lovers* comes from Cullercoats and has a Northumbrian burr. There are also many knowledgeable references to Newcastle in the first half of the book, where Side, New Gate and Broad Chare are mentioned. At a dramatic point in the narrative, Kinraid sings 'Weel may the keel row' in the streets of Acre in Palestine.

Charles Dickens had been in Newcastle in 1836 for the first performance of his *The Village Coquettes* and returned to act in a bill of three plays at the Assembly Rooms on 27 August 1852, with Wilkie Collins taking part. Dickens also gave readings at the Gaiety Theatre in Nelson Street in 1861, and remarked of Newcastle's citizens: 'Although the people are individually rough, they are an unusually tender and sympathetic audience, while their comic perception is quite up to the high London average.' Dickens also records being knocked flat and soaked by a mighty wave at Tynemouth on 4 March 1867. His great friend, John Forster, was born in Fenkle Street in Newcastle. He was also a friend of Mrs. Gaskell and persuaded her to entitle her notable novel *Mary Barton* rather than use the name of the murderer, John Barton. He also persuaded Tennyson to retain the famous opening lines of 'The Charge of the Light Brigade'. From 1837, Forster read in manuscript everything Dickens wrote and left these priceless documents to the nation. Forster is recognised as the first professional biographer in 19th-century England and his *Life of Dickens* (1872-4) is still regarded as a standard work. Dickens described Forster's London home as Mr. Tulkinghorn's residence in *Bleak House* and immortalised his pompous but lovable friend as Mr. Podsnap in *Our Mutual Friend*.

Harriet Martineau, also a friend of Dickens and a contributor to his magazines, became a major literary figure after the success of her *Illustrations of Political Economy*. She attended the meeting of the British Association in Newcastle in 1838, where her sister pretended to be Harriet, walking about the Green Market with an ear-trumpet to draw the throng away from Harriet herself. A mysterious ailment led to Harriet staying with her sister and brother-in-law, the celebrated doctor Thomas Michael Greenhow, at 28 Eldon Square, before moving to Tynemouth (57 Front Street) where she lived for nearly five years from 16 March 1840, producing at least three books. *Life in the Sick-Room* contains eloquent descriptions of the seascapes and views across the Tyne which her telescope afforded. Visitors included Richard Cobden and Thomas Carlyle, who found the inhabitants 'Scotch in features, in character and dialect'. In 1844, Harriet's controversial cure through mesmerism caused 'a family breach as absurd as it was lamentable' and she moved to Ambleside.

Jules Verne travelled through the North East coalfield by train in 1859 ('a terrifying nightscape') and was so impressed by the fact that some mines ran out under the sea-bed that in *Twenty Thousand Leagues Under the Sea* we find Captain Nemo's crew collecting coal from subterranean seams 'like the mines of Newcastle'. No major English writer reacted to the Industrial Revolution with other than distaste, however, and one of the few artists to celebrate it was William Bell Scott (1811-90) who resided at 14 St Thomas Crescent for 21 years from 1843 as head of the Government Design School. His famous *Iron and Coal* at Wallington Hall is a fine mural depicting Newcastle industry at this period. In Scott's *Autobiographical Notes* of 1892 we find interesting portraits of visitors like the poet Algernon Swinburne, a scion of the family at Capheaton Hall and a fierce Northumbrian patriot. With Scott holding his head, Swinburne had a 'mighty grinder' extracted bit by bit by a Newcastle dentist. Scott records that the manful little poet seemed almost indifferent to the pain. In

December 1862, Swinburne accompanied Bell Scott and his friends, probably including Dante Gabriel Rossetti, on a trip to Tynemouth. As they walked by the sea, Scott writes that Swinburne declaimed his great poems 'Hymn to Proserpine' and 'Laus Veneris' in his strange intonation, while the waves were 'running the whole length of the long level sands towards Cullercoats and sounding like far-off acclamations'. It was an appropriate spot. Swinburne detested Christianity and 'Hymn to Proserpine' contains his thrillingly sombre acceptance of eternal extinction:

> From too much love of living,
> From hope and fear set free,
> We thank with brief thanksgiving
> Whatever gods may be
> That no life lives for ever;
> That dead men rise up never;
> That even the weariest river
> Winds somewhere safe to sea.

In 1853, Rossetti, an important and influential figure in Victorian art and literature, spent several weeks with Bell Scott, whose poetry he greatly admired. Christina Rossetti came to Newcastle in 1858 and one modern biographer has detected in her poems of this time a frustrated passion for the handsome Bell Scott. The party went on a trip to Sunderland on 29 June and the doggerel manuscript poem Christina wrote on the occasion, entitled 'After the Pic-nic', begins:

> … From Newcastle to Sunderland
> Upon a misty morn in June
> We took the train: on either hand
> Grimed streets were changed for meadows soon.
>
> Umbrellas, tarts and sandwiches
> Sustained our spirits' temperate flow
> With potted jam, and cold as snow
> Rough-coated, sunburnt oranges.

Christina wrote on the same day the beautiful 'Up-Hill' and 'Today and Tomorrow', of all her poems the bleakest. She spent a day with the Trevelyans at Wallington Hall and also visited Marsden Bay with Scott. In October 1859, she travelled to Newcastle again in the company of Lady Pauline Trevelyan to stay with Laetitia Scott for a week.

A collier who won national fame was Joseph Skipsey. Born in Tynemouth, where his father was shot dead in a clash between pitmen and special constables,

Skipsey worked in the pits from the age of seven, and taught himself to read and write. In 1859, he published *Poems* in Morpeth, but the book seems not to be extant. In 1863 he moved to Newcastle and worked for a time as assistant librarian to the Literary and Philosophical Society. Skipsey initially edited the Canterbury Poets for the Newcastle publisher Walter Scott, whose Camelot series was an important feature of the Victorian reprint market. Interestingly, Ernest Rhys, later to become editor of the famous Everyman Library, was brought up in Newcastle and also worked as an editor for Scott.

In 1866, Skipsey published *Carols from the Coalfields*, praised by Rossetti and Oscar Wilde, who likened the poems to those of William Blake. Skipsey was appointed custodian of Shakespeare's Stratford birthplace on the recommendation of Tennyson, Rossetti, Bram Stoker and other eminent men, but he resigned two years later. The episode gave rise to Henry James' story 'The Birthplace'. Dignified and austere as a man, Skipsey could be windy and rhetorical as a writer. He is at his best when describing his own experience as a pitman. This poem Rossetti considered equal to anything in the language for quietly direct pathos:

> 'Get up!' the caller calls, 'Get up!'
>     And in the dead of night,
> To win the bairns their bite and sup,
>     I rise a weary wight.
>
> My flannel duddon donn'd, thrice o'er
>     My birds are kiss'd, and then
> I with a whistle shut the door,
>     I may not ope again.

In the 1870s, Newcastle was home to a novelist of world stature, the Portuguese writer Eça de Queiròs, one of the masters of 19th-century European fiction. Zola considered him to be greater than Flaubert, while others rank him alongside Dickens, Balzac and Tolstoy. Eça (pronounced Essa) worked in the consular service at 53 Grey Street from late 1874 until April 1879, among the most productive years of his career. He published the second version of *O Crime de Padre Amaro* (1876) and *O Primo Basilio* (1878), as well as working on a number of other projects. He even mentions the title of his masterpiece *Os Maias* in 1878, though this was largely written during his later residence in Bristol.

On a somewhat lower level of achievement, William Clark Russell (1844-1911) was the author of a series of immensely popular adventure tales. Doctor Watson in the Sherlock Holmes narrative 'The Five Orange Pips' is shown 'deep in one of Clark Russell's fine sea stories'. In about 1881, Russell worked for a time on the

*Newcastle Daily Chronicle* under the redoubtable Joseph Cowen, and his novel *A Sea Queen* (1884) contains tremendous descriptions of the sea at Tynemouth and the Black Middens, as well as an engaging description of the Side in Newcastle. Russell's heroine remarks:

> In the mouths of the lower orders, Newcastle English is … a very rugged and grotesque tongue, as unintelligible to the stranger as Dutch … On the other hand, there is nothing sweeter than the pronunciation of the educated Tynesider. There is something fascinating to listen to in the silken rippling of a Newcastle lady's speech, and the burr and an unconscious sprinkling of expressive local words will make the veriest commonplace attractive in a cultivated male speaker.

Curiously enough, the same year found Joseph Conrad in the Tyne, having his buttons sewn on by his Geordie captain's wife as he stayed aboard the *Palestine* off Percy Main, waiting to load West Hartley coal for Bangkok. This was his first fateful voyage to the exotic East. After interminable delays, the ship eventually caught fire off Java Head. Conrad's famous story 'Youth' is based on this episode.

The sea theme continues in the work of John Meade Falkner, who originally came to Newcastle as tutor to the children of Sir Andrew Noble at Jesmond Dene House. By 1916, he had risen to the top of the Armstrong-Whitworth armaments and shipbuilding colossus – hard though this is to equate with his poetry and his interest in heraldry and architecture. He

**13.3**   Joseph Conrad.

wrote a number of novels, including *The Nebuly Coat*, which has been seen as an influence on E.M. Forster, but his great claim to fame is the children's classic *Moonfleet* (1898), several times dramatised, filmed and televised. Many consider it to be more enjoyable than *Treasure Island*. Also very popular in his day was Henry Seton Merriman, born at 16 Rye Hill in 1862. Merriman wrote a whole series of exotic adventure stories, most notably the Napoleonic *Barlasch of the Guard* (1903).

Bernard Shaw (as he preferred to be called) describes a visit to St George's Church, Jesmond in the first issue of *The Savoy* in January 1896. Shaw had theatrical links with Newcastle; his *Caesar and Cleopatra* for example, was given its copyright performance on 15 March 1899 at the Theatre Royal by Mrs. Patrick Campbell's company. He was also a strong supporter of the People's Theatre, established by the Veitch family of actors in 1911 as an offshoot of the British Socialist Party. Its third production was Shaw's own *The Shewing-Up of Blanco Posnet* which had been banned by the Lord Chamberlain. Though the formal political connection ceased in 1915, the People's Theatre is still in existence in Stephenson Road, Heaton, and can claim to be the world's oldest amateur repertory company. Shaw visited the theatre's new premises in the Royal Arcade in 1921 for a production of *Man and Superman*, and it was in Rye Hill in 1936, at the age of 80, that he made his final stage appearance at the end of the People's performance of his play *Candida*. He spoke for about fifteen minutes and declared that for his last performance there was no theatre he would rather be in.

The exigencies of World War I brought a number of writers to Newcastle, including Kipling, in 1915, and Ivor Gurney, who was treated at the Newcastle General Hospital for gas inhalation and bought a Boswell in the town to cheer himself up. His opinion of the citizenry echoes that of Dickens. Gurney wrote a number of poems at his New Hartley camp, where J.R.R. Tolkien, it seems, was a fellow-soldier. In 1915, J.B. Priestley was billeted in Tynemouth, and spent all the time he could at the Newcastle theatres and music halls. As a prime industrial target, Newcastle and Tyneside suffered Zeppelin attacks in 1915-16, a fact ruefully commented upon by Yevgeni Zamyatin. Already a writer of some promise, he was also a marine specialist and was sent to England in 1916 to oversee the construction of a number of icebreakers for the Imperial Russian government. He lived at 19 Sanderson Road, Jesmond for nearly two years, and the initial culture shock of middle-class Jesmond society stung him into producing two novellas, *Islanders* and *A Fisher of Men*, in which he made savage fun of the Jesmondians' preference for conformity over spontaneity:

> The Sunday gentlemen were produced at one of the Jesmond factories and on Sunday mornings, thousands of them would appear on the streets with the Sunday edition of St Enoch's parish newspaper. Sporting identical canes and identical top-hats, the Sunday gentlemen strolled in dignified fashion along the street and greeted their doubles.

Back in Russia, however, where Zamyatin became a major literary figure, he was himself known as 'the Englishman', wore tweeds and smoked a pipe. In an

**13.4** Castle Stairs, *c.*1930. Zamyatin's 'Cobbler John's Alley'.

astonishing 1930 interview with the North East writer Harold Heslop in Leningrad, Zamyatin confessed that he liked the Geordies, particularly their musical dialect, though he couldn't manage it himself – apart from 'Sooth Shields'. The interview was astonishing because, in 1930, Zamyatin was under a dark political cloud and saw very few visitors. In fact, he was allowed to emigrate to Paris in 1931, after a courageous letter to Stalin. Zamyatin had nightmarishly extended the Newcastle novellas to produce *We*, written soon after his return to Russia in 1917, only to have it become the first book banned by the new revolutionary censorship. In *We*, the first great modern anti-utopia, privacy is non-existent in the One State and the city is walled-off from the free, dirty, natural and disorganised world outside. Life within, though not actually unhappy, is characterised by regimented obedience to the

Benefactor and his Guardians, and leaves no room for human variety and spontaneity. There are many hidden references in the novel to Newcastle and the working practices in the wartime Tyne shipyards; even the numbers of the main characters (no one has names) are taken from the specifications of Zamyatin's favourite icebreaker. *We* finally achieved publication in the USSR in 1988, along with Orwell's *Nineteen Eighty-Four*, appropriately enough. Orwell had read *We* in French, and his own book does exhibit striking parallels with Zamyatin's work. Thus Newcastle may be said to have instigated one, or indeed two of the most influential novels of the 20th century. It is a curious circumstance that Orwell's wife Eileen (born in South Shields) is buried in Jesmond. Orwell attended the funeral in April 1945, and visited the grave in May 1946, the year he reviewed Zamyatin's novel. He was of course unaware of how close he was to the very house where Zamyatin had toiled in 1916, as the Zeppelins droned over a darkened city.

It is the wartime experiences of Captain W.E. Johns which give such dramatic immediacy to his first air adventure stories, beginning in 1932. He was for long unique among children's writers in having Ginger Hebblethwaite, the son of a Northumberland miner, as an equal member of the Biggles team. *Biggles and the Black Peril* (1953) where Biggles and Algy meet Ginger for the first time, is set partly in the Newcastle of the '30s. Johns arrived in Newcastle late on 31 December 1924 and spent a horrific night at 15 Ellison Place, then a rat-infested disused private nursing home with no lights. He survived to serve a year in the Newcastle recruiting office, while living with Doris (Dol) Leigh in Whitley Bay.

Rosamond Lehmann began her best-selling first novel *Dusty Answer* (1927) in Newcastle. She had married Leslie Runciman of the Tyneside shipping family in December 1923, and the couple lived at 3 Sydenham Terrace (now demolished). Rosamond, though beautiful and popular, with a fine house and servants, was uneasy with her Newcastle existence (and relatives) and also found that her handsome, clever husband had no desire for children. Her second novel *A Note in Music* (1930) draws heavily on this experience, and is almost comically doleful. Trams constantly groan past the house and up Osborne Road; spring never comes. Trapped in an unhappy relationship, Grace, her main protagonist, retreats into complete passivity. The bustling characterful life of Newcastle (unnamed) and its people is kept at an irritatingly vague and unsympathetic distance.

Living in Newcastle at the same time was a writer who could analyse such class tensions with rueful precision. A plaque on 44 Third Avenue, Heaton marks the house where Jack Common was born, close to the rail-sheds where his father worked as an engine-driver. In 1928, Common began working for the *Adelphi* magazine in London, and his essays collected in, for example, *The Freedom of the Streets*, are a continual spur to thought. Common acutely divines that the intelligent young proletarian is 'a great fondler of wilful inhibition', unconsciously wishing to remain innocently detached from the calculating world of rulers and decision-making; he analyses the Jesmondians, and by implication, all middle-class suburbs far better than Zamyatin could. As a genuine proletarian, he could also perceive that his friend George Orwell was 'a sheep in wolf's clothing'. In pubs, the barman always called Orwell 'sir'. Common's writing is warm, ironic and intensely political in a non-abstract way, while being occasionally garrulous and couched in a quirky style which attempts to combine proletarian directness with intellectual rumination. Without employing dialect, he conveys something of the cadences of his local speech. Common won admirers throughout the 1930s as a writer with a genuine proletarian viewpoint, as distinct from the purveyors of middle-class Marxist fiction. V.S. Pritchett considered *The Freedom of the Streets* to be the most influential book in his life, and Orwell, reviewing the work in *New English Review* (16 June 1938) heard 'the authentic voice of the ordinary man, the man who might infuse a new decency into the control of affairs if only he could get there, but who in practice never seems to get much farther than the trenches, the sweatshop and the jail'.

*Kiddar's Luck* (1951), Common's best-known book, is a vivid account of street life in Edwardian Tyneside, as seen through the lens of his adult socialism. There are four chapters on his life before five years old – a feat of detailed memory – while his mother's alcoholism and the overbearing father whom Jack at length dramatically defies, form the dark background to the vigorous, at times bravura, narrative. Here he describes Bigg Market in Newcastle:

> The press of people coming into it became instantly ruddy-faced and bright-eyed as the naphtha-flares fanned out, eating the air just overhead, their smoke visibly coiling up to a brazen sky … Rival ice-cream wagons, their gilt and cream and blue almost a coloratura cry on the lit air, echoed to Italian-tinted Tyneside as their crews of brisk dark men flung bigger and bigger dollops into brass sandwich-makers.

In *The Ampersand* (1953) Common took the story further, but his publishers went into liquidation two years later. Neither book had been a commercial success and Common had not completed the trilogy with his long-promised *Riches and Rare*, a novel set in Newcastle at the time of the General Strike. Interestingly, Lawrence Bradshaw had used Common's brow as a model for his bust of Karl Marx in Highgate cemetery, saying that he found there a similar patience and understanding.

Too early (or too old) to be an angry young man of the 1950s, Common was unable to sustain a career in writing. His political attitudes were by now out of fashion, and his last manuscript, *In Whitest Britain* (1961), was said to have too much class distinction, and that the downtrodden, golden-hearted workman was a dated leading cliché. Thus Jack Common, perhaps the finest chronicler of the English working class to follow Robert Tressell, spent his last years in Newport Pagnell writing film treatments at poor rates. He died of lung cancer on 20 January 1968, leaving a mass of unpublished material, now held in the Robinson Library of the University of Newcastle upon Tyne.

Common's exhilarating descriptions of Newcastle are echoed by A.J. Cronin. He was in the city in 1925, when water from the Tyne broke into the mine workings near Scotswood, an idea he was to utilise in his first real triumph as a novelist, *The Stars Look Down* (1935). This is set partly in a mining community on the Northumberland coast ('Sleescale') and partly in Newcastle ('Tynecastle'). Cronin mentions a vast profusion of real Newcastle places and his portrait of Tynesiders is unpatronisingly warm-hearted. He even conveys the accent convincingly.

J.B. Priestley, on the other hand, was an unsympathetic observer (and auditor) and his *English Journey* (1934) has been oddly influential in establishing the 'depressed' image of the North East, even locally, for over sixty years. He is surprised at the fine buildings of Grainger-Dobson Newcastle, since, by sharp contrast with other places on his itinerary, he is utterly ignorant of the city's history; even Hadrian is mentioned only in connection with York. Priestley's enjoyment of Newcastle's theatres in 1915 is forgotten; he is astonished to find the People's Theatre (unnamed) rehearsing Euripides' *Trojan Women* at the *Bridge Hotel* and has left us a patronising account. The book in fact completely ignores the lighter side of Tyneside life, and concentrates relentlessly on the aesthetic cost of recession in the basic North East industries.

Representative of the lively theatre scene that Priestley missed was Esther McCracken, who acted with the Newcastle Repertory Company from 1924 until 1937. She was small, red-headed and full of spirit. On the BBC Brains Trust programme, the formidable Professor Joad (with whom Jack Common debated on radio) once asked her: 'Have you read Aristotle's *Poetics*?' She replied: 'Do I look like it?' Her first play *The Willing Spirit* was produced in 1936, but it was with *Quiet Wedding* in 1938 that her reputation as a writer of domestic comedy was made. Other successes included *Quiet Weekend* (1941) and *No Medals* (1944). Nancy Spain also did some radio acting, and records in her entertaining memoirs the enjoyable youth she spent at 7 Tankerville Place in Jesmond. The famous columnist and broadcaster also wrote a series of breezily amusing detective novels, including *Cinderella Goes to the Morgue* (1950), whose setting is a pantomime at the Theatre Royal.

Someone Priestley might usefully have contacted before his trip was the poet and critic Michael Roberts. Born in Bournemouth, Roberts taught at the Royal Grammar School in Newcastle for 16 years after 1925, apart from an interval in the early '30s in London. At first he lived at Red Lodge in Longbenton, where he papered a wall with rejection slips. Later, his anthologies *New Signatures* (1932) and *New Country* (1933), containing work by Empson, Auden, Spender, Day-Lewis and others, made him, in the words of T.S. Eliot, 'expositor and interpreter of the poetry of his generation'. Roberts edited the influential *Faber Book of Modern Verse* (1936). In 1935 he married Janet Adam Smith, also a gifted writer and anthologist, who edited the *Faber Book of Children's Verse* – still in print. The couple lived at 13 Fern Avenue, Jesmond, then at No. 73. Janet Adam Smith describes those years as 'a tale of poems, children, books, anthologies, reviews, climbing, ski-ing, school camps and holidays in Lakes, Highlands and Alps'. Roberts' own poetry is often about the mountains where he and his wife were very much at home, but 'H.M.S. Hero' and 'Temperance Festival: Town Moor, Newcastle' have local interest. Roberts was on the committee of the Newcastle Lit and Phil.

W.H. Auden was a lifelong devotee of the North Pennines near Newcastle. It was his 'great good place' and his 'symbol of us all'. He had written to Roberts in 1932 for advice on his teaching career and, later, about his play *The Ascent of F.6*. On 27 September 1937, curiously in the very week when the People's Theatre was performing the play, using the authentic climbing gear of the 1933 Everest expedition, Auden came to dinner at 13 Fern Avenue, when the couple's first baby was three weeks old. Always fascinated by medical matters, he talked much with the midwife in attendance, Nurse Laverick, and elicited a fund of stories drawn from her Newcastle experience. On 25 November 1937, Auden and Benjamin Britten were in Newcastle for the broadcast of their radio documentary *Hadrian's Wall*, from the studios in New Bridge Street. Thirty-five years later, on Sunday 17 December 1972, Auden was once more in Newcastle, reading in the University Theatre and staying at the *Turk's Head* in Grey Street. Sid Chaplin has left a touching and compassionate note of his meeting with Auden on this occasion.

Sid Chaplin (1916-86) can be said to have influenced a whole generation of post-war British working-class writers, including Keith Waterhouse and Stan Barstow. His book of stories *The Thin Seam* (1950) became the basis for a successful and moving musical play *Close the Coalhouse Door* by local writers Alan Plater and Alex Glasgow. Though his descriptions of conditions underground have a poignant immediacy, Chaplin's words on the fate of William Jobling, a miner hanged in 1832 at Jarrow Slake, have a generalising power given to few:

Lifted up to be degraded, turned into a 'white negro' covered from head to toe in pitch, strangely and fearfully encased in iron, he is transformed into a figure of almost archetypal power. A nonentity in life, he blossomed terribly in death.

From 1957, Chaplin lived at 11 Kimberley Gardens in Newcastle. Remarking that the term 'regional writer' made him spit blood, he wrote television scripts, including some for *When the Boat Comes In*. His two important novels *The Day of the Sardine* and *The Watcher and the Watched* are set among the working-class communities of Scotswood, Byker and Elswick.

Early in the 20th century, Lord North-cliffe's stated ambition for his newspapers had been to build up a national readership centred on London, and looking to London for its news and opinions. His success, coupled with the purchase of regional titles by metropolitan press barons, inevitably put an end to the independent voice and national influence of provincial owners such as Joseph Cowen of Newcastle. Great literary artists, however, showed that it was possible to achieve inter-national renown without the capital's sanction. Auden was a declared provincial, and Basil Bunting (1900-86), Britain's first modernist poet, was a Northumbrian patriot. He was born at 258 Denton Road, Scotswood, the son of a cultivated doctor, and attended the Royal Grammar School in Newcastle. By 1923 he was in Paris and had met Ezra Pound, who dedicated his *Guide to Kulchur* jointly to Bunting and Louis Zukofsky. Poverty was a constant pressure on Bunting, driving him to a multitude of shifts to make ends meet, and after a varied and remarkable war experience he found that

**13.5**  Sid Chaplin in Edinburgh.

**13.6**  Sid Chaplin with W.H. Auden and Philip Bomford at Chollerford, 1973.

**13.7** Basil Bunting in Rapallo, *c.*1931, probably on W.B. Yeats' balcony.

in Britain at least his work was out of fashion. He was working for the *Newcastle Evening Chronicle* when the local poet Tom Pickard persuaded him to write again. The result was his quasi-autobiographical masterpiece *Briggflatts*, first read in the Morden Tower on the medieval walls of Newcastle, venue for many stirring poetry evenings since. Critics, including Cyril Connolly and Hugh McDiarmid, ranked Bunting's work with Eliot's *Waste Land* and *Four Quartets*, while poets such as Allen Ginsberg and Thom Gunn have added their praise.

Though it ranges widely over Japanese, Persian and Latin sources, Bunting's writing is consciously Northumbrian – the 'We' of the poems as distinct from the Southrons of the Saxon south of England. He laments that Northumbrians should know about Eric Bloodaxe but seldom do because 'all the school histories are written by or for Southrons'. It is above all in *Briggflatts*, where themes of Northumbrian history, language and landscape mingle with personal memories beneath the wheeling stars, that we find the spare, complex music which makes reading Bunting an unforgettable experience:

> Great strings next the post of the harp
> clang, the horn has majesty,
> flutes flicker in the draft and flare.
> Orion strides over Farne.

Writers who adopted Newcastle continued to add lustre to the city's literary life. Penelope Gilliatt (1932-93) was brought up in Northumberland, and throughout her distinguished career as writer and film critic (she won an Oscar nomination for the screenplay of *Sunday, Bloody Sunday* in 1971) she championed the North. Her novel *Mortal Matters* (1983) is largely set in Northumberland and Newcastle, with mentions of the *Railway Hotel*, the Old Assembly Rooms, the Grainger Market and Grey Street. She writes at length about the famous vessels *Torrens* (Joseph Conrad's clipper), *Turbinia* and *Mauretania* (Kipling's 'nine-decked city'), while the South of England (exemplified in Harrow and the Stock Exchange) is portrayed as a sybaritic and corrupting influence: the North East is held up throughout as a model of acumen and courage.

Cecil Philip Taylor (1929-81), born in Glasgow, came to Newcastle in 1955, where he lived at 30 Lindale Road, Fenham, for many years. His first play was *Aa Went to Blaydon Races* (1962), while *Peter Pan Man* transfers Barrie's play to an Elswick estate. The Live Theatre in Newcastle premiered his *Bandits* (1977) which was also performed by the Royal Shakespeare Company. His most successful work was probably *Good* (1981), in which a liberal German professor's moral cowardice leads to his involvement with the Nazi war machine and Auschwitz. The Tyne-Tees production of *And a Nightingale Sang*, a bitter-sweet comedy set on wartime Tyneside, won a Prix Europa in 1990. Taylor's drama has also featured as a central theme of the Edinburgh Festival. He was the founding father of the Northern Playwrights Society (which still flourishes).

Jon Silkin (1930-97) was born in London, where he launched the quarterly magazine *Stand* in 1952, and sold it energetically himself in coffee bars. From 1966, he lived in Newcastle, where *Stand* was published until the poet's death. Though some of Silkin's output reflects his response to the Durham dales, he, like his magazine, strove to be international. The same can certainly be said of Bloodaxe Books of Newcastle, whose director Neil Astley takes pride in bringing out more new poetry titles than any other British imprint. Bloodaxe authors, including three Nobel laureates, have won almost every literary award since the enterprise began in 1978.

After World War II, the development of television greatly diminished the status of local live performance, while increasing the commissioning power of the capital (90 per cent of TV sitcoms are set in the London area, for example). Prominent local performers and writers felt a steady pressure to move south, and some local literary output began to take the form of scripts for memorable TV series such as *When the Boat Comes In*, followed by *The Likely Lads* and *Our Friends in the North*. Paradoxically, the very pervasiveness and appetite of television helped to emphasise a universality in such writing which in the shape of printed literature might have been ignored. The term 'regional writer' began to lose its pejorative sting and the hugely popular novels of Catherine Cookson, born on Tyneside and latterly resident in Newcastle, have proved ideal for television. The broadcast and print media have also given prominence to literary prizes, and North East writers such as Pat Barker, Jane Gardam and Barry Unsworth have won major awards. It is not generally known that the famous Chalet School books were written by Elinor Brent-Dyer of South Shields, but her North East successors in the field of children's literature – Sylvia Waugh, David Almond and Robert Westall are all prize-winners. The Centre for the Children's Book is to be located in Newcastle. The new millennium, in fact, is witnessing an upsurge of North East writing at all levels and in all genres of a variety and quality without precedent. Authors other than poets are still dependent on London publishers and distribution networks, but even here change may be at hand. It is quite possible that political devolution will be regional in the best sense of that word, involving, as Robert Hughes puts it, the full use of culture in the interest of local resources, somewhat after the manner of the Italian medieval city-states. No one in Lyons, Bologna or Barcelona is impressed by the cant of cultural empire or feels the need to prove themselves elsewhere. Similar confidence engendered by devolved decision-making may renew Newcastle publishing in a way not seen since the 18th century.

## Bibliography

Charleton, R., *A History of Newcastle on Tyne*, 2nd edition, Newcastle, 1989.
Blain, V., Clements, P., and Grundy, I. (eds.), *The Feminist Companion to Literature in English*, 1990.

# 14

# *Sociability and the City*

## BILL LANCASTER

June 1962 was a good month for T. Dan Smith. The rising star of British local government presided over one of the century's biggest events in Newcastle, an event that had been two years in the planning. Smith reached an emotional high, which inspired him to express his feelings in verse. According to Tyneside's McGonagall:

> Old Scotswood Road must live again
> To carry further still its fame
> We're soon to have a celebration –
> Let Tyneside rise in jubilation.[1]

The Blaydon Races Centenary Celebration was a remarkable phenomenon, culminating with the procession from Newcastle to the township of Blaydon on the city's western boundary, on the exact centenary of a raucous coach journey that never took place. Smith had chosen his day well. Saturday 9 June began with Hugh Gaitskell, the leader of the Labour Party, opening The Willows tower block at Cruddas Park before unveiling a piece of public sculpture nearby. Other tower blocks of the same design had already been built, occupied and opened at Shieldfield and Walker without fuss, all part of Smith's ambitious housing programme. But Cruddas Park, running alongside Scotswood Road, was the star development in Smith's plan for a northern Brasilia. Again poetry was used to express his ambition:

> From Cruddas Park to Rye Hill
> We are determined, have the will
> That horrid slums we shall erase
> With surgeons knife and then replace.[2]

He knew all too well the cultural significance of this west Newcastle site. Scotswood Road was renowned for its numerous pubs, for the terraced streets that

---

[1] Smith, T.D., *Autobiography* (1970), p.64.
[2] *Ibid.*, p.62.

climbed steeply from its northern side, for Armstrong's factory, long the city's largest employer, and above all for its arterial role in the Tyneside anthem *The Blaydon Races*. Half a million people participated in the festivity. Street parties, music, fireworks and, significantly during this era of restrictive licensing hours, all-day drinking.[3] Smith mixed a potent brew. The popularity of the event allowed him to dish the local Conservatives who had opposed the festival, a victory made sweeter when it was reported that many Tory council members were spotted enjoying the fun. Smith was playing with, and attempting to re-shape Britain's strongest local cultural tradition. Tynesiders were captivated by his ability to combine the cultural and physical renewal of the city. With a wide range of cultural events the celebrations lasted a week, many taking place in a large marquee on the Town Moor. On the Thursday in Dan's big tent a dinner dance at 21 shillings per head was organised for the many exiles temporarily returned from the Geordie diaspora. In that week in June 1962 something extraordinary took place. People took to the streets in their hundreds of thousands, and many travelled continents; for what? To celebrate the centenary of a fictitious proletarian bus ride to a shady unregulated 'flapping track'.[4] Or were deeper meanings being articulated – meanings perhaps rooted in the local cultural 'DNA' that can only be understood by witnessing the making of Newcastle's unique form of urban sociability? 'Party City' is a contemporary celebration that has brought national and international attention but it also expresses deep historic continuities. This essay is essentially an exploration in cultural archaeology, a search for those threads that link the present-day noise, banter, affability and exuberant sense of social ownership of the city's central area, with previous periods and generations. Cultures are made and are always in a process of re-making. New elements join the mix, but older ones remain and continue to enrich in sometimes very different circumstances. What follows is an attempt to chart the survival of Newcastle's old, but still potent cultural assets.

Crowds, as Dan Smith was well aware, have long been a central feature of Tyneside life. The Newcastle 18th-century crowd has received more attention by historians than that of any other provincial town. Keelmen, pitmen, freemen, patriots and radicals used the streets, public houses and open spaces of Newcastle for their activities.[5] Patricians and plebeians jostled for attention in an atmosphere of friendly

---

[3] *Evening Chronicle*, 6-11 June 1962.

[4] Tynemouth, W., *Centenary of Blaydon Race* (1962).

[5] Colls, R., *The Colliers Rant* (1977); Colls, R., *The Pitmen of the Northern Coalfield*, part three (1987); Levine, D. and Wrightson, K., *The Making of Industrial Society, Whickham 1560-1760* (1991); Ellis, J., 'Urban Conflict and Popular Violence: The Guildhall riots of 1740 in Newcastle upon Tyne', *International Review of Social History*, volume 25, part 3, 1980; Brewer, J., *The Pleasure of the Imagination: English Culture in the Eighteenth Century* (1997), chapter 13; Rogers, N., *Crowds, Culture and Politics in Georgian Britain* (1998); Wilson, K., *The Sense of the People: Politics, Culture and Imperialism in England, 1715-1775* (1995); Thompson, E.P., *Customs in Common* (1991).

banter. The Newcastle of Thomas Bewick was a vigorous centre of human creativity. The town pioneered musical concerts under the leadership of Charles Avison. It was the largest centre of English provincial publishing and supported newspapers and many periodicals.[6] Newcastle's 'Florists', gardeners who specialised in the cultivation of exotic bulbs which came into the town with most of the local fruit and vegetable supply from Holland, were masters at adapting the more tender species to the exigencies of the climate in 'the Northern Parts'.[7] The 'Auricula' was Newcastle's favourite and in the 1790s it was reported that locals were converting their melon frames for flower cultivation. This upsurge in popular horticulture was shared by many and generated exhibitions which were popular social occasions. Workers organised and participated in numerous July gooseberry shows, precursors to leek-growing competitions.[8]

Public houses often provided the venue for popular exhibitions, but more often, and particularly those near the river, were also part of a radical political culture that provided a safe haven for Jean Paul Marat during his exile from France prior to the revolution. There, Thomas Bewick once fought his friend, the radical writer Thomas Spence, with cudgels in a dispute on the nature of 'property'. They occupied a world that centred on local lecture rooms and quayside artisan hostelries that mixed beer with discourses on philosophy.[9] Naturally this radical hothouse was a frequent site for political disorder. The Guildhall riots of 1740, the Peterloo, Queen Caroline and Coronation disturbances of the early 1820s, the Reform protests of 1832 and '38-9, and the Town Moor Chartist demonstrations all bore witness to Newcastle's independent political tradition.[10]

Yet there was more to the popular than politics, and crowds, while rightly perceived by the authorities as potentially dangerous, have other more subtle functions than confrontation. Crowds don't just gather, they assemble for a purpose and few cities or towns assembled as many as Newcastle. Most were brought together by civic events rather than by local grievance. Newcastle Corporation was arguably one of the most ceremonial in the country. Its leading members and officers were the major players in this theatre that denoted the civic calendar. Corporate riches based upon its ancient control of the Tyne shipping trade allowed its elite to behave with all the pomp of a royal court.[11] Between 1561 and 1635 the Corporation kept

---

[6] Brewer, *Pleasure of the Imagination.*, chapter 13; Hudson, J., *The Florists Companion* (1794) frontispiece; see Charleton, R.J., *Newcastle Town* (1885), p.331 for the Dutch supply of fresh produce.

[7] Hudson, *Florists Companion.*

[8] *Newcastle Chronicle*, 2 August 1823.

[9] Brewer, *Pleasure of the Imagination.*

[10] Ridley, D., 'The Parliamentary Reform Crisis in Newcastle upon Tyne, 1832', *North East Labour History*, 26, 1992.

[11] Hodgekinson Hinde, J., 'Public Amusements in Newcastle', *Archaeologia Aeliana*, new series, volume 4, 1860, pp.229-33.

**14.1**   Barge Day, 1840: the mayor and his company beat the bounds.

a 'company of fools', a unique instance of a civic company, 'fools' usually being a phenomena of royal or, occasionally, aristocratic, households.[12] And Newcastle could stage events that were the equal of state occasions. The annual Ascension Day survey of the river was the most spectacular. Aboard the gilt-painted 'state' barge and surrounded by other sumptuous vessels, the Mayor and his officers would beat the bounds between Sparhawk and Hedwin Stream, the limits of Newcastle's corporate monopolistic privileges. River processions were the great events in the calendar and echoed the aquatic ceremonies of the early Hanoverians and the Doge of Venice.[13] Another significant elite event was the trooping out in full costume of the Sheriff, Mayor and other dignitaries to Sheriff Hill in Gateshead to greet and accompany the visiting judge to the Assizes. The Assizes were also the occasion for Newcastle's major society ball. Coronations, royal birthdays, horse race meetings, as well as religious festivals were all marked by civic pageantry.[14]

In other ways Newcastle differed from the normal format of provincial civic ceremony. Most towns staged events which offered roles for all citizens. Elite and

[12]   Southworth, J., *Fools and Jesters at the English Court* (1998), p.166.
[13]   Not so far fetched a comparison as might appear. See Lane, F.C., *Venice: A Maritime Republic* (1973), p.57.
[14]   Hodgekinson Hinde, 'Public Amusements'.

plebeians came together in civic pageants that expressed both a sense of historic place and social solidarity. Coventry's Godiva procession is, perhaps, the best known. Newcastle on the other hand went to great lengths to exclude plebeians from the centre stage of civic pageantry. The lower orders were expected to watch, drink to the health of their betters and move on.[15] The causes of this deep social divide lie beyond the range of this present volume, but are undoubtedly rooted in the Corporation's long defence of, and unwillingness to share or dilute, its ancient rights and powers. Disputes with the Freemen frequently demonstrated that Newcastle's hierarchy of Corporation, hostmen, merchant venturers and liveried companies formed a delicate equilibrium that was easily upset by external forces.[16]

Excluded from the festivals, plebeian Newcastle invented its own. The mock 'Mayors' Procession' staged by children on Michaelmas Day and the Cordwainers' coronation of Saint Crispin cocked a snook at civic ceremonial dignity.[17] By the early 19th century the time-honoured treat to the lower orders on occasions such as Coronation Day was more likely to be received as an insult than as an expression of civic patriotism. Note the contrast between the behaviour of the crowds at the Corporation-funded 'wine pant', to mark the coronations of George II in 1727 and George IV in 1821. In 1727 'the conduit running with wine all the time for the Populace' helped along celebrations, which concluded with 'Bonfires, Illuminations, ringing of Bells and all other demonstrations of joy'.[18] In 1821, against the background of the Queen Caroline affair, the Corporation's 'wine pant and ox roast' provoked a riot. The authorities had conducted the event with a lack of sensitivity. Lumps of hot meat were thrown to a crowd, which anyway was beginning to express sympathy for the 'injured queen'. The pant was smashed, one celebrant washed 'his posteriors' in the civic claret whilst another paraded the broken fountain spout 'as if it was a huge penis'.[19] The riot of 1821 was a major turning point. Future coronations were to be celebrated differently. The Corporation began to give up its street platforms and retreat to the more formal civic ceremonies. The Mayor in his barge, as Conservator of the Tyne, would continue to beat the bounds of the river on Ascension Day, but other elite public displays became rarities. By 1860 the deputy chairman of the Society of Antiquaries felt obliged to list the defunct events for publication.[20]

As the Corporation withdrew, plebeian Newcastle moved quickly to fill the vacuum and by the summer of 1823 the carnival was in full swing. The Corporation, the former 'keepers of fools', were now mocked as the 'Lords of Gotham' or

[15] Wilson, *Sense of the People*, p.297.
[16] Mackenzie, E., *A Descriptive and Historical Account of the Town and County of Newcastle upon Tyne* (1827), pp.709-14.
[17] *Newcastle Chronicle*, 16 August 1823.
[18] *Newcastle Courant*, 14 October 1727, cited in Wilson, *Sense of the People*, p.296.
[19] Rogers, *Crowds, Culture and Politics*, pp.268-9; Colls, *Pitmen*, pp.70-2.
[20] Hodgekinson Hinde, 'Public Amusements'.

**14.2** *The Sheriff's Procession* by T.M. Richardson.

'Gothams' Mayor' and the local militia as 'Gothams' Invincibles'.[21] Such irreverence breeds confidence. In July, for the first time since 1789, local shoemakers crowned 'King Crispin'. Great crowds thronged the streets as the procession of 'Heralds, Dukes, Yeomen, Lord Mayor, and Sheriffs' accompanied the 'King' on a journey which involved visiting a number of public houses. Young girls walked in front of the 'King', throwing flowers in his path. The parade ended when 'His Majesty and his Peers and Chief officers dined at the Chancellors Head in Newgate Street and there was a Ball in the evening'. The *Newcastle Courant* was disparaging about the event, remarking that the costumes had to be brought down from Scotland and many of them were somewhat tatty, though it did concede the 'Coronation's' popularity.[22]

[21]  The usage of the word 'Gotham' by Newcastle's early 19th-century radicals is a fascinating topic that warrants further investigation. See *Newcastle Garlands* (1821), especially 'Radical Monday, A Letter from Bob in Gotham; The Owl', by 'Skipper Wagstaff, Poet Laureate of Gotham'. Also *Kilts and Philibegs, The Northern Excusion of Geordie, Emperor of Gotham* (1821) and *Rhymes of Northern Bards* (1812), p.81.
[22]  *Newcastle Courant*, 2 August 1823.

A few weeks later the Free Gardeners' Friendly Society lodges took to the streets. Beginning at Mr. Price's public house in Gateshead, 'They walked in procession through the principle streets, dressed in their proper costume and carrying the various insignias of their lodges, with large branches of flowers …'. The St Oswald Melon Lodge of Free Gardeners carried 'colours and garlands and children with baskets of fruit and flowers were intermixed'. In a manner similar to St Crispin, the Gardeners concluded their parade by retiring to local hostelries.

As if kings and dukes 'garlanded gardeners' and girls throwing flowers were not enough, the most spectacular was yet to come. A week after the Gardeners, the Journeymen Tailors' Friendly Society celebrated their centenary with another procession, but the imagination of Newcastle's citizens was fired by the announcement in the press that, 'We hear that the Glassmakers etc. are to walk here on Friday 12th of September. Those of Sunderland and Shields have agreed to join the procession.' The region then was the centre of the British glass industry and, on the day, hundreds of workers met at Skinnerburn, at the western extreme of the Quayside.[24]

> At about twelve o'clock the procession moved forward in all its novel and variegated splendour, amidst the cheers of the assembled multitude, the firing of cannon and the ringing of bells. The men all wore sashes, and glass stars suspended from their necks, by chains, or drops of variegated colours; the great majority of them had glass feathers in their hats, and each individual carried a glass ornament in his hand. The sky was clear; and the rays of the sun falling upon the glittering column gave it a richness and grandeur that defy description. The first stop was the Mansion House, where a salute was fired from a glass cannon to the astonishment of every person present. The procession then moved to Gateshead as far as Mr Price's house; it then returned through the principal streets of this town and then to Mr Herron's at the *Cock Inn*, Head of The Side where the workmen belonging to four of the five glassworks [were] to dine. The public felt highly gratified with the spectacle.[25]

Many interpretations are possible. The Queen Caroline affair, coronation and Peterloo riots were still fresh in many memories. The Combination Acts of 1799-1800 had pushed trade unionists into other areas of occupational control and solidarity, particularly the friendly societies. Processions were also striking in their use of the 'carnival'. Of course, one could explain the surge in processions by reference to all these phenomena. Getting as much humour as possible into local

---

[23] *Newcastle Chronicle*, 16 August 1823.
[24] *Ibid.*
[25] *Newcastle Courant*, 2 September 1823.

politics was undoubtedly part of the summer parades. Plebeian Newcastle was not going to bring young girls bearing flowers and fruit to the fight, and artisans wearing glass feathers were not dressed for violence. The processions were what they said they were: high-summer, colourful, craft-based festivities that usually began and ended at a public house. They took place in what was still a 'walking city': a city of solidarities and sociabilities. Trade loyalties were still predominant and the parades could serve as industrial connecting points with workers from outside the town. In truth there wasn't much to fight about in the summer of 1823. These were people who were comfortable in their town, who could beat their own emotional bounds and did it without fear of hindrance.

Late-Georgian plebeian Newcastle was a masculine place. The hedonistic, boozy world of the wider coalfield, celebrated in the popular song *Bob Cranky*, became an integral part of local street life.[26] Keelmen, wherrymen, waggonmen and bonny pit laddies were all linked to coal, but in Newcastle coal was generally passing through on its way to somewhere else. The town economy was based more on commerce and services. And early 19th century Newcastle was not as masculine a public place as Victorian Britain was to become. Indeed Newcastle was possibly less segregated by gender than other towns. Women's friendly societies were very numerous. We have records of at least 32 that existed during this period.[27] Women also worked in occupations that contemporaries found highly novel. A woman artist from Edinburgh, passing through Newcastle in 1810, used her watercolourist skills to paint the women hod carriers employed on local building sites. Mackenzie, in 1827, lamented that

> The singular practice of engaging women as labourers to bricklayers and slaters impresses strangers with an unfavourable and erroneous idea of the delicacy and humanity of the inhabitants. As the gentlemen seem not to have sufficient gallantry to reform this abuse, we hope that the ladies will exert themselves, successfully in abolishing a custom so disgraceful to the town, and in providing employment more suitable and becoming for those poor girls than that of mounting high ladders, and crawling over the tops of houses.[28]

Mackenzie would, no doubt, have been equally critical of the women employed in quayside barbershops to shave male customers. The spectacle of strong working men offering up their necks and chins to these switchblade-wielding women was

---

[26] Colls, *Pitmen*, chapter 2.
[27] Newcastle Friendly Societies of Women (collection of articles, regulations, etc. of various Friendly Societies of Women in the North East) 1821-1830, Tyne and Wear Archives.
[28] Mackenzie, *Descriptive and Historical Account*, p.731.

**14.3** Women builders
and roofers, 1810.

a source of local jocular comment and was famously celebrated in the much-loved song *The Quayside Shaver*, where keelmen and 'pitmen with baskets and gay posy waistcoats' subjected themselves to the sharp edges of women's knives and tongues.[29] The Quayside shave was the prelude to the bonnie pit laddie's Saturday night drinking session and, with baskets and multicoloured waistcoats, they were truly bonnie. The 'fish wives', Newcastle's own *poissardes*, enjoyed a reputation for quick, often vulgar responses to male enquiries as they hawked their wares around the streets. Heuphy Scott, elected 'Queen of the Newcastle fish wives', was celebrated in Robert Emmery's scandalous song *Sandhill Oratory*. 'Drucken Bella Roy' played a similar role in the *Sandgate Lass*.[30] Most famous of all was 'Cushy Butterfield' of Gateshead, the subject of the Ridley song that became the anthem to local feminine raucousness:

[29] *Allan's Illustrated Edition of Tyneside Songs* (1891).
[30] See Harker, D., 'The Making of the Tyneside Concert Hall', in *Popular Music*, volume 1 (1981) for a discussion of these characters.

> She's a big lass, an' a bonny one,
> An' she likes her beer,
> An' the call her Cushy Butterfield,
> An' aw wish she was here.

These hard-working women – hod carriers, roof slaters, street vendors of fish and clay, barbers and ropery workers (this last group being particularly feared by single men) – all played a hugely visible role in the local economy.[31] The frequent mention of Newcastle women's variety of occupations in popular cultural sources such as songs and street literature underlines the failure of more orthodox historical records to account for the scale and importance of women to the local economy. Contemporary observers such as Mackenzie in 1827, as well as commenting on the incongruity of working women with the emerging middle-class redefinition of femininity, also noted these women's propensity for organisation. When on the march, radical and proletarian Newcastle was often led by the 'Winlaton Female Reformers', the women folk of 'Crowley's Crew', legendary armourers of local Chartism.[32] At a more mundane level, during an era when 'almost all Newcastle workers were involved in one kind of society or another', whose functions were as much social as economic, these institutions, particularly friendly societies, provided an important venue for female sociability.[33] Friendly societies in 1820s Newcastle were reported to have spent £12 per member, annually, on drink.[34] Women's friendly societies 'Head Meeting Days' were usually held monthly for formal accounting and disciplinary purposes. They typically concluded

> …when old ladies plied themselves with a plentiful supply of stimulants [and] would disport themselves on the likely, gay fantastic toe, to the pleasing scraping of Bobby's fiddle. To diversify their delight he would entertain them with a song, and a professor of moral ethics would have got a lesson had he seen how the more than innuendoes were received.[35]

The pageants of late 18th- and early 19th-century Newcastle acted as a lure to the surrounding districts. As early as 1702 the Puritan iron master, Ambrose Crowley, was so concerned by the temptations offered in Newcastle to his Winlaton work-force that he imposed a company rule which demanded of his managers, 'to inform me when any clerk or servant shall make a frequent practice of going much abroad,

---

[31] For a survey of women's work on Tyneside and a discussion of ropery workers see Knox, E., 'Keep Your Feet Still Geordie Hinney', in Colls, R. and Lancaster, B. (eds.), *Geordies. Roots of Regionalism* (1992).

[32] The Winlaton women led the 1819 protest against the Peterloo massacre. See 'Radical Monday', *op. cit.* On Crowley's Crew see Flinn, M.W., *Men of Iron* (1962).

[33] Mackenzie, *Descriptive and Historical Account*, p.567.

[34] *Ibid.*

[35] Quoted in Harker, 'Tyneside Concert Hall', p.33.

perticularly [*sic*] to Newcastle, which has been the ruin of several …'.[36] Not all regional employers were so censorious. The owners of the glass works in the 1823 procession obviously collaborated, allowing the men to utilise material in what appears to have been a trade-wide holiday. In the coalfield, trade celebrations were numerous. When a new colliery was opened, the first chauldron of coal was ceremoniously accompanied to the Tyne by pitmen, their families, viewers and coal owners, the waggons' arrival being followed by a day of festivities.[37]

Having gained the right to present its own street theatre, plebeian Newcastle was soon to turn the 'coaly Tyne' itself into the town's major stage. Tyne boat races were more than sporting contests. Coaches, ferry boats, steamers, and the spreading regional railway system brought in vast crowds from the Durham and Northumberland coalfield and beyond. Spectators (on both banks) often numbered between a quarter and half a million. Success for the 'Geordie Heroes' could produce near hysteria. Drink and gambling were closely associated with boat racing and local leisure entrepreneurs were quick to service these markets. The growing regional identity, whipped up by national and international success for the Tyne oarsmen, was given further expression in the remarkable number of songs about aquatic gladiators composed by local writers such as Corvan, Wilson and Ridley.[38] Newcastle's emerging music halls adopted a distinctly local style. In venues such as Balmbra's in the Bigg Market, the Newcastle songsmiths helped form England's most distinctive regional musical culture.[39]

This culture was more than a continuation of the old carnival. The city and the region were experiencing rapid economic and demographic expansion. The growth in population was assisted by a large influx of Irish, particularly after 1840. It has recently been estimated by one scholar that over 20 per cent of the population of present-day Tyneside are of Irish descent.[40] Such large influxes did create some tension, but thanks partly to the skill of local politicians Newcastle escaped the disfigurement of ethnic conflict that was to haunt Glasgow and Liverpool.[41] Perhaps the new musical culture also helped. Corvan, often regarded as the most gifted local rhymester, came to Newcastle with his Irish family as a child. Many of the most popular local songs were based upon Irish tunes and the emerging Geordie dialect absorbed Irish words and inflexions. By the 1860s, the streets, bars, music halls and

---

[36] Quoted in Flinn, *Men of Iron*, p.246.

[37] The opening of the railways was also accompanied by similar celebrations, see Hoole, K., *A Regional History of the Railways of Great Britain, Volume 4, The North East* (1974), p.188.

[38] Taylor, H., 'Sporting Heroes' in Colls and Lancaster, *Geordies*, pp.116-20.

[39] Harker, 'Tyneside Concert Hall', Little Billy Fane, *A Life of Ridley* (1985).

[40] Byrne, D., 'Immigrants and the Formation of the North East Industrial Working Class', *North East Labour Hisory*, 30 (1996).

[41] See Joan Hugman's chapter in this volume.

riverbanks were resounding with what the social anthropologist Pierre Bourdieu has termed the 'magicality of dialect'.[42]

As the 19th century progressed, Newcastle's commercial centre moved northwards, up the hill, into Grainger and Dobson's new development area. The grandeur of the honeystone facades, at least north of Grey Street, possessed a popular heart. Newcastle's role as a regional shopping centre has been discussed elsewhere, but it is worth noting the democratic character of the local retail sector.[43] For instance the new butchers' market, opened in 1835, contained 187 butcher's shops. This centralisation of food distribution into what was then the world's largest indoor market, served all social classes. Crowds came from all over Newcastle and beyond to intermingle in the common pursuit of meat and veg.[44] Grainger built sociability into his

**14.4**   Ned Corvan: 'the most gifted local rhymester'.

new town, erecting a music hall and 12 public houses close to the market. A town that shops together presents many business opportunities. First to spot the potential in the crowd that flocked to the market was Edward Muschamp Bainbridge, who opened his draper's shop in 1837 only thirty yards from the market entrance. Marked prices and cash-only trading were Bainbridge's hallmark reflecting trading practices inside the market over the road. Bainbridge's shop soon developed into the world's first department store.[45] Sixty years after Bainbridge's opening, the democratic nature of shopping in Newcastle was underlined when, a decade before Selfridge introduced the concept to London, the brothers Fred and Arthur Fenwick converted their father's up-market fashion house into Britain's first 'system Bon Marché' or 'Walk-Around' department store.[46]

Shopping was an important element in the democratisation of the new centre, but it is interesting how the buildings themselves managed to get under the skin of

[42]   Griffiths, B., *North East Dialect. Survey and Word List* (1999) is a useful, up-to-date account of regional dialect. See also his contribution to this volume.
[43]   Lancaster, B., 'Newcastle Capital of What?' in Colls and Lancaster, *Geordies*.
[44]   Woodward, P.J., 'The Evolution of the Indoor Food Market', University of Brighton PhD thesis (1998), chapter 4.
[45]   Lancaster, B., *The Department Store: A Social History* (1995), chapter 1.
[46]   *Ibid.*, pp.28-31.

**14.5**  Democratic shopping, Grainger Market, 1841.

Newcastle's citizens. Local songsmiths soon devised compositions that hailed the glories of the new centre, usually combining celebration of Newcastle's architecture with disparaging comments about London's.[47] Rivalry with the capital also found expression in songs honouring the Tyne's oarsmen, a crowd-pleasing tradition which continued through the 19th century and eventually found a permanent home in the growing crowds watching Newcastle United at St James's Park in the early 20th.

Although music hall appears to have survived longer in Newcastle than elsewhere, local anthems soon found new venues. Tyneside is fortunate in being close to the coastal beaches. Nearly three-quarters of a million visitors went to Tynemouth in 1875 by rail and steamboat, and these numbers increased rapidly with the subsequent electrification of the railway line to local resorts. The enormity of the building, and the numerous platforms still visible at Tynemouth railway station, are testimony to the seaside town's pulling power. Tynemouth, initially developed by the Duke of

---

[47]  Historians have commented on this topic, see both Colls and Harker, *op. cit.* This architectural chauvinism continued well into the 20th century: see the distinguished lawyer L. Wilks' *Tyneside Portraits* (1971), p.105.

Northumberland as an elite resort, had by the 1880s given up hope of being the 'Bournemouth of the North'.[48] In 1878 the resort's Winter Garden was opened as a concert hall and refined leisure venue for middle-class visitors. According to 'Musicous', the *Newcastle Daily Journal*'s music correspondent, within a year it had become little more than an 'ordinary music hall'. The management of the Aquarium and Winter Garden soon gave up any pretence of being the provider of middle-class cultural needs. They boosted attendance by selling combined entrance and return rail tickets from Newcastle, thus providing for a more popular clientele who were entertained with music-hall songs on Saturday half-holidays. The availability of alcoholic beverages was vital to the financial survival of the institution, but it was also a major source of contention amongst the company's directors. By the 1890s, the middle classes had retreated north to Alnmouth, where their beach activities were undisturbed by the gaze and the noise of working-class visitors. Some built chalets in the dunes and adopted a fashionable bohemian life-style.[49]

The local press had first reported working-class people going to the coast for leisure in the 1850s, many of them walking there. By the turn of the century, Newcastle sent tens of thousands to local resorts on summer weekends. Churches and chapels, trade unions, craft groups, friendly societies, pubs, clubs, horticultural groups and all other forms of associational life ran the 'trips'. Most went to the coast as part of a larger group. Typically the railway carriages, buses and steamer decks were filled with song.[50] Youngsters were teased that they were going to 'Byker Sands', an expression that became part of the vocabulary of local humorists and, reputedly, George Orwell's first choice destination ahead of 'Wigan Pier'. Occasionally the route was reversed and the pleasure seekers, travelling often by boat, visited the riverside meadow known as 'The Willows' at Ryton, or Blaydon's famous funfair 'Hoppins'.

Central Victorian Newcastle, with its bustling stores and markets, crowded pavements and noisy pubs remained a 'walking city'. There is a paradox here: the intermingling of classes on the beach had ceased by the 1890s and suburbanisation, as in most other British cities in this period, had adopted the geography of social class: Heaton and Byker for the workers, Jesmond and Gosforth for the well-to-do. But, 'Canny Newcastle', which for most people meant the centre, continued to play a major role in shaping their identity. As the city became larger, so did the crowd. Newcastle's citizens refused to allow urbanisation to erode their collective

[48] This account is based upon Affleck, A., 'Tyneside Aquarium: Class Divisions at the Seaside', *North East History*, Volume 31 (1997).
[49] *Alnwick Gazette*, 16 July 1898; Walton, J., *The British Seaside Resort* (2000), p.55, discusses this fashionable coastal lifestyle in a national context.
[50] *Newcastle Daily Chronicle*, 10 June 1862 has a near lyrical account of Whitsuntide crowds going to the coast.

sense. The faces may no longer have been so familiar to each other but their dialect and presence and shared understanding about how to behave expressed deep sympathies. Going, now, probably often involved public transport, but 'Passing the Folks alang the Road' indicates that this was no journey into the unknown.

Blaydon Races had been held on an island between Blaydon and Lemington on a few occasions prior to 1862. A member of the Cowen dynasty, whose family home overlooked the island in the Tyne, was the organiser, but this connection did not hide the fact that the event was essentially one of fun rather than 'turf science'. The horses had to swim over from Lemington and the spectators gained access by walking across a bridge of small boats. Early June was rapidly becoming Tyneside's unofficial holiday week. The Northumberland Plate, staged on the Town Moor, was a racing classic and the main attraction. The Blaydon Races on the other hand were more fun and 'The Fancy' rarely graced it. Blaydon's Hoppins, of which the races were just an added attraction, were of far greater importance. Two large beer tents on the island set the tone. The races themselves, which Ridley described a week before they took place, were a washout. Sent to cover the festivities, the *Chronicle*'s young reporter found himself seeking shelter in of the beer tents, where

> Hundreds of people crowded into the two booths … until the canvas was strained to its fullest stretch and people were crowded together as close as wax. The crowd swayed to and fro, as crowds will and as is usual under such circumstances, people bore their discomfiture with great good humour. A few of the gentler sex were safe under the guidance of their natural protectors, and as the pressure of the crowd allowed them no alternative, they were obliged to cling closely to the said protectors: and to do both parties justice they seemed quite resigned to the situation, which the exigencies of limited space had forced upon them.[51]

Back on dry land the revellers retreated to Blaydon Mechanics' Institute where Geordie Ridley regaled them with the song he had first sung the week before in Newcastle at Harry Clasper's retirement benefit concert. The rendition at the Mechanics' Institute included a new final verse recording the day's downpour.

The declining popularity of the Blaydon Races in the early 20th century coincided with the rise of Newcastle's own 'Hoppins' on the Town Moor during Race Week, the races themselves now being held at the new track at Gosforth Park.[52] Paradoxically, perhaps, the decline of the races was accompanied by the rising popularity of Ridley's song. Recorded in the early 1900s by Jimmy Cosgrove, *The*

[51] *Ibid.*
[52] Toulmin, V., 'Temperance and Pleasure at the Hoppings: A History of Newcastle Town Moor Fair', *North East Labour History*, 28 (1995).

**14.6**  *Blaydon Races* by William C. Irving, 1903.

*Blaydon Races* became the region's best known song, the wax version introducing many locals to the new music technology. This song also became the anthem of Newcastle United FC whose all conquering pre-war team was the most successful the club ever fielded.[53]

Soldiers sang it at Passchendaele, Ypres and Tyne Cot, but after 1918 there was little to celebrate. Local regiments had taken more than their fair share of casualties and the region's staple industries were in decline. Popular culture also underwent a process of change during the decade after the war. The strict wartime pub licensing laws continued to curtail drinking hours, but new pleasures were on offer. Newcastle shared in the national cinema boom and swung with the rest of the nation to the sound of jazz and the big bands.[54] New housing estates, improvements in home comforts and the rapid growth of radio ownership all had a profound effect on leisure patterns.[55] Tyneside followed the national trend of drinking less and smoking more, particularly cigarettes.[56] 'Staying in' for many was now a pleasure rather than an economic necessity. Much of the new was mechanically or electronically produced and the geography of leisure noticeably changed. But these innovations did not sweep away older cultural forms.

[53]  See Holt's and Physick's chapter in this volume, above.
[54]  Manders, F.W.W., *Cinemas of Newcastle: A Comprehensive History of the Cinemas of Newcastle upon Tyne* (1991)
[55]  Briggs, A., *The History of Broadcasting in the United Kingdom*, vol.11 (1965).
[56]  Hilton, M., *Smoking in British Popular Culture* (2000).

Music hall in Newcastle proved to be remarkably enduring. Balmbra's remained open until 1981.[57] For the vast majority of people, holidays were taken locally well into the 1960s, and for many 'trips' to the coast continued to be the norm. The Town Moor funfair held at Race Week attracted enormous crowds and local school breaks like Blackberry Week remained faithful to deep-rooted tradition. Newcastle United's occasional league or cup success could also re-kindle the sporting tribalism, articulating emotional themes that stretched back to Clasper the rower. Song also thrived. Children sang, in playgrounds and streets, dialect verses learnt from adults on journeys to the coast, at football grounds and in back lanes. Skipping songs and pavement games such as 'Bays' could all act as cultural conduits with previous generations. Above all, the living language of 'Geordie' helped to structure thoughts and feelings by connecting its users with their forebears. Local cultural hallmarks such as humour, irreverence and collective identity are largely rooted in dialect.[58] Space, place and movement are important elements of Geordie: 'gannin tappy lappy doon the lonnen, passin yem, howay wah gannin tu the toon, we flew past, aw went, an teuk …'. Strange to outsiders, but such words connect Blaydon to Cushy Butterfield, to the 'crystalmen' of 1823 and beyond.

Some, however, were no longer part of Newcastle's popular cultural thread. During the summer of 1931, members of the local aristocracy, gentry and business elite embarked upon a campaign to lift the city's doldrums. The centrepiece was a week long 'Historic Pageant of Newcastle and the North' held in Leazes Park. The organisers declared:

> We want to renew your interest in our past, we want you to relive our splen-
> did history, so that you may be confident, for the present and the future.
> Newcastle and the North are faced with troublesome times, but what are
> they to the terrible seventeen hundred years through which our fathers passed?
> They left us not only the heritage of a wonderful history, but qualities of
> fortitude and bravery, qualities which will make us win through as they did.

The sons and daughters of the Northumbrian elite brought their medieval costumes and horses to Leazes Park and local school children were recruited as a supporting cast.[59] But this was a far cry from the popular rituals of the unreformed Corporation, and locals seemed little interested in the event. It was not until the final day that greatly reduced entrance prices attracted the semblance of a crowd.

Locals preferred the more democratic amusements of the 'Hoppins' to the historic masquerades of the upper class. War victory and FA Cup celebrations again

---

[57] Lightburn, C., *Balmbra's The Hall that Outlived them All* (1998).
[58] Hadaway, T., 'Comic Dialect', in Colls and Lancaster, *Geordies*.
[59] *The Historic Pageant of Newcastle and the North, July 1931* (1931).

drew the crowd, but these were mere punctuations to an atmosphere of mid-century urban quietude. Cinema and radio served to create a high degree of cultural homogeneity throughout Britain. The regions with the richest particularities were generally sidelined by the hegemony of received pronunciation. Dialect, humour and song were still present, but the local stage appeared marginal and unimportant. Chinks of local colour did nevertheless start to appear. Mike Jeffreys, a former student from Newcastle University, opened a series of jazz clubs and music venues to cater for the city's burgeoning student population and local bohemia. "'Be-Bop" from the North East Coast' enjoyed a brief period of success in the early 1960s before being superseded by the new blend of pop and blues devised by groups such as the Animals in Jeffreys' Club-a-Go-Go. Geordie Rock would never rival its Mersey counterpart, but the local references in some of the Animals' work helped in the broader revival of local particularity.[60] Songs such as *Send You Back to Walker* echo the crowd-pleasing methods of the 19th-century archetype *Bob Cranky*.[61]

Paradoxically, it was the homogenising BBC which provided an important boost to cultural renewal. In the late 1950s the radio studio in Newcastle, under the presiding genius of Richard Kelly, produced programmes that successfully integrated local culture with the modern media. In particular Kelly's *Watcheor Geordie* featuring local comedian Bobby Thompson proved highly popular, enjoying audiences of more than a million. Kelly also pioneered the 'vox pop' form of radio documentary, utilising local themes and voices. Rising television audiences, a medium that failed to develop similar local initiatives, rapidly overtook prime-time radio listeners.[62]

Thompson's dialect humour was rich in irony and irreverence and expressed a cultural tradition that had first emerged in Newcastle's music halls in the mid-19th century. Cushy Butterfield would have found the city's streets in the 1950s empty of people sounds, but oral testimony suggests that she would have slipped comfortably into the company at 'Carters' in Nun Street, Newcastle's 'women's only' bar that traded until the 1970s. When Dan Smith announced that Newcastle was to become the 'Brasilia of the North' he claimed it was a slogan designed to lift regional ambitions. Smith, of course, knew all too well that he was stoking local chauvinism that had been a central part of Newcastle culture since the 18th century.

The efforts of Kelly and Smith did serve to produce a cultural revival. In 1961, Frank Graham, a local schoolteacher and Communist veteran of the Spanish Civil War, produced an improved guide to Lindisfarne. The success of this venture propelled Graham into starting a cottage publishing industry from his home in

---

[60] See *Northern Review*, volume 4 (1996) for a survey of Newcastle's 1960s cultural life.

[61] Colls, *Pitmen*, chapter 2.

[62] Sagar, P., 'The Development of Regional Identity in North East England 1800-1900', University of Northumbria MPhil thesis, chapter 4 *passim*, forthcoming.

Jesmond. The majority of his publications were 'local interest', covering the region from the Romans to the present period. Graham had a happy knack of mixing the serious and the scholarly with the popular and his books enjoyed a growing local market. By 1966, he was able to give up teaching and concentrate on publishing. Real commercial success, however, came in the late 1960s, when Graham teamed up with Scott Dobson, a former art teacher, painter, journalist, psychedelic light show operator and habitué of Newcastle bohemia. Dobson's *Larn yer sel Geordie* was the beginning of a flood of what Graham called 'Geordie Byuks'. By 1971, Graham had sold more than a quarter of a million of Dobson's works including *The Geordie Dictionary* and humorous items such as *Geordie Passports and Driving Licences*.[63] *Larn yer sel Geordie* has never been out of print. As Smith politicked, Dobson performed and wrote, and Graham published, another regional figure, Frank Atkinson, gathered together a plethora of objects and artefacts which by the end of the 1960s were to form the basis of Beamish, Britain's first open-air museum. In retrospect it was two men from a far-left background, Frank Graham and Dan Smith, and the bohemian Scott Dobson, together with the left-leaning Frank Atkinson, who served as impresarios of the post-war Geordie cultural revival.

Since the early 1960s Newcastle has undergone an ever-quickening process of social and economic change. Following the demise of Smith the city has also experienced a near collapse of local political life. This mixture has placed huge demands upon the thread that we have been following. Many turned to culture as an emotional prop, others as a form of self-representation. Rising living standards for the majority during recent decades have helped fuel the expansion and refurbishment of Newcastle's leisure industry. Beginning in the Bigg Market in the 1970s, a new generation of leisure entrepreneurs revitalised and gave new meaning to the propensity of locals to move quickly from one bar to another. They may be no match for the 'Crystal Men' and 'Gardeners' of the 1820s, but skimpily dressed in gaudy colours, more than a hint of the 'bonnie pit laddie and lassie' can be detected as they roam the city's southern central area and riverbank. The majority of the celebrants in the 'Party City' are dependent on the public and private tertiary sector for their livelihood. Many come from outside the city and there are always many students in the crowd. They have selected the hedonistic element of our cultural tradition and this is not necessarily negative: by turning the world upside down many women find partying to be a source of liberation. Others find a collective identity that expresses a refreshing particularity. Above all, the city, as it has done so often in the past, provides the venue for self and collective representation.

[63] *Newcastle Journal*, 21 August 1969; *The Northumbrian*, October/November 1971, p.96.

Some commentators have noted negative aspects of local popular culture, seeing it at best as a self-defence mechanism against a rapidly changing world and at worst an out-and-out escapism. This is particularly noticeable when cultural exuberance is juxtaposed with industrial decline. Interestingly, such sentiments were expressed at the 1962 Blaydon Races centenary. The local press had carried stories of expected redundancies at Vickers Armstrong's during the week prior to the event. In the midst of the festivities, on the day before the procession, the editor of the *Chronicle* sent Alan Armstrong, a young cub reporter, on a journey down Scotswood Road. Armstrong reported that:

> Usually I travel along Scotswood Road with my eyes closed to tradition and to the incongruous sight of modern skyscraper flats rising out of the rubble. Nearly everybody does. It's painful … there's nothing to sing or laugh about. Everything seems dirty, old and unwanted, uninhabitable homes stare out onto the road, broken and faceless windows. Shops are closing down because no one wants them any more.
>
> Armstrong's – its clang of hammers and bang of machinery – has gone on for years. Like the rest of the built up road it is black with the grime of industry and sadly needs a clean up …

His next encounter was the district known locally as Paradise

> … Paradise? More like Paradise Lost these days! But keep a careful eye open and you'll notice that many of the streets still bear pretentiously lyrical names.
>
> There's Sunset Street and the sun really has set on this street; Garden Street, not a blade of grass anywhere; Juliet Street; Violet Street; Aline Street – streets that are crumbling in decay, some of them banking up sharply from the main road below, almost as if they were trying to get away from it all.[64]

Mackenzie complained about women carrying hods of bricks, and in the mid-19th century the burgeoning temperance movement was highly critical of the drinking habits of Newcastle's citizens and the frequent proximity of prostitution to alcohol.[65] But, apart from female building labourers, these complaints were not unusual in 19th-century urban Britain. They did not express the same deep cultural unease felt by young Armstrong. Perhaps, in 19th-century Newcastle, cultural particularity was accompanied by its political and economic equivalents; it was part of a vibrant

[64] *Evening Chronicle*, 9 June 1962.
[65] Rewcastle, J., *Newcastle As It Is* (1854).

entity that could control its own destiny. The company that travelled the Scotswood Road in Ridley's song may have been journeying from a pub to a beer tent, but their starting point was the venue for a thriving local culture that produced its own sporting heroes, poets, comics, song writers, singers and musicians. The song was first performed in Balmbra's as part of a benefit concert to celebrate the retirement of Harry Clasper. Up Collingwood Street towards the world's first covered railway station, past Armstrong's factory, one of the fastest growing businesses in Britain and soon to be the world's largest manufacturer of arms, into 'Blaydon Toon' with its ancient 'Hoppins', and 'Geordie Ridley's Show' at the Mechanics' Hall. Built by Joseph Cowen and local artisans, this hall was a founding institution in the creation of mid-Victorian radical politics. It was also the place which introduced the Co-operative Movement to the North East. Blaydon 'Store', the region's first, was four years old when Ridley's bus rumbled past the bottom of Cuthbert Street, where it was located.

The disengagement of Newcastle's street carnival from direct political concerns began in the 1820s. Yet there was never a complete separation. The boozy, celebratory, street culture that has long been a feature of Newcastle was, in the 19th century at least, part of a larger milieu. It may have appeared to be autonomous, to be able to shape itself, but the parade was conducted within the geographical touchstones of economic, cultural and political institutions. Similarly, when not singing about real places, the lyricists celebrated real people: Ridley had to go into hiding for two weeks when Cushy Butterfield and her family, upset by suggestions in the song which questioned her morality, angrily searched the streets of Gateshead for their songsmith neighbour.[66]

Mackenzie's lament for aspects of local life has a contemporary echo. Some find local culture embarrassingly working-class and cast an envious eye at Leeds' claim for cosmopolitan status. Since the 1820s, when the populace took to the streets in droves, Newcastle has been a town whose culture has been working-class with some colourful plebeian continuities. To the uninitiated it is a unique mixture that can appear to be threatening and vulgar as well as colourful and noisy. One Whitehall mandarin justified a decision not to re-locate a government department to Newcastle on the grounds that senior staff could not be sent 'to an alien culture', a judgement that conflicts with the verdict of some Newcastle academics who have described Tyneside culture as a 'well nurtured myth', and dismiss the 'artificial "Geordie cult" of the North East'.[67]

Recently, planners and politicians have devised schemes to glass-roof the streets around the Grainger Market *à la* Leeds and drive out the foodstalls. Meat, fruit,

[66] Little Billy Fane, *Life of Ridley*.
[67] Rowe, D.J., 'The North East' in Thompson, F.M.L. (ed.), *Cambridge Social History of Britain*, vol.1 (1990); McCord, N. and Martin, R., *The Northern Counties from AD 1000* (1998), p.400.

vegetables, flowers and the banter and atmosphere of the cafes and pubs that have been 165 years in the making are to be replaced by espresso and 'festival shopping'. Unlike the academics, the planners find local culture all too real. In early 2000 Newcastle Council announced its new planning strategy 'Going For Growth', the crux of which is the wholesale demolition of the working-class West End and its replacement by two riverside villages designed for middle-class residents. The showpiece of this scheme will be the Elswick Wharf development, roughly demarcated by Skinnerburn and Scotswood Road.[68] Newcastle does face a very real problem. The city continues to lose population at an alarming rate, the middle classes in particular prefer the suburbs that lie outside the civic boundary. This is a problem common to many cities, but perhaps more acute in Newcastle.

The city is a nice place to *visit* with splendid architecture, lots of restaurants and the fun of the party afterwards. But living in the city is another matter. The other side of Geordie culture is not so endearing. The mannerisms can appear aggressive to outsiders and, coupled with dialect, can seem frighteningly tribal. John Ardagh, the noted travel writer, found in some of the rougher pubs an 'alien, vaguely menacing culture that I have felt in Moslem lands such as Iran or Algeria'.[69] Tommy Hepburn, the 19th-century miners' leader, warned against *Bob Cranky*'s drunken excesses and 'passion's fatal sway'. For Hepburn, Tyneside hedonism was potentially self-destructive and was capable of undoing all the positive gains that had been achieved by a culture of solidarity.[70] The problem is that the good comes mixed with the bad. Solidarity and hedonism helped to return the Corporation's insult at the wine pant in 1821 and this heady mixture seeped into Mr. Grainger's new town and colonised the streets of Victorian Newcastle. Recently it has re-defined the Quayside, claiming the post-modernist waterfront for the party. This is no mean achievement when we consider the fate of so many post-industrial city centres, particularly the bleak hulks of many American 'downtowns'. Away from the 'rougher pubs', Ardagh found the most compassionate and community-minded citizens of all the cities he visited.[71] Newcastle remains a beguiling, 'walking city' of 'rough spontaneity', where 'the dominant ethos, the "establishment" if you like, is – rarity! – working-class'.[72] But if Geordie *profond* is to avoid the fate of its Parisian and London cousins it will need to retain both *Cranky*'s 'passions' with Hepburn's ideals of mutuality and inclusiveness. Or else the sons and daughters of the crystalmen, fishwives, bonnie pit lassies and laddies, the Irish and all the others who have enriched local life during the last two centuries may not be able to continue to make Newcastle in their own image.

[68] 'Going for Growth', A Green Paper, Newcastle City Council (2000).
[69] Ardagh, J., *A Tale of Five Cities, Life in Provincial Europe Today* (1979), p.190.
[70] Colls, *Pitmen*, chapter 4.
[71] Ardagh, *Tale of Five Cities*, p.445.
[72] *Ibid.*, p.193.

# 15

# The Reconstruction of Newcastle

*Planning since 1945*

## DAVID BYRNE

Today it is accepted as good policy not to leave an area thoughtlessly to adapt itself to every changing condition, but to so control its development that the requirements of industry, transport, health, culture and recreation are fully co-ordinated to the mutual benefit of the citizen and the state, both in the present and the future. This is the object and purpose of the preparation of a Town Planning Scheme.

(Town Planning Sub-Committee, *Plan for Newcastle Upon Tyne*, 1945, 13)

### Three questions

The City and County of Newcastle is an ancient place which has been remade and extended. The remaking in the first half of the 19th century was so drastic, and growth in the second half of that century was so massive, that it makes sense to see Edwardian Newcastle as a new place laid over an old place. The new place was absolutely the product of industrialisation founded on the mining and utilisation of coal. The Newcastle created by carboniferous capitalism was an amalgam of three spatial elements. The first was the new city centre, 'Graingertown', the regional capital of the industrial North East, the locale of consumption and administration. The second comprised the elite suburbs of Jesmond and Gosforth (a separate local authority until 1974), the residential locales of the commercial, administrative and professional elites of the whole Tyneside conurbation. Finally there was the industrial city, the zone both of industrial production and residence for workers. Newcastle had industries within its 19th-century boundaries but in the early 20th century it acquired two industrial townships, Walker to the east and Benwell to the west, which greatly increased its area and population, and made it much more clearly an industrial as well as a commercial city.

One crucial factor must be grasped in any review of planning in 20th-century Newcastle. The city, with its long mercantile history, is embedded within a conurbation created by 19th-century industrialisation. To a considerable extent the history of Newcastle has been a history of antagonism by the commercial city to the rest of the conurbation, exemplified by the bitter disputes over the control of the River Tyne which were resolved by the progressive industrial capitalists of Tyneside wresting control from the reactionary and mercantile city with the establishment of the Tyne Improvement Commission in 1850. Throughout the history of Newcastle planning, those in control of the processes have systematically neglected the consequences of the city's industrial status – even when a leading figure was T. Dan Smith, a lad from Wallsend. Newcastle planners have at best been paternalistic about the industrial working class and at worst actively hostile to it. The needs of the industrial population have never been first on the agenda of Newcastle's planners, although in the one period when there was a significant element of conurbation-wide planning, during the life of the Tyne and Wear County Council from 1974 to 1986, things were different.

This chapter's review of planning in Newcastle from the end of the war to the present will be organised around three crucial questions:

- For whose benefit? – a question about distribution of resources.
- Who acted? – a question about political agency.
- What made it? – a question about underlying systemic determination (understood here as the setting of limits rather than as invariant causation).

## *1945-74: A city fit for cars to park in?*

The idea of 'planning' was an important component of wartime and immediate post-war radical political consciousness. The British wartime economy had been 'planned', more thoroughly than in the totalitarian societies of the USSR and Nazi Germany. Planning was seen as the technical basis for the progressive betterment of social conditions through the creation of the 'good city'. The failures of 'reconstruction' after 1919 were explicitly rejected by the electorate with the Labour victory of 1945. In some cases, notably Coventry's, wartime reconstruction plans were a response to massive bombing damage; in others, exemplified by Middlesbrough's Mathew Plan, there was a genuine commitment to the remaking of the industrial city as a place of social justice and progress. Even in reactionary and relatively undamaged Newcastle, there was some movement.

The Council's town-planning sub-committee produced a pamphlet in 1945 which explained both the necessity of interventionist social planning and the Council's views of the issues facing the city. At this time planning was the administrative and technical responsibility of the City Engineer's department and the 1945 plan already identified road traffic management as a primary component of the planning process. The pamphlet had no special legal status but the themes identified in it dominated city planning for the next thirty years and continue to be important today. These themes can be identified in the first plan proper, the *Written Statement* produced in 1951 by Percy Parr, City Engineer and Planning Officer when the City was under Conservative control. The first was that of the reorganisation of the road system so as to relieve traffic pressures on the city centre, bypass the city to the east and west for through traffic, and facilitate access for cars to the city centre. The actual road scheme identified in this plan has largely been realised in subsequent years. The second was the improvement of housing in the city through the reduction of residential densities. This would necessitate a substantial relocation of people to overspill estates to the east at Longbenton and to the west towards Ponteland. Finally, there was to be industrial development at Fawdon. However, *Report of The Survey* (1951), which provided the basis for the *Written Statement*, noted that nearly half of all Newcastle's employment base was in public and private services in contrast to less than a third in the Northern Region as a whole.

The authors of the *Report of The Survey* demonstrated a coherent grasp of the actual sectoral employment trends of the next twenty years. They predicted a major decline in mining and marine engineering employment, a growth in female industrial employment, and considerable growth in service employment. They did not envisage a 'post-industrial' future, but rather something very like the actual industrial structure of the early 1970s. Whereas all other North Eastern plans prepared in this period emphasised the need for a diversification of industrial employment, a constant theme in North Eastern public policy since the Special Areas investigations of the 1930s, in Newcastle service employment alone was seen as the basis for diversification. Industrial development had less saliency than elsewhere and over the years was to become even less important in Newcastle planning.

Not much of the plan was implemented in the 1950s. The priority was overspill housing construction, at Longbenton beyond the city's eastern boundaries. In the later 1950s speculative developers again began to build for owner occupation at Forest Hall and Westerhope as in the 1930s. In the 1950s what mattered was greenfield housing construction. Between 1951 and 1961 the city's population had a net loss of 39,600, of which 18,600 was the product of planned public sector overspill and much of the rest involved movement to new private housing beyond the city boundary. The 1960s were to be the period when the planners ruled the city.

## The North's Brasilia

Labour regained control of the city in 1958. Administrative change began with the appointment of the 37-year-old Wilfred Burns as Chief Planning Officer. In 1958 there had been nine planners attached to the City Engineer's department who dealt primarily with development control. By 1966 the new planning department had an establishment of 83 and was engaged in proactive planning for the future.[1] The engineers still had influence, as we shall see, and it is worth noting that Burns himself was a civil engineer by training. Burns' appointment was part of a 'modernization' of City Council functions although in practice service delivery continued much as before and the main focus of 'modernization' was to be physical planning.

The key document of this period is *Development Plan Review* of 1963 along with the supporting documents, *Housing: A Review of Current Problems and Policies* (1964), *The Social Plan for Newcastle Upon Tyne* (1962), and *Plan for the Centre of Newcastle* (1961). *The Development Plan Review* identified two main changes since 1951, viz. the massive growth in traffic and '... the prosperity of the nation which, because of changing demand and higher standards, reflects itself in the need for and possibilities of redevelopment and environmental improvement which were not contemplated in earlier days'. (1963, 23) Three conclusions were drawn. First, the road plans of 1951 should be implemented. Second, the city centre should be renewed, a process which Burns was careful to distinguish from comprehensive redevelopment:

> Urban renewal is taken to mean the process by which a large area of a town or city – say the whole town centre – slowly renews itself and thereby gradually changes its character to fit in with the needs of contemporary society. It is distinguished from the radical changes of redevelopment (which may of course take place in part of the town centre as part of the whole programme of urban renewal) as well as from the status quo of preservation and rehabilitation.[2]

Third, there should be a comprehensive redevelopment of inner housing areas, with 24,600 dwellings, 20 per cent of the total housing stock, being cleared and a further 12,000 being revitalised. It was not that Newcastle had large areas of slums; rather, as Burns put it:

> Newcastle has remarkably few slums for a great industrial city. In fact, one can say that in a year or two's [*sic*] time, the main areas of slums will no

---

[1] Davies, J.G., *The Evangelistic Bureaucrat* (1972), p.114.

[2] Burns, W., *New Towns for Old* (1963), p.14.

longer exist. The main problem is in dealing with houses that are socially outworn if not physically useless, and this calls for new thought in planning the housing programme.[3]

The first part of the scheme was the *City Centre Plan*, which prioritised the continued access of cars to the central area but which separated cars from pedestrians through the construction of elevated pedestrian areas. This came to fruition around the new Central Library with a new main traffic street constructed at ground level over the site of the old Central Library and running parallel to Northumberland Street. The car was to be kept out of the city centre as far as possible but brought close to it through the urban motorway system. Car-borne travellers were to have close access to the central area through a mix of long-stay car parks outside the motorway A system,[4] and short-stay car-parks and metered spaces within it. There were to be bus and railway stations but there was no other public transport innovation apart from the possibility of bus lanes on entry roads to the central area. The potential of the Quayside as part of the central area was recognised but, as Burns put it, any development scheme would '… be less successful if the river continues to run as an open sewer through Tyneside. But there is a scheme afloat whereby the river will gradually lose its unpleasant colour and objects and odours.'[5]

The *Central Area Plan* was the basis of the development of Eldon Square Shopping Centre and the All Saints Office Precinct. The other innovative development in it was the specification of higher education as a key central area function. In part this was a recognition of the existing location of the then Kings College between the central area and the Town Moor, but the new 'Central Education Precinct' was designated north of the existing Rutherford College. This is now the central site of the University of Northumbria.

The Central Education Precinct and the building of the adjacent Central Motorway East had considerable implications for residential areas. The far from slum working-class area of Shieldfield was demolished to accommodate them. Burns was ingenuous about 'socially outworn housing'. For him it had a remarkable tendency to be located in areas where central area-related developments were going to be put. The case for demolition of Rye Hill, the site of the main Newcastle College Campus today, was stronger. This area of early 19th-century housing for the affluent had descended into multi-occupied slums in the war years. It housed

[3] Burns, W., *Newcastle: A Study in Replanning at Newcastle upon Tyne* (1967), p.65.

[4] At this time the road plans involved the construction of an A-shaped system of motorways around the city centre with the eastern long limb of the A being the present Central Motorway East, the Western following the line of the new Boulevard from the Redheugh Bridge, and the crossbar running along the Quayside area. The limbs would be the Tyne and new Redheugh Bridges.

[5] Burns, *Newcastle*, p.37.

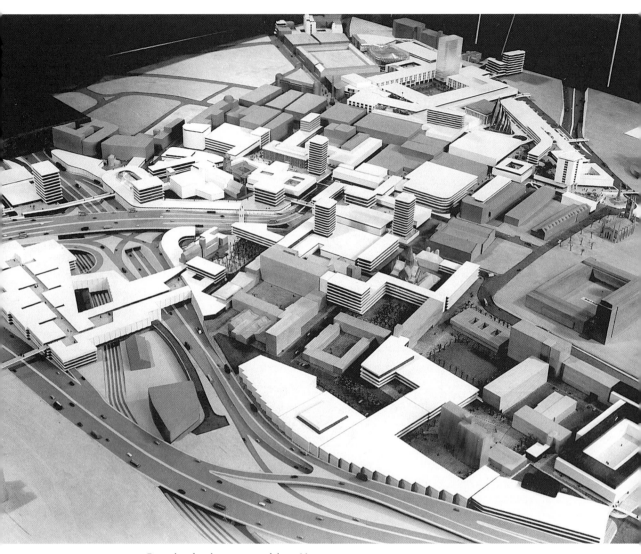

**15.1** Central redevelopment model, 1966.

the city's red-light district, although the great majority of the residents were respectable working-class people. This seems to be the kind of area which Burns had mind when be remarked:

> One result of slum clearance is that a considerable movement of people takes place over long distances, with devastating effect on the social groupings built up over the years. But, one might argue this is a good thing when we are dealing with people who have no initiative or civic pride. The task,

surely, is to break up such groupings even though the people seem to be satisfied with their miserable environment and seem to enjoy an extrovert social life in their own locality.[6]

There was slum clearance outside the influence of central area priorities, along the Scotswood Road in the west of the city, in Byker and Walker in the east, and in that part of Shieldfield beyond the motorway. These schemes were about improving housing standards. Housing densities in the original Tyneside flats of these redeveloped areas were so high that on site rebuilding could not accommodate existing populations. In the West End people were moved to overspill estates at Newbiggen Hall. More than two-thirds of the much larger number cleared from the East End were moved outside the city's boundaries into estates which are now in North Tyneside or Blyth Valley districts. Apart from those who had the bad luck to land up in the now demolished Killingworth Towers, their housing conditions and general environment were much improved and in Northumberland County Council's very well-planned Cramlington there was also significant industrial employment.

The planning strategy for the city's residential areas was built around the concept of neighbourhood units. This principle was applied in a wholesale way only in Shieldfield, Cruddas Park, Byker and parts of Walker. Shieldfield is a rather successful scheme with a health and social services neighbourhood facility providing an interesting core. Elsewhere the schemes vary from the dire (Cruddas Park) to the banal in Walker. Traffic management was central to planning even at this local level.

There was remarkable unanimity between political and technical views of planning in this period, with Smith as the politician and Burns as the technocrat who had added a sociological understanding to his engineer's tool kit. *Housing: a review of Current Problems and Policies* (1964) and the earlier *The Social Plan for Newcastle upon Tyne* (1962), both issued over Burns' signature as Chief Planner, are fascinating documents. In the *Social Plan* there was an exact specification of the issues: 'The current problems which have to be the concern of social planning are twofold: (a) evidence of social malfunctioning and (b) sociological change inherent in a dynamic society'. (p.3) Burns was influenced by the observational sociology of Zweig and it is worth quoting at length from the housing document:

> Sociologists have observed that in the growth of towns the trend has been for a continuous weakening of traditional structures such as family ties and local associations and the superimposition of an order resting on occupational and vocational interests. The contemporary characteristic is markedly of the

[6] Burns, *New Towns for Old*, pp.93-4.

weakening of kinship ties, the declining significance of the neighbourhood in local life and the undermining of many traditional bases of social solidarity. This is the new urbanism which we have to acknowledge and which influences the attitudes as to the social structure of urban areas and the goal in social planning … In considering the nature of this change in human relationships it is useful to recognize three main types of social group. The first is the familistic where the basis of membership depends on kinship ties. The second is the spatial group which is based on persons having a common area of residence. Both of these groups have been dominant in society in the past, but the third, the special interest group, is not necessarily connected with space or kinship and is entirely volitional in character. It is in fact a product of a mature urban society, and is perhaps one of its major benefits. (paras 5.2 and 5.3)

This is a remarkably postmodern conception of social organisation which prefigures in important respects (and much more lucidly and succinctly) contemporary theorising about urban social life. Burns cites Zweig on a very important consequence of this: 'Contemporary affluence and the revolution in housing expectations has brought about the family retreat to the home.' (para 5.6) In the 'affluent society' of the early 1960s we see a planning strategy informed by the sovereignty of the car-owning non-communal household as consumer. However, this is not an undifferentiated conception. The consumer may be sovereign and the right to drive may dominate transport policy, but the planner as expert provides solutions not only as road engineer but also as social engineer with an unquestioned dominance over the people whose lives depend on public provision. Burns was careful to point out that he thought multi-problem families constituted less than one per cent of the population (*Social Plan,* 1962, 4) but even the great majority of ordinary respectables would have to subordinate themselves to the planners.

The translation of these knowledge claims into practice provoked one of the most interesting sociological critiques of planning, J.G. Davies' *The Evangelistic Bureaucrats* (1972). This book combines an outstanding case study of the processes of planning implementation in one neighbourhood with a coherent critique of planning ideologies as a whole. Davies asserted that, 'In Newcastle … planning is an all-out effort to abolish the past and manufacture the future … Planning is, in its effect on the socio-economic structure, a highly regressive form of indirect taxation.'[7] I want to come back to the distributional effects of planning in Newcastle in the conclusion to this piece, but the idea of planning as the assertion of the form

---

7  Davies, J.G., *The Evangelistic Bureaucrats*, p.2.

**15.2** T. Dan Smith, Northern Planner, 1966.

of the future is extremely important. Davies developed his point in a most pertinent and interesting fashion:

> The ideological significance of futurism derives from the fact that it is the consumers of today who must pay for the commodities of the future; and in order to handle the conflict implicit in this situation planners have elaborated an idea of progress in which the future rewrites the present and in which they themselves accord unto themselves the role of the voice of that future.[8]

It is true, of course, that loan financing of major projects carries costs forward to the future, a real justification of the sensible local authority treatment of capital projects in contrast to central government's undifferentiated public sector borrowing requirement. However, the idea of the construction of the future with planners as the creative agents is crucial.

There is an extraordinary absence of 'politics' in Newcastle planning during this period, apart from some minimal Tory opposition to the general expense of developments. The crucial politician was T. Dan Smith and we have the advantage of his autobiography in explaining his role and motivations. Smith was just as much an elitist futurist as the planners. He did not have their technical background but his Trotskyist training had given him a belief in an expert elite and he was happy

---

[8] *Ibid.*, p.105.

to transfer the identification of that elite from the cadres of the Fourth International to architects and planners. Smith was the evangelistic bureaucrats' leading groupie of the '60s, asserting that Newcastle was to be, variously, another Brasilia, Milan or Venice. It is worth thinking about this charismatic and genuinely charming man's position at this time. He was a prosperous businessman with the appropriate lifestyle, including private education for his children, representing a very working-class ward in Walker with which he had no organic connection whatsoever, to this day a common phenomenon in Newcastle politics. What drove him was a sense of 'vision' – vision not so much of social justice as of the 'new' as 'good'. The vision was not his own. The chapter in his autobiography entitled 'Lets build a City' follows exactly the priorities of Newcastle's planners and engineers as stated since 1945, and begins with traffic management in the city centre: 'I have never been a traffic Canute – the modern city needs as much traffic as possible, and must deal with tomorrow's traffic problems today.'[9] Davies summarises the views of Newcastle's Principal City Officer in 1968 thus: 'The role of the elected member, according to this official, is to have the vision to go out and hire the best officers and to support them as they get on with the job.'[10] This seems to have been Smith's approach throughout this period. There was no political vision of any kind set against the technical vision of the planners.

In any discussion which involves Smith it is important to deal with the issue of corruption. It seems clear that criminal corruption played no part in the planning process or in the selection of architects for city centre development projects; this was Dan's dream, not his rice bowl.[11] Corruption there was, but that corruption was through the implementation of contracts and not in the planning process as such. Dan did not foul his own doorstep and operated far more outside Newcastle than in it.

In *Planning Progress and Policy* (1973), Galley, who replaced Burns on the latter's appointment as Chief Planner in the Ministry of Housing and Local Government, described the first half of the 1960s as the period of the formulation of policy, the second half as the period of implementation through legal and design processes, and the '70s as the period in which 'major works are being carried out on the ground'. (p.7) Cherry, an important planning academic, asserted that development was in the hands of a triumvirate of Chief Executive, City Planner and City Engineer – described as 'the men at the wheel'.[12] The car still ruled, but things were about to change.

---

[9]  Smith, T.D., *Dan Smith: An Autobiography*, Newcastle (1970), p.47.
[10]  Davies, *Evangelistic Bureaucrats*, p.91.
[11]  Fitzwalter, R. and Taylor, D. (1981), *Web of Corruption*, London: Granada Publishing.
[12]  Cherry, G., 'Newcastle: City with a Difference', *Local Government Chronicle* (1971), pp.21-76.

## *Tyne and Wear County – an attempt at planning for social justice*

In the 1960s Smith had argued for the establishment of a single unitary authority for Tyneside, still an excellent idea, but the majority report of the Royal Commission on Local Government, of which he was a member, recommended the establishment of a two-tier system in a new metropolitan county. The resulting Tyne and Wear County Council, which lasted from 1974 to 1986, was the strategic planning authority through the Structure Plan, with the new Metropolitan District of Newcastle City being responsible for local plans. The two-tier system generated conflict between County and City, with the City obdurately defending its traditional approaches against very different transport and economic development strategies adopted by the County. Things were to be further complicated by 'Inner City' policies after 1977, the establishment of a Tyneside Enterprise Zone in 1981 and the transfer of major planning powers to the QUANGO Tyne and Wear (Urban) Development Corporation in 1987.

Before the establishment of Tyne and Wear Council a consortium of Tyneside local authorities with the support of central government had commissioned the *Tyne and Wear Transport Plan for the 1980s* (1972). This important document was the first to suggest a public transport solution to traffic management on Tyneside through the development of the Tyne and Wear Metro. When the incoming County was set up and took over relevant highway powers, there was considerable support for cancelling much of the road programme and the Newcastle Central Motorway East was only able to proceed because contracts had already been let. However, important as this different transport strategy was to be, what was perhaps most significant was the County's very different conception of the purpose of planning.

This difference, in principle if not by any means so much in practice, is best illustrated by the *Draft Written Statement for Consultation* (1978) produced for the Structure Plan, in which it was stated that, 'The Strategy has two principal concerns: to increase the number and range of jobs in the County and to direct the greatest benefits to the most deprived members of the community.' (para 5.2 18) In practice there was little attention to redistribution but at least it was mentioned; job creation was taken very seriously. The Structure Plan was not an engineer's document. Newcastle's previous planning objectives were identified in the County Council's review of *Planning Policies in the former local authorities in Tyne and Wear* (1974) as: enhancing the role of Newcastle as a regional centre; balancing the need for redevelopment and conservation; large scale renewal and improvement of the older housing stock; and securing a balance between private and public transport. Jobs and social justice didn't figure for the City.

In practice the main dispute between City and County was over transport, with the County being firmly committed to the development of an integrated system of public transport and the City still endorsing the highway engineer's love of the car. In *District Council Comments on the Structure Plan* (1979), the main issue raised by Newcastle was the level of car parking in the city centre. Newcastle retained authority for detailed local plans and in 1978, in *Newcastle City Centre: Challenges for the Future*, reasserted the traditional commitment to the role of the City as 'Regional Capital' and key centre for administration, retail and commercial services.

In practice, apart from the development of the metro, planning was not innovative in this period. However, things began to change in 1977 with the shift in central government's resource allocation towards prioritising inner-city areas. This new principle of central allocation for special schemes was extremely important. Inner Newcastle and Gateshead were designated as 'inner city' partnership authorities and in subsequent years numerous schemes were funded by allocations under this heading. Partnership funds formed only a small part of total local authority resources but were disproportionately important because existing resources were committed to routine services. Only new money was available for innovation. DOE consultants noted that 45 per cent of Newcastle Inner City programme expenditure had gone on 'city wide projects':

> A large proportion of this borough wide expenditure has been on highly visible 'flagship' projects based in the city centre. Frequently, the aim of such projects has been to improve the city centre – in real and in image terms – as a centre for commerce and new office based service and retail uses and for leisure, entertainment and tourist uses. In such projects, there has often been an explicit focus upon boosting the city's image, both for potential investors and customers.[13]

In 1980 the Tory administration fundamentally changed the basis of planning in England and Wales through the 1980 Planning and Land Act. This represented a rejection both of the comprehensive principle in planning and of the role of local authorities. It was decidedly anti-planning. At the same time there was a fundamental shift in the spatial organisation of cities in advanced industrial countries – edge became at least as important as centre. These two things, taken together, have been of the greatest importance in the recent history of planning in Newcastle. Newcastle has two peripheries – a rural edge to the West and the River. The inner periphery along the River Tyne became available for development following the 1970s

---

[13] Dept of the Environment, *Assessing the Impact of Urban Policy* (1995), p.303.

implementation of the interceptor sewer scheme, proposed since the 1930s, which cleaned up the river and got rid of the colour, objects and smells identified by Burns in the 1960s. This has had profound implications for the Quayside area but developments here and in the east of the city have been primarily a UDC matter and we will deal with them in the next section. What mattered in the early 1980s was the designation in Newcastle and Gateshead of an Enterprise Zone on redundant industrial land.

The most important and immediate consequence of the Enterprise Zone was the development of the Metro Centre at Gateshead as a very serious 'Edge City' rival to Newcastle's retail functions. Equally significant has been extensive office park development, particularly on Team Valley and Newcastle Business Park, as 'Edge City' with extensive car parking. The city centre of Newcastle was comprehensively challenged as a location both for retail and for offices. The 'Edge' became extremely important. Enterprise Zone status meant that these developments occurred without any comprehensive frame of reference and outwith the strategic planning of the County. From 1945 until 1980 there had been a principle of comprehensive planning but now fragmentation was permitted and even actively encouraged through massive subsidies. Structure planning guidelines, which had some democratic content and foundation in participatory processes, could be ignored. This was the beginning of a period in which planning was subordinated to property development.

## *Property-led Urban 'Regeneration' – the rule of the Quango*

Tyne and Wear County Council was abolished in 1986 and the Tyne and Wear Development Corporation (TWDC), a nominated QUANGO, was established in 1987. The one was not a replacement for the other. The County Council had been charged with a comprehensive overview of the development process in the conurbation as a whole, with that process understood as serving democratically endorsed social goals of social justice and employment creation. TWDC was established with the remit of ensuring the redevelopment of a series of sites and was given local planning powers in order to facilitate that redevelopment. The order of priorities was reversed. A full account of the TWDC operations is given by Byrne.[14] The basic principle informing them was laid out by their expert witness at the public enquiry dealing with compulsory purchase on Newcastle East Quayside.

[14] Byrne, D.S., 'Property Development and Petty Markets Versus Maritime Industrialism: Past Present and Future' in Imrie, R. and Thomas, H. (eds), *British Urban Policy and the Urban Development Corporations* (first edition) (1993), pp.89-103; Byrne, D.S., 'Tyne and Wear UDC – turning the uses inside out' in Imrie, R. and Thomas, H. (eds.), *British Urban Policy and the Urban Development Corporations* (second edition) (1999), pp.128-43.

There is, in my opinion, a distinction to be drawn between 'regeneration' and 'redevelopment'. Redevelopment of a site will succeed in bringing land and buildings into whatever use the market determines as the most appropriate for that site at that time. Regeneration on the other hand, aims to create new markets by increasing confidence and attracting inward investment. A regeneration project is needed to rekindle economic and cultural vitality of the site itself and also creates similar betterment to its immediate environs. When combined with other such schemes, it will also be a catalyst for sustained improvement and growth in the whole city and indeed the region. (P.W. Jones, a director of Debenham, Tewson and Chinnocks, project advisors 1989, p.12, para 3.1.4.)

The task of the UDC was to subsidise from public funds the kick-starting of a private land market. In principle the comprehensive plan, with which local plans were supposed to conform, remained the Tyne and Wear Structure Plan but, after the abolition of the County Council, no body owned this plan and was willing to defend it. TWDC were able to ignore it and breached key elements in significant developments in North Shields and on Wearside. Within the Newcastle boundaries TWDC's developments were much less clearly breaches of the Structure Plan's details, but they did operate against its spirit if not its letter in relation to the redevelopment of the East Quayside, especially in terms of the traffic implications of large-scale office employment. In the West End developments were non-contentious in that the Vickers site was converted into a B1 business park which was quite compatible with the Structure Plan.

Downriver of the bridges developments were more radical. The elimination of the stench of the river made the central and East Quayside areas available for leisure. These sites had previously been the port of Newcastle, with the North Sea ferries docking at them until well into the 1960s. However, port functions were now concentrated downriver and there was no opposition in principle to the redevelopment of the site for other uses. An informal redevelopment had already occurred with the establishment of small 'metal bashing' businesses. The planning issues were, first, the elimination of these businesses and the employment provided in them, which was generally blue collar, in favour of office and leisure developments with a different employment base, and second, the retreat from public transport as the prime mode of urban access. There has been no study of the displacement effect of this redevelopment. The blue collar jobs may have relocated but they may just as well have disappeared. In any event the Quayside down to the Ouseburn is now a leisure area with substantial office employment and car access. Beyond this the only significant TWDC development is St Peter's basin, a less than wholly successful effort to create an exclusive marina/residential quarter on a redundant shipyard site.

There is an interesting case study of competing power in the Newcastle operations of the TWDC on East Quayside. Proctor and Gamble, a very large trans-national company, owned the former Hedley soapworks on East Quayside. Originally, Proctor and Gamble were assured by TWDC's Chief Executive that they would have a role in redevelopment, but it subsequently transpired that the scheme required the compulsory purchase of their site. The company took grave exception to what they regarded as at least 'economy with the truth' and triggered a massively expensive public enquiry into the compulsory purchase. TWDC got their way at the cost of considerable public embarrassment.

TWDC's operations were not the only non-democratic processes affecting Newcastle planning in the late '80s and early '90s. Business was given a considerable role by the City Council which operated willingly in partnership with the business-led 'Newcastle Initiative' in regeneration of those more peripheral parts of the central area which were suffering under Metro Centre competition. Most of this was non-contentious, but there was conflict between the City Council and the charismatic industrial entrepreneur Karl Watkins, who had purchased Newcastle's second theatre, the Tyne Theatre and Opera House, from the trust which had rescued it from near dereliction, and who disagreed radically with details of development in what had been designated 'the Theatre Village' area.

The character of planning in this period is identified by Wilkinson's distinction between the

> T. Dan Smith era [which] was concerned primarily with civic pride and a utopian version of the city as an urban machine fit for living in … essentially a modernist vision with a strong social welfare component, managed by the public sector on Keynesian functional principles [and] the post-modern city … characterized by a shift away from comprehensive redevelopment projects, characteristic of the 1960s and 1970s, towards the planning of urban fragments, evidenced in the mosaic effect created by the development of the new urban villages, flag-ship schemes, self-contained waterfront developments and cultural quarters. These islands of renewal also act as highly visible symbols of urban regeneration and, as such, they are regarded by public and private-sector agencies as vital ingredients in the place-marketing process.[15]

---

[15] Wilkinson, S., 'Towards a New City' in Healey, P., Davoudi, S., O'Toole, M., Tavsanoglu, S. and Usher, D., *Rebuilding the City* (1992), pp.177-8.

A certain degree of scepticism about 'place marketing' is in order here. Wilkinson is correct in identifying this as an important objective of planning during the 1980s and 1990s. Urban policy makers had bought from academic geographers an account of 'world cities' as nodes within a hierarchical global system. In this frame of reference the task of policy makers is to locate their place as favourably, which means as highly, as possible. However, actual developments in the fragmented and differentiated post-industrial city seem to have reflected much more the opportunities for profit derived from differentiated local consumption patterns. Of particular significance here is the spending power of young adults dependent on their parents for accommodation and/or financial support, but with money to spend on personal consumption. The East Quayside developments are to a considerable extent the location of nothing more global than a slightly older, staider, and classier version of the local consumption culture of the Bigg Market pubs.

There was another planning process in operation in the City during this period, the implementation of first 'City Challenge' and then 'Single Regeneration Budget' schemes. Three new principles were involved in City Challenge, launched in 1991 by Heseltine after his return to the Department of the Environment. These were, first, the principle of competition in which schemes were funded not on a basis of need as such but rather according to central government's judgement of their potential for success; second, the principle of consolidation so that the massive variety of complementary urban initiatives which had developed since 1977 could be drawn together in a coherent way – a principle taken to its logical conclusion in the Single Regeneration Budget scheme which has succeeded City Challenge; and third, the principle of 'people centredness' whereby urban regeneration was now seen as a process directed at populations rather than sites. However, one of the key criteria in selecting bids for funding remained the development potential of sites within Challenge areas and in some schemes, notably North Tyneside's, this element has predominated.

Newcastle's major City Challenge initiative was in the West End, in an area which seems to have become the UK's closest approximation to New York's South Bronx. The situation on the Armstrong Business Park, which has been a part of the Enterprise Zone, TWDC and City Challenge operations, is significant. This area has been successfully redeveloped as a site but offers minimal employment opportunities to local residents. The Single Regeneration Budget funded scheme in Newcastle's East End is a repeat process in the other 'industrial zone' of the city. Here, far more attention has been devoted, both politically and in public, to development control squabbles about supermarket siting than to the principles of planning for the future.

## *The Unitary Development Plan – the City goes West*

In the late 1980s a new planning system was introduced nationally to replace the virtually moribund system of county level structure and sub-district level local plans. Unitary districts were given the job of preparing a 'Unitary Development Plan' (UDP) which combined the two levels. On Tyneside the regional office of the DOE (later Government Office North East GONE) prepared a set of strategic planning guidelines as a framework for the conurbation in an effort to ensure some coordination in the preparation of Unitary Development Plans. This effort has not been successful to date, particularly in relation to the Newcastle UDP.

The DOE evaluation of the effects of the Urban Programme in Newcastle noted that in general in the North East large-scale incoming industry preferred peripheral greenfield sites[16] and that this had led Newcastle City to make a breach of the city's green belt – 'The Northern Development Area' of 1,127 hectares – the main element in its proposals. The Northern Development Area is a new initiative but it is worth noting that the Newcastle UDP has the same general priorities otherwise as Newcastle's first post-war plan of 1951 with the important exception of a reversal of position in relation to housing. In particular, as the *Report on Public Consultation* (1994) noted, 'It was widely felt that the UDP whilst in principle claiming to encourage measures for public transport, was in fact facilitating increased car use through highway improvement programmes.' Newcastle must be made a city fit for the car! In housing, whereas post-war plans sought to export population from the city, in the 1990s the distribution of Unified Business Rate on a per capita basis to local authorities has led City planners to propose massive housing development despite the existence of many designated housing sites in the city's commuter hinterlands. Much of this development is proposed for greenfield locations.

Newcastle's UDP has aroused much public controversy. It was bitterly opposed, not only by defenders of the green belt, but also by the City's constituency Labour Parties and Jim Cousins, MP for Newcastle Central, a leading light of the former County Council, who argued that the greenfield strategy would disadvantage working-class areas which elected the Labour councillors who wanted this plan implemented. As this scheme was about to be examined by a public inquiry, it was withdrawn and amended into a form emphasising public transport links.

[16]  DOE 1995, *op.cit.*, p.282.

## Conclusion

At the turn of the millennium Newcastle City Council published a green paper, *Going for Growth*. This identifies a long-term direction for the city towards the year 2020 and among the three options of 'managed decline', 'stability' and 'going for growth', opts for the last. The background is basically the financial problems caused for the local authority by the combination of a declining population and the flight of the middle classes outwith Newcastle's city boundaries. On present trends the current population of 276,000 in 1999 will fall to 259,000 by 2020. The intention is instead to have a population of 290,500 by that date.

The strategy has been presented through a video which makes it rather plain that the fundamental problem lies in the preference of many middle-class people who work in the city to live anywhere but Newcastle. Outside the prosperous enclaves of the far western suburbs and Jesmond/Gosforth/High Heaton, the city's population is falling and there are zones of urban disaster in the riverside wards. The intention is to tempt the commuters back by building middle income housing to replace existing social housing areas in the West End. The problem in all this is schools. Outside the enclaves, and excepting the Catholic system, Newcastle's schools are characteristically low-achieving and not likely to attract middle-class parents, many of whom resident in the city ship their children out to Ponteland or North Tyneside or use the private system. The people Newcastle needs in order to achieve its population target are the children of the respectable working class who have left the city or were moved out by overspill housing development forty years ago. They are to be tempted back to a West End cleansed of its existing population by major clearance and dispersal of social housing which means that the character of school intakes might change.

So, forty years on: For whose benefit? Who acted? What made it? – a question of distribution, a question of agency, and a question of cause – these are the questions which have to be considered in summarising the history of postwar planning in Newcastle. Let us take them in reverse order. It is plain that every city is going to be influenced by the character of the global capitalist system within which it exists, but there are variations possible in the form of the city even so. Places can be different, within limits. Even that is too passive a statement. The creation of post-industrial capitalism is as much a product of political agency, including crucial political agency at the local level, as of systemic forces.[17] Post-industrial status has local as well as global origins.

[17]  Nelson, J.I., *Post-Industrial Capitalism* (1995).

The question of who acted has two answers. From the '50s to mid-'70s the primary actors were planners as technicians, with road engineers always having a disproportionate influence. In Burns' day there was a genuine interest in social planning, but the planners always emphasised the commercial role of the city centre as the prime focus of Newcastle's plans. This was the period of the technical elite, of the evangelistic bureaucrats, with politicians as a mere chorus of approval. Only at the County level in the 1970s was there any political input which reflected the egalitarian objectives of the Labour Party. In the 1980s the planners were subordinated to the property developers, who had far more control over planning than was ever the case with elected politicians. Bizarrely, on reflection, I would conclude that the property developers did less damage, in Newcastle if not in other parts of the conurbation, primarily because the sovereignty of the market meant that there was little real demand for the kind of socially exclusive and excluding ghettos of the rich which they tried to develop in riverside Newcastle. This is why TWDC was a financial disaster lamentably failing to achieve the gearing ratio of £3 of private money invested for each £1 of public subsidy.

Who benefited? Not the industrial working-class people of the West and East Ends of Newcastle who have elected Labour councillors from Dan Smith to Jeremy Beecham, all of whom have singularly failed even to visualise a planning strategy directed towards their needs and ambitions. Many residents have been deported, those from the East End to authorities which are capable at least of providing decent state education, but those from the West End to dreadful outer estates. Their neighbourhoods are scarred by car access routes and the industrial jobs which provided both employment and identity have gone. We might say that car-borne consumers have benefited. If we discount the environmental impact of transport policies, to some extent they have. We must never forget that more of the children of the industrial working class of the 1940s and '50s live in owner occupied suburbs than in difficult to let estates. However, Edge City has been more beneficial to them, and in Edge City at least the old planning principle of separation of uses, of industry from housing and of residence from traffic, is much better achieved than in the city's central areas. 'Going for Growth' is about getting these people back but, given the increased significance of Edge City as the location of employment, a significance which will only be enhanced by the Northern Development Area near the airport and similar development at Newburn, why should they return from Whickham, Morpeth and the Tyne Valley to subject their children to the dreadful schools of inner Newcastle? Clearance in the West End must still involve the people who live there being housed somewhere within the city boundaries.

Newcastle may well have gone too far to come back as the mixed class city which city officers and councillors are now pinning their hopes on. The history of planning in the city should show us one of the major reasons why this is so. In the 1960s Alex Glasgow wrote a song, a line of which said that 'an older, better city bites the dust' whilst 'the architects and planners have all saved themselves a cottage in the hills'. He wasn't wrong.

# 16

# *Last Word: Dialect*

## BILL GRIFFITHS

Considerable issues in the development of dialect remain ambiguous: the role of early loan-words from Latin, the origin and significance of regional variation in language in the Anglo-Saxon period, the process of the assimilation of Viking (Old Norse) vocabulary into English, to name but some early examples. In the modern period, a striking case is the neglect of the study of the history of speech in industrial areas like Tyneside. So marked is this omission, it requires a little explanation …

The two major initiatives in dialect study have been the English Dialect Society, whose massive dictionary was published around 1900,[1] and the surveys conducted from Leeds University in the 1950s, the results of which are still being collated and published.[2] Both of these projects concentrated on rural informants and their vocabulary, in the knowledge that a way of life (and its speech) was quickly passing away, and in the belief that rural usage provided the best historical evidence of early usage. But was this justified, or have linguists paid too much attention to the myth of an unchanging countryside? What indeed does the family tree of a Word look like? Do the ancient families of Words really have their roots in the apparently static retreats of non-urban communities?

In this scheme of things, the cities are parvenues, places of lingos of uncertain descent and rather novel status, tainted not just with Standard English (no quarter of the world has escaped that influence) but with an admixture of peoples from different regions, different backgrounds, different cultures. It has been acknowledged that there might be legitimate topics for study here, but they would not constitute part of the *history* of dialect, let alone throw light on the pedigree of English, for *that* was the almost heraldic preserve of rural areas. The formula that 'countryside = older words' has never, to my knowledge, been challenged.

But, logically, why should 'old' words not be found in towns and cities? Would not a pitman adapt existing (agricultural) terminology to new contexts? Thus a *putter* (human pusher or hauler of coal-tubs) seems to descend from a verb *to put*, used of animal transitive action; a *goaf*, or underground space empty of coal retaining its

---

[1] Wright, Joseph (ed.), *English Dialect Dictionary* (6 vols., 1898-1905).
[2] For example, Upton, Clive *et al.* (eds.), *Survey of English Dialects: Dictionary and Grammar* (1994).

pit-props, apparently comes from the word for a bay in a barn, that is, a unit of wooden support structure. And so on. The range of technical words for ship-building attested in the Newcastle 'Noah' Play of the 15th or 16th century is already considerable, and was developed largely from existing terminology: innovation as modfication.[3]

But surely Tyneside speech – 'Geordie' for short – was something 'new', something 'modern', something (it is implied) that developed *after* the rise of industry? This 'alien' quality in the speech is certainly emphasised in an early account of the miners, their habits and speech, preserved in a poem, 'The Collier's Wedding', written by Edward Chicken, a Newcastle schoolmaster, around 1720.[4] This long poem is written in pretty fair standard English rhyming couplets, with very little indication of non-standard usage or pronunciation in the narrative text; but the speech of several 'low' characters is given in dialect, deliberately, to emphasis their uncouthness and roughness. This is satire, at the expense of the 'new' industrial sub-class, though it is an affable enough pose that Chicken takes. For instance, Tom and Jenny approach Jenny's mother for permission to marry:

> Lass, whe's that with ye? Whe shou'd it be?
> Sit still, says *Tom*, 'tis none but me;
> I came to have a little Clash:
> Hout Lad, get Hame, ye're nought but Fash:
> My Pipe's just out, then we'll to Bed;
> So, *Jenny*, come and loose my Head,
> And get some Coals, and mend the Fire,
> And lay my Cods a little higher;
> And, *Tom*, be sure that ye get Hame,
> And give my Service to your Dame:
> De'il scratch your Arse, what brought you here;
> Ye've kept our Daughter up I fear.

What is this old gorgon speaking? *Fash* ('to trouble') is from French, *cod* ('pillow') from Old Norse, *hame* ('home') Northern English, *head* for pinned-up hair, slang. None of this would have been acceptable to an educated city dweller of the 18th century, for whom written and increasingly spoken English adhered to a Southern norm. Thus and thus only is Chicken able to present the talk (and the customs) of the workers of Benwell as strange and amusing. (A few such workers would hardly

---

[3] The original text of the Noah Play was printed by Henry Bourne in his *History of Newcastle-upon-Tyne* (Newcastle, 1736). Most later editors discuss the dating and vocabulary of this piece, including my booklet version *Noah's Ark – the Newcastle Mystery Play* (Seaham, 1998).

[4] Chicken, Edward, *The Collier's Wedding, A Poem* (Newcastle, 1764).

merit notice, but of course pits and shipping were employing tens of thousands of men by Chicken's day, and it was steadily growing.) 'Geordie' was so noticeable not because it was 'slang', or 'vulgar' – though these elements could be present – but because it was unlike, in fact it was *older* than, educated city speech. The industrial workers probably came from *all* the surrounding areas, more or less rural or more or less industrial, but much less influenced by 'standard' English than the dominant classes in their suddenly challenged town culture.

An exact source for 'Geordie' it would be unprofitable to seek. The speakers came potentially from varying minor settlements; the location and density of their population was a new feature, but their talk was more 'traditional' than we might expect. It has its share of Old Norse-based words (*at bank, bowk, bleck, goaf, kirve, kist, marra, skeets, skep, skip, swalley* …) just as rural speech would, and its story is just as interesting, perhaps more dramatic in many ways. For a start, the many inputs into urban speech, though adding to the 'confusion', contribute to (or demonstrate) its flexibility and richness.

Maritime vocabulary, if it is right to talk of such a concept, seems to have played a role – specifically through a smattering of (common) words that may have come from Dutch, presumably by trade contact, through seafarers between say the 15th and 18th centuries. Here we may tentatively list: *cant, elsin, geck, gliff, haar, hoy, kit, knack, mafted, mizzle, plote, pluff, pubble, scudder, yuke* … That is to say, Geordie grows, absorbing words from sources not available to country-dwellers, and probably not of direct concern to the educated classes, so that by the end of the 18th century a recognisable industrial speech is forming, similar to older, traditional modes of speech, but with a specific typical core of vocabulary that is soon to be emulated by workers in neighbouring areas, as mining and ship-building spread. A coherence is established, a special identity even, to be reinforced by printers of dialect songs and poems in the early 19th century.

By the 1840s this speech merited a popular dictionary of its own, John Brockett's *Glossary of North Country Words*,[1] notable for its familiarity with Newcastle usage, and capable, like any dictionary, of shaping what it aims to describe. It is a substantial, two-volume work, and includes many terms that have proved to be transitory:

BEND-UP, a signal to draw away in a coal mine. 'Bend up the crab.'

BYE-BOOTINGS, or SHARPS, the finest kind of bran; the second in quality being called TREET, and the worst CHIZZEL.

---

[1] Brockett, John Trotter, *A Glossary of North Country Words with their etymology, and affinity to other languages; and occasional notices of local customs and popular superstitions* (3rd edition, 2 vols., Newcastle, 1846).

CROCKEY, a little Scotch cow.

DUB-SKELPER, a bog-trotter; a term applied to Borderers.

How much of this is authentic English, how much local invention? *Chisel* for 'bran' goes back to an Old English word for grit-like material, and so is not merely a trade-term or brand-name, though its use here may be a specialised one; *dub-skelper* means literally 'pool-slapper', a neat compound insult. Very definitely, Geordie contains a lot of 'new' words, that is, terms not recorded previously, and with no known 'root' among other languages. This is the important 'slang' or inventive element, which may be motivated by new technology, community experiences, or pure whimsy. Such terms are descriptive, for example, *bullets* for sweets, *cottrils* for coins; or 'fashionable', for example, *kitty* for a lock-up (after Kidcote jail?), or potentially mocking, like *skilly* for porridge. Older words can be altered or used in new combinations, and there is often an onomatopoeic (imitative) effect, e.g. *bang* for 'to hit, defeat'. Why did they bother? Slang is essentially 'private' language, a code, and especially likely to flourish among the group-loyalties of a big city. This would normally be dubbed invalid in a dictionary sense, but is surely a needed generative process. Much of it fails to last: it is noted but soon goes out of currency again. Oaths – the ultimate in fashion – seem to change decade by decade. Yet some of it sticks, and becomes accepted usage to puzzle the etymologist (what is the source of *O.K.*? or, for that matter, where does the word *dog* come from?).

Physically, too, Newcastle changes. The built environment has experienced repeated upheavals, from the days of packed tenements on the Quayside, to the 19th-century rebuilding of its main streets, the spread of population out to the suburbs, or the demolitions from the 1960s and '70s that continue. Already, in the 1880s, James Horsley was looking back with nostalgia on the earlier times:

> They axed if the Whittle Dene wettor wis still
> Supplied te the folks at se much a gill;
> If the pipes elwis burst when thor come a bit thaw,
> and the wives weshed thor claes wiv a pailful o' snaw.

There is also his half plaintive

> … They've torned the Quay intiv a fair; on Sunday they begin
> Te gammel wi' teetotums, an' the Swing Bridge roon' they spin;
> They want te set the toon on fire, an' seun, on sum dark neet,
> They'll bleeze up Earl Grey's moniment wi' Swan's electric leet.[6]

---

[6] Horsley, James, *Lays of Jesmond and Tyneside Songs and Poems* (Newcastle, 1891), pp.87 and 129.

The 19th century was also the age of migration. There may be an assumed input from the many Irish and Scottish settlers in cities such as Newcastle and Sunderland, but this came relatively 'late' – say the mid-19th century – too late, perhaps, to influence core vocabulary, though it may have modulated intonation and syntax. When Mike Shields typifies Mid-Tyne speech as more conventional, and perhaps more influenced by the Irish population, we can only lament the lack of detailed recordings, even from the 1970s.[7] There may be many contributions to Tyneside vocabulary that we will now find it hard to trace: there is possible evidence of Romany connections (*gadgie, shive, chawvor, faw?*) but at what period or in what context is hard to say.

But Geordie – by which I mean the industrial speech of the whole North East – is more than just a matter of sources, intriguing and important as these can be. It is also a question of what language becomes, what it makes itself, what it is used for and what it is perceived to represent. And here there is no doubt the growing numerical, economic and cultural importance of the labouring classes on Tyneside from the 18th century onwards is represented by the rise in status of their 'dialect' speech. We should be careful not to overstate the isolation of this traditional local manner of talking. It is constantly in communication with other forms of English – notably 'standard' English (and, now, American English) – and reacting with them,[8] but it also made a big point of its difference from the standard.

For regional dialect also had a political dimension. Newcastle was a great centre of radicalism (republicanism, Chartism) in the century astride 1800, and local writers were soon emulating the proud achievements of Burns and Scottish assertiveness in 19th-century North East songs, poems and performance pieces. Who can deny the exultation of verses like these, noted by Bell in 1812?[9]

> If I had another penny
>   I would have another gill,
> I would make the fiddler play
>   'The Bonny Lads of Byker Hill'.
> Byker Hill and Walker Shore,
>   Collier lads for ever more!
> Byker Hill and Walker Shore,
>   Collier lads for ever more!

---

[7]  Shields, Mike, 'Dialects of North-Eastern England', *Lore & Language*, 10 (Sheffield University, 1974), pp.3-9.

[8]  An example is the yielding of *Aa'z* (*I'se*) to *Aa'm* (*I'm*). For further discussion of many of these points, see my *North East Dialect: Survey and Word List* (Newcastle, 1999).

[9]  Bell, John, *Rhymes of Northern Bards* (Newcastle, 1812).

Some of this aggression relaxed in the later 19th century as a new democracy emerged, but awareness of identity and dialect would have been reinforced and sharpened by regionalism – and even by an emerging academic interest in dialect – as the century drew to a close. In the 20th century, the role of industrial dialect has been increasingly tied to the image of a 'working class'; in a positive sense, dialect was the proud badge of the heavy industries and their workers up to the 1960s and beyond, when the region still seemed to glow with its own confidence, security and optimism. Sadly, the sudden decline of heavy industry thereafter may have major implications for dialect too: where is the economic basis of worker unity now? Has dialect become so identified with an industrial base as to risk its own survival? It is hard to imagine so long a tradition failing altogether for, paradoxically, Geordie is the best evidence we have for the pre-industrial, pre-modern speech of the region, come down not in a pure, lineal descent as imagined in rural contexts, but by a very convoluted, indirect and tortuous path; yet from the same ultimate styles of the speech of Angle and Viking. It is changing – being eroded, some would say – at an alarming rate; but many of its features, its sounds and intonations, its sentence-patterns, its key words, even its humour, show little sign of diminution.

# Index

Aberdeen, 41
Adams, David, 74,
Adams, W.E., 82, 122
Adamson, John, 302
Admiralty, 41, 53, 58
Airey, John, 25
Aitken, Andy, 206-7
Akenside, Mark, 296-7
Albion Row School, 236
Alcohol, 167-92
Alder, Jim, 199
All Saints Office precinct, 345
Allendale, 8
Almond, David, 318
Alnmouth, 332
Alnwick, 250
Alston Moor, 8
Amber Associates, 262
American Civil War, 114
Anderson Place, 222, 224, 226
Anglicanism, 93-112
Angus, George, 45
Animals, 336
Anti State Church Association, 121
*Archaeologia Aeliana,* 302
Ardagh, John, 339
Armstrong Business Park, 67, 356
Armstrong College, 259
Armstrong Whitworth Ltd, 44, 47, 49, 51, 62
Armstrong, Henry, Medical Officer of Health, 79-80, 148-50
Armstrong, Sir William, 30, 32, 40-1, 81, 85, 99, 116, 203, 264, 268, 275, 289
Armstrong's factory, 34-5, 44, 48-9, 51, 59, 69, 252, 267, 320
*Art International*, 256
*Art News*, 256
Arts and Crafts movement, 229, 235
Ashington, 208
Ashington Group, 258
Assay Office, 214
Assembly Rooms, 215-16, 273, 286
Association football, 204-11
Astell, Mary, 298
Astley, Neil, 317
Athletics, 197-9, 211
Atkinson, Frank, 337
Auden, W.H., 294, 314-15

Austin, Thomas, 229
Avison, Charles, 301, 321

Baily, Edward Hodges, 264
Bainbridge's department store, 37, 38, 39, 62, 70, 330-1
Baker's Coffee and Dining Rooms, 287
Balleine, G.R., 99
Balmbra's, 329
Baltic, 264, 265
Baltic Flour Mills, 261-2
Baltic Sea, 3, 7, 48
Baltimore, 260
Bank of England, 35, 214
Barber, Joseph, 296
Barclays Bank, 35
Barge Day celebrations, 322
Baring, Bishop, 103, 109, 111
Barker, Pat, 318
Barnett's Bank, 34, 35
Barry, John, 130
Bath, 16, 22, 214
Batson, William, 222
BBC, 336
Beamish Museum, 291, 337
Beaumont, Augustus, 119
Beecham, Jeremy, 359
Beer Act, 1830, 168
Beer Houses, 169
Beilby, Ralph, 117
Bell, Isaac Lothian, 32, 72, 73, 79, 87, 275
Bell, John, 302
Bell, Matthew, 24, 25, 275
Bell, Thomas, 42
*Bell's Life*, 198
Benn, Morris, 199
Benton, 215
Benwell, 27, 43, 215, 234
Benwell Club, 181
Benwell Colliery, 34
Berwick, 10
Bewick, Thomas, 117-18, 246-8, 258, 295, 298, 302, 321
Bewley, Jon, 260
Bigg Market, 191, 214, 356
Biggar, Joseph, 130
Biggles, 311
Biggs, Lewis, 260

Biggs, Matthew, 42
Bilbao, 265
Billiards, 171
Birmingham Mechanics' Institute, 277
Birmingham railway line, 269
Birth rate, 142
Black Gate, 283
Blackberry Week, 335
Blackett family, 8
Blagdon, 215
Blake, William, 307
Blakey, Robert, 119
Blaydon, 121
Blaydon Co-operative Society, 124
Blaydon Hoppins, 332
Blaydon Manure and Alkali Co., 45
Blaydon Mechanics' Institute, 123-24, 333
Blaydon Races, 193, 333-4
Blaydon Races Centenary Celebration, 319-20, 338
Blenkinsop, John, 269
Bloodaxe Books, 317
Blyth, 59
Blyth Valley, 347
Board of Health, 78-79
Boswell, James, 300-1
Bourne, Henry, 221, 295
Bowes, George, 299
Bowes, John, 34
Bowes Museum, 265
Boxing, 210-11
Bradford, 51
Bradlaugh, Charles, 122
Bradley, Paul, 262-3
Bradshaw, Lawrence, 312
Bragg, Charles, 38
Bramble, Tabitha, 300
Brand, John, 295
Brandling Park, 83, 238
Brandling, Charles (Sir), 21
Brandling, Charles John, 72
Brandling, John, 72
Brantwood, 122
Brennan, Frank, 209
Brent-Dyer, Elinor, 318
Brighton, 22
Bristol, 1, 2, 3, 7, 19, 22, 51
British Fokker Douglas Aircraft Ltd., 58

British Union of Fascists, 184
Britten, Benjamin, 314
Brockett, John Trotter, 302, 363
Brockett, W. H., 277
Brown, John, 299
Brown, William, 24
Browne, Benjamin, 40
Bruce, Dr. Collingwood, 268, 278
Brunel, I.K., 269, 287
Brutalism, 240
Buddle, John, 99
*Builder, The*, 290
Building Societies Association, 91
Bull Park, 83
Bunting, Basil, 294, 315-16
Burns, Robert, 365
Burns, Wilfred, 243, 344, 346-8, 350
Burt, Thomas, 128
Burton, Andrew, 260-61
Burtons Ltd, 57
Butcher Market, 224
Butt, Isaac, 130
Butterfield, Cushy, 327-8
Button, Joseph, 296
Byker, 150, 234, 237, 258

C & A Modes, 63, 64
C.W.S. warehouse, 237, 261
Cairn Shipping Line, 39
Cairns, Councillor, 88
Callcott, Augustus Wall, 248
Campbell, Mrs. Patrick, 309
Carliol House, 53, 219
Carlisle, 9, 20
Carlyle, Thomas, 305
Carmichael, John Wilson, 249
Carolina, 6
Carr, Ralph, 4, 5, 23
Carrick, Thomas, 249
Castle, 247, 261
Castle Garth, 276
Catholicism, 95, 101, 107
Central Control Board, 179
Central Exchange, 278
Central Library, 82, 240, 345
Central Station, 83, 217, 230, 252,
    272, 283, 285, 286, 287
Centre for the Children's Book, 318
Chamber Music Society, 109
Chamber of Commerce, 62
Chamberlain, Joseph, 116
Chambers, Robert, 196
Chantrell, R.D., 217
Chapel House Estate, 189
Chaplin, Sid, 314-15
Chapman, William, 269
Charlton, Bobby, 208
Charlton, Jack, 208
Charnley, Emmerson, 257

Charnley, William, 295
Chartism, 119-21, 126, 129, 143, 145,
    321, 284-5
Chat Moss, 274
Cherry, Gordon, 350
Cheshire, 23
Chester, 217
Chicago, 33, 55
Chichester, 10
Chicken, Edward, 297, 303, 362-3
China, 60
Chinatown, 243
Cholera, 78-9, 145, 304
Church of England Institute, 108
Churches: All Saints', 216, 301; All
    Saints', Gosforth, 230; St Andrew,
    12, 97, 221; St Anne, 215-16; St
    George, Jesmond, 309; St John,
    12, 221; St Mary the Virgin, 221;
    St Matthew, 230; St Michael and
    All Angels, 230; St Nicholas
    Cathedral, 110, 214, 240, 247,
    264; St Thomas, 95, 109, 217-18,
    265; Venerable Bede, 232
City Challenge, 356
*CIU Journal*, 179
Civic Centre, 219, 241-2, 244
Civil Engineers, Institute of, 275,
    277
Clark, Thomas, 41
Clarke Chapman Ltd., 58
Clasper, Harry, 196, 212, 333
Clayton, John, 34, 72, 90, 224
Clayton, Lucy, 57
Clayton, Richard, 35, 104
Clephan, James, 268, 277
Cleveland, John, 294-5
Closegate, 7, 25
Club-a-Go-Go, 336
*Clubmen*, 188
Cobbett, William, 303
Cobden, Richard, 305
Colebrook, James (Sir), 24
College Sweets, 55
Collingwood, Lord Cuthbert, 281
Collins, Wilkie, 304
Commercial Union Office, 240
Common, Jack, 311-13
Connolly, Cyril, 316
Conrad, Joseph, 308
Consett Iron Co., 39
Consul, Samuel, 55
Cook, Ann, 300
Cook, John, 43
Cookson & Co., 25-6
Cookson, Catherine, 318
Cookson, John, 24, 25
Co-operative movement, 115, 124-6,
    152, 219, 339

Corbridge, 20
Corbridge, James, 213-20
Cordwainers' Society, 323
Corporation of Newcastle, 48, 321-4,
    340
Corvan, Ned, 329
Cosgrove, Jimmy, 333-4
Cousins, Jim, MP, 357
Coutts, Charles, 41, 42, 49
Couves, L.J., 219
Coventry, 52, 342
Coventry Ordnance Works, 49
Cowell, Bobby, 210
Cowen family, 333
Cowen, Joseph, 31, 73, 82, 83, 85,
    87, 105, 109, 111, 113-32, 264,
    268, 308, 315, 339
Cowen, Joseph Sr., 73, 116-17, 121,
    123, 125, 128
Cowgate, 235
Coxlodge Colliery, 269
Craig, James, 44
Cram, Steve, 199
Cramlington, 214, 347
Crass, John, 50, 51
Crawhall, Joseph, 81
Cricket, 203
Crimean War, 41
Crispin, King celebration, 324
Cronin, A. J., 313
Crowe, Charlie, 209
Crowley Ironworks, 17, 23
Crowley, Ambrose, 8, 328-9
Crowley's Crew, 328
Crown, 59
Croydon, 64
Cruddas, George, 34, 40
Cullercoats, 250-1, 256
Cumberland, 11
Cunningham, John, 298
Cycling, 197

Darlington, 57, 269
David, Elizabeth, 300
Davies, J.G., 348-9, 350
Davies, Wyn, 210
Davy, Sir Humphrey, 272
Dawes, Richard, 299
Dawson, Abraham, 72
Deacon, Richard, 261
Death rate, 144-6
Defoe, Daniel, 1, 2, 9, 11, 26, 296
Democratic Federation, 131
*Democratic Revue*, 120
Demography, 133-66
Department of the Environment,
    356
Derby, Lord, 273
Derwent, River, 8

Detroit, 52
Deucher, James, 181
Devyr, T.A., 284
Dialect, 361-6
Dibdin, Thomas Frognall, 246, 249, 257, 283, 302
Dick, Robert Burns, 219, 231, 232-3, 235, 238
Dickens, Charles, 304-5
Dilke, Ashton, 131
Diphtheria, 151-2
Dobson, John, 217-36, 276, 278, 330
Dobson, Scott, 337
Dog racing, 198
Donkin, Armorer, 34, 72
Doubleday, Thomas, 75, 126
Douglas, Earl of, 293
Drewry, John, 37
Drunkenness, 172, 184-7
Duke of Northumberland, 275
Dunbar, David, 249, 304
Duncan, Reverend Thomas, 104
Dunn, A.M., 229, 236
Dunston, 196
Durham, 10, 11, 19, 40
Durham Cathedral, 265
Durham Miners' Association, 132

Edinburgh, 120, 214, 225-6, 272, 276
Edison & Swan United Electric Light Company, 44
Egremont, Lord, 280
Ekins, L.G., 219
Eldon Square, 222-3, 226-7, 239, 265, 285
Eldon Square shopping centre, 64, 65, 66, 345
Elgin, Lord, 279
Eliot, T.S., 294, 316
Ellis, Baxter, 91
Elstob, Elizabeth, 298
Elswick, 40-1, 45, 49, 52, 58, 216, 234-5, 253
Elswick Hall, 216, 233, 276
Elswick Ordnance Co., 41
Elswick Park, 83
English Dialect Society, 361
*English Republic*, 122
Exhibition Park, 233

FA Cup finals, 207, 209-10, 335-6
Factory Act, 1924, 56
Family structure, 164-6
Faulkner, John Meade, 308
Fawdon, 56
Federation of Northern Art Societies, 254
Female employment, 141, 152, 155
Fenham, 216, 234-5

Fenham Park Grounds, 198
Fenwick's department store, 38, 39, 62, 64, 66, 330
Ferry, Brian, 254
Fertility, 141-2
Fiennes, Celia, 11, 296
Fife, Sir John, 72, 76, 96
Finland, 4
First World War, 44, 48, 49, 53
Fisher, Ann, 299
Fitzgerald, John, 177
Fleming Hospital, 109
Food supply, 152-4
Football Association, 204-11
Ford, Henry, 52
Foreign Affairs Committee, 122
Forster, E. M., 308
Forsyth, Jimmy, 258, 259
Forth Banks, 26, 40, 41, 50
Forth Bridge, 272
Forth fields, 83
Forth works, 271
Foster, Brendan, 199
Foster, John, 217, 305
Frampton, George, 264
France, 22
Friendly Society parades, 325
Froissart, Jean, 293
Fujitsu, 65
Fulcher, Raf, 261

Gaitskell, Hugh, 319
Gallacher, Hughie, 207-8, 212
Gambling, 171
Gardam, Jane, 318
Garden City movement, 235
Garibaldi, 114, 122, 124
Gascoigne, Paul, 210
Gaskell, Mrs, 303-4, 305
Gateshead, 7, 8, 9, 10, 16, 22, 30, 31, 76, 214, 265, 276
Gateshead East Quayside, 264
Gateshead Mechanics Institute, 277
*Gateshead Observer*, 119, 275, 277
Gateshead Riverside Sculpture Park, 261
Geck, Stefan, 260
General Hospital, 309
Geordie Dialect, 362-3, 364, 366
George II coronation, 323
George IV coronation, 323
Germany, 29, 42, 43
Gibson, George Tallantire, 234
Gibson, Reverend Marsden, 109
Gilbert, Alfred, 264
Gillespie, Hyndman, 56
Gilliatt, Penelope, 317
Ginsberg, Alan, 316
Gladstone, W., 249

Glasgow, 50, 265
Glasgow, Alex, 314, 360
Glasse, Hannah, 300
Glassmakers' parade, 325
Goldsmith, Alexander, 296
Goldsmith, Oliver, 300
Golf, 199-200, 201
Gomeldon, Francis, 299
Gomeldon, Jane, 299
Gormley, Antony, 265
Gosforth, 216, 234
Gosforth Park, 194, 200-1
Government Office North East, 357
Graham, Frank, 336-7
Graham, Gillespie, 218
Grainger Market, 38, 224, 330, 339-40
Grainger, Richard, 22, 34, 213-44, 249, 257, 278, 285, 330, 340
Grainger Town, 243
Grand Junction Railway, 273
*Graphic, The*, 288
Gray, Thomas, 246
Great North Run, 198
Green, Benjamin, 224, 249
Green, John, 224, 237, 249, 278
Greenhow, Dr. Thomas, 98, 305
Gregson, Thomas, 77, 82, 88
Grey, William, 295
Grey's Monument, 249, 250, 264, 275, 277, 284, 287
Grieve, George, 19
Grigson, Jane, 300
*Guardian*, 189, 289
Guildhall, 74, 220
Guildhall riots, 321
Guilot, Claud, 296
Gunn, Thom, 316
Gurney, Ivor, 309

Hackworth, Timothy, 271, 273
Hadrian's Wall, 293
Hall, Sir John, 204, 210, 243
Hamilton, Richard, 254-5
Hamilton, Thomas, 218
Hancock Museum, 109
Hanover Square, 98
Hanover Street , 262
Hanover Street warehouses, 236
Harney, George Julian, 120-1, 122, 127
Harris, J.J., 74
Harris, Joseph, 22
Harris, Richard, 261
Harrison, T.E., 278
Harrison, Thomas, 217
Harrison, Tom, 259
Harton Coal Co., 34
Hartwell, C. L., 264-5

Harvey, F. W., 236
Harvey, Joe, 210
Hatoum, Mona, 260
Hatton Art Gallery, 258
Hawks, Crawshay, 267
Hawks Family, 8
Hawthorn, 34, 39, 40, 41, 267
Hawthorn & Leslie, 49, 50, 59
Hawthorn Company, 26
Hawthorn, Robert, 26, 34
Hawthorn, William, 26
Haydon, Benjamin Robert, 279-80
Headlam, Thomas, 72, 77, 81
Health of Towns Commission, 83
Healy, Timothy, 130
Heaton, 183, 234-5
Heaton Anti-Licensing Council, 175
Heaton Hall, 85, 215
Heaton Park, 85
Hebblethwaite, Ginger, 311
Hebburn, 40
Hedley & Sons, 55
Hedley, Ralph, 257-8
Hedley, Thomas, 72
Hedley, William, 269, 273
Henderson, Arthur, 50, 74
Hepburn, Tommy, 340
Herbert, Simon, 260
Hernaman, John, 303
Heseltine, Michael, 356
Heslop, Harold, 310
Hetton, 269
Hexham, 20
Hicks, H.L., 232
Hicks, W.S., 229
Higginbottom, A.H., 177
High Bridge Chapel, 97
High Heaton, 236
High Level Bridge, 228, 238, 262, 283, 285, 287
Hinde, John Hodgson, 276
HMS Greyhound, 20
HMS Martin, 20
Hockey, 201
Hockin, C., 237
Hodgkin's Bank, 34, 35
Hodgson, 284
Hodgson, James, 72
Hodgson, John, 216
Holland, 3, 51, 57
Holland, Sir Henry, 303
Holy Cross, 232
Holy Jesus Hospital, 238
Holyoake, G.J., 122, 126
Homer, Winslow, 256
Hone, William, 97
Horse racing, 193-4, 333
Horsley, John, 299
Hospital of Mary Magdalene, 109

Household structure, 164-6
Housing, 87-8, 165-6, 235
Howden, 18
Howick, Lord, 272
Hudson, George, 268-9, 272, 287
Hudspeth, Frank, 207
Hugh of Newcastle, 293
Hughes, Robert, 260, 318
Hull, 10, 20, 21
Hume, Cardinal Basil, 209
Hunter, Jill, 199
Hunting & Sons Ltd., 64
Hurry family, 18
Hyndman, H.R., 131

Illustrated London News, 287
Imperial Group Ltd., 56, 237
India, 60
Industrial Bank Ltd., 35
Infant mortality, 146-8
Inter-Cities Fairs Cup, 210
Ireland, 128-31
Irish Home Rule, 114
Irish migrants, 79, 105, 114, 129-30, 151, 155, 159-63, 329-30, 365
Irish Republican Brotherhood, 129
Italy, 51

Jackson the Tailor, 57
Jacobsen, Arne, 239
Jacobson, Lionel, 57
James, Henry, 307
Japan, 59
Jarrow Staithes, 48
Jeffreys, Mike, 336
Jesmond, 216, 234
Jesmond Dene, 85
Jesmond Vale, 182
Joad, Professor, C.E.M., 313
Jobling, William, 314
Johannesburg, 45
John, Goscombe, 264
Johns, W. E., 311
Johnson, R.J., 229-30, 236
Johnson, Samuel, 296, 300, 301
Joicey, J. & G., 40
Jonson, Ben, 294

Kapoor, Anish, 265
Keegan, Kevin, 210
Kelly, Richard, 336
Kenyon, George, 241-2
Killingworth, 214, 269, 347
Kimpster, J.J., 37
King's College, 254, 256, 345
Kingsley, Charles, 247
Kinraid, Charley, 304
Kipling, Rudyard, 309
Kirkup, Wendy, 260

Knox, John, 294
Kockums, 59
Konttinen, Sirkka-Liisa, 258
Korean War, 59
Kossuth, 114, 122, 124

Labour Representation Committee, 132
Lacy, Richard, 19
Laing, Alexander, 177
Laing Art Gallery, 177, 245, 254, 258, 265
Laird, Joseph Cuthbert, 73
Lambert, R., 34
Landells, Ebenezer, 302
Larkin, Charles, 119
Laverick, Mary, 72
Lawrence, Jim, 207
Le Corbusier, 244
Leazes Park, 83, 243
Leazes Terrace, 223, 276
Leeds, 39, 45, 51, 57, 66, 217, 269
Lehmann, Rosamond, 311
Leigh, Doris, 311
Lemington, 25
Leslie, Andrew, 40, 41
Leventon, Rosie, 262
Lewis & Albany, 37
Liberation Society, 122
Libraries, 81-3
Liddel, Henry George, 275
Liddel, Henry Thomas, First Earl Ravensworth, 275
Lightfoot, Bishop, 111
Linton, W. J., 121-2
Lisbon, 6
Listener, The, 258
Literary and Philosophical Society, 99, 118, 168, 277, 286, 301, 314
Live Theatre, 317
Liverpool, 20-2, 24, 51, 217, 219, 260, 273
Livesey, Joseph, 169
Lloyd George, David, 49, 50
Lloyds, 35, 36
Local Government, 71-92
Locke, Joseph, 273, 287
Lockhart's Cocoa Rooms, 200
Locus+, 260
Lord's Day Observance Society, 108
Lomas, John, 43
London, 2, 3, 9, 13, 21, 22, 23, 24, 29, 39, 41, 44, 55, 56, 64, 66, 225
London and North Eastern Railway, 33
London Lead Company, 8
Londonderry, Lord, 99
Longbenton, 66
Losh, James, 72, 99, 102

Losh, William, 25, 31, 40, 42, 43
Lough, John Graham, 267-92 *passim*
Lyon, Robert, 259

Macdonald, Malcolm, 210
Mackenzie, E., 102, 222, 326, 328, 339
Macklin, Thomas Eyre, 265
Macky, John, 12
Madge, Charles, 259
Malmö, 59, 265
Malory, Sir Thomas, 293
Malton, 21
Manchester, 22, 40, 51, 217, 219, 273, 274, 269
Mansion House, 74
Marat, Jean Paul, 299-300, 321
Marks and Spencer, 63-4
Marks, Sir Croydon, MP, 50
Marriage, 138-141
Marseilles, 6
Martin, John, 245-6, 248, 264, 265
Martin, John, MP, 130
Martineau, Harriet, 305
Marx, Karl, 312
Matthew, Sir Robert, 239-40
Maude, Thomas, 19
Maudslay Son & Field, 41
Mazzini, 114, 120-1
McColl, Bob, 206-7
McCracken, Bill, 207
McCracken, Esther, 313
McDiarmid, Hugh, 316
McLellan, J.C., 53
McLeod, Mike, 199
MEA House, 240
Mechanical Engineers, Institute of, 275
*Mechanics Magazine*, 273
Medical Officer of Health, 79-80, 283
Melbourne, 33
Melville, James, 294
Merriman, Henry Seton, 308
Merz & McLellan, 33, 53
Merz, Charles, 33, 34, 43, 55
Merz, Theodore, 44, 53
Mess, Henry, 47
MetroCentre, Gateshead, 214, 353, 355
Middle Street School, 236
Middlesbrough, 57, 342
Middleton, Jane, 299
Migration, 137, 154-63
Milbanke, Judith, 9
Milburn, Jackie, 198, 208-9, 211-12
Mill, John Stuart, 114
Mitchell & Co, Charles, 41
Mitchell, Charles, 40, 41, 42
Mitchell, W.A., 119
Mitford Street School, 236
Modern Movement, 232
Modernism, 236

Montagu colliery, 48, 68
Montagu, Elizabeth, 24, 300
Moot Hall, 220
Morden Tower, 316
Morley, John, 132
Morpeth, 1
Morpeth to Newcastle road race, 198
Morris, William, 294
Morrison, Robert, 41
Mortality, 141-52
Mosley Street, 12
Mott, Hay and Anderson, 232
Motum, Hill, 90
Municipal Corporation Act 1835, 71, 75
Munitions, Ministry of, 53
Munitions of War Act, 1915, 49
Murray, Grace, 301
Murray, Matthew, 269
Murray, Reverend James, 97-8, 118, 300-1
Museum of Natural History, 286
Music halls, 329-30, 335

Naldi, Pat, 260
Nash, J., 22, 225
*Nation*, 130
National Land League of Great Britain, 130
Natural History Society, 99
Neville Hall, 229
New York, 5, 9
New Zealand Shipping and Federal Line, 51
Newburn, 7
Newburn Club, 180
Newcastle and Carlisle Railway, 31, 272
Newcastle and Darlington Junction, 272
Newcastle & District Electrical Lighting Co., 33
Newcastle and Gateshead Gas Company, 72
Newcastle and Gateshead Tramways and Carriage Company Limited, 86
Newcastle and Gateshead Union Gas Co., 34
Newcastle and Gateshead Water Co. (previously Whittle Dean Water Co.), 34
Newcastle and the North, Historic Pageant of, 335
Newcastle, Berwick and North Shields Railway, 236
Newcastle Breweries, 182
Newcastle Brown Ale, 184, 189
Newcastle Business Park, 353
Newcastle Central Motorway, 351

Newcastle Chamber of Commerce, 30, 31
*Newcastle Chronicle*, 115, 118, 126-7, 130, 172, 286, 333
Newcastle City Council, 60, 65, 68, 127, 339
Newcastle College, 345
Newcastle Co-operative Society, 63
Newcastle Corporation, 48, 321-4, 340
*Newcastle Courant*, 119, 324
*Newcastle Daily Chronicle*, 73, 105
Newcastle, Diocese of, 111
Newcastle Dispensary, 145
Newcastle East End Football Club, 204-6
*Newcastle Evening Chronicle*, 338
Newcastle Free Public Library, 257
Newcastle initiative, 355
*Newcastle Journal*, 118
Newcastle Liberal Association, 130, 131, 132
Newcastle Mechanics' Institute, 99, 123, 277
Newcastle Polytechnic, 66
Newcastle Protection & Indemnity Association, 36
Newcastle Repertory, 313
Newcastle, Shields and Union Bank, 35
Newcastle Ship Building Company, 50
Newcastle Society of Antiquaries, 275, 302
*Newcastle Standard*, 119
Newcastle Stock Exchange, 66
Newcastle Trades Council 1973-74, 74
Newcastle United FC, 204-10, 331, 243
Newcastle University, 66
Newcastle-upon-Tyne Electric Supply Company (NESCo), 33, 34, 53
Newcastle upon Tyne Permanent Building Society, 63
*Newcastle Weekly Chronicle*, 122, 179
Newcastle West End Football Club, 204-6
Newcastle Working Men's Club, 177
Newton, David, 301
Newton, Dr. Henry, 78, 82, 83
Newton, William, 215-20, 277-8
Noble, Andrew, 44
Noble, Sir Andre, 308
Nonconformity, 93-112
Norman, F.R., 112
North British Railway, 272
North East Electrical Supply Company, 53, 219
North Eastern Banking Co., 35
North Eastern Railway, 32, 267, 278, 286

North Midland railway line, 269
North of England Home Service, 57
North of England Institute of
    Mining and Mechanical
    Engineers, 286
North of England Iron Steam Ship
    Association, 36
North of England Temperance
    League, 171
North Shields, 7, 16, 17, 18, 19, 20,
    76, 354
North Tyneside, 347
Northern Clubs Federation Brewery,
    181, 188
Northern Counties Bank, 35
Northern Counties Building Society,
    63
*Northern Democrat*, 132
Northern Development Area, 359
Northern Industrial Group (NIG),
    58, 60
*Northern Liberator*, 119
Northern Political Union, 119
Northern Reform Union, 125
Northern Rock Building Society, 64,
    67
*Northern Star*, 119
Northern Stock Exchange, 66
*Northern Temperance Advocate*, 168-9
*Northern Tribune*, 122, 132
Northern Union of Mechanics
    Institute, 124
Northumberland, 10, 11, 24, 25
Northumberland and Durham
    District Bank, 34
Northumberland County Council,
    232, 347
Northumberland Hussars Yeomanry,
    275
Northumberland Public House
    Trust, 176
Northumberland Street, 62, 63, 64,
    66, 276
Northumberland, Duke of, 275, 280
Norwich Union Office, 240
Nun's Field, 221, 226

Occupational structure, 134-5
O'Connor, Feargus, 119, 284
Olav V, King, Norway, 242
Oliver Leeson & Wood, 230
Oliver, Thomas, 222, 226-7, 231,
    276
Openshaw, 49
Orwell, George, 311-12, 332
Oslo City Hall, 242
Ouseburn, 9, 25, 41, 249, 354
Owen, Robert, 99
Oxclose Colliery, 40

Paine, Thomas, 118
Palmer, Charles Mark, 116
Pandon Dene, 77
Parker, Henry Perlee, 248, 251, 256,
    258
Parks, 83-5
Parr, Percy, 342
Parson's, 51, 59, 60
Parsons Ltd, C.A., 238
Parsons, Charles Algernon, 34, 51,
    58, 116
Party City, 191-2, 321
Pasmore, Victor, 254-5
Pease family, 34-5, 100
Pease, Edward, 271
Pedestrianism, 194-5, 198
Pendower Estate, 235
Penydarran, Merthyr Tydfil, 269
People's Theatre, 309, 313, 314
Pevsner, Sir Nikolaus, 238
Philipson, Hilton, 44
Phillipson, Ralph Park, 90
Pickard, Tom, 316
*Planet*, 271
Plater, Alan, 314
Playfair, W.H., 218
Plummer, Benjamin, 79-80, 81
Plummer's Flax Mill, 236
Pollock, Jackson, 266
Poor Law Guardians, 78-9
Pope Pius II, 293
Population growth, 135-8
Portsmouth, 16
Potshare bowling, 195
Potter, A.L., 34, 40
Potter, Addison, 81, 85
Pound, Ezra, 315
Priestley, J.B., 213, 218, 309, 313,
    314
Pritchett, C.I., 312
Proctor and Gamble, 55, 355
Prostitution, 172
Public Health Act 1848, 78
Public Health Act 1872, 80
Public Houses: Addison, 177;
    Adelaide, 167; Argyle House, 171;
    Carters, 336; Corner House, 183;
    County Hotel, 181; Crows Nest,
    190; Delaval Arms, 176; Denton
    Hotel, 183; Dues Bar, 170;
    Empress, 189; Freemasons Arms,
    187; Grace Inn, 170; Grand
    Hotel, 177, 181; Green Tree, 182,
    185; Gun, 187; Howlett Hall, 187;
    Hydraulic Crane, 187; Joe
    Wilson's, 167; Mechanics, 187;
    Moulders, 187; New Hawk Inn,
    173; North British, 190;
    Northumberland Arms, 189;

Nursery Cottage, 176; Portland
    Arms, 173, 176; Queen's Head,
    275; Raby, 177; Rifle, 187; Royal
    Station Hotel, Byker, 170; Royal
    Turk's Head, 181; Runnymede,
    187; Shipwrights, 187; Turnpike,
    187; Wheatsheaf Hotel, 183

Quayside, 48, 63, 67, 68, 191, 196,
    214, 230, 236, 237, 240, 260-3,
    283, 296, 327, 340, 345, 353-4,
    355, 356
Quayside Explosion of 1854, 80-1
Queen Caroline disturbances, 321,
    323
Queen Victoria, 264, 303
Queirós, Eça de, 307
Quoits, 171

Rabbit coursing, 198
Race Week, 169
Rainhill trials, 269, 271, 273
Ravensworth, Lord, 268, 278
*Red Republican*, 120
Redheugh Bridge, 261
Reid, Dr. D.R., 77, 83, 145, 150
Reid, John, 265
Religious attendance, 1881, 106
Religious Census, 1851, 93-4
Renforth, James, 196
Rennie, John, 19
Reynolds, Sir Joshua, 279
Reyrolle Ltd., 58
Rhys, Ernest, 307
Rich, F.W., 230, 236
Richardson, Edward, 42
Richardson, John Wigham, 33, 41,
    42, 45
Richardson, Joshua, 273
Richardson, T.M. Jr., 249
Richardson, Thomas Miles, 248-9,
    250-1, 253
Ridley family, 25
Ridley, Geordie, 193, 327-8, 329
Ridley, Lord, 58, 64
Ridley, (Sir) Mathew White, 25, 215,
    275, 280
Roberts, Michael, 314
Robinson, J., 62
Robson, Joseph, 303
Rock Building Society, 63, 64
Roker Park, 206
Rose, Colin, 261
Rossetti, Christina, 306
Rossetti, Dante Gabriel, 306-7
Rowe, William, 18
Rowing, 195-7
Rowntree Mackintosh, 56
Royal Academy, 279

Royal Arcade, 22, 222, 232, 238, 240, 309
Royal Commission on the Health of Towns 1845, 81
Royal Mint, 214
Royal Ordnance, 49
Rugby League, 204
Rugby Union, 203-4
Runciman, Lesley, 311
Ruskin, John, 246-7, 290
Russell, William Clark, 307-8
Rutherford College, 345
Rutherford Grammar School, 236
Rutherford, Dr. J. H., 79
Rutherford, Jackie, 207
Ryle, J. C., 99
Ryton Willows, 332

Safety lamp, 272
St Anthony's Quay, 17, 26
St James's Hall, 210
St James's Park, 204-5
St Mary's Place, 217
St Peter's Basin, 354
St Peter's Engine Works, 50
St Peter's Marine Engine Works, 41
Sallyport Tower, 261
Sanderson, Richard Burdon, 81
Sandgate, 6, 9, 14, 383
Sandhill, 2
Sanitary Association, 78
Saturday Flesh Market, 10
Scandinavia, 10, 47
Scarborough, 2
Scarlet fever, 151-2
School of Art, 286
School of Design, 253
School sports, 201-2
Scotland, 31
Scotswood, 48, 58, 60
Scotswood Road, 64, 176, 182, 186-7, 319-20, 338-9
Scott, Sir Walter, 276, 294, 303
Scott, Walter (publisher), 307
Scott, William (Lord Stowell), 300
Scott, William Bell, 252-4, 257, 287, 305-6
Scottish and Newcastle Breweries Ltd., 189
Scottish migrants, 105, 159-63, 365
Scotus, John Dunns, 293
Seaham, 30
Second World War, 40, 48, 55, 56, 57
Sefton, Lord, 273
Seven Years War, 24
Sewers, 150
Shaw, George Bernard, 309
Shearer, Alan, 210
Sheffield, 8, 23

Shelley, Mary, 303
Shepherd, Jack, 254
Sheppard, R., 238
Sheriff Hill, Gateshead, 322
Shieldfield, 182
Shipbuilding Employers' Federation, 51
Shopping, 330-1
Shotley Bridge, 250
Siddeley Deasey Motor Company, 52
Siddons, Mrs, 280
Sidney, Sir Philip, 294
Siemens Ltd., 60, 65
Silkin, John, 317
Single Regeneration Budget, 356
Sitwell, Osbert, 291
Skinnerburn Glassworks, 25
Skipsey, Joseph, 306-7
Slack, Thomas, 298
Slums, 347
Smallpox, 145, 150
Smiles, Samuel, 268-9, 273
Smith, Janet Adam, 258, 314
Smith, T. Dan, 64, 65, 66, 243, 319-20, 336-7, 342, 347, 349-50, 355, 359
Smiths Dock, 59
Smollett, Tobias, 296, 300
Social Security, Ministry of, 66
Society of Antiquaries, 275, 302
Sorsbie, Benjamin, 236
South Africa, 55
South Shields, 7, 16, 17, 18, 19, 20, 30, 76
Spain, Nancy, 313
Spence, Sir Basil, 239-40
Spence, Thomas, 97, 117, 302, 321
Spiller's Mill, 55
Sport, 193-212
Sport centres, 202
Stephen, John, 75
Stephens, Superintendent, 284
Stephenson & Co., Robert, 39
Stephenson, David, 216-20, 276, 301
Stephenson, George, 25, 99, 116, 251, 267-92
Stephenson, Ian, 254
Stephenson, John, 224
Stephenson, Robert, 31, 116, 252, 269, 276, 278
Stephenson, William Haswell, 73, 82
Stephenson's & Hawthorn's Works, 83
Stevenson, James Cochran, 44
Stock and Shareholders Association, 36
Stock Exchange, The, 67
Stockholm City Hall, 242
Stockton, 38, 76, 269, 271
Stoker, Bram, 307

Stokoe, John, 216, 220
Stokoe, William, 216
Storey, David, 254
Strakers family, 40
Strakers, John Coppin, 35
Studio, 256
Suez crisis, 59
Sullivan, Alex, 130
Sunderland, 16, 23, 30, 76
Sunderland Football Club, 206, 207
Surtees, Aubone, 34
Sutherland, Duke of, 280
Swalwell, 8, 18
Swan, Anne, 42
Swan House, 240-1
Swan Hunter Ltd, 39, 42, 57, 58, 59, 238
Swan, (Sir) Joseph, 43, 116
Swimming, 202
Swinburne, Algernon, 305-6
Swing Bridge, 261

Talbot, Neil, 261
Tall Ships Race, 261
Tate Gallery, 265
Taylor, Cecil Philip, 317
Taylor, P.A., 126
Team Valley, 353
Teesside, 35
Temperance Hotel, 287
Temperance movement, 171-4, 175-7
Tennis, 199-200
Tennyson, Lord Alfred, 305-7
Theatre Royal, 12, 220, 224, 278, 309, 313
Theatre Village, 243, 355
Thompson, Mark, 262
Thornycroft, Hamo, 264
Tolkien, J.R.R., 309
Town Hall, 89
Town Improvement Act, 1865, 150
Town Improvement Committee, 272
Town Moor, 83, 118, 175, 193-4, 243, 285, 320, 333, 335
Town Planning, 238-44, 341-60
Tramways, 85-7
Trevelyan, Julian, 259
Trevelyan, Lady Pauline, 306
Trevithick, Richard, 269, 273
Trotter, Thomas, 168
Turf, 275
Turner, Reverend William, 98-9, 250, 301, 303-4
Tuxedo Royale, 262
Tweed, John, 113, 264
Tyne and Wear County Council, 342, 350-53
Tyne and Wear Development Corporation, 67-8, 261-3

Tyne and Wear Metro, 33, 351
Tyne and Wear Urban Development
    Corporation, 351, 353, 354, 355,
    356, 359
Tyne Bridge, 17, 19, 68, 232, 238, 262
Tyne Improvement Act 1850, 76, 91
Tyne Improvement Commission, 19,
    30, 31, 48, 116-17, 286, 342
*Tyne Mercury*, 119, 277
Tyne Theatre and Opera House,
    109, 355
Tynemouth, 10, 16, 17, 18, 20, 30,
    44, 76, 331-2
Tyneside Dilution Commission, 50
Tyneside Enterprise Zone, 351
Tyneside Flats, 234-5, 347
Tyneside Glass Company, 25
Typhoid, 151-2

Udall, John, 294
Unemployment in Newcastle 1971-
    91 (table), 61
Union Club, 287
Unitarian Church of the Divine
    Unity, 232
United Alkali Co., 43
United Kingdom Alliance, 182
University of Northumbria, 345
Unsworth, Barry, 318
USA, 42

Van Mildert, Bishop, 100
Veitch, (family), 309
Veitch, Colin, 207, 211
Verne, Jules, 305
Versailles, Treaty of, 51
Vickers-Armstrong's, 49, 51, 58, 59,
    60, 338, 354
Victoria Grounds, 197-8
Viola, Bill, 265
Virginia, 9
Visual Arts UK, 264, 265

Walbottle Colliery, 40
Walker, 27, 40, 41, 42, 60, 234-5

Walker Alkali Co., 42, 43
Walker, George, 224
Walker, John A., 254-6, 266
Walker Iron Foundry, 42
Walker Ironworks, 25
Walker Jubilee Club, 188
Wallington Hall, 287
Wallis, Andre, 260
Wallsend, 42, 237
Wallsend Slipway Co., 39
Wardle and Walker, 278
Wardle, John, 224
Washington, Tyne & Wear, 214
Wasney, Robert, 99
Water supply, 80-1, 150
Watkins, Karl, 355
Watson, Alderman Angus, 188
Watson, 'Seaman' Tommy, 173, 210
Watson, Robert Spence, 53, 131, 132
Waugh, Sylvia, 318
Waverley Memorial, 276
Wearside, 354
Webb, Beatrice, 74
Webb, Sidney, 74, 81
Welford, R., 278
Wellington, Duke of, 279-80
Wesley, John, 14, 96, 300-1
West Jesmond Metro station, 234
Westall, Robert, 318
Westerhope Club, 90
Westgate, 7, 150
Westgate Hill School, 236
Westgate Road, 12, 267
Westmorland, 11
Whickham View School, 236
White, Gilbert, 247
White, T.H., 293
White, William, 287
Whitefield, George, 96
Whitehaven, 9
Whitehead Torpedo Company, 52
Whittaker, Thomas, 169
Wigham Richardson Ltd., 39
Wilberforce, Bishop Ernest, 111
Wilde, Oscar, 307

William Beardmore & Co. Ltd, 49
Willington Dene, 249, 250
Wills factory, 56, 237
Wilson & Bell, 40
Wilson, George, 194-5
Wilson, Joe, 176, 177, 192, 196, 329
Wilson, Pilcher & Co., 44
Wilson, Richard, 260, 262
Wilson, Thomas, 42, 85, 303
Wine and Beer House Act, 1869,
    171-2
Winlaton, 8, 120-1
Winlaton Female Reformers, 328
Winlaton Sanitary Association, 123
Winthrop Laboratories Ltd., 56
Wodiczko, Krzysztof, 262-3
Women's football, 211
Women's Friendly Societies, 326, 328
Women's sports, 202-3, 211
Women's work, 326-8
Wood Memorial Library, 286
Wood, (Sir) Lindsay, 34
Wood, Nicholas, 276
Woods & Co., 34, 35
Woods, William, 31, 32, 35
Woolsington, 58
Wordsworth, Dorothy, 303
Wordsworth, William, 303
Workers' Educational Association,
    259
Working Men's Club and Institute
    Union (CIU), 177-9
Working Men's Clubs, 183-4
Workmen's Protection League, 179
Wright, Frank Lloyd, 232
Wylam, 269
Wyllie, William Lionel, 256

York, 21, 33
York-Newcastle-Berwick Railway,
    269, 272
Yorkshire, 11
Young, Arthur, 15, 23

Zamyatin, Yevgeni, 309-11